The Age of Justin

Theodora

A History of the Sixth Century A.D.

(Volume 1)

William Gordon Holmes

Alpha Editions

This edition published in 2024

ISBN : 9789366383040

Design and Setting By
Alpha Editions
www.alphaedis.com
Email - info@alphaedis.com

As per information held with us this book is in Public Domain.
This book is a reproduction of an important historical work. Alpha Editions uses the best technology to reproduce historical work in the same manner it was first published to preserve its original nature. Any marks or number seen are left intentionally to preserve its true form.

(VOLUME 1)

PREFACE

ALTHOUGH the age of Justinian is the most interesting and important in the whole series of the Byzantine annals, no comprehensive work has hitherto been devoted to the subject. The valuable and erudite "Vita Justiniani" of Ludewig is more of a law book than of a biography, and less of a circumstantial history than of either. The somewhat strange medley published by Isambert under the title "Vie de Justinien" is scarcely a complete chronology of the events, and might be called a manual of the sources rather than a history of the times.[1] Excellent accounts, however, of Justinian are to be found in some general histories of the Byzantine Empire as well as in several biographical dictionaries, whilst monographs of greater or lesser extent exist under the names of Perrinus, Invernizi, and Padovani, etc., but any student of the period would decide that it deserves to be treated at much greater length than has been devoted to it in any of these books. In the present work the design has been to place before the reader not only a record of events, but a presentment of the people amongst whom, and of the stage upon which those events occurred. I have also attempted to correlate the aspects of the ancient and the modern world in relation to science and progress.

W. G. H.

LONDON,
February, 1905.

PREFATORY NOTE TO SECOND EDITION

This work has now been carefully revised and slightly enlarged. I am indebted to suggestions from various reviewers of the first edition for several of the improvements introduced. Occasionally, however, they are in error and at variance among themselves on some of the points noted. A few of my critics have accused me of being too discursive, especially in my notes, an impression which is the natural result of my not having expressed it definitely anywhere that my object was to present not merely the sociology and events of a particular period, but also to illustrate, in an abridged sense, the history of all time.

W. G. H.

LONDON,
August, 1912.

PROEM

THE birth and death of worlds are ephemeral events in a cycle of astronomical time. In the life history of a stellar system, of a planet, of an animal, parallel periods of origin, exuberance, and of extinction are exhibited to our experience, or to our understanding. Man, in his material existence confined to a point, by continuity of effort and perpetuity of thought, becomes coequal and coextensive with the infinities of time and space. The intellectual store of ages has evolved the supremacy of the human race, but the zenith of its ascendancy may still be far off, and the aspiration after progress has been entailed on the heirs of all preceding generations. The advancement of humanity is the sum of the progress of its component members, and the individual who raises his own life to the highest attainable eminence becomes a factor in the elevation of the whole race. Familiarity with history dispels the darkness of the past, which is so prolific in the myths that feed credulity and foster superstition, the frequent parents of the most stubborn obstacles which have lain in the path of progress. The history of the past comprises the lessons of the future; and the successes and failures of former times are a pre-vision of the struggles to come and the errors to be avoided. The stream of human life having once issued from its sources, may be equal in endurance to a planet, to a stellar system, or even to the universe itself. The mind of the universe may be man, who may be the confluence of universal intelligence. The eternity of the past, the infinity of the present, may be peopled with races like our own, but whether they die out with the worlds they occupy, or enjoy a perpetual existence, transcends the present limits of our knowledge. From century to century the solid ground of science gains on the illimitable ocean of the unknown, but we are ignorant as to whether we exist in the dawn or in the noonday of enlightenment. The conceptions of one age become the achievements of the next; and the philosopher may question whether this world be not some remote, unaffiliated tract, which remains to be annexed to the empire of universal civilization. The discoveries of the future may be as undreamt of as those of the past,[2] and the ultimate destiny of our race is hidden from existing generations.

In the period I have chosen to bring before the reader, civilization was on the decline, and progress imperceptible, but the germs of a riper growth were still existent, concealed within the spreading darkness of mediaevalism. When Grecian science and philosophy seemed to stand on the threshold of modern enlightenment the pall of despotism and superstition descended on the earth and stifled every impulse of progress for more than fifteen centuries. The Yggdrasil of Christian superstition spread its roots throughout the Roman Empire, strangling alike the nascent ethics of Christendom, and the germinating science of the ancient world. Had the leading minds of that epoch, instead of expending their zeal and acumen on theological inanities, applied themselves to the study of nature, they might have forestalled the march of the centuries, and advanced us a thousand years beyond the present time. But the atmosphere of the period was charged with a metaphysical mysticism whereby all philosophic thought and material research were arrested. The records of a millennium comprise little more than the rise, the progress, and the triumph of superstition and barbarism. The degenerate Greeks became the serfs and slaves of the land in which they were formerly the masters, and retreated gradually to a vanishing point in the vast district from the Adriatic to the Indus, over which the eagle-wing of Alexander had swept in uninterrupted conquest. Unable to oppose their political solidarity and martial science to the fanaticism of the half-armed Saracens, they yielded up to them insensibly their faith and their empire, and their place was filled by a host of unprogressive Mohammedans, who brought with them a newer religion more sensuous in its conceptions, but less gross in its practice, than the Christianity of that day. But the hardy barbarians of the North, drinking at the fountain of knowledge, had achieved some political organization, and became the natural and irresistible barriers against which the waves of Moslem enthusiasm dashed themselves in vain. The term of Asiatic encroachment was fixed at the Pyrenees in the west, and at the Danube in the east by the valorous Franks and Hungarians; and on the brink of the turning tide stand the heroic figures of Charles Martel and Matthias Corvinus. Civilization has now included almost the whole globe in its comprehensive embrace; both the old world and the new have been overrun by the intellectual heirs of the Greeks; in every land the extinction of retrograde races proceeds with measured certainty, and we appear to be safer from a returning flood of barbarism than from some astronomical catastrophe. The mediaeval order of things is reversed, the ravages of Attila reappear under a new aspect, and the descendants of the Han and the Hun alike are raised by the hand, or crushed under the foot of aggressive civilization.

In the infancy of human reason intelligence outstrips knowledge, and the mature, but vacant, mind soon loses itself in the dark and trackless wilderness of natural phenomena. An imaginative system of cosmogony, baseless as the fabric of a dream, is the creation of a moment; to dissipate it the work of ages in study and investigation. Less than a century ago philosophic scepticism could only vent itself in a sneer at the credibility of a tradition, or the fidelity of a manuscript; and the folklore of peasants, encrusted with the hoar of antiquity, was accepted by erudite mystics as the solution of cosmogony and the proof of our communion with the supernatural. An illegible line, a misinterpreted phrase, a suspected interpolation, in some decaying document, the proof or the refutation, was often hailed triumphantly by ardent disputants as announcing the establishment or the overthrow of revelation. But the most signal achievements of historic research or criticism were powerless to elucidate the mysteries of the universe; and the inquirer had to fall back perpetually on the current mythology for the interpretation of his objective environment. In the hands of science alone were the keys which could unlock the book of nature, and open the gates of knowledge as to the enigmas of visible life. A flood of light has been thrown on the order of natural phenomena, our vision has been prolonged from the dawn of history to the dawn of terrestrial life, an intelligible hypothesis of existence has been deduced from observation and experiment, idealism and dogma have been recognized as the offspring of phantasy and fallacy, and the mystical elements of Christianity have been dismissed by philosophy to that limbo of folly which long ago engulfed the theogonies of Greece and Rome. The sapless trunk of revelation lies rotting on the ground, but the undiscerning masses, too credulous to inquire, too careless to think, have allowed it to become invested with the weeds of superstition and ignorance; and the progeny of hierophants, who once sheltered beneath the green and flourishing tree, still find a cover in the rank growth. In the turn of the ages we are confronted by new Pagans who adhere to an obsolete religion; and the philosopher can only hope for an era when every one will have sufficient sense and science to think according to the laws of nature and civilization.

The history of the disintegrating and moribund Byzantine Empire has been explored by modern scholars with untiring assiduity; and the exposition of that debased political system will always reflect more credit on their brilliant researches than on the chequered annals of mankind.

CHAPTER I
CONSTANTINOPLE IN THE SIXTH CENTURY[3]

THE Byzantine peninsula has been regarded from a very early date as an ideal situation for a capital city. Placed at the junction of two great seas which wash the shores of three continents, and possessed of a safe and extensive anchorage for shipping, it might become the centre of empire and commerce for the whole Eastern hemisphere. Yet, owing to an adverse fate, the full realization of this splendid conception remains a problem of the future. Byzantium as an independent city was little more than an outpost of civilization; as a provincial town of the Roman Empire its political position allowed it no scope for development; as the metropolis of the same Empire in its age of decadence its fitful splendour is an unsubstantial pageant without moral or political stability. Lastly, in the hands of the Turk its growth has been fettered by the prejudices of a nation unable to free itself from the bondage of an effete civilization.

I. HISTORY

The first peopling of the site of Constantinople is a question in prehistoric research, which has not yet been elucidated by the palaeontologist. Unlike the Roman area, no relics of an age of stone or bronze have been discovered here;[4] do not, perhaps, exist, but doubtless the opportunities, if not the men, have been wanting for such investigations.[5] That the region seemed to the primitive Greeks to be a wild and desolate one, we learn from the tradition of the Argonautic expedition;[6] and the epithet of "Axine,"[7] or inhospitable, applied in the earliest times to the Euxine or Black Sea. By the beginning, however, of the seventh century before the Christian era these seas and maritime channels had been explored, and several colonies[8] had been planted by the adventurous Greeks who issued from the Ionian seaport of Miletus. Later than the Milesians, a band of Dorians from Megara penetrated into these parts and, by a strange choice, as it was afterwards considered, selected a point at the mouth of the Bosphorus on the Asiatic shore for a settlement, which they called Chalcedon.[9] Seventeen years later[10] a second party from Megara fixed themselves on the European headland, previously known as Lygos,[11] nearly opposite their first colony. The leader of this expedition was Byzas,[12] and from him the town they built was named Byzantium.[13] The actual limits of the original city are now quite unknown, but doubtless they were small at first and were gradually extended according as the community increased in wealth and prosperity.[14] During the classic period of Greek history the town rose to considerable importance, as its commanding position enabled it to impose a toll on ships sailing to and from the Euxine sea; a power of which, however, it made a very sparing use.[15] It was also enriched by the countless shoals of fish[16] which, when the north winds blew, descended from the Euxine and thronged the narrow but elongated gulf called, most probably for that reason, *Chrysoceras* or Golden Horn.[17] Ultimately Byzantium became the largest city in Thrace, having expanded itself over an area which measured four and a half miles in circumference, including, probably, the suburbs.[18] It exercised a suzerainty over Chalcedon and Perinthus,[19] and reduced the aboriginal Bithynians to a state of servitude comparable to that of the Spartan Helots.[20] Notwithstanding its natural advantages, the town never won any pre-eminence among the Hellenic communities, and nothing more unstable than its political position is presented to us in the restless concourse of Grecian nationalities. In the wars of Persians with Greeks, and of Greeks with Greeks, it always became the sport of the contending parties; and during a century and a half (about 506 B.C. to 350 B.C.) it was taken and re-taken at least six times by Medes, Spartans, Athenians, and Thebans, a change of constitution following, of course, each change of political connection.[21] In 340 B.C., however, the Byzantines, with the aid of the Athenians, withstood a siege successfully, an occurrence the more remarkable as they were attacked by the greatest general of the age, Philip of Macedon. In the course of this beleaguerment, it is related, on a certain wet and moonless night the enemy attempted a surprise, but were foiled by reason of a bright light which, appearing suddenly in the heavens, startled all the dogs in the town and thus roused the garrison to a sense of their danger.[22] To commemorate this timely phenomenon, which was attributed to Hecate, they erected a public statue to that goddess and, as it is supposed, assumed the crescent for their chief national device. For several centuries after this event the city enjoyed a nominal autonomy, but it appears to have been in perpetual conflict with its civilized or barbarous neighbours; and in 279 B.C. it was even laid under tribute[23] by the horde of Gauls who penetrated into Asia and established themselves permanently in Galatia. After the appearance of the Roman legionaries in the East the Byzantines were always the faithful friends of the Republic, while it was engaged in suppressing the independent potentates of Macedonia and Asia Minor. For its services Byzantium was permitted to retain the rank of a free city,[24] and its claim to indulgence was allowed by more than one of the Roman emperors,[25] even after A.D. 70, when Vespasian limited its rights to those of a provincial town.[26]

Of all the ancient historians one only has left us a description capable of giving some visual impression as to the appearance of old Byzantium. "This city," says Dion Cassius,[27] "is most favourably situated, being built upon an eminence, which juts out into the sea. The waters, like a torrent, rushing downwards from the Pontus impinge against the promontory and flow partly to the right, so as to form the bay and harbours, but the main stream runs swiftly alongside the city into the Propontis. The town is also extremely well fortified, for the wall is faced with great square stones joined together by brazen clamps, and it is further strengthened on the inside through mounds and houses being built up against it. This wall seems to consist of a solid mass of stone,[28] and it has a covered gallery above, which is very easily defended. On the outside there are many large towers, perforated with frequent loopholes and ranged in an irregular line, so that an attacking party is surrounded by them and exposed on all sides at once. Toward the land the fortifications are very lofty, but less so on the side of the water, as the rocks on which they are founded and the dangers of the Bosphorus render them almost unassailable. There are two harbours within the walls,[29] guarded by chains, and at the ends of the moles inclosing them towers facing each other make the passage impracticable to an enemy. I have seen the walls standing and have also heard them speaking; for there are seven vocal towers stretching from the Thracian gates to the sea. If one shouts or drops a pebble in the first it not only resounds itself or repeats the syllables, but it transmits the power for the next in order to do the same; and thus the voice or echo is carried in regular succession through the whole series."[30]

At the end of the second century the Byzantines were afflicted by the severest trial which had ever come within their experience. In the tripartite struggle between the Emperor Severus and his competitors of Gaul and Asia, the city unfortunately threw in its lot with Niger, the Proconsul of Syria. Niger soon fell, but Byzantium held out with inflexible obstinacy for three years and, through the ingenuity of an engineer named Priscus, defied all the efforts of the victor. During this time the inhabitants suffered progressively every kind of hardship and horror which has been put on record in connection with sieges of the most desperate character. Stones torn from the public buildings were used as projectiles, statues of men and horses, in brass and marble, were hurled on the heads of the besiegers, women gave their hair to be twisted into cords and ropes, leather soaked in water was eaten, and finally they fell on one another and fed on human flesh. At last the city yielded, but Severus was exasperated, and his impulse of hostility only ceased with the destruction of the prize he had won at such a cost in blood and treasure. The garrison and all who had borne any public office, with the exception of Priscus, were put to death, the chief buildings were razed,[31] the municipality was abolished, property was confiscated, and the town was given over to the previously subject Perinthians, to be treated as a dependent village. With immense labour the impregnable fortifications were levelled with the ground, and the ruins of the first bulwark of the Empire against the barbarians of Scythia attested the wisdom and temperance of the master of the East and West.[32]

But the memory of Byzantium dwelt in the mind of Severus and he was attracted to revisit the spot. In cooler moments he surveyed the wreck; the citizens, bearing olive branches in their hands, approached him in a solemn and suppliant procession; he determined to rebuild, and at his mandate new edifices were reared to supply the place of those which had been ruined. He even purchased ground, which had been previously occupied by private gardens, for the laying out of a hippodrome,[33] a public luxury with which the town had never before been adorned. But the hateful name of Byzantium was abolished and the new city was called Antonina[34] by Severus, in honour of his eldest son; a change, however, which scarcely survived the life of its author. Through Caracalla,[35] or some rational statesman acting in the name of that reprobate, the city regained its political privileges, but the fortifications were not restored, and for more than half a century it remained defenceless against the barbarians, and even against the turbulent soldiery of the Empire. Beginning from about 250 the Goths ravaged the vicinity of the Bosphorus and plundered most of the towns, holding their own against Decius and several other short-lived emperors. Under Gallienus a mutinous legion is said to have massacred most of the inhabitants, but shortly afterwards the same emperor gave a commission to two Byzantine engineers to fortify the district, and henceforward Byzantium again appears as a stronghold, which was made a centre of operations against the Goths, in the repulse of whom the natives and their generals even played an important part.[36] In 323 Licinius, the sole remaining rival of Constantine, after his defeat in a great battle near Adrianople, took refuge in Byzantium, and the town again became the scene of a contest memorable in history, not for the magnitude of the siege, but for the importance of the events which it inaugurated. Licinius soon yielded, and a new era dawned for Byzantium, which in a few years became lastingly known to the nations as the City of Constantine.

The tongue of land on which Constantinople is built is essentially a low mountainous ridge, rising on three sides by irregular slopes from the sea. Trending almost directly eastward from the continent of Europe, it terminates abruptly in a rounded headland opposite the Asiatic shore, from which it is separated by the entrance of the Bosphorus, at this point a little more than a mile in width. This diminutive peninsula, which is bounded on the north by the inland extension of the Bosphorus, called the Golden Horn, and on the south by the Propontis or Sea of Marmora, has a length of between three and four miles. At its eastern extremity it is about a mile broad and it gradually expands until, in the region where it may be said to join the mainland, its measurement has increased to more than four times that distance. The unlevel nature of the ground and reminiscences of the seven hills of classical Rome have always caused a parallel to be drawn between the sites of the two capitals of the Empire, but the resemblance is remote and the historic import of the Roman hills is totally wanting in the case of those of Constantinople. The hills of the elder city were mostly distinct mounts, which had borne suggestive names in the earliest annals of the district. Every citizen had learned to associate the Palatine with the Roma Quadrata of Romulus, the Aventine with the ill-omened auspices of Remus, the Quirinal with the rape of the Sabine women, the Esquiline with the murder of King Servius, the Capitol with the repulse of the Gauls by Manlius; and knew that when the standard was raised on the Janiculum the comitia were assembled to transact the business of the Republic. But the Byzantine hills are little more than variations in the face of the slope as it declines on each side from the central dorsum to the water, and have always been nameless unless in the numerical descriptions of the topographer. On the north five depressions constitute as many valleys and give rise to six hills, which are numbered in succession from the narrow end of the promontory to the west. Thus the first hill is that on which stood the acropolis of Byzantium. Two of the valleys, the third and fifth, can be traced across the dorsum of the peninsular from sea to sea. A rivulet, called the Lycus, running from the mainland, joins the peninsula near its centre and then turns in a south-easterly direction so as to fall into the Propontis. The valley through which this stream passes, the sixth, bounds the seventh hill, an elevation known as the Xerolophos or Dry-mount, which, lying in the south-west, occupies more than a third of the whole area comprised within the city walls.[37] From every high point of the promontory the eye may range over seas and mountains often celebrated in classic story—the Trojan Ida and Olympus, the Hellespont, Athos and Olympus of Zeus, and the Thracian Bosphorus embraced by wooded hills up to the "blue Symplegades" and the Euxine, so suggestive of heroic tradition to the Greek mind. The Golden Horn itself describes a curve to the north-west of more than six miles in length, and at its extremity, where it turns upon itself, becomes fused with the estuary of two small rivers named Cydarus and Barbyses.[38] Throughout the greater part of its course it is about a quarter of a mile in width, but at one point below its centre, it is dilated into a bay of nearly double that capacity. This inlet was not formerly, in the same sense as it is now, the port of Constantinople; to the ancients it was still the sea, a moat on a large scale, which added the safety of water to the mural defences of the city; and the small shipping of the period was accommodated in artificial harbours formed by excavations within the walls or by moles thrown out from the shore.[39] The climate of this locality is very changeable, exposed as it is to north winds chilled by transit over the Russian steppes, and to warm breezes which originate in the tropical expanses of Africa and Arabia. The temperature may range through twenty degrees in a single day, and winters of such arctic severity that the Golden Horn and even the Bosphorus are seen covered with ice are not unknown to the inhabitants.[40] Variations of landscape due to vegetation are found chiefly in the abundance of plane, pine, chestnut, and other trees, but more especially of the cypress. Earthquakes are a permanent source of annoyance, and have sometimes been very destructive. Such in brief are the geographical features of this region, which the caprice of a prince, in a higher degree, perhaps, than its natural endowments, appointed to contain the metropolis of the East.

When Constantine determined to supplant the ancient capital on the Tiber by building a new city in a place of his own choice,[41] he does not appear to have been more acute in discerning the advantages of Byzantium than were the first colonists from Megara. It is said that Thessalonica first fixed his attention; it is certain that he began to build in the Troad, near the site of Homeric Ilios; and it is even suggested that when he shifted his ground from thence he next commenced operations at Chalcedon.[42] By 328,[43] however, he had come to a final decision, and Byzantium was exalted to be the actual rival of Rome. This event, occurring at so advanced a date and under the eye of civilization, yet became a source of legend, so as to excel even in that respect the original foundation by Byzas. The oracles had long been lapsing into silence,[44] but their place had been gradually usurped by Christian visions, and every zealot who thought upon the subject conceived of Constantine as acting under a special inspiration from the Deity. More than a score of writers in verse and prose have described the circumstances under which he received the divine injunctions, and some have presented to us in detail the person and words of the beatific visitant.[45] On the faith of an ecclesiastical historian[46] we are asked to believe that an angelic guide even directed the Emperor as he marked out the boundaries of his future capital. When Constantine, on foot with a spear in his hand, seemed to his ministers to move onwards for an inordinate distance, one of them exclaimed: "How far, O Master?" "Until he who precedes me stands," was the reply by which the inspired surveyor indicated that he followed an unseen conductor. Whether Constantine was a superstitious man is an indeterminate question, but that he was a shrewd and politic one is self-evident from his career, and, if we believe that he gave currency to this and similar marvellous tales, we can perceive that he could not have acted more judiciously with the view of gaining adherents during the flush of early Christian enthusiasm.[47]

The area of the city was more than quadrupled by the wall of Constantine, which extended right across the peninsula in the form of a bow, distant at the widest part about a mile and three-quarters from the old fortifications.[48] This space, by comparison enormous, and which yet included only four of the hills with part of the Xerolophos, was hastily filled by the Emperor with buildings and adornments of every description. Many cities of the Empire, notably Rome, Athens, Ephesus, and Antioch, were stripped of some of their most precious objects of art for the embellishment of the new capital.[49] Wherever statues, sculptured columns, or metal castings were to be found, there the agents of Constantine were busily engaged in arranging for their transfer to the Bosphorus. Resolved that no fanatic spirit should mar the cosmopolitan expectation of his capital the princely architect subdued his Christian zeal, and three temples[50] to mythological divinities arose in regular conformity with pagan custom. Thus the "Fortune of the City" took her place as the goddess Anthusa[51] in a handsome fane, and adherents of the old religion could not declare that the ambitious foundation was begun under unfavourable auspices. In another temple a statue of Rhea, or Cybele, was erected in an abnormal posture, deprived of her lions and with her hands raised as if in the act of praying over the city. On this travesty of the mother of the Olympians, we may conjecture, was founded the belief which prevailed in a later age that the capital at its birth had been dedicated to the Virgin.[52] That a city permanently distinguished by the presence of an Imperial court should remain deficient in population is opposed to common experience of the laws which govern the evolution of a metropolis. But Constantine could not wait, and various artificial methods were adopted in order to provide inhabitants for the vacant inclosure. Patricians were induced to abandon Rome by grants of lands and houses, and it is even said that several were persuaded to settle at Constantinople by means of an ingenious deception. Commanding the attendance in the East of a number of senators during the Persian war, the Emperor privately commissioned architects to build counterparts of their Roman dwellings on the Golden Horn. To these were transferred the families and households of the absent ministers, who were then invited by Constantine to meet him in his new capital. There they were conducted to homes in which to their astonishment they seemed to revisit Rome in a dream, and henceforth they became permanent residents in obedience to a prince who urged his wishes with such unanswerable arguments.[53] As to the common herd we have no precise information, but it is asserted by credible authority that they were raked together from diverse parts, the rabble of the Empire who derived their maintenance from the founder and repaid him with servile adulation in the streets and in the theatre.[54]

By the spring of 330[55] the works were sufficiently advanced for the new capital to begin its political existence, and Constantine decreed that a grand inaugural festival should take place on the 11th of May. The "Fortune of the City" was consecrated by a pagan ceremony in which Praetextatus, a priest, and Sopater, a philosopher, played the principal parts;[56] largess was distributed to the populace, and magnificent games were exhibited in the Hippodrome, where the Emperor presided, conspicuous with a costly diadem decked with pearls and precious stones, which he wore for the first time.[57] On this occasion the celebration is said to have lasted forty days,[58] and at the same time Constantine instituted the permanent "Encaenia," an annual commemoration, which he enjoined on succeeding emperors for the same date. A gilded statue of himself, bearing a figure of Anthusa in one hand, was to be conducted round the city in a chariot, escorted by a military guard, dressed in a definite attire,[59] and carrying wax tapers in their hands. Finally, the procession was to make the circuit of the Hippodrome and, when it paused before the cathisma, the emperor was to descend from his throne and adore the effigy.[60] We are further told that an astrologer named Valens was employed to draw the horoscope of the city, with the result that he predicted for it an existence of 696 years.[61]

After the fall of Licinius it appears most probable that Constantine, as a memorial of his accession to undivided power, gave Byzantium the name of Constantinople.[62] When, however, he transformed that town into a metropolis, in order to express clearly the magnitude of his views as to the future, he renamed it Second, or New Rome. At the same time he endowed it with special privileges, known in the legal phraseology of the period as the "right of Italy and prerogative of Rome";[63] and to keep these facts in the public eye he had them inscribed on a stone pillar, which he set up in a forum, or square, called the Strategium, adjacent to an equestrian statue of himself.[64] To render it in all respects the image of Rome, Constantinople was provided with a Senate,[65] a national council known only at that date in the artificial form which owes its existence to despots. After his choice of Byzantium for the eastern capital Constantine never dwelt at Rome, and in all his acts seems to have aimed at extinguishing the prestige of the old city by the grandeur of the new one, a policy which he initiated so effectively that in the century after his death the Roman Empire ceased to be Roman.[66]

Constantine is credited with the erection of many churches[67] in and around Constantinople, but, with the exception of St. Irene,[68] the Holy Cross,[69] and the Twelve Apostles,[70] their identification rests with late and untrustworthy writers. One, St. Mocius,[71] is said to have been built with the materials of a temple of Zeus, which previously stood in the same place, the summit of the Xerolophos, outside the walls. Another, St. Mena, occupied the site of the temple of Poseidon founded by Byzas.[72] Paganism was tolerated as a religion of the Empire until the last decade of the fourth century, when it was finally overthrown by the preponderance of Christianity. Laws for its total suppression were enacted by Theodosius I, destruction of temples was legalized, and at the beginning of the fifth century it is probable that few traces remained of the sacred edifices which had adorned old Byzantium.[73]

After the age of Constantine the progress of New Rome as metropolis of the east was extremely rapid,[74] the suburbs became densely populous, and in

413 Theodosius II gave a commission to Anthemius,[75] the Praetorian Prefect, to build a new wall in advance of the old one nearly a mile further down the peninsula. The intramural space was thus increased by an area more than equal to half its former dimensions; and, with the exception of some small additions on the Propontis and the Golden Horn, this wall marked the utmost limit of Constantinople in ancient or modern times. In 447 a series of earthquakes, which lasted for three months, laid the greater part of the new wall in ruins, fifty-seven of the towers, according to one account,[76] having collapsed during the period of commotion. This was the age of Attila and the Huns, to whom Theodosius, sooner than offer a military resistance, had already agreed to pay an annual tribute of seven hundred pounds of gold.[77] With the rumour that the barbarians were approaching the undefended capital the public alarm rose to fever-heat, and the Praetorian Prefect of the time, Cyrus Constantine, by an extraordinary effort, not only restored the fortifications of Anthemius, but added externally a second wall on a smaller scale, together with a wide and deep fosse,[78] in the short space of sixty days. To the modern observer it might appear incredible that such a prodigious mass of masonry, extending over a distance of four miles, could be reared within two months, but the fact is attested by two inscriptions still existing on the gates,[79] by the Byzantine historians,[80] and by the practice of antiquity in times of impending hostility.[81]

II. TOPOGRAPHY

Having now traced the growth of the city on the Golden Horn from its origin in the dawn of Grecian history until its expansion into the capital of the greatest empire of the past, I have reached the threshold of my actual task— to place before the reader a picture of Constantinople at the beginning of the sixth century in its topographical and sociological aspects. The literary materials, though abundant, are in great part unreliable and are often devoid of information which would be found in the most unpretentious guide-book of modern times.[82] On the other hand the monumental remains are unusually scanty, insignificant indeed compared with those of Rome, and few cities, which have been continuously occupied, have suffered so much during the lapse of a few centuries as Constantinople. Political revolution has been less destructive than that of religion, and Moslem fanaticism, much more than time or war, has achieved the ruin of the Christian capital. On this ground, the same calamities which Christianity inflicted on paganism in the fourth century, she suffered herself at the hands of Islam in the fifteenth.

The modern visitor, who approaches Constantinople, is at once impressed by the imposing vista of gilded domes and minarets, which are the chief objective feature of the Ottoman capital. It is scarcely necessary to say that in the sixth century the minaret, uniquely characteristic as it is of a Mohammedan city, would be absent, but the statement must also be extended to the dome, the most distinctive element in Byzantine architecture, which at the date of my description scarcely yet existed even in the conception of the builder.[83] If we draw near from the Sea of Marmora (the Propontis) at the time of this history, we shall observe, extending by land and sea from the southernmost point, the same ranges of lofty walls and towers, now falling into universal ruin, but then in a state of perfect repair. Within appear numerous great houses and several tall columns interspersed among a myriad of small red-roofed dwellings, densely packed; and here and there the eye is caught by a gleam of gilded tiles from the roof of a church or a palace. In order to inspect the defences on the land side, the aspect of the city most strongly fortified, we must disembark near the south-west corner of the Xerolophos, the locality now known as the Seven Towers. Without the city, towards the west, the ground consists of flowery meadows diversified by fruit-gardens and by groves of cypress and plane trees.[84] Almost at the water's edge is an imposing bastion, which from its circular form is called the Cyclobion.[85] Proceeding inland we shall not at this date find a road winding over hill and dale from sea to sea as at the present day.[86] Most of the country is occupied by walled *philopatia* or pleasaunces in which landscape gardening has been developed with considerable art, suburban residences of the Byzantine aristocracy.[87] In a grove about a mile from the shore we come upon a certain well, which is regarded as sacred and frequented by sufferers from various diseases on account of the healing virtue attributed to its waters.[88] Northwards the extramural district abutting on the Golden Horn is called Blachernae from the chief of a Thracian tribe, which formerly occupied this quarter.[89] Here, contiguous to the wall, we may notice a small summer palace on two floors, built of brick with rows of stone-framed, arched windows, now undergoing restoration and extension by the Emperor Anastasius.[90] A few paces further on is a Christian chapel dedicated to the Theotokos or Mother of God, founded by Pulcheria,[91] the pious but imperious sister of Theodosius II, and finally the maiden wife of the Emperor Marcian. Hard by is a natural well,[92] which from its interesting associations is now beginning to ripen into sanctity.

The scheme of fortification consists of three main defences: (1) a foss, (2) an outer wall with frequent towers, and (3) an inner wall, similar, but of much greater proportions.

(1) Since the moat necessarily follows the trend of the ground as it rises on either side from the beach to the dorsum of the peninsula, this canal, instead of maintaining a uniform level, consists of a number of sections divided by cross-walls, the distances between which are determined by the exigences of ascent or descent. In its course it outlines the contour of the walls, which advance on the peninsula from each end in the form of a bow. The average width of this foss is about sixty, and its depth about thirty feet. It is lined on both sides from the bottom with substantial stone walls, but, whilst that on the outside only reaches the level of the ground, the wall next the city, with a crenellated top, rises for several feet,[93] so as to convey the impression of a triple wall of defence. In peace time the water is allowed to run low, but if an assault is apprehended the trench can be quickly flooded by means of earthenware pipes concealed within the partition walls. From these conduits the

city also derives a secret supply of water not likely to be tampered with by a besieging army.[94]

(2) At a distance of about twenty yards from the inner edge of the moat, rising to a height of nearly thirty feet, with dentated parapets, stands the lesser wall. Towers of various shapes, square, round, and octagonal, project from its external face at intervals of about fifty yards. Each tower overtops the wall and possesses small front and lateral windows, which overlook the level tract[95] stretching from the foss. High up in each tower is a floorway having an exit on the intramural space behind, and they have also steps outside which lead to the roof. The vacant interval between the walls is about fifty feet wide, usually called the *peribolos*.[96] It has been artificially raised to within a few feet of the top of the wall by pouring into it the earth recovered in excavating the moat.[97] This is the special vantage-ground of the defenders of the city during a siege: from hence mainly they launch their missiles against the enemy or engage them in a hand-to-hand fight should they succeed in crossing the moat and planting their scaling-ladders against the wall.[98]

(3) Bounding the *peribolos* posteriorly lies the main land-wall of Constantinople, the great and indisputable work of Theodosius II. In architectural configuration it is almost similar to the outer wall, but its height is much greater, and its towers, placed so as to alternate with the smaller ones in front, occupy more than four times as much ground. Built as separate structures, but adherent to the wall behind, they rise above it and project forwards into the interspace for more than half its breadth. Most of the towers are square, but those of circular or octagonal shape are not infrequent. In level places offering facilities for attack the wall has a general height of seventy feet, but in less accessible situations, on rising or rugged ground, it attains to little more than half that elevation.[99] As in the case of the outer defences, the wall and towers are crested by an uninterrupted series of crenellated battlements.

The towers are entered from the city at the back, and within each one is a winding stone staircase leading to the top. Here, sheltered by the parapet, there is room for sixty or seventy men to assail an enemy with darts or engines of war. There is also a lower floor from which a further body of soldiers can act on the offensive by means of front and side windows or loopholes. At intervals certain of the towers have an exit on the *peribolos* for the use of those militants who have their station on that rampart. In time of peace these towers serve as guard-houses, and the sentries are enjoined to maintain their vigilance by passing the word of each successive hour from post to post during the night.[100] The usual thickness of this wall is about eight feet, but no regular rampart has been prepared along the summit, the defensive value of such an area being superseded by the *peribolos*. Hence the top, the width of which is limited to less than five feet by the encroachment of the parapet, has no systematic means of access from the ground or from the towers. Hewn stone, worked in the vicinity, has been used for the construction of these fortifications,[101] and in some places close to the city the ground may be seen to have been quarried into hills and hollows[102] for the supply of the builders.[103]

At about every half mile of their length these walls are pierced by main gateways for the passing to and fro of the inhabitants. In these situations the inner wall is increased to more than treble its ordinary thickness, and the passage is flanked by a pair of the greater towers, which here approximate at much less than their usual distance. The thoroughfare consists of a deep and lofty archway, which on occasion can be closed by ponderous doors revolving on huge iron hinges. Opposite each gate the moat is crossed by wooden drawbridges easily removable in case of a siege. The most southerly entrance, being opposite the holy well, is called the Gate of the Fountain; next comes the Gate of Rhegium, then that of St. Romanus, fourthly the Charsios or oblique Gate,[104] and lastly the Xylokerkos Gate—that of the wooden circus. Between the third and fourth gates the moat is deficient and the walls are tunnelled for the transit of the streamlet Lycus, which, though almost dry in summer, swells to a considerable volume in winter. The second and last portals bear metrical inscriptions, differing verbally, but each declaring the fact that the Prefect, Cyrus Constantine, built the wall in two months.[105] On the second gate, that of Rhegium, the circumstance is recorded in a Latin tristich as well as in a Greek distich.[106]

Besides these popular approaches there is another series of five gates, architecturally similar, but designed only for military or strategic purposes. About intermediate in position and in line with neither roads nor bridges, they are closed to the general public and named merely in numerical succession from south to north.[107] Just above the third gate, that is, about half way between the Golden Horn and the Propontis, the walls dip inwards for a distance of nearly one hundred yards, forming a crescent or, as the Greeks call it, Sigma.[108]

The first strategic gate, first also of the land-wall, being scarcely a furlong from the Propontis, offers a notable exception to the constructive plainness of all the other entries. Intended only as a state entry to the capital for the display of Imperial pomp, it has been built and adorned with the object of rendering it the most splendid object in this part of the city. A pair of massive towers, each one hundred feet high, advance from a façade of equal altitude, which is traversed by three arched portals, that in the centre being elevated to sixty feet. The whole is constructed in white marble, and this chaste and imposing foundation is made resplendent by the addition of gilded statues, bas-reliefs, and mouldings. From a central pedestal above rises a figure of Victory[109] with flowing draperies, her hand extended offering a laurel crown. At her feet stands an equestrian statue of Theodosius the Great,[110] and from the extremity of each tower springs the two-headed Byzantine eagle.[111] Below, the surfaces of the monument are ensculptured all round with mythological designs,[112] among which we may recognize Prometheus the Fire-giver, Pegasus, Endymion, the labours of Hercules and many others. Corinthian columns of green-veined marble[113] bound the main portal, within which is erected a great cross.[114] In the fore area are placed a pair of marble elephants, recalling those used by Theodosius in his triumphal procession after the defeat of Maximus of Gaul; and behind these his grandson,[115] the builder of the gate, has raised a column bearing a statue of himself. Profusely gilded, this elaborate pile is popularly and officially known as the Golden Gate.[116]

To proceed with our survey we may re-embark on the Propontis and skirt the promontory by water from end to end of the land-wall, passing through the mouth of the Bosphorus between Europe and Asia and finishing our circuit in the upper reaches of the Golden Horn. The single south wall, rising from the brink of the sea, is similar to that of Anthemius, and the towers exhibit the same diversity of form.[117] Courses of rough stones immersed in the water lie along its base and form a kind of primitive breakwater, which saves its foundations from being sapped by the waves in tempestuous weather. These are said to have been quarried from the tops of the hills during the process of levelling the ground for the extension of the city, and then, at the suggestion of Constantine, sent rolling down the slopes until they became lodged in their present position.[118]

Several gates in this wall give access to the water, but they possess no architectural distinction. Westerly is the Porta Psamathia or Sand-gate, so called because an area of new ground has been formed here by silting up of sand outside the wall.[119] Near the opposite extremity is the Porta Ferrea or Iron-gate, thus designated from the unstable beach having been guarded by rails of iron to enable it to sustain the ponderous burdens imported by Constantine.[120] Towards the centre of this shore is situated the Gate of St. Aemilian, named from its proximity to a church sacred to that martyr.[121] More noticeable in this range of wall are the entrances to two excavated harbours, each closed by a chain stretching between a pair of containing towers. The first, at the foot of the Xerolophos, dates from the time of Constantine, who called it the Port of Eleutherius[122] after his master of the works. Remade by Theodosius I, it has since been most commonly associated with the name of that emperor.[123] Paved at the bottom and surrounded by a stone quay,[124] it is about a Roman mile in circuit,[125] and is divided centrally by a dike into an inner and outer basin.[126] More easterly is another similar but smaller harbour, having only one basin, designated Port Julian[127] from its Imperial founder, but it is more often spoken of as the New Port.[128] Owing, however, to the exceptional suitability for shipping of the north side of the city, both these harbours have gradually fallen into disuse and, becoming choked with sand, have been looked on merely as fit receptacles for the rubble accumulated in clearing building sites.[129] But the Port of Julian is soon to be reopened, for, at the direction of Anastasius, rotatory pumps have been fixed to empty it of its water and dredging operations are in progress.[130] To insure its continued patency a mole is even in course of construction in the Propontis over against its mouth.[131] Passing the Porta Ferrea, as we begin to round the headland, a large mansion or palace comes into view, substituted apparently for the wall in about fifty feet of its length. Fronted along its base with slabs of white marble, the edifice presents a lofty stone balcony overhanging the water,[132] and opening on to it, a central group of three rectangular windows or doors with jambs and lintels of sculptured stone. Above, a row of seven nearly semicircular windows indicates the uppermost floor of the building, which is known as the palace of the Boukoleon. Contiguous, to the west, we observe a small but very ornate harbour, formed on quite a different plan from those previously seen. Curved piers of masonry, enriched with marbles, extending from the land, inclose about an acre of water, which is approached from the city by flights of white marble steps.[133] On the intervening quay rests a handsome group of statuary representing a lion and a bull in the agonies of a death struggle.[134] This is the exclusive port of the Imperial Palace,[135] an important segment of which adjoins the wall at this point. Both palace and harbour have taken the name of Boukoleon from the piece of sculpture which so conspicuously marks the site.[136] In this vicinity, behind the wall on the city level, is the palace of the once famous Persian refugee, Prince Hormisdas.[137]

Farther on is a small entry from the water leading to a chapel sacred to the Theotokos, surnamed the Conductress, another foundation of the devout Pulcheria.[138] Here are preserved a portrait of the Virgin painted by St. Luke, the swaddling-clothes of Jesus, and other recondite memorials of Gospel history[139] grafted by imposture on the credulity of the age. This Conductress,[140] by virtue of a holy fount, is credited with being able to point out the way for the blind to receive their sight;[141] and a retreat for the blind, therefore, has been established on the spot.[142]

As soon as we turn the north-east point, which marks the beginning of the Golden Horn, we exchange the inhospitable aspect of a fortified coast for a busy scene of maritime life. The wall recedes gradually to some distance from the waterline and forms an inconspicuous background to the impressive spectacle, which indicates the port of entry of a vast city. In the course of over a mile the shore has been fashioned into wharves from which three sets of stairs of ample width descend to the water's edge to facilitate the unloading of vessels. The first stair, named from its constructor, is that of Timasius;[143] next comes that of Chalcedon;[144] and lastly the stairs of Sycae,[145] a region of the city on the opposite side of the gulf. Alternating with the stairs are placed the entrances of two excavated harbours: the Prosphorian Port[146] for the landing of all kinds of imported provisions, and the Neorian Port, used chiefly as a naval station and for ship-building. The quays of the latter port, which are distinguished by the brazen statue of an ox, are also habitually frequented by the merchants of Constantinople, who make it their principal Exchange.[147] Similarly the vacant spaces about the Prosphorian Port are set apart for a cattle market.[148]

The first issue from the city on this side is called the Gate of Eugenius,[149] and is situated in the retreating portion of the wall. More remarkable is the Tower of Eugenius, called also the Centenarian Tower,[150] a massive pile closer to the bank, which corresponds to a similar erection across the water. These structures are the work of Constantine, who raised them to serve as the points of attachment of a ponderous iron chain, which should close the Golden Horn against the attack of a hostile fleet. So far, however, no enemy has been encountered so adventurous as to necessitate the practical application of this means of defence.[151]

Beyond the stairs of Sycae the locality is called the Zeugma.[152] This tract is reserved for the storage of wood, which, coal being unknown, is the only fuel available for cooking, heating of baths, and all other purposes. Immense quantities have, therefore, to be brought down by sea from the wild countries bordering on the Euxine[153] and deposited here for the use of the Constantinopolitans. At this point we have reached the limits of the wall of Byzantium and henceforth to the end of the land-wall at Blachernae this side of the city lies open to the water. Deeming it improbable that the town should ever be assaulted from this sequestered inlet, Constantine and his successors have omitted to fortify this bank. Originally this shore was indented by a number of small creeks,[154] but the teeming population, overflowing into every available space, has now so crowded the strand with houses that the outer rank, founded on piles, extends beyond the water's edge.[155] In the further part of this district the stream becomes narrower, and from a projecting point a wooden bridge has been thrown across to the opposite shore.[156] In its vicinity a brazen dragon commemorates or suggests a legend of virgins ravished and devoured until the destruction of the monster by St. Hypatius.[157] A slight expansion of the Golden Horn at Blachernae is called the Silver Bay.[158]

Having inspected the outside of Constantinople, it now remains for us to enter the city and pass in review its principal streets, buildings, and open spaces, whence we shall be led to make some acquaintance with the manners and customs of its inhabitants. From the Gate of Eugenius we can proceed directly to the most aristocratic quarter, where a majority of the public buildings are clustered round the Imperial Palace. Inside we shall find that thoroughfares of three kinds intersect the city for the purposes of general traffic: (1) main or business streets; (2) squares or market-places; and (3) lanes or side-streets for private residents.

(1) A main street consists of an open paved road, not more than fifteen feet wide, bounded on each side by a colonnade or portico. More than fifty of such porticoes are in existence at this date, so that a pedestrian can traverse almost the whole city under shelter from sun or rain.[159] Many of them have an upper floor, approached by wooden or stone steps, which is used as an *ambulacrum* or promenade. They are plentifully adorned with statuary of all kinds, especially above,[160] and amongst these presentments of the reigning emperor are not infrequent. The latter may be seen in busts of brass and marble, in brazen masks, and even in painted tablets.[161] Such images are consecrated and are sometimes surreptitiously adored by the populace with religious rites.[162] They are also endowed with the legal attribute of sanctuary, and

slaves not uncommonly fly to them for refuge as a protest against ill-treatment by their masters.[163] Portraits of popular actors, actresses, and charioteers may also be observed, but they are liable to be torn down if posted close to the Imperial images or in any position too reputable for their pretensions.[164] On the inside the porticoes are lined for the most part by shops and workshops.[165] Opening on to them in certain positions are public halls or auditoriums, architecturally decorative and furnished with seats, where meetings can be held and professors can lecture to classes on various topics.[166] Between the pillars of the colonnades next the thoroughfare we find stalls and tables for the sale of all kinds of wares. In the finer parts of the city such stalls or booths must by law be ornamentally constructed and encrusted outside with marbles so as not to mar the beauty of the piazza.[167] At the tables especially are seated the money-changers or bankers, who lend money at usury, receive it at interest, and act generally as the pawnbrokers of the capital.[168] Such pleasant arcades have naturally become the habitual resort of courtezans,[169] and they are recognized as the legitimate place of shelter for the houseless poor.[170]

(2) The open spaces, to which the Latin name of *forum* is applied more often than the Greek word *agora*, are expansions of the main streets, and, like them, are surrounded on all sides by porticoes. They are not, however, very numerous and about a dozen will comprise all that have been constructed within the capital. They originate in the necessity of preserving portions of the ground unoccupied for use as market-places, but the vacant area is always more or less decorative and contains one or more monuments of ornament or utility. Each one is named distinctively either from the nature of the traffic carried on therein or in honour of its founder, and most of them will deserve special attention during our itinerary of the city.

(3) The greater part of the ground area of Constantinople is, of course, occupied by residential streets, and these are usually, according to modern ideas, of quite preposterous narrowness.[171] Few of them are more than ten feet wide, and this scanty space is still more contracted above by projecting floors and balconies. In many places also the public way is encroached upon by *solaria* or sun-stages, that is to say by balconies supported on pillars of wood or marble, and often furnished with a flight of stairs leading to the pavement below. In such alleys low windows, affording a view of the street, or facile to lean out of,[172] are considered unseemly by the inmates of opposite houses. Hence mere light-giving apertures, placed six feet above the flooring, are the regular means of illumination. Transparent glass is sometimes used for the closure of windows, but more often we find thin plates of marble or alabaster with ornamental designs figured on the translucent substance.[173] Simple wooden shutters, however, are seen commonly enough in houses of the poorer class.[174]

Impatient to see the immense vacant area which he added to Byzantium covered with houses Constantine exercised little or no supervision over private builders; necessary thoroughfares became more or less blocked, walls of public edifices were appropriated as buttresses for hastily erected tenements, and the task of evolving order out of the resulting chaos was imposed on succeeding rulers.[175] On Constantinople becoming the seat of empire, as a resident of the period remarks, "such a multitude of people flocked hither from all parts, allured by military or mercantile pursuits, that the citizens out of doors and even at home are endangered by the unprecedented crush of men and animals."[176] In 447 Zeno, taking advantage of an extensive fire, promulgated a very stringent building act, contravention of which renders the offending structure liable to demolition, and inflicts a fine of ten pounds of gold on the owner. The architect also becomes liable in a similar amount, and is even subjected to banishment if unable to pay.[177] By this act, which remains permanently in force throughout the Empire, the not very ample width of twelve feet is fixed for private streets, *solaria* and balconies must be at least ten feet distant from similar projections on the opposite side, and not less than fifteen feet above the pavement; whilst stairs connecting them directly with the thoroughfare are entirely abolished. Prospective windows also are forbidden in streets narrower than the statutory allowance of twelve feet. These enactments, however, too restricted in their practical application, have done but little to relieve the congested thoroughfares. Thus, long afterwards, another resident complains that every spot of ground is occupied by contiguous dwellings to such an extent that "scarcely can an open space be discovered, which affords a clear view of the sky without raising the eyes aloft."[178]

These by-streets, of which there are more than four hundred[179] in the capital, consist chiefly of houses suitable for single families of the middle or lower classes. There are also, however, a large number of dwellings for collective habitation, which cover a greater area and rise by successive stories to an unusual height; but by law they are not allowed to exceed an altitude of one hundred feet.[180] When one side of such buildings is situated next a portico the adjacent part of the ground floor is usually fitted up as a range of shops.[181]

Besides the ordinary domiciles, which constitute the bulk of the city, there are the mansions or palaces of the wealthy, situated in various choice and open positions throughout the town. Such residences are generally two-storied, and have ornamental façades on which sculptured pillars both above and below are conspicuous. The windows, arched or rectangular, are divided by a central pilaster, and the roof, usually slanting, is covered with wood or thin slabs of stone. Within, a lofty hall is supported on tall columns surmounted by gilded capitals, and the walls are inlaid with polished marbles of various colours and textures. Throughout the house the principal apartments are similarly decorated, and even bedrooms are not destitute of the columnar adornments so dear to luxurious Byzantines. Ceilings are almost invariably fretted and liberally gilt. In houses of this class a central court, contained by a colonnade, giving air and light to the whole building, is considered a necessity. Much wealth is often expended in order to give this space the appearance of a landscape in miniature. Trees wave, fountains play, and artificial streams roll over counterfeited cliffs into pools stocked with tame fish.[182]

Within the gate of Eugenius we are on the northern slopes of the first hill, whereon was placed the citadel of Byzantium. Rounding it to the east we soon approach a tall Corinthian column of white marble, bearing on its summit a statue of Byzas,[183] a memorial of the victories by land and sea of Venerianus or other Byzantine generals over the marauding Goths about 266.[184] "Fortune has returned to the city," so runs the inscription on the base, "since the Goths have been overcome."[185] But these events have now passed into oblivion, and the vicinity is given up to low taverns, whilst in the popular mind the monument is associated with the more signal exploits of Pompey the Great in his Mithridatic wars.[186] To the south of this pillar, and close to the eastern wall, is situated the Imperial arsenal or Manganon, founded by Constantine, a repertory of weapons of all descriptions, and of machines used in the attack and defence of fortifications.[187] It contains, besides, a military library.[188]

Passing the Cynegium, a deserted amphitheatre of pre-Constantinian date,[189] and a small theatre, we may make the circuit of the first hill on the south side and enter the chief square of the city. This area, the ancient market-place of Byzantium,[190] is called the Augusteum,[191] that is the Imperial Forum; and it forms a court to those edifices which are particularly frequented by the Emperor. Around it are situated his Palace, his church, his Senate-House, and a vast Circus or Hippodrome, where the populace and their ruler are accustomed to meet face to face. Almost all the public buildings at this date, which aspire to architectural beauty, are constructed more or less exactly after the model of the classical Greek temple; that is, they are oblong, and have at each end a pediment corresponding to the extremities of a slanting roof. The eaves, projecting widely and supported on pillars, form a portico round the body of the building, which, in the most decorative examples, is excavated externally by a series of niches for the reception of statues.[192] The vestibule of the Palace, which opens on the southern portico of the Augusteum, is a handsome pillared hall named Chalke, or the Brazen House, from being roofed with tiles of gilded brass.[193] An image of Christ, devoutly placed over the brazen gates which close the entrance, dates back to Constantine,[194] but the remainder of the building has lately been restored by Anastasius.[195] This vestibule leads to several spacious chambers or courts which are rather of an official than of a residential character. Amongst these most room is given to the quarters of the Imperial guards, which are divided into four companies called Scholars, Excubitors, Protectors, and Candidates respectively.[196] The latter are distinguished by wearing white robes when in personal attendance on the Emperor.[197] Here also we find a state prison, the Noumera, a great banqueting hall, the Triclinium of Nineteen Couches, and a Consistorium or Throne-room.[198] Three porphyry steps at one end of this apartment lead to the throne itself, which consists of an elaborately carved chair adorned with ivory, jewels, and precious metals. It is placed beneath a silver *ciborium*, that is, a small dome raised on four pillars just sufficiently elevated to permit of the occupant standing upright. The whole is ornamentally moulded, a pair of silver eagles spread their wings on the top of the dome, and the interior can be shut in by drawing rich curtains hung between the columns.[199]

Beyond Chalke, the term includes its dependencies, we enter a court, colonnaded as usual, which leads on the right to a small church dedicated to St. Stephen,[200] the upper galleries of which overlook the Hippodrome. On the left, that is on the east of this court, is an octagonal hall, the first chamber in a more secluded section of the palace called Daphne.[201] It derives its name from a notable statue of Daphne, so well known in Greek fable as the maiden who withstood Apollo.[202] On the domed roof of this second vestibule stands a figure, representing the Fortune of the City, erected by Constantine.[203] The palace of Daphne contains the private reception rooms of the Emperor and Empress, whose chief personal attendants are a band of nobles entitled Silentiaries. The duty of these officers, amongst whom Anastasius was included before his elevation to the purple,[204] is to keep order in the Imperial chambers.[205] The terraces and balconies of Daphne, which face the west, overlook the Hippodrome. Adjoining the Palace on the south is an area fitted up as a private circus, which is used by members of the Court for equestrian exercises.[206]

Passing through Daphne to the east we enter a further court, and find ourselves opposite a third vestibule which, being of a semi-elliptical form, is called the Sigma of the Palace.[207] The division of the Imperial residence to which this hall introduces us is specially the Sacred or "God-guarded" Palace, because it contains the "sacred cubicle" or sleeping apartment of the Emperor.[208] In this quarter a numerous band of cubicularies or eunuchs of the bed-chamber have their principal station, controlled by the Praepositus of the sacred cubicle.[209] Here also are a crowd of vestiaries or dressers who are occupied with the royal apparel, including females of various grades with similar titles for the service of the Empress. At the eastern limit of the Palace stands the Pharos, a beacon tower afterwards, if not now, the first of a series throughout Asia Minor by which signals were flashed to and from the capital.[210] The Tzykanisterion,[211] Imperial Gardens, large enough to be called a park, occupies a great part of the south-eastern corner of the peninsula.[212] It is surrounded, or rather fortified, by substantial walls which join the sea walls of the city on the east and south.[213] The western section, which terminates on the south near the palace of Hormisdas and Port Julian, is surmounted by a covered terrace named the Gallery of Marcian,[214] the emperor who caused it to be constructed. A detached edifice within this inclosure, close to the Bucoleon Port, possesses considerable historical interest. It is called the Porphyry Palace, and Constantine is said to have enjoined on his successors that each empress at her lying-in should occupy a chamber in this building.[215] Hence the royal children are distinguished by the epithet of Porphyrogeniti or "born in the purple." The edifice is square, and the roof rises to a point like a pyramid. The walls and floors are covered with a rare species of speckled purple marble imported from Rome.[216] Hence its name. All parts of the Imperial palace are profusely adorned with statues, some mythological, others historical, representing rulers of the Empire, their families, or prominent statesmen and generals. Chapels or oratories dedicated to various saints are attached to every important section of the building.[217]

The north side of the Augusteum, opposite the vestibule of Chalke, is occupied by an oblong edifice with an arched wooden roof,[218] the basilica of St. Sophia,[219] commonly called the Great Church. The entrance faces the east,[220] and leads from a cloistered forecourt to a narrow hall, named the *narthex*, which extends across the whole width of the church. The interior consists of a wide nave separated from lateral aisles by rows of Corinthian columns, which support a gallery on each side. At the end of the nave stands the pulpit or *ambo*,[221] approached by a double flight of steps, one on each side. Behind the *ambo* the body of the church is divided from the *Bema* or chancel by a lofty carved screen, decorated with figures of sacred personages, called later the *Iconostasis* or image-stand. Three doors in the *Iconostasis* lead to the *Bema*, which contains the altar,[222] a table of costly construction enriched with gold and gems, and covered by a large and handsome *ciborium*. The edifice is terminated by an apse furnished with an elevated seat, which forms the throne of the Patriarch or Archbishop of Constantinople.[223] Light enters through mullioned windows glazed with plates of translucent marble. Every available space in the church is adorned with statues to the number of several hundreds, the majority of them representing pagan divinities and personifications of the celestial signs. Among them is a nearly complete series of the Roman emperors, whilst Helena, the mother of Constantine, appears thrice over in different materials, porphyry, silver, and ivory.[224] Close to St. Sophia on the north is the church of St. Irene, one of the earliest buildings erected for Christian worship by Constantine. It is usually called the Old Church.[225] Between these two sacred piles stands a charitable foundation, Sampson's Hospital, practically a refuge for incurables reduced by disease to a state of destitution.[226] Yet a third place of worship in this locality to the north-west of the Great Church may be mentioned, Our Lady (Theotokos) of the Brassworkers, built in a tract previously devoted to Jewish artisans of that class.[227]

On the east side of the Augusteum are situated two important public buildings, viz., the Senate-house, and, to the south of it, a palatial hall, the grand triclinium of Magnaura.[228] The latter stands back some distance from the square in an open space planted with trees,[229] and consists of a pillared façade, from whence we pass into a vast chamber supported on marble columns. It is the largest of the State reception rooms, and is the established rendezvous of Imperial pageantry whenever it is desirable to overawe the mind of foreign ambassadors.[230]

Next to Chalke on the west is placed the handsomest public bath in the city, that of Zeuxippus, the most ambitious work of Severus during his efforts at restoration.[231] It is compassed by ample colonnades which are conjoined with those of the Palace,[232] and are especially notable for their wealth of statuary in bronze and marble, dating from the best period of Grecian art. Within and without, in the palatial halls and chambers encrusted with marble and mosaic work, and in the niches of the porticoes, are to be found almost all the gods and goddesses, the poets, politicians, and philosophers of Greece and Rome, as celebrated by the Coptic poet Christodorus in a century of epigrams.[233] Amongst these a draped full-length figure of Homer is particularly admired: with his arms crossed upon his breast, his hair and beard unkempt, his brows bent in deep thought, his eyes fixed and expressionless in token of blindness, the bard is represented as he lived, absorbed in the creation of some sublime epic.[234] The bath, or institution,[235] as it may properly be called, is brilliantly illuminated during the dark hours of night and morning on an improved system devised by the Praefect Cyrus Constantine.[236]

On the west side of the Augusteum the ground is chiefly taken up by a large covered bazaar, in which dress fabrics of the most expensive kind, silks, and cloth of gold, are warehoused for sale to the Byzantine aristocracy. It is known as the House of Lamps, on account of the multitude of lights which are here ignited for the display of the goods after nightfall.[237] Close by is the Octagon, an edifice bordered by eight porticoes. It contains a library and a lecture theatre, and is the meeting-place of a faculty of erudite monks, who constitute a species of privy council frequently consulted by the Emperor.[238] Preferment to the highest ecclesiastical dignities is the recognized destiny of its members. In the same vicinity is a basilica named the Royal Porch, wherein is preserved a library founded by the Emperor Julian.[239] Here principally judicial causes are heard, and its colonnades have become the habitual resort of advocates, who for the greater part of each day frequent the place in expectation of, or consulting with, clients.[240]

In the open area of the Augusteum we may notice several important monuments. South of St. Sophia are two silver statues raised on pedestals, one on the west representing the great Theodosius,[241] and another on the east opposite the Senate-house, a female figure in a trailing robe, the Empress Eudoxia, wife of Arcadius. This is the famous statue round which the populace used to dance and sing so as to disturb the church service in the time of Chrysostom, whose invectives against the custom were deemed an insult by the Court, and made the occasion of his deposition and banishment.[242] Adjoining is a third statue, that of Leo Macella, elevated by means of a succession of steps, whereon popular suitors for Imperial justice are wont to deposit their petitions. These are regularly collected and submitted to the Emperor for his decision, whence the monument is called the Pittakia or petition-stone.[243] Near the same spot is a fountain known as the Geranium.[244] The most important structure, however, is the Golden Milestone or Milion,[245] situated in the south-west corner of the square. This is merely a gilded column to mark the starting-point of the official measurement of distances, which are registered systematically on mile-stones fixed along all the main roads of the Empire. But, in order to signalize its position, a grand triumphal arch, quadrilateral, with equal sides, and four entries, has been erected above it. The arch is surmounted by figures of Constantine and his mother holding a great cross between them. This group is of such magnitude that it is not dwarfed by equestrian statues of Trajan and Hadrian, which are placed behind it.[246] Beneath the arch a flying group, representing the chariot of the Sun, drawn by four flame-coloured horses, is elevated upon two lofty pillars.[247]

The Hippodrome or Circus commences near the Milion, whence it stretches southwards towards the sea and terminates in the vicinity of the Sigma of Julian,[248] a crescentic portico verging on the harbour of that name. It is an artificially constructed racecourse having an external length of about a quarter of a mile, and a breadth of nearly half that distance. This elongated space, straight on the north and round at the opposite end, is contained within a corniced wall decorated outside with engaged Corinthian columns, thirty feet in height.[249] Owing to the declivity of the ground as it sinks towards the shore, the circular portion of the architectural boundary is supported on arcades which gradually diminish in altitude on each side as they approach the centre of the inclosure.[250] Interiorly, except at the straight end, a sloping series of marble benches[251] runs continuously round the arena, the level of which is maintained in the *sphendone* or rounded part by the vaulted substructions based on the incline of the hill.[252] The northern extremity is flanked by a pair of towers, between which, on the ground level, lies the Manganon,[253] offices for the accommodation of horses, chariots, and charioteers. Above the Manganon is placed the Kathisma,[254] the name given to the seat occupied in state by the Emperor, when viewing the races. It is situated in a covered balcony or lodge fronted by a low balustrade, and is surrounded by an ample space for the reception of guards and attendant courtiers. In advance of the Kathisma, but on a lower level, is a square platform sustained by marble columns called the Stama, which is the station of a company of Imperial guards with standard-bearers.[255] Behind the Kathisma is a suite of retiring rooms, from whence a winding staircase[256] leads, by the gallery of St. Stephen's chapel, to the colonnades of Daphne. This is the royal route to the Circus.[257] The whole of the edifice superimposed on the Manganon is named the Palace of the Kathisma or of the Hippodrome.[258] A narrow terrace constructed in masonry, about three feet high, extends along the centre of the arena equidistant from all parts of the peripheral boundary. This Spine, as it was called in the old Roman nomenclature, but now renamed the Euripus,[259] serves to divide the track of departure from that of return. It is adorned from end to end with a range of monuments of great diversity. In the middle stands an Egyptian obelisk, inscribed with the usual hieroglyphs, resting on four balls sustained in turn by a square pedestal. An inscription at the bottom of the pedestal, illustrated by diagrams, exhibits the engineering methods adopted under the great Theodosius for the erection of the monolith on its present site; higher up elaborate sculptures show the Emperor in his seat presiding at the games.[260] Farther to the south is a still loftier column of the same shape, covered with brass plates, called the Colossus.[261] Intermediately is the brazen pillar, ravished from the temple of Delphi, composed of the twisted bodies of three serpents, whose heads formerly supported the golden tripod dedicated to Apollo by the Grecian states in memory of the defeat of the Persians at Plateia.[262] The names of the subscribing communities can still be read engraved on the folds of the snakes. Adjacent is a lofty pillar bearing the figure of a nymph with flowing robes, who holds forth a mail-clad knight mounted on horseback with one hand.[263] Near the south end is a fountain or bath with a central statue, known as the Phial of the Hippodrome.[264] Contiguous is an aedicule raised on four pillars, in which is displayed the laurelled bust of the reigning Emperor.[265] Above the obelisk, on a column, is a celebrated statue of Hercules Trihesperus by

Lysippus; the hero of colossal size, in a downcast mood seated on his lion's hide.[266] There are also several pyramids in various positions along the Spine as well as numerous figures of famous charioteers interspersed among the other ornaments.[267] To these are to be added the necessary furniture of the Spine of a Roman Circus, viz., the narrow stages raised on a pair of pillars at each end, the one supporting seven ovoid bodies, by the removal or replacing of which the spectators at both extremities are enabled to see how many laps of the course have been travelled over by the chariots; the other, seven dolphins,[268] ornamental waterspouts through which water is pumped into the Phial beneath.[269] At each end of the Euripus are the usual triple cones,[270] figured with various devices, the "goals" designed to make the turning-points of the arena conspicuous. Over the Manganon, on each side external to the Kathisma, are a pair of gilded horses removed by Theodosius II from the Isle of Chios.[271] The Podium, or lower boundary of the marble benches, is elevated about twelve feet above the floor of the arena by a columnar wall;[272] at the upper limit of these seats a level terrace or promenade is carried completely round the Circus. This walk is crowded with statues in brass and stone, many of them inscribed with their place of origin, from whence they have been carried off.[273] A number of them are deserving of special mention: a bronze eagle with expanded pinions rending a viper with its talons, and engraved with mystic symbols beneath the wings, said to have been erected by the arch-charlatan or illusionist, Apollonius Tyaneus, as a charm against the serpents which infested Byzantium;[274] a group representing the semi-piscine Scylla devouring the companions of Ulysses, who had been engulfed by Charybdis;[275] the figure of a eunuch named Plato, formerly a Grand Chamberlain, removed from a church notwithstanding a prohibition cut on the breast: "May he who moves me be strangled";[276] a man driving an ass, set up by Augustus at Actium in memory of his having met, the night before that battle, a wayfarer thus engaged, who, on being questioned, replied, "I am named Victor, my ass is Victoria, and I am going to Caesar's camp;"[277] the infants Romulus and Remus with their foster-mother the wolf;[278] a Helen of the rarest beauty, her charms enhanced by the most captivating dress and ornaments; a factitious basilisk crushing an asp between its teeth; a hippopotamus, a man grappling with a lion, several sphinxes,[279] a well-known hunchback in a comic attitude,[280] statues of emperors on foot and on horseback, and various subjects from pagan mythology, the whole representing the spoliation of more than a score of cities looted in time of peace at the caprice of a despot.[281] Four handsome arched gateways, two on each side, with containing towers,[282] give the public access to the interior of the Hippodrome.[283] That on the south-east is named the Gate of the Dead,[284] a term which originated at the time when a special entry was reserved for removing the bodies of those slain in the fatal, but now obsolete, combats of gladiators. The Sphendone, however, is now frequently used for the execution of offenders of rank, not always criminal, and this portal has still, therefore, some practical right to its name.[285] When necessary, the Circus can be covered with an awning as a protection against the sun or bad weather.[286]

From the western arch of the Milion we enter the Mese, that is, the Middle, Main, or High Street of the city, which traverses the whole town from east to west with a southerly inclination between the Augusteum and the Golden Gate. It is bounded in almost all of its course by porticoes said to have been constructed by Eubulus, one of the wealthy Romans who were induced to migrate by Constantine. The same patrician gifted the city with two other colonnades which extend for a considerable distance along the eastern portion of the north and south shores.[287] The Mese proceeds at first between the north of the Hippodrome and the Judicial or Royal Basilica with the adjacent buildings already mentioned. Contiguous to the Royal Porch is a life-size statue of an elephant with his keeper, erected by Severus to commemorate the fact that the animal had killed a money-changer, who was afterwards proved dishonest, to avenge the death of his master.[288] Near the western flank of the Circus is the Palace of Lausus, said to be one of those reared by Constantine to allure some of the Roman magnates to reside permanently in his new capital.[289] Subsequently, however, it was transformed into an inn for the public entertainment of strangers.[290] In its vestibule and galleries were collected many gems of Grecian statuary, but most of these have been destroyed by the great fire which raged in this quarter under Zeno.[291] Amongst them were the celebrated Venus of Cnidos in white marble, a nude work of Praxiteles;[292] the Lindian Athene in smaragdite; the Samian Hera of Lysippus; a chryselephantine, or ivory and gold statue of Zeus by Phidias, which Pericles placed in the temple at Olympia;[293] an allegorical figure of Time by Lysippus, having hair on the frontal part of the head, but with the back bald; and also many figures of animals, including a cameleopard.[294]

Proceeding onwards for about a quarter of a mile we pass on our right the Argyropratia, that is, the abode of the silversmiths,[295] and arrive at the Forum of Constantine, which presents itself as an expansion of the Mese. This open space, the most signal ornament of Constantinople, is called prescriptively the Forum; and sometimes, from its finished marble floor, "The Pavement." Two lofty arches of white Proconnesian marble, opposed to each other from east to west, are connected by curvilinear porticoes so as to inclose a circular area.[296] From its centre rises a tall porphyry column bound at intervals with brazen laurel wreaths. This pillar is surmounted by a figure of Constantine with the attributes of the Sun-god, his head resplendent with a halo of gilded rays.[297] The mystic Trojan Palladium, furtively abstracted from Rome, is buried beneath the monument, on the base of which an inscription piously invokes Christ to become the guardian of the city.[298] The sculptural decorations of this Forum are very numerous: the Fortune of the City, called Anthusa, was originally set up here, and adored with bloodless sacrifices;[299] a pair of great crosses inscribed with words of the Creed and Doxology are erected on opposite sides; Constantine with his mother Helena, and a pair of winged angels form a group about the one, whilst the sons of the same emperor surround the other.[300] Here also may be seen Athene, her neck encircled by snakes emanating from the Gorgon's head fixed in her aegis; Amphitrite distinguished by a crown of crab's claws; a dozen statues of porphyry ranged in one portico, and an equal number of gilded sirens or sea-horses in the other; and lastly the bronze gates bestowed by Trajan on the temple of Diana at Ephesus, embossed with a series of subjects illustrating the theogonies of Greece and Rome. These latter adorn the entrance to the original Senate-house which is situated on the south side of the Forum.[301]

If we diverge from the Mese slightly to the north-east of the Pavement, we shall enter a large square named the Strategium, from its forming a parade-ground to the barracks of the Palatine troops.[302] Amongst several monuments a Theban obelisk conspicuously occupies the middle place,[303] but the most striking object is an equestrian figure of Constantine with the pillar alongside it by which Constantinople is officially declared to be a second Rome.[304] This locality is associated in historic tradition with Alexander the Great, of whom it contains a commemorative statue.[305] From hence he is said to have started on his expedition against Darius after holding a final review of his forces. On this account it was chosen by Severus as a permanent site for military quarters.[306] The public prison is also located in this square.[307]

Continuing our way beneath the piazzas of the Mese beyond the Forum of Constantine we reach the district known as the Artopolia or public bakeries which lie to the north of the main street. A strange group of statuary, allegorizing the fecundity of nature, is collocated in this region, viz., a many-headed figure in which the faces of a dozen animals are seen in conjunction; amongst them are those of a lion, an eagle, a peacock, a ram, a bull, a crow, a mouse, a hare, a cat, and a weasel. This eccentric presentment is flanked by a pair of marble Gorgons.[308] Adjacent we may also observe a paved area in which a cross stands conspicuously on a pillar, another record of the hybrid piety of Constantine.[309]

Farther on by a couple of furlongs is the great square of Taurus, also called the Forum of Theodosius, through its being specially devoted to memorials of that prince. It covers an oblong space, extending from level ground on the south up the slope of the third hill, the summit of which it includes in its northern limit.[310] This eminence, in accordance with the conception of making Constantinople a counterpart of Rome, is called the Capitol, and is occupied by an equivalent of the Tabularium, that is, by a building which contains the Imperial archives.[311] Similarly, this site has been chosen for an edifice composed of halls and a lecture-theatre assigned to a faculty of thirty professors appointed by government to direct the liberal studies of the youth of the capital—in short, for the University, as we may call it, of Constantinople.[312] The principal monument in Taurus is the column of Theodosius I, the sculptural shaft of which illustrates in an ascending spiral the Gothic victories of that Emperor.[313] But the equestrian statue which originally crowned this pictured record of his achievements, having been overthrown by an earthquake, has lately been replaced by a figure of the unwarlike Anastasius.[314] To the north of this column, on a tetrapyle or duplex arch, Theodosius the Less presides over the titular Forum of his grandfather.[315] But in the fading memory of the populace the figure of this Emperor is already confounded with a horseman said to have been abstracted from Antioch, whom some imagine to be Jesus Nava,[316] and others Bellerophon.[317] Facing each other from east to west on opposite sides of the square are arches supporting figures of those degenerate representatives of the Theodosian dynasty, Arcadius and Honorius.[318] To the western of these arches we may observe that an assortment of troublesome insects, counterfeited in brass, have been carefully affixed— another charm of Apollonius Tyaneus intended to protect the inhabitants against such diminutive pests.[319] In this vicinity is also a palace, built by Constantine, in which strangers from all parts are hospitably entertained without expense or question.[320]

From the west side of Taurus we may perceive the great aqueduct of Valens, which crosses the third valley, and is here conjoined with the chief *Nymphaeum*, a decorative public hall built around a fountain.[321] Several of these *Nymphaea* exist in the city, and they are often made use of for private entertainments, especially nuptial festivals, by citizens who have not sufficient space for such purposes in their own homes.[322] The water supply of the town is under the care of a special Consul, and very stringent laws are in force to prevent waste or injury to the structures necessary for its storage and distribution.[323] With the exception, however, of that of Valens, aerial aqueducts (so conspicuous at Rome) have not been carried near to, or within, the walls of Constantinople; and subterranean pipes of lead or earthenware are the usual means of conveying the precious liquid from place to place.[324] The public cisterns are in themselves a striking architectural feature of the city. Some of these are open basins, but many of them possess vaulted roofs, upborne by hundreds of columns whose capitals are sculptured in the varied styles of Byzantine art.[325] Most of these receptacles for water are distinguished by special names; thus, beneath the Sphendone of the Hippodrome, we have the Cold cistern,[326] and near to the palace or *hospice* of Lausus the Philoxenus, or Travellers' Friend.[327] By a law of Theodosius II, the wharf dues, paid for the use of the various stairs on the Golden Horn, are applied to the repair of the aqueducts, the supply of water from which is free to the public.[328] In connection with the cisterns a group of three storks in white marble is pointed out as a further result of the fruitful visit of Apollonius Tyaneus to Byzantium; owing to the district becoming infested by serpents, flocks of these birds were attracted hither, and caused a terrible nuisance through having contracted a habit of casting the dead bodies of the reptiles into the water reservoirs; but the erection of this monument speedily achieved their perpetual banishment from the city.[329]

If we step aside a short distance from Taurus, both on the north and south sides, we shall in each case come upon an interesting monument. 1. On the far side of the Capitol, overlooking the Zeugma, on a marble pillar, is a noted statue of Venus, which marks the site of the only *lupanar* permitted by Constantine to exist in his new capital.[330] Around, each secluded within its curtained lattice, are a series of bowers consecrated to the illicit, or rather mercenary, amours of the town. The goddess, however, who presides here is credited with a remarkable leaning towards chastity; for, it is believed, that if a wife or maid suspected of incontinence be brought to this statue, instead of denying her guilt, she will by an irresistible impulse cast off her garments so as to give an ocular proof of her shamelessness.[331] 2. To the south, elevated on four pillars, is a lofty pyramid of bronze, the apex of which sustains a female figure pivoted so as to turn with every breath of wind. The surfaces of the pyramid are decorated with a set of much admired bas-reliefs; on one side a sylvan scene peopled with birds depicted in flight or song; on another a pastoral idyl representing shepherds piping to their flocks, whilst the lambs are seen gambolling over the green; again, a marine view with fishers casting their nets amid shoals of fish startled and darting in all directions; lastly, a mimic battle in which mirthful bands of Cupids assault each other with apples and pomegranates. This elaborate vane, which is visible over a wide area, is known as the *Anemodulion*, or Slave of the Winds.[332]

Beyond Taurus the Mese leads us to the *Philadelphium*, a spot dedicated to brotherly love and embellished by a group representing the three sons of Constantine in an affectionate attitude. The monument commemorates the last meeting of these noble youths, who, on hearing of the death of their father, encountered each other here prior to assuming the government of their respective divisions of the Empire.[333] Opposite is another group of the same princes, who ultimately destroyed each other, erected by Constantine himself with the usual accompaniment of a large gilt cross.[334] A few paces farther on, our route is again interrupted by a square, the entrance to which is marked by a Tetrapyle, or arch of four portals, executed in brass. Above the first gateway is affixed a significant symbol, namely, a modius or measure for wheat standing between a pair of severed hands. It records the punishment by Valentinian I of an unjust dealer who ignored his law that corn should be sold to the people with the measure heaped up to overflowing.[335] The Forum on which the Tetrapyle opens is called the *Amastrianum*, perhaps from a wanderer belonging to Amastris in Paphlagonia, who was found dead on this spot.[336] It is the usual place of public execution for the lower classes, whether capital or by mutilation.[337] This square, which is close to the streamlet Lycus,[338] is no exception to the rule that such open spaces should be crowded with statues. Among them we may notice the Sun-god in a marble chariot, a reclining Hercules, shells with birds resting on the rim, and nearly a score of dragons.[339]

Yet two more open spaces on the Mese arrest our progress as we proceed to the Golden Gate. The first is the Forum of the Ox, which contains a colossal quadruped of that species brought hither from Pergamus.[340] This is in reality a brazen furnace for the combustion of malefactors condemned to perish by fire, and has the credit of having given some martyrs to the Church, especially under the Emperor Julian.[341] Farther on is the last square we shall find it necessary to view, the Forum of Arcadius, founded by that prince.[342] Its distinguishing monument is a column similar in every way to that in Taurus,[343] but the silver statue which surmounts it is the figure of Arcadius himself.[344] We are now on the top of the Xerolophos, and the colonnades which lead hence to the walls of Theodosius are named the *Porticus Troadenses*.[345] But about halfway to the present Imperial portal we pass through the original Golden Gate,[346] a landmark which has been spared in the course of the old walls of Constantine. The extensive tract added by Theodosius II to the interior of the city was formerly the camping ground of the seven bodies of Gothic auxiliaries, and for that reason was divided into seven districts, denoted numerically from south to north. The whole of this quarter is now spoken of as the *Exokionion*, that is, the region outside the Pillar, in allusion to a well-known statue of Constantine which marks the border.[347] But, in order to particularize the smaller areas of this quarter, some of the numbers are still found indispensable, and we often hear of the Deuteron, Triton, Pempton, and Hebdomon. Adjacent to the Golden Gate is situated the great monastery of St. John Studii, which maintains a thousand monks.[348]

On entering the *Exokionion* the Mese gives off a branch thoroughfare which leads to the Gate of the Fountain, skirting on its way the church of St. Mocius, a place of worship granted to the Arians by Theodosius I when he established the Nicene faith at Constantinople.[349] By this route also we arrive at a portico which adorns the interior of the mural Sigma,[350] and contains a monument to Theodosius II erected by his Grand Chamberlain, the infamous eunuch Chrysaphius.[351]

If we now retrace our steps to the Philadelphium and diverge thence from the Mese in a north-westerly direction, we shall soon reach the church of the Holy Apostles, the most imposing of the Christian edifices founded by Constantine. It is contained within an open court surrounded by cloisters, on which give the numerous offices required for the guardians of the sacred precincts. This church is one of the first of those constructed in the form of a cross.[352] Outside it is covered with variegated marbles, and the roof is composed of tiles of gilded brass. The interior is elaborately decorated with a panelled ceiling and walls invested with trellis-work of an intricate pattern, the whole being profusely gilded. Cenotaphs ranged in order are consecrated to the honour and glory of the Twelve Apostles, and in the midst of these is a porphyry sarcophagus wherein repose the remains of Constantine himself and his mother. The building is in fact a *heroon* or mausoleum designed to perpetuate the fulminating flattery of the period by which Constantine was declared to be the "equal of the Apostles."[353] Subsequently, however, this religious pile was adopted as the customary place of interment of the Imperial families, and many tombs of royal personages are now to be seen scattered around. Amongst them lie the sons of Constantine, Theodosius I and II, Arcadius, Marcian, Pulcheria, Leo I, and Zeno.[354] On leaving this spot, if we turn to the south for a short distance, we shall be enabled to examine a tall column with a heavy capital elaborately sculptured in a Byzantino-Corinthian style. An inscription on the pedestal testifies to its having been erected by the Praefect Tatian to the memory of the Emperor Marcian.[355]

The region of Sycae, built on the steep slope of the hill which rises almost from the water's edge to the north of the Golden Horn, is considered to be an integral part of the city. It is particularly associated with the brother of Arcadius, the enervated Honorius, who ruled the Western Empire for more than thirty years, an effigy rather than the reality of a king. Thus the Forum of Honorius constitutes its market-place, and its public baths are also distinguished by the name of the same prince. It possesses, moreover, a dock and a church with gilded tiles, and is fortified in the usual way by a wall with towers.[356]

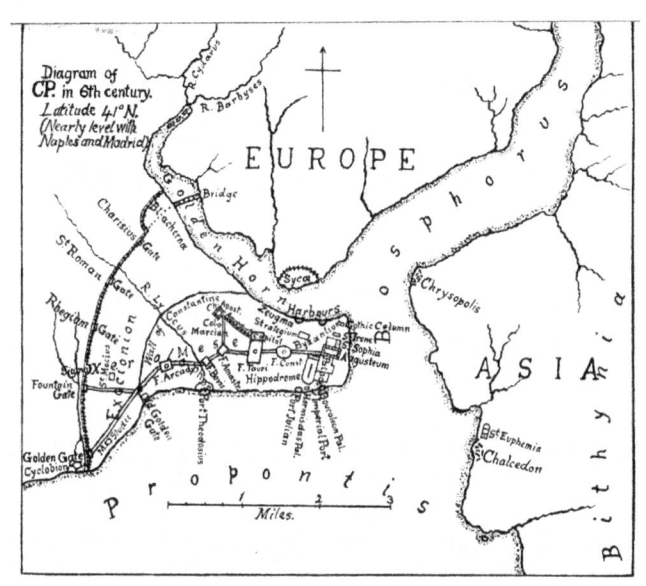

**Diagram of CP. in 6th century.
Latitude 41° N. (Nearly level with Naples and Madrid)**

- 35 -

Rome was divided by Augustus into fourteen regions or parishes, to each of which he appointed a body of public officers whose functions much resembled those of a modern Vestry.[357] The municipal government of the new Rome is an almost exact imitation of that instituted by the founder of the Empire for the old capital. Here are the same number of regions, named numerically and counted in order from east to west, beginning at the end of the promontory. The last two of these, however, are outside the wall of Constantine, that is to say, Blachernae on the north-west and Sycae over the water. To each division is assigned a *Curator* or chief controller, a *Vernaculus* or beadle, who performs the duties of a public herald, five *Vicomagistri*, who form a night patrol for the streets, and a considerable number of *Collegiati*, in the tenth region as many as ninety, whose duty it is to rush to the scene of fires with hatchets and water-buckets.[358] At night the main thoroughfares are well lighted by flaring oil-lamps.[359]

One remarkable feature of the city, to be encountered by the visitor at every turn, is an elevated shed which can be approached on all sides by ranges of steps. These "Steps," as they are briefly called, are stations for the gratuitous daily distribution of provisions to the poorer citizens. Every morning a concourse of the populace repairs to the Step attached to their district, and each person, on presenting a wooden *tessera* or ticket, inscribed with certain amounts, receives a supply of bread, and also a dole of oil, wine, and flesh.[360] More than six score of such stations are scattered throughout the town, and the necessary corn is stored in large granaries which are for the most part replenished by ships arriving every season from Alexandria.[361] More than twenty public bakeries furnish daily the required demand of bread.[362] Besides free grants of food and houses for the entertainment of strangers, the city contains various other charities under the direction of state officials, the chief of which are hospitals for the sick and aged, orphanages, poor-houses, and institutions for the reception of foundlings.[363] A medical officer, entitled an arch-physician, with a public stipend, is attached to each parish to attend gratuitously to the poor.[364]

The civic authorities are well aware that disease arises from putrid effluvia, and hence an elaborate system of deep drainage has been constructed so that all sewage is carried by multiple channels into the sea.[365] Since the introduction of Christianity, cremation has become obsolete, and burial in the earth is universally practised.[366] Public cemeteries, however, are not allowed within the walls, but churches and monasteries are permitted to devote a portion of their precincts to the purpose of interment. Such limited space is necessarily reserved for members of the hierarchy and persons of a certain rank, who have been beneficiaries of the church or order.[367]

We may here terminate our exploration of the topography of Constantinople, content to leave a multitude of objects, both interesting and important, beyond the limits of our survey. Were I to attempt the description of everything worthy of notice in the city, my exposition would soon resemble the catalogue of a museum, and the reader's attention would expire under the sense of interminable enumerations. Our picture has been filled in with sufficient detail to convey the impression of a vast capital laid out in colonnaded squares and streets, to the adornment of which all that Grecian art could evolve in architecture and statuary has been applied with a lavishness attainable only by the fiat of a wide-ruling despot.

III. Sociology

To make this chapter fully consonant to its title it now remains for us to pass in review the sociological condition of the inhabitants, whilst we try to learn something of their mode of life, their national characteristics, and their mental aptitudes. We have already seen that in the case of the Neo-Byzantines or Lesser Greeks,[368] the path of evolution lay through a series of historical vicissitudes in which there was more of artificial forcing than of the insensible growth essential to the formation of a homogeneous people. Owing to its geographical position it was perhaps inevitable from the first that Byzantium should become a cosmopolitan town, whose population should develop little political stability or patriotic coherence. In addition, however, it happened that the Megareans, their chief progenitors, had gained an unenviable notoriety throughout Greece; they were generally esteemed to be gluttonous, slothful, ineffective, and curiously prolific in courtesans, who, for some reason which now escapes us, were peculiarly styled "Megarean sphinxes."[369] Once established on the Golden Horn the Byzantines seem to have found life very easy; their fisheries were inexhaustible and facile beyond belief;[370] whilst the merchants trading in those seas soon flocked thither so that port dues furnished an unearned and considerable income. As a consequence the bulk of the populace spent their time idling in the market-place or about the wharves, each one assured of meeting some visitor to whom for a valuable consideration he was willing to let his house and even his wife, whilst he himself took up his abode in the more congenial wine-shop. So firmly did this dissolute mode of life gain a footing, that when the town was besieged the citizens could not be rallied to defend the walls until the municipal authorities had set up drinking-booths on the ramparts.[371] Law was usually in abeyance,[372] finance disorganized,[373] and political independence forfeit to the leading power of the moment, whether Greek or Persian.

Such was the community whose possession of a matchless site decided Constantine to select them as the nucleus of population for his new Rome, the meditated capital of the East. And, in order to fill with life and movement the streets newly laid out, he engrafted on this doubtful stock a multitude of servile and penurious immigrants, whom he allured from their native haunts by the promise of free residence and rations.[374] Nevertheless a metropolis constituted from such elements was scarcely below the level of the times, and was destined to prove a successful rival of the degenerate Rome which Constantine aspired to supplant.

The impressions of life and colour which affect a stranger on entering a new city arise in great part from the costume of its inhabitants. At Constantinople there prevails in this age a decency in dress foreign to Rome during the first centuries of the Empire, and even to Greece in the most classic period. Ladies invested with garments of such tenuity as to reveal more than they conceal of their physical beauties, to the confusion of some contemporary Seneca, are not here to be met with in the streets;[375] the Athenian maiden, with her tunic divided almost to the hip, or the Spartan virgin displaying her limbs bare to the middle of the thigh, have no reflection under the piazzas of renascent Byzantium. A new modesty, born of Christian influences, has cast a mantle of uniformity over the licence as well as over the simplicity of the pagan world. In observing the costume of this time a modern eye would first, perhaps, note the fact that in civil life the garb of men differs but little from that of women. Loose clothing, which hides the shape of the body, and in general the whole of the lower limbs, is common to both sexes. Men usually shave, but a moustache is often worn; their hair is cropped, but not very close.[376] Head-gear is an exception, and so, for the lower classes, are coverings for the feet. A workman, an artisan, or a slave, the latter a numerous class, wears a simple tunic of undyed wool, short-sleeved, girt round the waist and reaching to the knees, with probably a hood which can be drawn over the head as a protection against the weather.[377] This garment is in fact the foundation dress of all ranks of men, but the rich wear fine materials, often of silk and of varied hues, have long sleeves, and use girdles of some costly stuff. They, in addition, are invested in handsome cloaks reaching to the ankles, which are open for their whole length on the right side and are secured by a jewelled clasp over the corresponding shoulder. Shoes often highly ornamented,[378] and long hose, coloured according to taste, complete the dress of an ordinary Byzantine gentleman. On less formal occasions a short sleeveless cloak, fastened at the neck, but open down the front, is the customary outer vestment. The tunic or gown of women reaches to the feet, and, in the case of ladies, is embroidered or woven with designs of various patterns and tints. The latter usually consist of some small variegated device which is repeated in oblique lines all over the garment. Shawls, somewhat similar in colour and texture to the gown, thrown over the back and shoulders or wound round the bust, are habitually worn at the same time. Gloves, shoes and stockings of various hues, and a simple form of cap which partly conceals the hair, are also essential to the attire of a Byzantine lady. As in all ages, jewellery is much coveted, and women of any social rank are rarely to be seen without heavy necklaces, earrings of an elaborate spreading design,[379] and golden girdles.[380] A less numerous class of the community are male ascetics, celibates of a puritanical cast, who love to placard themselves by wearing scarlet clothing and binding their hair with a fillet;[381] also virgins devoted to the service of the churches, who are known by their sombre dress, black hoods, gray mantles, and black shoes.[382] Philosophers adopt gray, rhetoricians crimson, and physicians blue, for the tint of their cloaks.[383] To these may be added the courtesans who try to usurp the costume of every grade of women, even that of the sacred sisterhood.[384] Such is the population who usually crowd the thoroughfares and lend them a gaudy aspect which is still further heightened by numbers of private carriages—literally springless carts—bedizened with paint and gilding, and most fashionable if drawn by a pair of white mules with golden trappings. Such vehicles are indispensable to the outdoor movements of matrons of any rank;[385] and in each case a train of eunuchs in gorgeous liveries, and decked with ornaments of gold, mark the progress of a great lady.[386] Occasionally we may see the Praefect of the City, or some other man of signal rank, passing in a silver wagon drawn by four horses yoked abreast.[387] Often we meet a noble riding a white horse, his saddle-cloth embroidered in gold; around him a throng of attendants bearing rods of office with which they rudely scatter all meaner citizens to make way for their haughty master.[388] A person of any consequence perambulating the city is followed by at least one slave bearing a folding seat for incidental rest.[389] In some retired nook we may encounter a circle of the populace gazing intently at the performance of a street mountebank; he juggles with cups and goblets; pipes, dances, and sings a lewd ballad; the bystanders reward him with a morsel of bread or an obole; he invokes a thousand blessings on their heads, and departs to resume his display in some other spot.[390]

The Byzantine Emperor and Empress are distinguished in dress from all their subjects by the privilege of wearing the Imperial purple.[391] The Emperor is further denoted by his jewelled shoes or slippers of a bright scarlet colour, a feature in his apparel which is even more exclusive than his cloak or his crown. The latter symbol of majesty is a broad black hoop expanding towards the top, bordered above and below with a row of pearls, thickly studded with gems all round, and bearing four great pendent pearls which fall in pairs on the nape of the neck. His ample purple robe, which falls to his feet, is fastened by a costly shoulder-clasp of precious stones. Its uniformity is diversified by two squares or tables of cloth of gold embroidered in various colours, which approach from the back and front the division on the right side. Purple hose and a white tunic, sleeved to the wrists and girt with a crimson scarf, complete the civil attire of the Emperor. When sitting in state he usually bears a globe surmounted by a cross[392] in his left hand. His attendant nobles, a new order of patricians who are styled the Fathers of the Emperor,[393] are garbed all in white, but the tables of their gowns are of plain purple, their girdles are red, and their shoes are black. His Protectors or guards wear green tunics, with red facings, and are shod in black with white hose; a thick ring of gold, joined to a secondary oval one in front, encircles the neck of each one; they are armed with a long spear, and carry an oval shield bordered with blue and widely starred from the centre in black on a red ground. Their Count or Captain is distinguished by a red and purple breasted tunic, and by the Christian monogram of his shield in yellow on a green ground. The dress of the Empress is very similar to that of her consort, but her crown is more imposing, being heightened by sprays of jewels, and laden with strings of pearls which fall over her neck and shoulders.[394] Her purple mantle is without tables, but is brocaded with gold figures around the skirt; she wears besides an under-skirt embroidered in bright hues, golden slippers with green hose, and all jewels proper to ladies of the most costly description.[395] Two or three patricians usually wait on the Empress, but her Court is chiefly composed of a bevy of noble matrons or maids, female patricians who act as her tire-women; the leader[396] of these is distinguished by her purple gown.[397]

Every morning at seven o'clock the Grand Janitor of the Palace,[398] taking his bunch of keys, proceeds with a company of guards and Silentiaries to open all the doors which lead from the Augusteum to the Consistorium. After the lapse of an hour the Primicerius or captain of the watch knocks at the door of the Emperor's private apartments. Surrounded by his eunuchs the prince then sallies forth and first, standing before an image of Christ in a reverential attitude, recites a formal prayer. On the completion of this pious office he takes his seat on the throne and calls for the Logothete[399] or steward of the royal household. Upon this the Janitor, pushing aside the variegated curtains which close the door leading to the antechamber, passes out, and in a short time returns with the desired official. The Logothete first drops on one knee and adores the majesty of the Emperor, after which he rises and transaction of business for the day begins. By this time the antechamber of the Throne room has become crowded with dignitaries of state, patricians, senators, praefects, and logothetes of various denominations. The Emperor commands the presence from time to time of such of these as he wishes to confer with, and all of them at their first entrance salute him with the same form of submissive obeisance, except those of patrician rank, who merely bow profoundly, and are greeted by the Emperor with a kiss.[400] Codicils or commissions for the appointment of officers of state or rulers of provinces are presented by the Master of the Rolls,[401] and the Emperor signs the documents in purple ink, the use of which is forbidden to subjects.[402] Such codicils are illustrated in colours with various devices symbolical of the dignity or duties of the office conferred.

Those of praefects and proconsuls of the highest rank display a draped *abacus* or table on which rests a framed image of the Emperor lighted by wax tapers; in addition, busts of the Emperor with his imperial associates or heirs on a pedestal, and a silver quadriga—insignia of office, which adorn the local vestibule or denote the vicegerent of the sovereign in his progress through the public ways. The provinces or districts are indicated by female figures or busts labelled with various names; in many instances by rivers, mountains, indigenous animals, and miniature fortresses representing the chief towns. In the case of rulers of lesser rank—dukes, vicars, correctors, counts, presidents—a portly volume inscribed with the initials of a conventional sentence[403] supplants the painted image. For Masters of the Forces the codicils are illustrated with weapons of war or with the numerous designs, geometrical or pictorial, which distinguish the shields of the cohorts under their command. Dignitaries of civil rank, financial or secretarial, are suitably denoted on their diplomas by vessels loaded with coin, purses, writing-cases, and rolls of manuscript.[404] In addition to those assigning administrative appointments honorary codicils are also issued, by which the prerogative or precedence only pertaining to various ranks is conferred. These documents are also called "nude," as they are not illustrated with those figures which indicate that the holder is in authority over particular districts. They are equivalent to patents of nobility, and are granted for service to the state, general esteem, and probably also by mere purchase.[405] Among the throng at the Emperor's receptions are always a number of officers of a certain rank, who, on vacating their posts, have the privilege of waiting on the Emperor in order to adore or kiss his purple.[406] In the absence of urgent business the audience closes at ten o'clock; at a sign from the Emperor the Janitor passes into the antechamber with his keys, which he agitates noisily as a signal of dismissal. The Palace is then shut up, but at two o'clock it is reopened with the same formalities for the further transaction of affairs. At five o'clock it is again closed and the routine of Imperial reception is at an end for the day. On the *Dominica* or Sunday the assembly is most numerous, and the company repairs in procession to one of the adjoining halls to attend the performance of a brief divine service.[407] As a concession to the holiness of this day adoration of the Emperor is less formal. When the Emperor or Empress drives through the streets the carriage is drawn by four white horses or mules,[408] the vehicle and the trappings of the animals being ornate in the highest degree.[409] Public processions on festal days of the Church are regular and frequent; and on these occasions, as well as on those of national rejoicing, the Emperor rides a white horse amidst his train of eunuchs, nobles, and guards. At such times the Praefect of the City enjoins a special cleansing and decoration of the streets on the prescribed route. The way is adorned from end to end with myrtle, rosemary, ivy, box, and flowers of all kinds which are in bloom at the season. The air is filled with the odour of incense, and from private windows and balconies particoloured and embroidered fabrics are suspended by the inhabitants. Wherever the royal cavalcade passes, cries of "Long live the Emperor" rise from every throat.[410] At night the thoroughfares are illuminated by frequent lamps displayed from windows and doorways. But on occasions of public calamity, such as ruinous earthquakes or prolonged drought, this scene of splendour is reversed; and the Emperor, on foot and uncrowned, proceeds amidst the clergy and populace, all clad in sombre garments, to one of the sacred shrines outside the walls to offer up supplications for a remission of the scourge.[411] And again the Emperor may be seen as a humble pedestrian, whilst the Patriarch, who usually rides upon an ass, is seated in the Imperial carriage, on his way to the consecration of a new church, or holding on his knees the relics of some saint prior to their deposition in one of the sacred edifices.[412]

At this date conventional titles of distinction or adulation have attained to the stage of full development. The Emperor, in Greek *Basileus* or *Autocrator*, the sole Augustus, is also styled Lord and Master, and is often addressed as "Your Clemency."[413] His appointed heir receives the dignity of Caesar and perhaps the title of *Nobilissimus*, an epithet confined to the nearest associates of the throne.[414] Below the Imperial eminence and its attachments the great officers of state are disposed in three ranks, namely, the *Illustres*, *Spectabiles*, and *Clarissimi*. The Illustrious dignitaries are termed by the Prince and others "Most Glorious," and are variously addressed as "Your Sublimity," "Magnificence," "Eminence," "Excellence," "Highness," "Serenity," or "Sincerity," etc. The two lower ranks are similarly addressed, but only the less fulsome of such expressions are applied to them. Consonant to the same scheme the clergy receive the epithets of "Most Holy," "Blessed," "Reverend," "Beloved of God"; and are addressed as "Your Beatitude," "Eminence," etc., the emphasis being graduated according as they may happen to be Patriarchs, Archbishops, Metropolitans, Bishops, or simple clericals.[415]

In the assemblies of the Hippodrome popular fervour reaches its highest pitch, whether in times of festive or political excitement. From Daphne, by the gallery of St. Stephen's and the Cochlea, the Emperor, surrounded by courtiers and guards, gains his throne in the Kathisma.[416] On his entry the Protectors, already assembled in the Stama or Pi, elevate the Standards which have previously been lying on the ground.[417] Before seating himself on his throne the Emperor, advancing to the balustrade of the Kathisma, greets the assembled populace by making the sign of the cross in the air. As soon as the answering cries of adulation subside, a set hymn[418] is intoned from each side of the Circus in alternate responses by particular bodies of the people called *Demes*, whose importance, not merely agonistic, but above all political, renders a special account of them here necessary.

The Demes or factionaries of the Hippodrome occupy the benches at the end of the arena on each side adjacent to the Kathisma,[419] and are called the *Veneti* and *Prasini*, that is, the Blues and Greens.[420] These bodies, which are legally incorporated as guilds,[421] consist of the contending parties in the chariot races, and of such others as elect to enroll themselves as their followers, and to wear the colours of the respective sides. Each Deme has a subdivision, or rather, a pendant, to which the colours white and red are attached respectively.[422] The chief or president of each faction is entitled the Demarch.[423] These two parties form cabals in the state, who are animated by a fierce rivalry engendering an intensely factious disposition. Every consideration is subordinated to a strained sense of personal or party honour, whence is evolved a generally uncompromising defiance to the restrictions of law and order. Ties of blood and friendship are habitually set at naught by the insolent clanship of these factions; even women, although excluded from the spectacles of the Circus, are liable to become violent partisans of either colour, and that in opposition sometimes to the affinities of their own husbands and families. Nor does the Emperor by an equal distribution of his favours seek to control the intemperate rivalry of the Demes, but usually becomes the avowed patron of a particular faction.[424] At the present time the Greens are in the ascendant, and fill the benches to the left of the Kathisma, a position of honour assigned to them by the younger Theodosius.[425] Every town of any magnitude has a Circus with its Blue and Green factions, and these parties are in sympathetic correspondence throughout the Empire.[426]

The throng of spectators within the Hippodrome, who can be accommodated with seats around the arena, amounts to about 40,000, but this number falls far short of the whole mass of the populace eager to witness the exhibition. From early dawn men of all ages, even if maimed or crippled, assault the gates; and when the interior is filled to repletion the excluded multitude betake themselves to every post of vantage in the vicinity which overlooks the Circus. Then windows and roofs of houses, hill-tops and adjacent eminences of all kinds are seized on by determined pleasure seekers.[427]

Public entertainments are given regularly in the Hippodrome and the theatre during the first week of January, in celebration of the Consul being newly installed for the year. They are given also on the 11th of May, the foundation day of the city, and on other occasions to celebrate some great national event, such as the accession of an emperor, the fifth or tenth anniversary of his reign,[428] the birth or nomination of a Caesar or successor to the throne, or the happy termination of an important war.[429] Several Praetors, officers who were formerly the chief oracles of the law, are nominated annually, their judicial functions being now abrogated in favour of organizing and paying for the amusements of the people.[430]

Twelve chariot races take place in the morning, and, after an interval of retirement, a similar number in the afternoon;[431] between the races other exhibitions are introduced, especially fights of men with lions, tigers, and bears,[432] rope walking,[433] and matches of boxing and wrestling.[434] In the contests between two-or four-horse chariots, the competitors make the circuit of the arena seven times, whence the whole length of the course traversed amounts to about a mile and a half.[435] The start is made from the top of the Euripus on the right-hand side, where a rope is stretched across to keep the horses in line after their exit from the Manganon, until the signal is given by the dropping of a white cloth or *mappa*.[436] The races are run with great fury, and the charioteers, standing in their vehicles, make every effort to win, not merely by speed, but by fouling each other so as to pass in front or gain the inmost position of the circuit. Hence serious and fatal accidents are of habitual occurrence, and help to stimulate the popular frenzy to the highest pitch.[437] The antagonists, however, pay but little attention to the clamours of the spectators, looking only to the Emperor's eye for their meed of approval or censure.[438] At the conclusion of the games, amid the chanting of various responsions by the factions and the populace, the victors, supported by delegates from the four Demes bearing crosses woven from fresh flowers, wait upon the Emperor in the Kathisma, and receive from his hand the awards of their prowess.[439]

Less frequently the Circus may be contemplated under a more serious aspect, as the focus of national agitation. In the year 491, during Easter week, Constantinople was thrown into a great commotion by a report that the Emperor Zeno had died somewhat suddenly,[440] and that no successor had yet been nominated for the throne. The people, the Demes, and the Imperial guards at once rushed to the Hippodrome, where all took up the stations allotted to them for viewing the Circensian games. On all sides an incessant clamour then arose, and the cry, addressed to those in authority, was vociferously repeated: "Give an Emperor to the Romans." Simultaneously the great officers of the Court, the Senate, and the Patriarch assembled hastily within the Palace in order to decide on what course to pursue. In this convention the counsel of the chief eunuch Urbicius, Grand Chamberlain, had most weight; and, fearing a riot, it was resolved that the Empress Ariadne, on whose popularity they relied, should proceed immediately to the Kathisma, and, by a suitable address, attempt to pacify the populace. On the appearance of the Empress in the Hippodrome, with the retinue of her supreme rank, the clamours were redoubled. Exclamations arose from every throat: "Ariadne Augusta, may you be victorious! Lord have mercy on us! Long live the Augusta! Give an orthodox Emperor to the Romans, to all the earth!" The widow of Zeno addressed the multitude at some length, by the mouth of a crier, who read her speech from a written document. "Every consideration," said she, "shall be shown to the majesty of the people. We have referred the matter to the Lords of the Court, to the Sacred Senate, and to the Heads of the Army; nor shall the presence of the Holy Patriarch be wanting to render the election valid. An orthodox Emperor shall be given to you and one of blameless life. Restrain yourselves for the present and be careful not to disturb the tranquillity of our choice." With such promises and exhortations, often interrupted, Ariadne left the Circus amid the renewed shouts of the vast assembly. Within the Palace the council was reformed, and, after some debate, Urbicius carried his proposition that the election of an Emperor should be referred to the widowed Empress. Upon this Ariadne put forward a much respected officer of the Court, the Silentiary Anastasius, a man of about sixty years of age. Her nominee was about to be accepted unanimously when the Patriarch interposed his authority and demanded that Anastasius should give him an engagement to uphold the orthodox faith. The Silentiary was, in fact, suspected of a strong leaning towards the monophysite heresy, which declared that Christ was possessed of only one nature.[441] His proposition was entertained, and thereupon a guard of honour was sent to summon Anastasius from his house, and to escort him to the Palace; but before any formal question was put they all set about performing the obsequies of the deceased Emperor Zeno. The next day Anastasius presided in the Consistorium to receive the officers of state, all of whom waited on him clad in white robes. He subscribed the document as required by the Patriarch, and took an oath to administer the Empire with a true conscience. He was then conducted to the Hippodrome, where he appeared in the undress of an emperor, but wearing the red buskins. Amid the acclamations of the populace he was exalted on a buckler, and a military officer crowned him with a golden collar removed from his own person.[442] Anastasius then retired to the antechamber of the Kathisma to be invested, by the Patriarch himself, with the Imperial purple, and to have a jewelled crown placed upon his head. Again he sought the presence of the assembled multitude, whom he addressed in a set speech which was read out to them by a crier. Finally the newly-elected Autocrator departed to the Palace amid repeated cries of "God bless our Christian Emperor! You have lived virtuously, Reign as you have lived!"[443]

But the proceedings in the Hippodrome were not always merely pleasurable or peacefully political. The Circus was also the place where sedition was carried to the culminating point; and the same Anastasius, in his long reign of twenty-seven years, had to experience on more than one occasion the fickle humour of the Byzantine populace. About 498, during the progress of the games, a cry arose that certain rioters, who had been committed to prison for throwing stones inside the arena, should be liberated. The Emperor refused, a tumult arose, and the Imperial guards were ordered to arrest the apparent instigators of the disorder. Stones were immediately flung at Anastasius himself, who only escaped injury or death by his precipitate flight from the Kathisma. The mob then set fire to the wooden benches of the Hippodrome, and a conflagration ensued, which consumed part of the Imperial Palace in one direction, and ravaged a large tract of the city as far as the Forum of Constantine on the other.[444] Again in 512, when the Emperor, yielding to his heretical tendencies to confound the persons of the Trinity, proclaimed that in future the Trisagion[445] should be chanted with the addition "Who wast crucified for us," the populace rose in a fury, set fire to the houses of many persons who were obnoxious to them, decapitated a monk suspected of suggesting the heresy, and, marching through the streets with his head upon a pole, demanded that "another Emperor should be given to the Romans." Anastasius, affrighted, rushed into the Hippodrome without his crown, and protested his willingness to abdicate the purple. The spectacle, however, of their Emperor in such an abject state appeased the excited throng, and, on the withdrawal of the offensive phrase, peace was restored to the community.[446]

The Byzantine theatre, in which there are usually diurnal performances,[447] is by no means a lineal descendant of that of the Greeks and Romans. The names of Aeschylus, Sophocles, and the rest of those inimitable playwrights, are either altogether unknown, or are heard with complete indifference. Pantomime, farce, lewd songs, and dances in which troops of females[448] virtually dispense with clothing, monopolize the stage to the exclusion of the classic drama. Ribaldry and obscenity, set off by spectacular displays,[449] constitute the essence of the entertainment; and women even go through the form of bathing in a state of nudity for the delectation of the audience.[450] A contemporary music-hall, without its enforced decency, would probably convey to a modern reader the most correct impression of the stage as maintained in Christian Constantinople. Actress and prostitute are synonymous terms, and all persons engaged in the theatrical profession are regarded in the eye of the law as vile and disreputable.[451] Nevertheless, the pastimes of the public are jealously protected; and the amorous youth who runs away with an actress,[452] equally with him who withdraws a favourite horse from the Circensian games for his private use,[453] is subjected to a heavy fine. A woman, however, who wishes to reform her life on the plea of religious conviction, is permitted to quit the stage, but is not afterwards allowed to relapse into her former life of turpitude.[454] Should she betray any inclination to do so, it is enacted that she shall be kept in a place of detention until such time as the decrepitude of age shall afford an involuntary guarantee of her chastity.[455] The Byzantine aristocracy, from the rank of Clarissimus upwards is prohibited from marrying an actress or any woman on a level with that class.[456]

A particular form of amusement among the Byzantines is the installation of a Consul every year on the Calends of January in imitation of the old republican function at Rome. The person nominated assumes a gorgeous robe decorated with purple stripes and gold embroidery,[457] grasps a sceptre surmounted with a figure of Victory,[458] and proceeds in state to the Hippodrome, where he displays his authority by manumitting a number of slaves specially provided for the purpose.[459] He presides at the games from the Kathisma, and for the moment, if not the Emperor himself, as frequently happens, the pretence is made of regarding him as the sovereign of the Empire.[460] The year is legally distinguished by his name and that of his colleague of the West,[461] a series of public spectacles are exhibited for seven days,[462] he scatters golden coin as largess among the citizens,[463] and emissaries are dispatched in all directions throughout the provinces to announce his elevation,[464] and to deposit in the local archives his diptychs, a pair of ivory plates inscribed with his likeness or insignia.[465] Immediately afterwards, the office relapses into a sinecure, and the Consul resumes his ordinary avocations in life.

On Sunday there is a cessation of business and pleasure throughout the city, though not of agricultural labour in the rural districts.[466] At the boom of the great *semantron*,[467] a sonorous board suspended in the porch of each church, and beaten with mallets by a deacon, the various congregations issue forth to attend their respective places of worship. In the forecourt they are met by a crowd of mendicants, exemplifying every degree of poverty and every form of bodily infirmity, who enjoy a prescriptive right to solicit alms at this time and place. This practice has, in fact, been encouraged by the early Fathers of the Church, in order that the heart may be melted to pity and philanthropy at the sight of so much human misery as the most fitting preparation for the order of divine service.[468] The centre of the same inclosure is occupied by a fountain of pure water, in which it is customary to wash the hands before entering the sacred edifice.[469] In the narthex or vestibule, in a state of abject contrition, are found the various penitents, who, for some offence, have been cut off from the communion of the faithful, condemned to advance no farther than this part for a term of years proportionate to the heinousness of their sin.[470] The males of the congregation make use of the central or Beautiful Gate of the church, in order to gain their station in the nave, whilst the females, passing through the doors on each side, ascend to the galleries which are set apart for their special accommodation.[471] The liturgy consists of reading from the Scriptures, of prayers, and of hymns sung in responses;[472] after which the Patriarch, coming forward from his throne in the apse to the ambo,[473] preaches a homily based on some portion of the Bible. Finally the Eucharist is administered to the whole congregation, a spoon being used to give a portion of wine to each person.[474] Ladies, to attend public worship, bedeck themselves with all their jewels and finery,[475] whence female thieves, mingling amongst them, often take the opportunity to reap their harvest.[476] Men, in the most obvious manner, betray their admiration for the women placed within their range of vision.[477] The general behaviour of the audience is more suggestive of a place of amusement than of a holy temple; chattering and laughter go on continually, especially among the females; and, as a popular preacher makes his points, dealing didactically or reprehensively with topics of the day, the whole congregation is from time to time agitated with polemical murmurs, shaken with laughter, or bursts into uproarious applause.[478] Contiguous to each church is a small building called the Baptistery, for the performance of the ceremonial entailed on those who wish to be received among the Christian elect. The practice of the period is to subject the body to complete immersion in pure water, but separate chambers or times are set apart for the convenience of the two sexes. Here on certain occasions nude females of all ages and ranks descend by steps into the baptismal font, whilst the ecclesiastics coldly pronounce the formulas of the mystic rite,[479] a triumph of superstition[480] over concupiscence pretended more often perhaps than real.[481]

The luxury of the rich, especially in the use of the precious metals and ivory, is in this age maintained at the maximum. Practically all the furniture in the house of a wealthy man, as far at least as the visible parts are concerned, is constructed of those costly materials. Gilding or plates of gold or silver are applied to every available surface—to tables, chairs, footstools, and bedsteads; even silver night-urns are essential to the comfort of the fastidious plutocracy.[482] For banqueting the Byzantines make use of a large semicircular table,[483] on the convex side of which they recline at meals, still adhering to the custom of the earlier Greeks and Romans.[484] By this table is set a ponderous gold vase with goblets of the same metal for mixing and serving out the wine. Rich carpets are strewn over the mosaic pavement; and troops of servants, either eunuchs or of barbarian origin, permeate the mansion.[485] These domestics are costumed and adorned as expensively as are their masters, and in the largest establishments are retained to the number of one or two thousand.[486] Like animals they are bought and sold; and, male and female alike, are as much the property of their owner as his ordinary goods and chattels; their life is virtually in his hands, but the growth of humanity under the Empire, and the tenets of Stoicism,[487] have considerably ameliorated their condition since the time of the old Republic.[488] In this, as in every other age, the artificial forms of politeness, which spring up as the inseparable concomitant of every aspect of civilization, have developed in social circles; and the various formalities and affectations of manners and speech familiar to the modern observer as characteristic of the different grades of society may be noted among the Constantinopolitans.[489]

The Byzantine wife is in possession of complete liberty of action, and is entirely the mistress in her own household. She is, as a rule, devoted to enervating luxury and enjoyments, which she gratifies by extravagance in dress and jewels, by the use of costly unguents and the artificial tinting of her countenance,[490] and by daily visits to the public baths and squares for the purpose of display and gossip.[491] At home she is often a tyrant to her maidservants, and not infrequently whips them severely with her own hand.[492] Precisely the reverse of this picture is the condition of the Byzantine maiden in her father's house; before her coverture she is persistently immured in the women's apartments, and seldom passes the outer door of the dwelling; never unless under strict surveillance.[493] In most instances, however, her state of seclusion is not of long duration; for, at the age of fourteen or fifteen she is considered to be marriageable.[494] She then becomes an article of traffic in the hands of the professional match-maker, who is usually an old woman of low social grade, but remarkable for her tactful and deceptive aptitudes.[495] By her arts a suitable family alliance is arranged, but unless by a subterfuge, the proposed husband is not permitted to behold his future wife.[496]

Once a marriage has been decided on,[497] it is considered fitting that all the innocence of the ingenuous damsel should be put to flight on the threshold of the wedded state. In the dusk of the evening the bride is fetched from her home by a torchlight procession to the sound of pipes and flutes and orgiastic songs. Although women are not allowed to attend the theatre, on this occasion the theatre is brought to the houses of the contracting parties; and the installation of a wife takes place amid a scene of riot and debauchery, of lewdness and obscenity, which tears the veil from all the secrets of sexual co-habitation.[498]

Mental culture, even in the mansions of wealthy Byzantines, occupies a very subordinate place. Everywhere may be seen dice and draughts, but books are usually conspicuous by their absence. Bibliophiles there are, however, but they merely cherish costly bindings and beautiful manuscripts, and seldom take the trouble to study their literary contents. They only value fine parchments dyed in various tints, especially purple, and handsomely inscribed with letters of gold or silver; these they delight to have bound in jewelled covers or in plates of carved ivory, and to preserve them in cabinets, whence they are drawn out on occasion in order to afford a proof of the taste and affluence of the owner.[499]

Popular superstitions are extremely rife at this time in the Orient; a few examples of such may be here given. In choosing a name for a child it is the practice to light a number of candles, and to christen them by various names; the candle which burns longest is then selected to convey its appellation to the infant as an earnest of long life.[500] Another custom is to take a baby to one of the public baths and to sign its forehead with some of the sedimental mud found there as a charm against the evil eye and all the powers of enchantment.[501] Amulets are commonly worn, hung about the neck, and of these, miniature copies of the Gospels are in great favour, especially for the protection of infants.[502] Should a merchant on his way to business for the day first meet with a sacred virgin, he curses his luck and anticipates a bad issue to any pending negotiations; on the contrary, should the first woman he encounters be a prostitute, he rejoices in the auspicious omen with which his day has opened.[503] At funerals the old Roman custom of hiring females to act as mourners, who keep up a discordant wailing and shed tears copiously at will, is still maintained.[504] Black clothes are worn as a mark of sorrow for the dead.[505] Great extravagance is often shown in the erection of handsome sepulchral monuments.[506]

That the capital of the East, and by inference the whole Empire, is a hotbed of vice and immorality will impress itself on the mind of the most superficial reader. The dissoluteness of youth is in fact so appalling that the most sane of fathers resort to the extreme measure of expelling their sons from home in a penniless state, with the view that after a term of trial and hardship they may return as reformed and chastened members to the family circle.[507] Yet to complete the picture one other sin against morality must be mentioned, which travels beyond the belief and almost eludes the conception of any ordinary mind. The incredible perversion of sexual instinct named paederasty is still more than ever rife in the principal cities of the East. Idealized by the Greek philosophers,[508] tolerated by the later Republic,[509] and almost deified[510] under many of the pagan emperors,[511] it has withstood the pronouncements of Trajan and Alexander,[512] the diatribes of the Christian Fathers,[513] and even the laws of Constantius and Valentinian, by which such delinquents are condemned to be burnt alive.[514] Preaching at Antioch a century before this time, the earnest and fearless Chrysostom cannot refrain from expressing his amazement that that metropolis, in its open addiction to this vice, does not meet with the biblical fate of Sodom and Gomorrah.[515] Nor is there any evidence to refute the assumption that Constantinople at the beginning of the sixth century is in this respect less impure than the Syrian capital.[516]

The Byzantine coinage, which has been recast by Anastasius, consists of gold, silver, and copper. The standard gold coin, the *aureus* or *solidus*, subdivides the pound[517] of gold into seventy-two equal parts, and is, therefore, to be valued at nearly twelve English shillings. Halves and thirds of the *aureus* are regularly minted for circulation. There is also a silver *solidus* which weighs nearly fifteen times as much as that of gold.[518] Twelfths, twenty-fourths, and forty-eighths of this coin are issued; they are named the *milliaresion*, the *siliqua*, and the *half-siliqua* respectively. In the copper coinage at the head of the list stands the *follis*, two hundred and ten of which are contained in the *solidus*.[519] Hence the *milliaresion* is not much less in value than a shilling, whilst the *follis* represents but little more than a halfpenny. Yet the *follis* is divided hypothetically into forty *nummia*, but pieces of five *nummia* are the smallest coins in actual use,[520] approximately quarter-farthings, and less even than continental centimes, etc. The money of old Byzantium was generally figured with a crescent and a star, or with a dolphin contorted round a trident,[521] but the Imperial coinage of Constantinople is stamped on the obverse with the bust of the reigning emperor,[522] and on the reverse, in the case of gold or silver pieces, with a figure of Victory bearing a cross and a crown or some similar device. On the reverse of copper coins, with accompanying crosses and even crescents, we find a large letter—M, K, I, or E—indicating that they contain 40, 20, 10, or 5 *nummia* respectively. As specimens of art the coinage of this epoch appears degraded to the most uncritical eye.[523]

The population of Constantinople in the sixth century is unknown, but it may be estimated with some approach to accuracy at considerably over a million of inhabitants.[524] The suburbs also are extremely populous, and for many miles around the capital, both in Europe and Asia, are covered with opulent country villas, farmhouses, and innumerable habitations of meaner residents.[525] In this district are situated immense reservoirs for water, and many of the valleys are spanned by imposing aqueducts raised by a double series of lofty arches to a great height.[526] At a distance of thirty-two miles westwards from the city is situated the Long Wall, a stupendous bulwark against the inroads of barbarians, built by Anastasius in 512. It stretches between the Euxine and Propontis, a range of nearly fifty miles, and forms also a safe and facile road for those travelling from sea to sea.[527]

The description of manners given in this chapter, although nominally applied only to Constantinople, may be received as illustrating at this date the social features of the whole Roman Empire; or, to speak more accurately, of the Grecian fragment of that empire which once extended universally over Latins and Greeks.

Before concluding this sociological exposition of the Graeco-Roman people during the period I am treating of, a brief reference to their language may be deemed essential to the integrity of the subject. Viewed from the philological side the aspect of the Byzantines is peculiar and, perhaps, unique,[528] since to them may fairly be applied the epithet of a trilingual nation. By the union of the Roman and Greek factors of the Empire the Latin tongue, as the official means of expression, became engrafted on the Eastern provinces;[529] and in the lapse of centuries a third mode of speech, a popular vernacular,[530] has been evolved, which often has little affinity with the first two. Sustained by the solid foundations of laws and literature, Latin and Greek of a more or less classical cast[531] are the requisite equipment of every one who aims at civil or military employment in any governmental department,[532] or who even pretends to recognition as a person of average culture. In the pride of original supremacy we may perceive that citizens of Latin lineage despise the feeble Greeks who forfeited nationality and independence, whilst the latter, pluming themselves on their inheritance of the harmonious tongue in which are enshrined all the masterpieces of poetry and philosophy, contemn the uninspired genius of the Romans, whose efforts to create a literature never soared above imitation and plagiarism.[533]

CHAPTER II
THE ROMAN EMPIRE UNDER ANASTASIUS: THE INHERITANCE OF JUSTINIAN

THAT a spirit of dominion was implanted in the breasts of those early settlers or refugees who rallied around Romulus, when, about 750 B.C., he raised his standard on the Palatine hill, is made plain by the subsequent history of that infant community; and the native daring which first won wives for a colony of outcasts, foreshadowed the career of conquest and empire which eventually attached itself to the Roman name.[534] Contemned, doubtless, and disregarded by their more reputable neighbours as a band of adventurers with nothing to lose, in despair of being respected they determined to make themselves feared; and the original leaven was infused through every further accretion of population, and was entailed as an inheritance on all succeeding generations who peopled the expanding city of the Tiber. When their kings threatened to become despotic they drove them out; when the patricians attempted to maintain an exclusive control the more numerous plebs revolted and gradually achieved the establishment of a republic, in which political honours and aristocracy became synonymous with the ability to fill, or the energy to gain, a ruling position. They devoted themselves with enthusiasm to the task of self-government, and sacrificed their private interests to the welfare of the Republic. Without history and without science, inflated by ambition within their narrow sphere, they applied the conception of immortality, which millenniums would not justify, to being acclaimed in the ephemeral fervour of the populace or to being remembered for a few decades in the finite language of poetry and rhetoric.

While the Roman state was in its cradle a citizen and a soldier were equivalent terms, and every man gave his military service as a free contribution to the general welfare of the public. But as wars became frequent and aggressive, and armies were compelled to keep the field for indefinite periods, a system of payment[535] was introduced in order to compensate the soldier for the enforced neglect of his family duties. By the continued growth of the military system, war became a profession, veteran legions sprang into existence, and generals, whose rank was virtually permanent, became a power among the troops and a menace to the state. Finally the transition was made from a republic governed by a democracy to an empire ruled by the army. In the meantime the dominion of Rome had been extended on all sides to the great natural barriers of its position on the hemisphere; to the Atlantic ocean on the west, to the Rhine, the Danube, and the Euxine on the north, to the Euphrates on the east, and on the south to the securest frontier of all, the impassable deserts of Libya and Arabia.

The first emperors affected to rule as civil magistrates and accepted their appointment from the Senate, but their successors assumed the purple as the nominees of the troops, and often held it by right of conquest over less able competitors.[536] Concurrently the Imperial city had been insensibly undergoing a transformation; by the persistent influx of strangers of diverse nationalities its ethnical homogeneity was lost;[537] a new and more populous Rome, in which the traditions of republican freedom were dissipated, was evolved; and the inhabitants without a murmur saw themselves deprived of the right to elect their own magistrates.[538] The laws of the Republic were submitted for ratification to the citizens, but in the ascent to absolutism the emperor became the sole legislator of the nation.[539] The elevation of an emperor seemed at first to be an inalienable privilege of the metropolis, and the original line of Caesars necessarily descended from a genuine Roman stock; but in little more than a century the instability of this law was made plain, and many an able general of provincial blood was raised to the purple at his place of casual sojourn.[540] In the sequel, when men of an alien race, who neither knew nor revered Rome, obtained the first rank, they chose their place of residence according to some native preference or in view of its utility as a base for military operations. The simultaneous assumption of the purple by several candidates in different localities, each at the head of an army, foreboded the division of the Empire; and after the second century an avowed sharing of the provinces became the rule rather than the exception. As each partner resided within his own territory, Rome gradually became neglected and at last preserved only a semblance of being the capital of the Empire.[541] But after Constantine founded a capital of his own choice even this semblance was lost, and the new Rome on the Bosphorus assumed the highest political rank. From this event we may mark the beginning of mediaevalism, of the passing of western Europe under the cloud of the dark ages; and the disintegration of the Roman Empire in the West was achieved by the barbarians within the following century and a half. In 395 a final partition of the Empire, naturally halved as it was by the Adriatic sea, was made; and the incapable sons of Theodosius, Arcadius and Honorius,[542] were seated as independent sovereigns on thrones in the East and West. During this period a central administrative energy to uphold Rome as an Imperial seat was entirely wanting; and a succession of feeble emperors maintained a mere shadow of authority while their provinces were being appropriated by the surplus populations of the north. Italy and south-west Gaul became the prey of East and West Goths; the valorous Franks under Clovis founded a kingdom which made itself permanently respected under the name of France; Vandals, with kindred tribes, gained possession of Spain and even erected a monarchy in north Africa, which extended beyond the limits of ancient Carthage; Britain, divested of Roman soldiers in 409, for centuries became the goal of acquisitive incursions by the maritime hordes who issued from the adjacent seaboards, Saxons, Angles, and Danes.

In the change from a nominally popular or constitutional monarchy to a professed despotism, a reconstitution of all subordinate authority was regarded as a matter of necessity. At first the Empire was administered in about forty provinces, but under the later scheme of control it was parcelled out into nearly three times that number. In earlier times a Roman proconsul in his spacious province was almost an independent potentate during his term of office,[543] the head alike of the civil and military power. But in the new dispensation no man was intrusted with such plenary authority, and each contracted province was ruled by a purely civil administrator, whilst the local army obeyed a different master. For further security, each of these in turn was dependent on a higher civil or military officer, to whom was delegated the collective control of a number of his subordinates. Again a shift of authority was made, and the reins of government were delivered into fewer hands, until, at the head of the system, the source of all power, stood the Emperor himself. In order to perfect this policy the army itself was treated in detail on a similar plan; and for the future no homogeneous body of troops of considerable number was collocated in the hands of a single leader. A typical Roman legion had previously consisted of about six thousand foot, seven hundred horse, and of a band of auxiliaries drawn from foreign or barbarian sources, in all, perhaps, ten thousand men. Each legion was thus in itself an effective force; and as it yielded implicit obedience to a single praefect, the loyalty or venality of a few such officers in respect of their common general had often sufficed to seat him firmly on the throne. To obviate the risk, therefore, of revolt, usurpation, or even of covert resistance to the will of the Emperor, existing legions were broken up into detachments which were relegated to different stations so as to be dispersed over a wide area. As a consequence the praefect of the legion could only exist in name, and that office was soon regarded as obsolete. Consistently, when new legions had to be enrolled for the exigences of defence or warfare, their number was limited to about one fifth of the original amount.[544] To complete the fabric of autocracy all the pomp and pretensions of Oriental exclusiveness were adopted by Diocletian, so that henceforward the monarch was only accessible to the subject under forms of such complexity and abasement as seemed to betoken a being of more than mortal mould.[545]

Another signal divergence from the simple manners of the first emperors was the permanent establishment of eunuchs in high offices about the royal person.[546] The Grand Chamberlain, as the constant attendant on the privacy of the monarch, generally became his confidant, and sometimes his master.[547] Ultimately, by habitude, or perhaps with a feeling for the vicious propensities of the times, the Emperor developed an almost feminine reserve in relation to the "bearded" or masculine sex; and in his movements he was guarded by his staff of eunuchs with as much jealousy as if his virtue were something as delicate as that of a woman.[548]

Having dismissed these general considerations, I will now attempt to depict briefly the state of the remaining moiety of the Empire, of the Eastern provinces, at the beginning of the sixth century. In order to render my descriptions more compact and intelligible, I shall treat the subject under three distinct headings, viz., Political, Educational, and Religious.

I. POLITICAL

The dominions of Anastasius the elder,[549] for there was a later emperor of that name, corresponded generally to those ruled during the first quarter of the past century by the Ottoman sultans, who were the last to conquer them, and who became possessed of the whole in 1461.[550] Proceeding from east to west, the northern boundary of the Empire followed the coast of the Euxine in its sweep from the mouth of the Phasis (adjacent to the modern town of Batoum) to the estuaries of the Danube, as it delimits Asia on the north and Europe on the east, by the bold curve of its unequal arms. From the latter point, taking the Danube for its guide, the northern frontier stretched westwards to its termination on the banks of that river in the neighbourhood of Sirmium.[551] The western border, descending from thence almost due south, was directed in part of its course by the river Drina, and halved nearly vertically the modern principality of Montenegro as it struck towards the shores of the Adriatic. The coast of Greece, with its associated islands on this aspect, traced the western outline of the Empire for the rest of its course, excepting a small portion to be reached by crossing the Mediterranean to the Syrtis Major, where at this date the confines of Roman Africa were to be found. In this vicinity the Egyptian territory began, and the southern frontier coincided for the most part with the edge of the Libyan desert as it skirts the fertile lands of the north and east, that is, the Cyrenaica and the valley of the Nile. An artificial line, cutting that valley on a level with the first cataract and the Isle of Philae, marked the southern extension of Egypt as far as claimed by the Byzantine emperors.[552] From a corresponding point on the opposite shore of the Red Sea the Asiatic border of their dominions began. Passing northwards to regain that part of the Euxine from whence we started, the eastern frontier pursued a long and irregular track, at first along the margin of the Arabian desert as it verges on the Sinaitic peninsula, Palestine, and Syria; then crossing the Euphrates it gained the Tigris, so as to include the northern portion of Mesopotamia. Finally, returning to the former river, it joined it in its course along the western limits of Armenia,[553] whence it reached the Phasis on the return journey, the point from which we set out.[554] Considered in their greatest length, from the Danube above Sirmium, to Syene on the Nile, and in their extreme width, from the Tigris in the longitude of Daras or Nisibis, to the Acroceraunian rocks on the coast of Epirus, these ample dominions stretch from north to south for nearly eighteen hundred miles, and from east to west for more than twelve hundred. In superficial area this tract may be estimated to contain about half a million of square miles, that is, an amount of surface fully four times greater than that covered by Great Britain and Ireland.[555] At the present day it is calculated that these vast regions are peopled by only about twenty-eight millions of inhabitants,[556] but their modern state of decay is practically the reverse of their condition in the sixth century, when they were the flourishing, though already failing, seat of the highest civilization at that time existing on the earth; and there is good reason to believe that they were then considerably more, perhaps even double as, populous.[557]

For the purposes of civil government the Empire was divided into sixty-four provinces, each of which was placed under an administrator, who was usually drawn from the profession of the law.[558] These officers were, as a rule, of nearly equal rank, but in three instances the exceptional extent and importance of the provinces necessitated the bestowal of a title more lofty than usual on the governors.

1. The whole of Greece, including Hellas proper and the Peloponnesus, though now no longer classical, was ruled under the name of Achaia by a vicegerent, to whom was conceded the almost obsolete dignity of a proconsul. 2. Similarly, the central maritime division of Asia Minor, containing the important cities of Smyrna and Ephesus with many others and grandiosely named "Asia,"[559] was also allowed to confer on its ruler the title of proconsul. This magistrate had the privilege of reporting directly to the Emperor without an intermediary, and had also jurisdiction over the governors of two adjacent provinces, viz.: the Hellespont, which abutted on the strait of that name, and The Islands, a term applied collectively to about a score of the Cyclades and Sporades. 3. The main district of Lower Egypt, adorned by the magnificent and populous city of Alexandria, the second capital of the Empire, was placed under an administrator bearing the unique title of the Augustal Praefect. The sixty-one remaining provinces were intrusted to governors of practically the same standing; of these, twenty-seven were called consulars, thirty-one presidents, two correctors, and one duke, the latter officer being on the southern frontier of Egypt, apparently in both civil and military charge.[560]

To enumerate severally in this place all the petty provinces of the Empire would be mere prolixity, but there are a few whose designations present peculiarities which may save them from being passed over without notice. The comprehensive names of Europe and Scythia, which in general suggest such vast expansions of country, were given to two small portions of Thrace, the first to that which extended up to the walls of Constantinople, and the second to the north-east corner which lay between the Danube and the Euxine.[561] With parallel magniloquence, a limited area adjoining the southeast border of Palestine was denominated Arabia. The maritime province of Honorias on the north of Asia Minor, perpetuated the memory of the despicable Emperor of the West, Honorius. The name of Arcadia awakens us to reminiscences of Mount Cyllene with Hermes and "universal" Pan,[562] of Artemis with her train of nymphs heading the chase through the woods of Erymanthus, or of the historic career of Epaminondas and the foundation of Megalopolis. But the Arcadia officially recognized in the Eastern Empire had no higher associations than the feeble son of Theodosius, brother of the above-named, and we may be surprised to find it in central Egypt with Oxyrhyncus and Memphis for its chief towns.

By a second disposition of the Empire of an inclusive kind the provinces were grouped in seven Dioceses, namely: three European, Dacia,[563] Thrace, and Macedonia; three Asiatic, the Asian, the Pontic, and the Orient; and one African, Egypt. The first of these obeys the Praetorian Praefect of Illyricum, the sixth the Count of the Orient or East, and the last the Augustal Praefect, whilst the rulers of the remaining four are entitled Vicars.[564] When I add that the Orient, the most extensive of these divisions, comprised in fifteen provinces the whole of Palestine and Syria as well as the southern tract of Asia Minor, from the Tigris to the Mediterranean, and the island of Cyprus, the limits of the other dioceses may be conjectured from their names with sufficient accuracy for our present purpose.[565] By a final partition the dominions of the Byzantine Emperor were assigned, but very unequally, to two officers of the highest or Illustrious rank, viz.: the Praetorian Praefects of the East and of Illyricum. Dacia and Macedonia fell to the rule of the latter, whilst the remaining five dioceses were consolidated under the control of the former minister.[566] The Praefect of the East is in general to be regarded as the subject in closest proximity to the throne, in fact, the first minister of the crown.[567] The Imperial capital, as being outside all these subordinate arrangements, was treated as a microcosm in itself; and with its Court in permanent residence, its bureaus of central administration, and its special Praefect of Illustrious rank, may almost be considered as a third of the prime divisions of the Empire. Here, as a rule, through the long series of Byzantine annals, by the voice of the populace and the army, or by the intrigues of the Court, emperors were made or unmade.

The whole Empire was traversed by those narrow, but solidly constructed roads, the abundant remains of which still attest how thoroughly his work was done by the Roman engineer.[568] The repair and maintenance of these public ways was enjoined on the possessors of the lands through which they passed; and similarly in the case of waterways, the care of bridges and banks was an onus on the shoulders of the riparian owners.[569] On all the main roads an elaborate system of public posts was studiously maintained; and at certain intervals, about the length of an average day's journey, *mansions* or inns were located for the accommodation of those travelling on the public service.[570] Each of such stations was equipped with a sufficient number of light and heavy vehicles, of draught horses and oxen, of pack-horses, sumpter mules, and asses for the exigences of local transit.[571] Stringent rules were laid down for the equitable loading of both animals and carriages, and also for the humane treatment of the former. Thus a span of four oxen was allowed to draw a load of fifteen hundred pounds, but the burden of an ordinary pack-horse was limited to thirty.[572] It was forbidden to beat the animals with heavy or knotted sticks; they were to be urged onwards by the use only of a sharp whip or rod fit to "admonish their lagging limbs with a harmless sting."[573] In addition to the mansions there were usually four or five intermediate stations called *mutations*, where a few relays were kept for the benefit of those speeding on an urgent mission.[574] The abuse of the public posts was jealously guarded against, and only those bearing an order from the Emperor or one of the Praetorian Praefects could command their facilities, and then only to an extent restricted to their purely official requirements. A Vicar could dispose of a train of ten horses and thirteen asses on a dozen occasions in the year, in order to make tours of inspection throughout his diocese; legates from foreign countries and delegates from provincial centres, journeying to Constantinople to negotiate a treaty or to lay their grievances before the Emperor, were provided for according to circumstances.[575] The highways were constantly permeated by the Imperial couriers bearing dispatches to or from the capital.[576] These emissaries were also deputed to act as spies, and to report at head-quarters any suspicious occurrences they might observe on their route,[577] whence they were popularly spoken of as "the eyes of the Emperor."[578] They were known by their military cloak and belt, their tight trousers,[579] and by a spray of feathers[580] in their hair to symbolize the swiftness of their course. One or two were appointed permanently to each province with the task of scouring the district continually as inspectors of the public posts.[581] There was also a regular police patrol on the roads, called Irenarchs, whose duty it was to act as guardians of the peace.[582]

A Roman emperor of this age, as an admitted despot subjected to no constitutional restraints, could formulate and promulgate whatever measures commended themselves to his arbitrary will. But such authority, however absolute in theory, must always be restricted in practice by the operation of sociological laws. Although a prince with a masterful personality might dominate his subordinates to become the father or the scourge of his country, a feeble monarch would always be the slave of his great officers of state. Yet even the former had to stoop to conciliate the people or the army, and a sovereign usually stood on treacherous ground when attempting to maintain a balance between the two.[583] The army, as the immediate and effectual instrument of repression, was generally chosen as the first stay of the autocracy, and there are few instances of a Byzantine emperor whose throne was not on more than one occasion cemented with the blood of his subjects. But many a virtuous prince in his efforts to curb the licence of the troops lost both his sceptre and his life.[584]

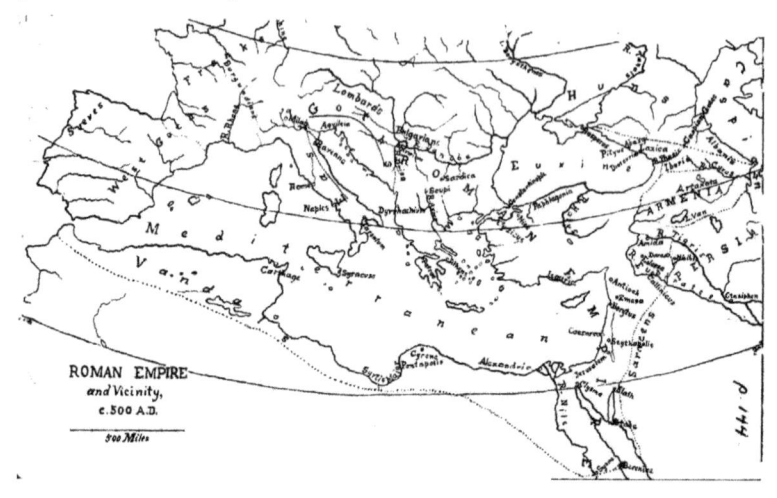

**ROMAN EMPIRE
and Vicinity, c. 500 A.D.**

The Council of the Emperor, besides the three Praefects already mentioned, consisted of five civil and of an equal number of military members, all of Illustrious dignity.[585] Their designations were severally: 1. Praepositus of the Sacred Cubicle, or Grand Chamberlain, Master of the Offices, Quaestor, Count of the Sacred Largesses, and Count of the Privy Purse. 2. Five Masters of Horse and Foot,[586] two at head-quarters,[587] and one each for the Orient, Thrace, and Illyricum. To these may be added the Archbishop or Patriarch of Constantinople, always a great power in the State. In the presence of a variable number of these ministers it was usual for the Emperor to declare his will, to appeal to their judgment, or to act on their representations, but the time, place, and circumstances of meeting were entirely in the discretion of the prince.[588] The formal sittings of the Council were not held in secret, but before an audience of such of the Spectabiles as might wish to attend.[589] The legislation of the Emperor, comprised under the general name of Constitutions, fell naturally into two classes, viz., laws promulgated on his own initiative and those issued in response to some petition. Edicts, Acts, Mandates, Pragmatic Sanctions, and Epistles usually ranked in the first division; Rescripts in the second.[590] A Rescript was granted, as a rule, in compliance with an *ex parte* application, and might be disregarded by the authority to whom it was addressed should it appear to have been obtained by false pretences, but the Court which set it aside did so at its own peril.[591]

The Senate of Constantinople, created in imitation of that of Rome, was designed by Constantine rather to grace his new capital than to exercise any of the functions of government.[592] Like the new order of patricians, the position of Senator was mainly an honorary and not an executive rank. All the members enjoyed the title of Clarissimus, that of the third grade of nobility, and assembled under the presidency of the Praefect of the city.[593] As a body the Senate was treated with great ostensible consideration by the Emperor, and was never referred to in the public acts without expressions of the highest esteem, such as "the Venerable," "the Most Noble Order," "amongst whom we reckon ourselves."[594] This public parade of their importance, however, endowed them with a considerable moral power in the popular idea; and the subscription of the impotent Senate was not seldom demanded by a prudent monarch to give a wider sanction to his acts of oppression or cruelty.[595] During an interregnum their voice was usually heard with attention;[596] and a prince with a weak or failing title to the throne would naturally cling to them for support.[597] They were sometimes constituted as a High Court for the trial of criminal cases of national importance, such as conspiring against the rule or life of the Emperor.[598] They could pass resolutions to be submitted for the approval of the crown;[599] they had a share in the nomination of some of the higher and lower officials; and they performed generally the duties of a municipal council.[600]

In addition to the Imperial provinces there was also, to facilitate the work of local government, a subsidiary division of the Empire into Municipia. Every large town or city, with a tract of the surrounding country, was formed into a municipal district and placed under the charge of a local Senate or Curia. The members of a Curia were called Decurions,[601] and were selected officially to the number of about one hundred from the more reputable inhabitants of the vicinity. They not only held office for life, but transmitted it compulsorily to their heirs, so that the State obtained a perpetual lien on the services of their descendants. In each Municipium the official of highest rank was the "Defender of the City,"[602] who was elected to his post for five years by the independent suffrage of the community. His chief duty was to defend the interests of his native district against the Imperial officers who, as aliens to the locality, were assumed to have little knowledge or concern as to its actual welfare. He became *ex officio* president of the Curia; and in conjunction with them acted as a judge of first instance or magistrate in causes of lesser importance.[603]

A provincial governor, generally called the Rector or Ordinary Judge, held open court at his Praetorium and sat within his chancel every morning to hear all causes brought before him.[604] His chancellors guarded the trellis, which fenced off the outer court against the onrush of eager suitors;[605] within, the advocates delivered their pleadings, whilst a body of scribes and actuaries took a record in writing of the whole proceedings.[606] The precincts were crowded with his apparitors,[607] officers upon whom devolved the duty of executing the judgements of the court. With the aid of his assessor,[608] a legal expert well versed in the text of the law, the Rector elaborated his judgment, a written copy of which he was bound to deliver to each litigant.[609] But if his decision were asked in cases which seemed too trivial for his personal attention, he was empowered to hand them over to a class of petty judges called *pedanei judices*.[610] From the provincial court an appeal lay to the Vicar of the Diocese, or even to the Emperor himself,[611] but appellants were severely mulcted if convicted of merely contentious litigation.[612] At certain seasons the Rector went on circuit throughout his province to judge causes and to inspect abuses.[613]

I. The permanent existence of any community in a state of political cohesion depends on its possession of the means to defray the expenses of government; and, therefore, the first duty of every primary ruler or administrative body in chief is to collect a revenue for the maintenance of a national treasury. The Roman or Byzantine system of raising money or its equivalent, by means of imposts laid on the subjects of the Empire, included every conceivable device of taxing the individual for the benefit of the state. The public were called on not only to fill the treasury, but were constrained to devote their resources in kind, their time, and their labour to the needs of the government. To obtain every requisite without purchase for the administration was the economical policy of the ruling class. Food and clothing, arms and horses, commuted to a money payment if the thing were unattainable, were levied systematically for the use of the civil and military establishment. The degree of personal liability was determined by the assessment of property, and those who were possessed of nothing were made liable for their heads. Social distinctions and commercial transactions were also taxed under well-defined categories. A considerable section of the community was, however, legally freed from the regular imposts. This indulgence was granted especially to the inhabitants of cities, whose facilities for combination and sedition were always contemplated with apprehension by the jealous despot. But immunity from taxation was also extended with some liberality to all who devoted themselves to art or learning.

1. The financial year began with the first of September, and was spoken of numerically as an *indiction*, according to its place in a perpetually recurring series of fifteen. Properly an indiction was the period of fifteen years[614]

which separated each new survey and revaluation of the private estates throughout the Empire. At the beginning of such a term the Imperial Censitors or surveyors pervaded the country districts, registering in their books and on their plans all the details of the new census.[615] Their record showed the amount of the possessions of each landowner; the quality of the land; to what extent it was cultivated or lay waste; in what proportions it was laid out in vineyards and olive-grounds; in woods, pastures, and arable land. The number and magnitude of the farm and residential buildings were carefully noted, and even the geniality of the climate, and the apparent fecundity of the fruit-bearing trees, which were separately counted and disposed in classes, exercised the judgement of the Censitor in furnishing materials for a just estimate as to the value of an estate. Essential also to the *cataster*, or assessment, was a list of the flocks and herds possessed by the owner.[616] The particulars supplied by the Censitor passed into the hands of another official named a *Peraequator*. He divided the district into "heads" of property, each computed to be of the value of 1,000 solidi,[617] and assigned to each landowner his census, that is, the number of heads for which in future he would be taxed. This assessment was not based on a mere valuation of the property of each person; it was complicated by the principle of Byzantine finance that all land should pay to the Imperial exchequer. It was the duty, therefore, of a Peraequator, to assign a nominal possession in barren or deserted land to each owner in fair proportion to his apparent means. Thus the possessor of a valuable farm was often encumbered with a large increment of worthless ground, whilst the owner of a poor one might escape such a burthen.[618] Yet a third official, called an *Inspector*,[619] came upon the scene, but his services were not always constant or comprehensive. He visited the province in response to petitions or appeals from dissatisfied owners, or was sent to solve matters of perplexity.[620] His acquirements were the same as those of a Peraequator, but, whereas the latter was obliged to impose a rate on some one for every hide of land, the Inspector was allowed considerable discretion. After a strict scrutiny he was empowered to give relief in clear cases of over-assessment, and even to exclude altogether any tracts of land which could not fairly be imposed on any of the inhabitants of the district. Before final ratification, the cataster had to pass under the eyes of the local Curia, the provincial Rector, and the Imperial financiers at the capital. The *polyptica* or censual books were then closed, and remained immutable until the next indiction.[621]

2. Appended to the land survey was a register of the labourers, slaves, and animals employed by the possessors of estates; and upon every ordinary adult of this caste a poll-tax was imposed.[622] Similarly with respect to every animal which performed a task, horses, oxen, mules, and asses for draught purposes, and even dogs.[623] For this demand the landowner alone was dealt with by the authorities, but he was entitled to recover from his labourers whatever

he paid on account of themselves or their families. As this capitation was very moderate, the individual was freed from it by the possession of the smallest holding, and subjected to the land-tax instead;[624] but the farmer still paid vicariously for his work-people, even when assessed on property of their own. Slaves were always, of course, a mere personal asset of their masters, and incapable of ownership. A sweeping immunity from poll-tax was conferred on all urban communities,[625] whence nobles and plutocrats escaped the impost for the hosts of servants they sometimes maintained at their city mansions; but even in the rural districts, virgins,[626] widows, certain professional men, and skilled artizans generally, were exempt.[627]

3. Port or transit dues, called *vectigalia*,[628] were levied on all merchandise transported from one province to another for the sake of gain, that is, for resale at a profit; but for purely personal use residents were permitted to pass a limited quantity of goods free of tax. In this category may be included licenses for gold-mining, which cost the venturer about a guinea a year.[629] Taxes of this class were let out by public auction for a term of three years to those who bid highest for the concession of collecting them.[630] Export of gold from the Empire was forbidden, and those who had the opportunity, were exhorted to use every subterfuge in order to obtain it from the barbarians.[631]

4. A tax, peculiar in some respects to the Byzantine Empire, was the *lustral collation* or *chrysargyron*, a duty of the most comprehensive character on the profits of all commercial transactions.[632] Trade in every shape and form was subjected to it, not excepting the earnings of public prostitutes, beggars, and probably even of catamites.[633] The *chrysargyron* was collected every fourth year only, and for this reason, as it appears, was felt to be a most oppressive tax.[634] Doubtless the demand was large in proportion to the lapse of time since the last exaction, and weighed upon those taxed, like a sudden claim for accumulated arrears. When the time for payment arrived, a wail went up from all the small traders whose traffic barely sufficed to keep them in the necessaries of life. To procure the money, parents frequently, it is said, had to sell their sons into servitude and their daughters for prostitution.[635] There were limited exemptions in favour of ministers of the orthodox faith and retired veterans, who might engage in petty trade; of artists selling their own works; and of farmers who sold only their own produce.[636] The most popular and, perhaps, the boldest measure of Anastasius, was the abrogation of this tax.[637] Fortifying himself with the acquiescence of the Senate, he proclaimed its abolition, caused all the books and papers relating to this branch of the revenue to be heaped up in the sphendone of the Hippodrome, and publicly committed them to the flames.[638] The chrysargyron was never afterwards reimposed.

5. With some special taxes reaped from dignitaries of state, the income derived from crown lands and state mines, and with fines, forfeitures, and heirless patrimonies, the flow of revenue into the Imperial coffers ceased. From a fiscal point of view there were four classes of Senators, or to consider more accurately, perhaps, only two: those who were held to contribute something to the treasury in respect of their rank, and those who were absolved from paying anything. Wealthy Senators, possessed of great estates, paid an extraordinary capitation proportioned to the amount of their property, but lands merely adjected to fill up the census were exempt under this heading; those of only moderate means were uniformly indicted for two *folles*, or purses of silver, about £12 of our money; whilst the poorest class of all were obliged to a payment of seven *solidi* only, about £4, with a recommendation to resign if they felt unequal to this small demand.[639] Members who enjoyed complete immunity were such as received the title of Senator in recognition of long, but comparatively humble, service to the state; amongst these we find certain officers of the Guards, physicians, professors of the liberal arts, and others.[640] Not even, however, with their set contributions were the Senators released from the pecuniary onus of their dignity, for they were expected to subscribe handsome sums collectively to be presented to the sovereign on every signal occasion, such as New Year's day, lustral anniversaries of his reign, birth of an heir, etc.[641] When any of the great functionaries of state, during or on vacating office, were ennobled with the supreme title of patrician, an offering of 100 lb. of gold (£4,000) was considered to be the smallest sum by which he could fittingly express his gratitude to the Emperor; this accession of revenue was particularly devoted to the expenses of the aqueducts.[642] An oblation of two or three horses was also exacted every five years for the public service from those who acquired honorary codicils of ex-president or ex-count.[643] Finally a tax, also under the semblance of a present, was laid on the Decurions of each municipality, who, in acknowledgement of their public services, were freed from all the lesser imposts. To this contribution was applied the name of *coronary gold*, the conception of which arose in earlier times when gold, in the form of crowns or figures of Victory, was presented to the Senate, or to the generals of the Republic who had succeeded in subjecting them, by conquered nations in token of their subservience.[644] These presentations were enjoined on every plausible occasion of public rejoicing and the Imperial officials did not forget to remind the local Curiae of their duty to overlook no opportunity of conveying their congratulations in a substantial manner to the Emperor. The Imperial demesnes lay chiefly in Cappadocia, which contained some breadths of pasture land unequalled in any other part of the Empire.[645] The province was from the earliest times famous for its horses, which were considered as equal, though not quite, to the highly-prized Spanish breeds in the West.[646] Mines for gold, silver, and other valuable minerals, including marble quarries,

were regularly worked by the Byzantine government in several localities both in Europe and Asia; but history has furnished us with no precise indications as to the gains drawn from them.[647] Under the penal code, to send criminals to work in the mines was classed as one of the severest forms of punishment.[648]

The *exaction* of the *annones* and *tributes*, expressions which virtually included all the imposts, was the incessant business of the official class. At the beginning of each financial year the measure of the precept to be paid by each district was determined in the office of the Praetorian Praefect, subscribed by the Emperor, and disseminated through the provinces by means of notices affixed in the most public places.[649] A grace of four months was conceded and then the gathering in of the *annones* or canon of provisions, which included corn, wine, oil, flesh, and every other necessary for the support of the army and the free distributions to the urban populace, began. Delivery was enjoined in three instalments at intervals of four months,[650] but payments in gold were not enforced until the end of the year.[651] The *Exactors*, who waited on the tributaries to urge them to performance, were usually decurions or apparitors of the Rector.[652] The Imperial constitutions directed with studied benignity that no ungracious demeanour should be adopted towards the tax-payers,[653] that no application should be made on Sundays,[654] that they should not be approached by *opinators*, that is, by soldiers in charge of the military commissariat,[655] that they should, when possible, be allowed the privilege of *autopragias* or voluntary delivery,[656] and that, if recalcitrant, they should not be sent to prison or tortured, but allowed their liberty under formal arrest.[657] Only in the last resource was anything of their substance seized as a pledge, to be sold "under the spear" if unredeemed,[658] but in general any valid excuse was accepted and the tributaries were allowed to run into arrears.[659] Consonantly, however, to the prevailing principle every effort was made by the Exactors to amass the full precept from the locality, and those who could pay were convened to make up for the defaulters.[660] The actual receivers of the canon were named *Susceptors*, and their usual place of custom was at the mansions or mutations of the public posts.[661] Scales and measures were regularly kept at these stations,[662] and on stated occasions a Susceptor was in attendance accompanied by a *tabularius*, a clerk who was in charge of the censual register which showed the liability of each person in the municipality.[663] The *tabularius* gave a receipt couched in precise terms to each tributary for the amount of his payment or consignment, particulars of which he also entered in a book kept permanently for the purpose.[664] The system of *adaeratio*, or commutation of species for money, was extensively adopted to obviate difficulties of delivery in kind; and this was especially the case with respect to clothing or horses for the army, or when transit was arduous by reason of distance or rough country.[665] The transport of the annones and tributes to their destination was a work of some magnitude, and was under the special supervision of the Vicar of the diocese.[666] Inland the *bastagarii*, the appointed branch of the public service, effected the transmission by means of the beasts of burden kept at the mansions of the Posts;[667] by sea the *navicularii* performed the same task. The latter formed a corporation of considerable importance to which they were addicted as the decurions were to the Curia. Selected from the seafaring population who possessed ships of sufficient tonnage, their vessels were chartered for the conveyance of the canon of provisions as a permanent and compulsory duty.[668] Money payments, in coin or ingots, went to the capital;[669] provisions to the public granaries of Constantinople or Alexandria, the two cities endowed with a free victualling market,[670] or were widely dispersed to various centres to supply rations for the troops.[671] Besides the ordinary officials engaged in exaction there were several of higher rank to supervise their proceedings: *Discussors*, the Greek *logothetes*, who made expeditions into the provinces from time to time to scrutinize and audit the accounts;[672] surveyors of taxes, Senators preferably, whose duties were defined by the term *protostasia*,[673] to whom the *Susceptors* were immediately responsible; and lastly *Compulsors*, officers of the central bureaucracy, *Agentes-in-rebus*, palatines attached to the treasury, even Protectors, who were sent on special missions to stimulate the Rectors when the taxes of a province were coming in badly.[674]

As to the revenue of the Roman Empire at this or at any previous period, the historian can pronounce no definitive word, but it concerns us to note here one important fact, viz., that Anastasius during the twenty-seven years of his reign saved about half a million sterling per annum, so that at his death he left a surplus in the treasury of nearly £13,000,000.[675]

II. The political position of the Roman Empire in respect of its foreign relations presents a remarkable contrast to anything we are accustomed to conceive of in the case of a modern state. Having absorbed into its own system everything of civilization which lay within reach of its arms, there was henceforth no field in which statesmanship could exert itself by methods of negotiation or diplomacy in relation to the dwellers beyond its borders. Encompassed by barbarians, to live by definite treaty on peaceful terms with its neighbours became outside the range of policy or foresight; and its position is only comparable to that of some great bulwark founded to resist the convulsions of nature, which may leave it unassailed for an indefinite period, or attack it without a moment's warning with irresistible violence. The vast territories stretching from the Rhine and the Danube to the frontiers of China, nearly a quarter of the circumference of the globe, engendered a teeming population, nomads for the most part, without fixed abodes, who threatened continually to overflow their boundaries and bring destruction on every settled state lying in their path. Among such races the army and the nation were equivalent terms; the whole people moved together, and inhabited for the time being whatever lands they had gained by right of conquest. But their career was brought to a close when they subdued nations much more numerous than themselves, with fixed habitations and engaged in the arts of peace; and they then possessed the country as a dominant minority, which, whilst giving a peculiar tincture to the greater mass, was gradually assimilated by it. In classical and modern times conquest usually signifies merely annexation, but in the Middle Ages it implied actual occupation by the victors. Such was the fate of the Western Empire, when Italy, Africa, Spain, Gaul, and Britain were dissevered from each other by various inroads; and those countries at the time I am writing of are found to be in such a transitional state.[676] Nor can Thrace and Illyricum, though forming a main portion of the Eastern Empire, be properly omitted from this list; for, exposed to barbarian incursions[677] during more than two centuries, they enjoyed a merely nominal settlement under the Imperial government; and if we contemplate the Long Wall[678] of Anastasius, at a distance of only forty miles from the capital, we shall need no further evidence that the Byzantines exercised no more than a shadow of political supremacy in these regions.[679] But an exception to the foregoing conditions was generally experienced by the Romans on their eastern frontier, where the Parthian or Persian power was often able to meet them with a civil and military organization equal to their own.[680]

The elaborate scheme for the defence of the Empire against its restless and reckless foes was brought to perfection under Diocletian and Constantine. Armies and fleets judiciously posted were always ready to repel an attack or to carry offensive operations into an enemy's country. A chain of muniments guarded the frontiers in every locality where an assault could be feared. Forts and fortified camps sufficiently garrisoned lined every barrier, natural or artificial, at measured distances. Suitable war vessels floated on the great circumscribing waterways; and where these were deficient their place was supplied by walls of masonry, by trenches, embankments, and palisades, or even by heterogeneous obstructions formed of felled trees with their branches entangled one with the other.[681] Border lands were granted only to military occupants, who held them by a kind of feudal tenure in return for their service on the frontier.[682] Every important station was guarded by from 2,000 to 3,000 soldiers; and in the Eastern Empire the division of the army to which such duties were assigned may have amounted to over 200,000 men of all soldiers, arms,[683] etc. These forces were called the *Limitanei Milites*, or Border Soldiers, and in each province of the exterior range were under the command collectively of a Count or Duke.[684] Such were the stationary forces of the Empire, of whose services the frontiers could not be depleted should a mobile army be required to meet the exigences of strategic warfare. Large bodies of troops were, therefore, quartered in the interior of the country, which could be concentrated in any particular locality under the immediate disposition of the Masters of the Forces. This portion of the army was organized in two divisions to which were given the names of *Palatines* and *Comitatenses*. The former, which held the first rank, were stationed in or near the capital under the two Masters[685] at head-quarters; and, in accordance with their designation, were identified most nearly with the conception of defending the Imperial Palace or heart of the state. The latter were distributed throughout the provinces under the three Masters whose military rule extended over the East, Thrace, and Illyricum respectively. The *Palatine* troops comprised about 50,000 men, the *Comitatenses* about 70,000.[686] Cavalry formed a large proportion of all the forces, and may be estimated at about one third of the *Limitanei* and nearly one fourth of the other branches. In addition to these troops a fourth military class, the highest of all, was formed, the Imperial Guards already mentioned,[687] viz., the Excubitors, Protectors, Candidates, and Scholars. The latter body consisted of seven troops of cavalry, each 500 strong, 3,500 in all.[688] Owing their position solely to birth or veteran service, the three former groups were probably much less numerous, but their actual number is unknown.[689] The usual division of the infantry was the legion of 1,000 men, that of the horse the *vexillatio* containing 500.[690] The various bodies of foot soldiers were distinguished by the particular emblems which were depicted on their brightly painted shields,[691] but amongst horse and foot alike each separate body was recognizable by an ensign of special design, for the former a *vexillum*, for the latter a dragon. The Imperial standard, or that of the general in chief command, was a purple banner embroidered with gold and of exceptional size. The *vexilla* were dependent horizontally from a cross-bar fixed to the pole or spear by which they were elevated. Mounted lancers displayed small pennons or streamers near the points of their weapons,[692] but these were removed as an encumbrance on the eve of battle.[693] Full armour was worn, in some troops even by the horses.[694] Besides the weapons adapted for close conflict, much reliance was placed on missiles, javelins and slings, but especially bows and arrows in the hands of mounted archers.[695] In replenishing the ranks great discrimination was exercised; and not only the physical fitness of the recruit,[696] but the social atmosphere in which he had sprung up was made the subject of strict inquiry. No slave was accepted as a soldier,[697] nor any youth whose mind had been debased by menial employment or by traffic for petty gains in the slums of a city.[698] The sons of veterans were impressed into the service,[699] and the landowners had periodically either to provide from their own family or to pay a computed sum for the purchase of a substitute among such as were not liable to conscription.[700] Many of the turbulent barbarian tribes on being subdued were obliged by the articles of a treaty to pay an annual tribute of their choicest youths to the armies of the Empire.[701] In addition to the regular forces, barbarian contingents, called *foederati*,[702] obeying their own leaders, were often bound by a league to serve under the Imperial government. In Europe the Goths, in Asia the Saracens, were usually the most important of such allies. Of the former nation Constantine at one time attached to himself as many as 40,000, an effort in which he was afterwards emulated by the great Theodosius.[703] The warships of the period were mostly long, low galleys impelled by one bank of oars from twenty to thirty in number, built entirely with a view to swiftness and hence called *dromons* or "runners." The smaller ones were employed on the rivers, the larger for operations at sea.[704] After a period of service varying from fifteen to twenty-four years the soldier could retire as a veteran with a gratuity, a grant of land, and exemption from taxation on a graduated scale for himself and his family.[705]

Such was the carefully digested scheme of military defence bequeathed to his successors by Constantine, who doubtless anticipated that he had granted a lease of endurance to the regenerated Empire for many centuries to come. But in the course of a hundred and fifty years this fine system fell gradually to pieces; and by the beginning of the sixth century no more than a *cento* of the original fabric can be discerned in the chronicles of the times. The whole forces were diminished almost to a moiety of their full complement;[706] the great peripheral bulwark of the *Limitanei*, scarcely discoverable on the Illyrian frontier, in other regions was represented by meagre bodies of one or two hundred men;[707] whilst the *Palatines* and *Comitatenses* betrayed such an altered character that they could claim merely a nominal existence.[708] The very name of legion, so identified with Roman conquest, but no longer available in the deteriorated military organization, became obsolete. In a Byzantine army at this period three constituents exist officially, but with little practical distinction. They appear as the *Numeri*,[709] the *Foederati*, and the *Buccellarii*. 1. The *Numeri* are the regular troops of the Empire, horse and foot, enrolled under the direct command of the Masters of the Forces, but the principle of strict selection has been virtually abandoned, applicants are accepted indiscriminately,[710] and even slaves are enlisted and retained under any plausible pretext.[711] 2. The *Foederati* now consist of bodies of mercenaries raised as a private speculation by soldiers of fortune, with the expectation of obtaining lucrative terms for their services from the Imperial government.[712] Such regiments were formed without regard to nationality, and might be composed mainly, or in part, of subjects of the Empire, or be wholly derived from some tribe of outer barbarians who offered themselves in a body for hire. On being engaged, each band received an *optio* or adjutant, who formed the connecting link between them and the central authorities, and arranged all matters relating to their *annones* and stipend.[713] But the tie was so loose that even on a foreign expedition they might arbitrarily dissolve the contract for some trivial reason, and possibly join the enemy's forces.[714] 3. The *Buccellarii*[715] are the armed retainers or satellites of the Byzantine magnates, whether civil or military, but especially of the latter. Officially they are reckoned among the *Foederati*,[716] and are obliged to take an oath of allegiance, not only to their actual chief, but also to the Emperor.[717] Their number varied according to the rank and wealth of their employers, and in the case of the Praetorian Praefects, or the Masters of the Forces, might amount to several thousands.[718] In each company they were divided into two classes, named respectively the lancers and the shieldmen. The former were selected men who formed the personal guard of their leader, the latter the rank and file who were officered by them.[719] The lancers were invariably cavalry, the shieldmen not necessarily so. These satellites were recruited preferably amongst the Isaurians,[720] a hardy race of highlanders, who, though within the Empire, always maintained a quasi-independence in their mountain fastnesses, and devoted themselves openly to brigandage.[721] To check their depredations a military Count was always set over that region, which thus resembled a frontier rather than an interior province. A fleet of warships was not kept up systematically at this epoch, but in view of an expedition, owing to the small size of the vessels, a navy could be created in a few weeks.[722]

From the foregoing specification it will be perceived that the method of enrollment constituted the only practical difference between the three classes of soldiers who marched in the ranks of a Byzantine army. The maintenance of the Empire rested, therefore, on a heterogeneous multitude, trained to the profession of arms no doubt, but without the cohesion of nationality or uniform military discipline.[723] In the multifarious host the word of command was given in Latin, which Greek and barbarian alike were taught to understand.[724]

Every student of ancient history is familiar with the methods of warfare among the Greeks and Romans; with the impenetrable, but inactive, phalanx which subdued the eastern world; and with the less solid, but mobile, legion which ultimately succeeded in mastering it.[725] Such armies consisted mainly of infantry; and the small bodies of cavalry attached to them, amounting to one tenth, or, perhaps, to as little as one twentieth part of the whole, were intended merely to protect the flanks of each division, or to render more effective the pursuit of a flying enemy. In those times, therefore, the horsemen were only an auxiliary force, which never engaged in battle as an independent army. But in the multiple operations against elusive barbarians in the wide circuit of the Roman Empire, experience made it evident that the mobility of cavalry was indispensable in order to deal effectively with such wary and reckless foes.[726] Early in the fourth century the number and importance of the cavalry had increased to such an extent that they were relegated to a separate command: and the Master of the Horse was regarded as of superior rank to his colleague of the infantry.[727] In the East, however, both branches of the service were soon combined under a single commander-in-chief; and henceforward the first military officers are entitled Masters of the Horse and Foot, or, collectively, of the Forces.[728]

At the period I am writing about, the usual routine of a pitched battle is to range the infantry in the centre with large squadrons of cavalry on either flank.[729] Both armies first exhaust their supply of missiles, after which a general engagement at close quarters ensues. By the aid of various evolutions, concealed reserves, and unexpected manœuvres, the opposing generals strive to take each other at a disadvantage, and victory rests with the most skilful or fortunate tactician. Single combats in the interspace between the two armies are not unfrequently initiatory to a battle;[730] and sometimes a campaign is decided by conflicts of cavalry alone.[731]

The various classes of Imperial guards still exist as a fourth division of the army, but, owing to the introduction of a system of purchase, these corps have degenerated into the condition of being mere figures to be mechanically paraded in the course of state pageantry; soldiers apparently, and in resplendent uniforms, but unversed in war, who would sooner buy their release for a large sum than enter on a campaign.[732]

The wars of Anastasius may be reviewed briefly in this section. They were four in number. 1. At the outset of his reign he found himself opposed within the capital by a strong faction of turbulent Isaurians, the relations and adherents of the late Emperor Zeno. Some of these held high office, and had even aspired to the throne.[733] On their dismissal and banishment from Constantinople the leaders fled to Isauria, where they levied large forces, and raised a rebellion by the aid of arms and treasure which Zeno had seen fit to amass in his native province.[734] The insurgents kept up hostilities for a long period with declining success against the Imperial generals, and the revolt was not fully suppressed till the seventh year (498).[735] In the fourth year of the war, however, the ringleaders were captured and decapitated, and their heads were sent to Constantinople, where they were exhibited to the populace fixed on poles in the suburb of Sycae.[736] The pacification of the province was achieved by this war more effectually than on any previous occasion, and the Isaurians do not again appear in history as refractory subjects of the Empire.[737]

2. In 502 the Persian king, Cavades,[738] applied to Anastasius for the loan of a large sum of money which he required in order to cement an alliance with the barbarian nation of the Nephthalites or White Huns.[739] For politic reasons this loan was refused, and the exasperated potentate immediately turned his arms against the Empire. He invaded the western portion of Armenia, which was under Roman suzerainty,[740] and took one or two towns of minor importance before an army could be sent against him. The principal

feature of this war, which lasted about four years, was the capture and recovery of Amida, a strongly fortified city of considerable size, situated in northern Mesopotamia, on the banks of the Tigris. Although ill-garrisoned, and neither armed nor provisioned to stand a siege, the inhabitants received the Persians with the most insulting defiance and made a very determined resistance for some months. The massive walls withstood the attacking engines, and all the devices of the besiegers were baffled by the ingenuity of those within the city. In despair Cavades had already given orders to raise the siege when the downfall of Amida was brought about by a very singular circumstance, as related by the chief historian of the period.[741] In the excess of popular frenzy at the news of the proposed retreat, the harlots of the town hastened to the battlements in order to jeer at the Persian monarch as he passed on his rounds, by making an indecent exposure of their persons. This obscene conduct so impressed the Magi in attendance that they gave it a mystical signification, and imparted their opinion to the King that "everything hidden and secret in Amida would shortly be laid bare." The departure was countermanded, and ultimately, through the supineness or treachery of some monks, to whom the guard of one of the main towers had been confided, an entry was made. A vengeful massacre of the vanquished then took place,[742] which was only stayed by the wit of a suppliant priest, who, in answer to the irate question of Cavades, "How did you dare to resist me so violently?" replied, "That the city might be won by your valour and not by our cowardice." Two years later, as a result of a protracted but ineffective siege, the Persians agreed to evacuate the town for a payment of one thousand pounds of gold (£40,000). On entering, the Romans discovered to their chagrin that such a state of destitution prevailed as would have compelled the surrender of the stronghold within a few days. The conclusion of this war was brought about by an invasion of the Huns,[743] who threatened Persia from the north; and hence Cavades was glad to make peace for seven years, on terms which left both parties in the same position as before the commencement of hostilities. The issue of this conflict was, on the whole, favourable to Anastasius, who, in the sense of being the superior power, soon proceeded to infringe the articles of the treaty by erecting commanding fortresses against his late foes along his eastern border. Especially as a counterpoise to the impregnable Nisibis, which had been ceded to the Persians a century and a half previously by the inept Jovian,[744] he raised the insignificant village of Daras to the rank of an important town, and surrounded it with bastions of imposing strength.[745] The impotent protests of the Persians were disregarded, and the two empires did not again come into martial collision for more than twenty years.

3. In 505 Anastasius and Theodoric, the Gothic king in Italy, by mutual inadvertence, as it may be judged, became involved in a conflict. Simultaneously the Master of the Forces in Illyricum and the Gothic general

Petza were engaged in suppressing their several enemies in that region.[746] The antagonist of the Byzantine general was Mundo, a bandit chief of the blood of Attila, who, with a body of Hunnish marauders, was preying on the country. He, on the point of being worsted, craved the assistance of Petza, who, seeing in him a natural ally of kindred race, joined him with his forces. The Goth had, in fact, just achieved the object of his expedition and probably made this move in the heat of success. Together they routed the Imperial army, which was shattered beyond all chance of reparation.[747] To avenge this defeat, Anastasius in 508 fitted out a naval expedition, which conveyed a landing force of 8,000 soldiers to the Italian coast. Making an unforeseen descent on Tarentum, they ravaged the vicinity with piratical ferocity, and returned as hastily as they came.[748] Theodoric, however, did not feel equal to pitting himself against the forces and resources of the East, and decided not to resent these reprisals. He deprecated the wrath of the Emperor in deferential language, and these encounters were soon forgotten as merely fortuitous disturbances of the peace.[749]

4. In 514 the studied economy of Anastasius provoked an upheaval of the incongruous elements of the state, which threatened the immediate collapse of his administration. From the hordes of barbarians massed on the banks of the Danube, troops were continually detached to take service under the Empire as *Foederati*; and their numbers had increased to such an extent that the annones due to them became an intolerable drain on the revenue. A sweeping reduction of these supplies was, therefore, decreed;[750] a measure judicious in itself, which would probably have been supported in sullen silence by the barbarians had not Count Vitalian, a Goth, and their principal leader, perceived that a specious means of retaliation was to hand. Taking advantage of the religious intractability of Anastasius, which was the bane of his rule and had alienated from him most of his pious subjects, he announced himself as the champion of orthodoxy, and proclaimed a holy war against the heretical Emperor.[751] The cry was taken up universally, and, especially within the capital, all the factious fanatics clamoured for Vitalian as the legitimate occupant of the throne. An immense host of *Foederati* followed the standard of the rebel; a great battle was fought in Thrace, with the result that the Imperial army was cut to pieces, suffering a loss, it is said, of more than sixty thousand.[752] A fleet was placed at the disposal of the pretender, whereupon Vitalian moved on the capital and blockaded Constantinople by land and sea. Against this attack the Emperor concerted measures within the city with some Athenian philosophers, their chemical knowledge was utilized effectively, galleys which ejected bituminous combustibles were launched against the hostile ships, and the investing fleet retreated precipitately amid volumes of fire and smoke.[753] The diplomacy of the almost nonagenarian monarch during this revolt was marked by much temporizing and duplicity; he disarmed the *Foederati* by a liberal donative,[754] and by raising their captain

to the rank of Master of the Forces in Thrace;[755] he mollified the orthodox ecclesiastics by promises and prepared instruments for the recall of exiled bishops; and he appealed to Pope Hormisdas praying that a synod should meet at Heraclea in order to appease the dissensions of the Church.[756] The synod met after protracted negotiations, but the combination was already dissolved, and the head of rebellion was broken; the concessions offered by the Emperor were presented and found to be illusory, and the futile assembly separated without any tangible result.[757] Anastasius had carried his point; active, yet impotent discontent reigned everywhere, but he had yielded nothing; and soon afterwards, in extreme old age, he sank into the grave[758] amid the familiar waves of sedition which for twenty-seven years had raged ineffectually round his throne.[759]

III. The commercial activities of the ancient world, as far as they come within the vision of history, were almost confined to these countries which encircle the basin of the Mediterranean; and in the early centuries of our era the varied regions to be measured between the Ganges and Gades were conceived to represent approximately the whole extent of the habitable earth.[760] Although the theory of a globe was held by advanced geographers and astronomers, the fact had not been established by circumnavigation and survey; and the idea was so far from being realized by the masses, that the notion of antipodes seemed to them to be little less than preposterous.[761] In the obscurity of prehistoric times the arts and sciences appear to have originated in the East; and from thence, by the aid of Greece and Rome, civilization extended until it included almost all the known parts of Western Africa and Europe. Before the beginning of the sixth century, however, owing to the incursions and settlements of Goths and Vandals, those western countries had retrograded nearly to the same level of barbarism from which they had been rescued formerly by the civilizing arms of Rome.

In the earliest ages the trade of the Mediterranean was entirely in the hands of the Semitic race; and from their great ports of Tyre and Sidon the Phoenicians penetrated with their well-laden ships even as far as Spain and Britain,[762] disposing of their native manufactures and imported wares on every coast within their reach.[763] But with the rise and spread of Hellenic civilization, commerce became more cosmopolitan; and by the conquests of Alexander the Greeks were made practically cognizant of a Far East teeming with productions which could minister to the needs of increasing wealth and luxury. At the same period, about 330 B.C., the foundation of Alexandria by that monarch gave them the command of Egypt, and they began to explore the borders of the Arabian Gulf or Red Sea as far as the Gulf of Aden and the confines of equatorial Africa. Concomitantly the laborious voyage of Nearchus,[764] undertaken at the instigation of the Macedonian conqueror, along inhospitable shores from the mouth of the Indus to the head of the

Persian Gulf, revealed to the Greeks the existence of a chain of navigable seas by which the treasures of the Indies might be brought by water to the wharves of the new capital. Through the establishment of this commerce Alexandria became the greatest trading centre of the Mediterranean, and distributed its exports to every civilized community who peopled the extended littoral of that sea.[765]

The first merchants who crossed the Indian ocean, embarking in small ships of light draught, timidly hugged the shore during their whole voyage, dipping into every bight for fear of losing sight of land. But in the reign of Claudius a navigator named Hippalus discovered the monsoons, and noted their stability as to force and direction at certain seasons of the year.[766] Thenceforward the merchants, furnishing themselves with larger vessels,[767] boldly spread their sails to the wind, ventured into mid-ocean, and made a swift and continuous passage from the southern coast of Arabia to some chosen port in the vicinity of Bombay.[768] Such was the southern, and, within the Christian era, most frequented trade route between the Roman Empire and the Indies. There were, however, two other avenues, more ancient, but less safe and less constant, by which merchandise from the far East, mainly by inland transit, could enter the Empire. By the first of these, which traversed many barbarous nations, the eastern shores of the Euxine were brought into communication with northern India through the Oxus, the Caspian Sea, and the Cyrus. From a bend in the latter river, the emporium of the trade, the town of Phasis, was easily attainable.[769] The second, intermediately situated, was the most direct and facile of the three, but, as it lay through the Persian dominions, the activity of commerce by this route depended on the maintenance of peace between the two empires.[770] The Byzantine government, jealous of the intercourse of its subjects with their hereditary enemies, fixed Artaxata, Nisibis, and Callinicus[771] as marts beyond which it was illegal for Roman merchants to advance for the purposes of trade on this frontier.[772]

In the sixth century the Ethiopian kingdom of Axume,[773] nearly corresponding with Abyssinia, became the southern centre of international trade; and its great port of Adule was frequented by ships and traders from all parts of the East.[774] Ethiopian, Persian, and Indian merchants scoured the Gangetic Gulf, and, having loaded their vessels with aloes, cloves, and sandalwood, obtained at Tranquebar and other ports, returned to Siedeliba or Ceylon[775] to dispose of their goods. There transhipments were effected, and sapphires, pearls, and tortoise-shell, the chief exports of that island, were added to the cargoes of ships westward bound. In the same market a limited supply of silk was obtained from such Chinese merchants as were venturesome enough to sail so far.[776] From Ceylon such vessels voyaged along the Malabar coast between Cape Comorin and Sindu, near the mouth of the Indus, receiving on board at various places supplies of cotton and linen fabrics for clothing, copper and rare woods, together with spices and aromatics, musk, castor, and especially pepper. In the harbours of that seaboard they also met with the merchants from Adule, most of whom sailed no farther, and provided them with the freight for their homeward voyage.[777]

The traders of Axume were not, however, wholly dependent for supplies on their intercourse with the Indies. Adjacent to their own borders lay wide tracts of country which were to them a fruitful source of the most valuable commodities; and with such their ships were laden when outward bound for the further East. Journeying to the south-east they entered an extensive but wild region called Barbaria,[778] part of which was known as the Land of Frankincense, from its peculiar fecundity in that odoriferous balsam. In this region cinnamon and tortoise-shell were also obtained; black slaves were purchased from various savage tribes; elephants were hunted by the natives for food; and ivory was supplied in greatest quantity to the markets of the world.[779] Every other year a caravan of several hundred merchants set out from Axume, well armed and equipped for a distant expedition. For six months continuously they travelled southward until they had penetrated far into the interior of the African continent. Gold was the object of their journey, and they took with them a herd of oxen as well as a quantity of salt and iron to barter for the precious metal. On arriving at the auriferous region they slaughtered the oxen and cut up the flesh into joints which they arranged along with the other objects of trade on the top of a specially erected barrier formed of thorn bushes. They then retreated to some distance, upon which the inhabitants, who had been watching their proceedings, came forward and placed pellets of gold on such lots as they wished to purchase. On the savages retreating the traders again advanced and removed or left the gold, according as they accepted or refused the amount offered. In this way, after various advances and retreats, bargains were satisfactorily concluded.[780] In the southern parts of Arabia bordering on the ocean, myrrh and frankincense were gathered in considerable quantity, whence the country acquired the epithet of Felix or Happy.[781] The richest source of emeralds lay in the uncivilized territory between Egypt and Axume, where the mines were worked by a ferocious tribe of nomads called Blemmyes. From them the Axumite merchants obtained the gems, which they exported chiefly to northern India. Amongst the White Huns, the dominant race in that region, they were esteemed so highly that the traders were enabled to load their ships with the proceeds of a few of these precious stones.[782]

Down the Red Sea to Adule resorted the Byzantine merchants, engaged in the home trade, in great numbers.[783] After loading their vessels they again sailed northward, a proportion of them to the small island of Jotabe,[784] situated near the apex of the peninsula of Mount Sinai, which separated the Elanitic from the Heroopolitan gulf. At a station there they were awaited by the officials of the excise, who collected from them a tenth part of the value of their merchandise.[785] Some of these ships proceeded up the eastern arm of the sea to Elath; the rest of them chose the western inlet and cast anchor at Clysma.[786] The wares landed at these ports were intended chiefly for the markets of Palestine and Syria.[787] By far the greater portion of the fleet, however, terminated their northward voyage at Berenice,[788] the last port of Egypt, on the same parallel with Syene. Here they discharged their cargoes and transferred the goods to the backs of camels, who bore them swiftly to the emporium of Coptos on the Nile.[789] A crowd of small boats then received the merchandise and made a rapid transit down stream to the Canopic arm of the river, from which by canal they emerged on lake Mareotis,[790] the inland and busiest harbour of Alexandria. The maritime traffic between the Egyptian capital and all other parts of the Empire, Constantinople especially, was constant and extensive, so that commodities could be dispersed from thence in every direction with the greatest facility.

Within the Eastern Empire itself there were manufactories for the fabrication of everything essential to the requirements of civilized life, but production was much restricted by the establishment universally of a system of monopolies. Several of these were held by the government, who employed both men and women in the manufacture of whatever was necessary to the Court and the army.[791] At Adrianople, Thessalonica, Antioch, Damascus, and other towns, arms and armour were forged, inlaid with gold when for the use of officers of rank; the costly purple robes of the Imperial household emanated from Tyre,[792] where dye-works and a fleet of fishing-boats for collecting the murex were maintained; these industries were strictly forbidden to the subject. There were, besides, at Cyzicus[793] and Scythopolis,[794] official factories for the weaving of cloth and linen. The military workshops were under the direction of the Master of the Offices, the arts of peace under that of the Count of the Sacred Largesses. Public manufacturers or traders were incorporated in a college or guild controlled by the latter Count, the privileges of which were limited to some five or six hundred members.[795] Among the staple productions of the Empire we find that Miletus[796] and Laodicea[797] were famous for woollen fabrics, Sardes[798] especially for carpets, Cos[799] for cotton materials, Tyre[800] and Berytus[801] for silks, Attica[802] and Samos[803] for pottery, Sidon[804] for glass, Cibyra[805] for chased iron, Thessaly[806] for cabinet furniture, Pergamus[807] for parchment, and Alexandria[808] for paper. The fields of Elis were given over to the cultivation of flax, and all the women at Patrae were engaged in spinning and weaving it.[809] Hierapolis[810] in Phrygia was noted for its vegetable dyes; and Hierapolis[811] in Syria was the great rendezvous for the hunters of the desert, who captured wild animals for the man and beast fights of the public shows. Slave dealers, held to be an infamous class, infested the verge of the Empire along the Danube, but at this date Romans and barbarians mutually enslaved each other.[812] On this frontier, also, consignments of amber and furs were received from the shores of the Baltic and the Far North.[813] With respect to articles of diet, almost every district produced wine, but Lesbian and Pramnian were most esteemed.[814] A wide tract at Cyrene was reserved for the growth of a savoury pot-herb, hence called the Land of Silphium.[815] Egypt was the granary of the whole Orient.[816] Dardania and Dalmatia were rich in cheese,[817] Rhodes[818] exported raisins and figs, Phoenicia[819] dates, and the capital itself had a large trade in preserved tunnies.[820]

China was always topographically unknown to the ancients, and about the sixth century only did they begin to discern clearly that an ocean existed beyond it.[821] The country was regarded as unapproachable by the Greek and Roman merchants,[822] but nevertheless became recognized at a very early period as the source of silk. Fully four hundred years before the Christian era the cocoons were carried westward, and the art of unwinding them was discovered by Pamphile of Cos, one of the women engaged in weaving the diaphanous textiles for which that island was celebrated.[823] Owing to the comparative vicinity of the Persian and Chinese frontiers, the silk exported by the Celestial Empire always tended to accumulate in Persia, so that the merchants of that nation enjoyed almost a monopoly of the trade.[824] Hence Byzantine commerce suffered severely during a Persian war, and strenuous efforts would be made to supply the deficiency of silk by stimulating its importation along the circuitous routes. Such attempts, however, invariably proved ineffective[825] until the invention of the compass and the discovery of the south-east passage opened the navigation of the globe between the nations of the East and West.

IV. In general condition the Byzantine people exhibit, almost uniformly in every age, a picture of oppressed humanity, devoid of either spirit or cohesion to nerve them for a struggle to be free. With the experience of a thousand years, the wisdom of Roman statesmen and jurists failed to evolve a political system which could insure stability to the throne or prosperity to the nation. Seditious in the cities, abject in the country, ill-disciplined in the camp, unfaithful in office, the subjects of the Empire never rose in the social scale, but languished through many centuries to extinction, the common grave of Grecian culture and Roman prowess.

In the rural districts almost all the inhabitants, except the actual landowners, were in a state of virtual slavery. The labourers who tilled the soil were usually attached, with their offspring, to each particular estate in the condition of slaves or serfs. They could neither quit the land of their own free will, nor could they be alienated from it by the owner, but, if the demesne were sold, they were forced to pass with it to the new master.[826] The position of a serf was nominally superior to that of a slave, but the distinction was so little practical that the lawyers of the period were unable to discriminate the difference.[827] Any freeman who settled in a neighbourhood to work for hire on an estate lost his liberty and became a serf bound to the soil, unless he migrated again before the expiration of thirty years.[828] The use and possession of arms was interdicted to private persons throughout the Empire, and only such small knives as were useless for weapons of war were allowed to be exposed for sale.[829]

In every department of the State the same principle of hereditary bondage was applied to the lower grades of the service, and even in some cases to officials of considerable rank. Here, however, a release was conceded to those who could provide an acceptable substitute, a condition but rarely possible to fulfil.[830] Armourers, mintmen, weavers, dyers, purple-gatherers, miners, and muleteers, in government employ[831] could neither resign their posts nor even intermarry[832] with associates on a different staff, or the general public, unless under restrictions which were almost prohibitive. Within the same category were ruled the masters or owners of freight-ships,[833] chartered to convey the annones and tributes, of which the Alexandrian corn-fleet[834] constituted the main section. Those addicted to this vocation in the public interest were necessarily men of some private means, as they were obliged to build and maintain the vessels at their own expense; but they were rewarded by liberal allowances, and were almost exempt in respect of the laws affecting the persons and property of ordinary citizens. The lot of this class of the community appears to have been tolerable, and was even, perhaps, desirable,[835] but that of the Decurions, the members of the local senates, was absolutely unbearable.[836] In relation to their fellow townsmen their duties do not seem to have been onerous, but as collectors of the revenue they were made responsible for the full precept levied four-monthly on each district, and had to make good any deficiency from their own resources.[837] As natives of the locality to which their activities were constrained, their intimate knowledge of the inhabitants was invaluable to the government in its inquisitorial and compulsive efforts to gather in the imposts; and, subordinated to the Imperial officials resident in, or on special missions to, the provinces, they became consequently the prime object of their assaults when dealing with the defaulting tributaries. In view of such hardships, municipal dignities and immunities were illusory; and, as the local senates were very numerous, there were few families among the middle classes, from whom those bodies were regularly replenished, whose members did not live in dread of a hereditary obligation to become a Decurion. In every ordinary sphere of exertion, not excepting the Court, the Church, or the army, men, long embarked on their career, were liable to receive a mandate enjoining them to return to their native town or village in order to spend the rest of their lives in the management of local affairs.[838]

Occupation of the highest offices of State, or many years' service in some official post, could alone free them from the municipal bond.[839]

Life under accustomed conditions, though with restricted liberty, may be supportable or even pleasant, but the Byzantine subject could seldom realize the extent of his obligations or foresee to what exactions he might have to submit. He might review with satisfaction a series of admirable laws which seemed to promise him tranquillity and freedom from oppression, but experience soon taught him that it was against the interest of the authorities to administer them with equity. By an ineradicable tradition, dating from the first centuries of the expansion of the Empire, it was presumed that the control of a province offered a fair field to a placeman for enriching himself.[840] Hence the prevalence of a universal corruption and a guilty collusion between the Rector and all the lesser officials, who afforded him essential aid in his devices for despoiling the provincials.[841] While the fisc never scrupled to aggravate the prescribed imposts by superindictions,[842] its agents were insatiate in their efforts at harvesting for themselves. The tyranny of the first emperors was local and transient, but under the rule of the Byzantine princes the vitals of the whole Empire were persistently sapped. In the *adaeratio* of the annones a value was set upon the produce far above the market price;[843] taxes paid were redemanded, and receipts in proper form repudiated because the *tabellio* who had signed them, purposely removed, was not present to acknowledge his signature;[844] unexpected local rates were levied, to which the assent of the Decurions was forced, with the avowed object of executing public works which were never undertaken;[845] sales of property at a vile estimate were pressed on owners who dared not provoke the officials by a refusal;[846] decisions in the law courts were ruled by bribery, and suitors were overawed into not appealing against unjust judgements;[847] forfeitures of estates to the crown were proclaimed under pretence of lapse of ownership or questionable right of inheritance, and their release had to be negotiated for the payment of a sufficient ransom;[848] even special grants from the Imperial treasury for reinstatement of fortifications or other purposes were sometimes embezzled without apprehension of more serious trouble, if detected, than disgorgement.[849] In all these cases the excess extorted was appropriated by the rapacious officials. Such were the hardships inflicted systematically on the small proprietors who, if unable to pay or considered to be recalcitrant, were not seldom subjected to bodily tortures. For hours together they were suspended by the thumbs,[850] or had to undergo the application of finger-crushers or foot-racks,[851] or were beaten on the nape of the neck with cords loaded with lead.[852] Nevertheless, remainders accumulated constantly, and a remission of hopeless arrears for a decade or more was often made the instance of Imperial indulgence. But the old vouchers were habitually secreted and preserved by the collectors so that the ignorant rustics might be harassed persistently for debts which they no longer owed.[853] The existence of such frauds was patent even to the exalted perceptions of the Court; and hence Anastasius, in order to render his abolition of the chrysargyron effective, resorted to an artifice which appealed to the avarice of his financial delegates throughout the country.[854] But an emperor, however well-intentioned, could rarely attempt to lighten the burdens of even the humblest of his subjects. His immediate ministers had sold the chief posts in the provinces[855] and were under a tacit convention to shield their nominees unless in the case of some rash and flagrant delinquent who abandoned all discretion. The public good was ignored in practice; to keep the treasury full was the simple and narrow policy of the Byzantine financier, who never fostered any enlightened measure for making the Empire rich.[856] Zeno essayed to remedy the widespread evil of venality, but his effort was futile; although his constitution was re-enacted more than once and permanently adorned the statute-book.[857] According to this legislator every governor was bound to abide within his province in some public and accessible place for fifty days after the expiration of his term of office. Thus detained within the reach of his late constituents when divested of his authority, it was hoped that they would be emboldened to come forward and call him to account for his misdeeds. The reiteration of the law at no great intervals of time sufficiently proves that it was promulgated only to be disregarded.[858]

Without legitimate protectors from whom they might seek redress, the wretched tributaries either tried to match their oppressors in craft, or yielded abjectly to all their demands. Some parted with whatever they possessed, and finally sold their sons and daughters into slavery or prostitution;[859] others posted their holdings against the visits of the surveyors with notices designating them as the property of some influential neighbour.[860] Such local magnates, who maintained, perhaps, a guard of Isaurian bandits, were wont to bid defiance to the law as well as to the lawlessness of the Rector and his satellites.[861] To their protection, in many instances, the lesser owners were impelled to consign themselves unconditionally, hoping to find with them a haven of refuge against merciless exaction. The patron implored readily accepted the trust, but the suppliant soon discovered that his condition was assimilated to that of a serf.[862] The web of social order was strained or ruptured in every grade of life; traders joined the ranks of the clergy in order to abuse the facilities for commerce conceded to ministers of religion;[863] the proceedings of the Irenarchs among the rustic population were so vexatious, that they were accounted disturbers, instead of guardians of the peace,[864] and the simple pastor had to be denied the use of a horse, lest it should enable him to rob with too much security on the public highways.[865]

II. Educational

Superstition flourishes because knowledge is still the luxury of the few. By education alone can we hope to attain to the extinction of that phase of mind termed belief, or faith, which has always been inculcated as a virtue or a duty by the priest, and condemned as a vice of the intellect by the philosopher. In every age, the ability to discern the lines of demarcation which separate the known from the unknown is the initial stage of advancement; and in the training of youth, the prime object of the educator should be to confer this power on every individual; for in the uninformed minds of a great majority of mankind, fact and fancy are for the most part inextricably entangled. The efforts of authority to dispel or perpetuate error are most potent when acting on the impressionable faculties of early life. In a sane and progressive world the first conception to be engrafted in the expanding mind should be that knowledge has no foothold beyond the causeways pushed by science into the ocean of the unknown.[866]

I do not design to produce under this heading a lengthy disquisition on paedagogics among the Byzantines, but merely to indicate, by some broad lines, upon what stock of common knowledge the foundations of civilization rested in this age. The student of early Roman history will scarcely need to be reminded that the virtues of the Republic were not derived from the schools of art or philosophy; or that the aesthetic tastes of those blunt citizens only developed in proportion as they found themselves lords over the culture as well as over the country of the Greeks.[867] Towards the middle of the second century B.C., Greek professors of literature and eloquence began to establish themselves at Rome, where they held their ground for some decades on a very precarious footing, owing to the strong disfavour with which they were regarded by those who considered the preservation of ancient manners as the salvation of the state.[868] Gradually, however, the new discipline prevailed; eminent teachers were accorded recognition by the government, and before the end of the first century A.D., the privilege of maintaining at the public expense a faculty of professors to impart higher instruction to the rising generation, was granted to every town of any magnitude throughout the Empire.[869] To facilitate, therefore, the prosecution of *liberal studies*, for such they were officially named, suitable buildings were erected in every populous centre. Architecturally, a state school comprised a handsome hall or lecture theatre, with class-rooms attached, the whole being surrounded essentially by a portico.[870] The extent and decorative elaboration of these edifices depended doubtless on their local or general importance. The greater institutions, as denoted by their being the resort of a large concourse of students, were liberally provided with the adornments of painting and statuary.[871] Objective instruction was given by means of tabular expositions of the subjects taught affixed to the walls of the colonnades, among which maps conveying not only geographical, but also historical information, were particularly conspicuous.[872] Until the barbarian invasion of Greece by Alaric at the close of the fourth century, Athens maintained an easy pre-eminence as a centre of polite learning, and bestowed the greatest prestige on those who passed through her schools.[873] The most pronounced effort for the advancement of higher education in the East at this epoch was the definite constitution of the schools of Constantinople in an Auditorum on the Capitol, almost as the counterpart of a modern University, by Theodosius II, in 425. The teaching staff of this college consisted, under their official titles, of three Orators and ten Grammarians for the Latin language; of five Sophists and ten Grammarians for the Greek tongue; of one Philosopher; and of two Jurists, thirty-one members in all.[874] To insure the success of this foundation, the decree for its establishment was accompanied by an injunction against the public lecturing of professors other than those appointed to hold forth within its walls.[875] A body of scriveners, technically named antiquarians, was also maintained for the multiplication of copies of manuscripts in the public libraries of the capital, which were rich in literature.[876]

In addition to these teachers, who were settled in various localities, the itinerant professor, who travelled from place to place delivering public harangues and taking pupils for a short course of instruction, was a feature in the life of the period. With considerable vanity they distinguished themselves by wearing a long beard, carrying a staff, and enfolding themselves in a cloak of an unusual tint.[877] Rhetoricians affected a garb of scarlet or white, philosophers of gray, and physicians of blue.[878] When addressing an audience, they usually presented themselves crowned with flowers, reeking with perfumes, and displaying a gold ring of remarkable size.[879] The advent of these self-ordained instructors of the public into a provincial town was often the occasion of much local enthusiasm, and a throng of citizens advanced to meet them for some distance, in order to conduct them to their lodgings.[880] All professors, whether in the pay of the state or otherwise, enjoyed a complete immunity from the civil duties and imposts enforced on ordinary individuals, thus presenting the singular contrast of being licensed to live in a condition of ideal freedom under a political system which restricted personal liberty at every turn.[881] Such material advantages inevitably became liable to abuse through imposture, and the country was permeated by charlatans in the guise of philosophers, who coveted distinction and emolument at the easy price of a merely personal assertion of competence.[882] In the fourth century this evil was scarcely checked by Imperial enactments which required that professors of every grade should procure credentials as to character and attainments from the Curia of their native place.[883] The cost of education is a somewhat obscure subject, but we are justified in assuming that all the state seminaries were open gratuitously to the youth of the district; and we know that even private teachers of eminence were accustomed to remit the fees to students who were unable to pay.[884]

The ancients, like the moderns, assigned certain courses of instruction to pupils according to their age and the estimated development of their intelligence. As with us, the recipient of a full liberal education passed through three stages, adapted respectively to the capacity of the child, the boy, and the youth, which may be discussed under the headings of Elementary, Intermediate, and Final. To these must necessarily be added, in the case of those destined for a special vocation, a fourth stage, viz., the Professional. Their conception, however, of the periods of early life was more defined, and differed somewhat from our own, the first terminating at twelve, the second at fourteen, the third at twenty, and the fourth at twenty-five years of age.[885] Primary education began at from five to seven, and the pupils were usually sent to a day-school in the charge of a slave, named a paedagogue. There they were taught to read, write, and to count; and suitable pieces were given to them to learn by rote. A wooden tablet faced with wax, upon which they scratched with a style, took the place of the modern slate or copy-book. Calculation was restricted to some simple operations of mental arithmetic, owing to the cumbersome method of figuring employed by the ancients, which did not lend itself easily to the manipulation of written numbers.[886] The schoolmasters who presided over such preparatory establishments did not rank as professors, and were not accorded any privileges beyond those of ordinary citizens.[887]

II. At twelve the work of mental cultivation commenced seriously, and the pupil entered on the study of the *seven liberal arts*, viz., grammar, dialectic, rhetoric, geometry, arithmetic, astronomy, and music.[888] These subjects were taken in two stages, which in the West were beginning to be called the *Trivium* and *Quadrivium*.[889] Two years were devoted to the *Trivium*, the scope of which may be apprehended from a brief summary. 1. The grammar of the period dealt with the eight parts of speech in a sufficiently exhaustive manner; conveyed some notions, often crude and erroneous, as to the derivation of words; and, in the absence of precise anatomical or acoustic science, attempted in a primitive fashion a classification of the letters and a physiology of vocalization. The construction of sentences was analyzed with considerable minuteness; and passages selected from eminent writers were set for the student to parse with an exactitude seldom called for at the present day.[890] The laws of poetical metre were taught as a leading branch of the subject; and a familiarity with literature was promoted by reading the best authors, especially Homer.[891] The copious Latin grammarian Priscian flourished at Constantinople under Anastasius, and his monumental work in eighteen books is still extant.[892]

2. In the province of dialectics it was sought to instill the art of reasoning correctly into the mind of the pupil. Thus he was introduced to the elementary principles of logic; the categories, or the modes of regarding and classifying phenomena, were explained to him; and he was exercised in the practice of accurate deduction according to the various forms of the syllogism.

3. Without a practical acquaintance with the art of rhetoric it was considered that no one could pretend to occupy any desirable position in the civil service of the Empire.[893] This course was the extension and application of the two previous ones of grammar and logic, upon which it was based. The rules of composition and the arts of argument, which the ingenuity of the Greeks had unravelled and defined under a hundred apposite names, were exemplified to the student,[894] who wrote extracts to dictation chosen from various illustrative authors. The sophist or rhetorician addressed his class on some stated theme, and spoke alternately on both sides of the question. The management of the voice and the use of appropriate gesture were systematically taught.[895] Finally the pupils were set to compose speeches of their own and to debate among themselves on suitable subjects.[896]

III. The four divisions of the *Quadrivium* were grouped together as the mathematical arts; and six years were allotted to their study. 1. In geometry the discipline did not include the learning of theorems and problems as set forth in the Elements of Euclid, but merely an acquaintance with the definitions and with the ordinary plane and solid figures.[897] The teaching in this section, however, was mainly of geography.[898] It was asserted doubtfully that the earth was a globe and that there was an inferior hemisphere of which nothing certain could be predicated.[899]

2. Arithmetic was not practised methodically by the setting of sums to be worked out by the pupils, but consisted chiefly in demonstrating the more obvious properties of numbers, such as odd, even, prime, perfect, etc., together with many fanciful absurdities.[900] Operations with figures were indicated verbally in a disconnected manner; multiplication tables to be learnt by heart had not been invented; the higher rules and decimal fractions were unknown.

3. Systematic astronomy at this period and for long after, as is well known, was conceived of on false principles which, whilst admitting of the correct solution of some problems, such as the prediction of eclipses, left the vastness of the universe and its physical constitution totally unapprehended.

All the heavenly bodies were regarded as mathematically, if not teleologically disposed about the earth, to which as a centre even the fixed stars, at varying and immeasurable distances as they are, were constrained fantastically by a revolving sphere of crystal.[901] The reasoning, however, by which these views were upheld was not sufficiently convincing to gain universal acceptance; and the outlines of the science communicated to students generally received some modifications from the minds of individual teachers.[902] Much of the course was taken up with treating of the constellations and the zodiac, not without a tincture of astrology, and some primitive observations on meteorology were included.[903]

4. Music as known to us is virtually a modern creation; and that of the Greeks would doubtless impress us as a wild and disorderly performance, adapted only to the ears of some semi-barbaric people of the East. Their most extended scale did not range beyond eighteen notes;[904] in order to obtain variety their only resource was a shift of key, that is, a change of pitch, or the adoption of a different mode, that is, of a gamut in which the semitones assumed novel positions; and their harmony was restricted to the consonance of octaves. Time was not measured according to the modern method, but there was a rhythm fixed in relation to the various metres of poetic verse. Their usual instruments were the pipe or flute, the lyre, a simple form of organ,[905] and, of course, the human voice. Practically, therefore, their music consisted of melody of a declamatory or recitatival type, to which a peculiar character was sometimes given by the use of quarter tones; and choral singing was purely symphonic. But the vibrational numbers of the scale had been discovered by Pythagoras when making experiments with strings; and each of the eighteen notes and fifteen modes had received a descriptive name. Hence the limited scope of the art did not prevent the theory of music from ultimately becoming elaborated with a complexity not unworthy of the native subtlety of the Greeks.[906] In practice the musical training of pupils consisted in their learning to sing to the lyre.[907]

Such in brief were the component parts of a liberal education, with which, however, under the name of philosophy, it was considered essential that a complement of ethical teaching should be conjoined. This complement was digested into three branches, under which were discussed the duty of the individual to himself, to the household, and to the community at large or to the state.[908]

IV. It now remains for us to glance at the more protracted training of those who had resolved to devote their lives to some particular sphere of activity. Aspirants for the position of professor of the liberal arts, or who wished to utilize their acquirements in a political career, would continue and extend their studies on the lines above indicated; but those who intended to follow the professions of law or physic, or engage in practice of art proper, had to direct their energies into new channels.

1. As the administration of the Empire was almost monopolized by the members of the legal profession, it may be inferred that the throng of youths intent on becoming lawyers fully equalled in number the students of every other calling. Hence we find that not only were schools of law established in every city of importance, notably Constantinople, Alexandria, and Caesarea, but that a provincial town of minor rank obtained a unique celebrity through the teaching of jurisprudence. Berytus, on the Syrian coast, in the province of Phoenicia, with an academic history of several centuries[909] at this date, had attained to that position; and was habitually spoken of as the "mother" and "nurse of the laws."[910] Four jurists of eminence, double the number allotted to any other school, under the title of Antecessors, lectured in the auditorium;[911] and a progressive course of study was arranged to extend over five years. In each successive year the candidate assumed a distinctive designation which marked his seniority or denoted the branch of law on which he was engaged.[912] Before the sixth century the legal archives of the Empire had been swollen to such proportions that it had become an almost impossible task to thread the maze of their innumerable enactments. During the lapse of a thousand years the constitutions of the emperors had been engrafted on the legislation of the Republic, and the complexity of the resultant growth was capable of bewildering the most acute of legal minds. On three occasions, beginning from the time of Constantine, attempts had been made to separate and classify the effective laws;[913] and the Code of Theodosius II, published in 438, the only official one, was at present in force. But this work, executed in a narrow spirit of piety which decreed that only the enactments of Christian emperors should be included, was universally recognized as both redundant and insufficient. A still wider entanglement existed in the literature which had accumulated around the interpretation and application of the statutes; during the administration of justice a myriad of perplexing points had arisen to exercise the keenest forensic judgement in order to arrive at equitable decisions; and it was estimated that two thousand treatises, emanating from nearly forty authors, contained in scattered passages matter essential to a correct apprehension of the principles and practice of the law.[914] Such was the arduous prospect before a legal student who desired to win a position of repute in his profession.[915]

2. As Berytus had become famous for its law school, so Alexandria, and even some centuries earlier, had gained a noted pre-eminence as a centre of medical education;[916] but with respect to the course of study and the methods of instruction no details have come down to us. We have seen that the regulations for the establishment of the auditorium at Constantinople did

not provide for a chair of physic, whence it may be inferred that it was left entirely to those who had attained to the position of senior or arch-physician to organize the teaching and training of pupils. The public medical officers, who attended the poor at their own homes or in the *nosocomia* or hospitals existing at this date,[917] would doubtless have excellent opportunities for forming classes and rendering students familiar with the aspect and treatment of disease. The medical and surgical science of antiquity had come to a standstill by the end of the second century, when the indefatigable Galen composed his great repertory of the knowledge of his own times. That knowledge comprised almost all the details of macroscopic anatomy, but had advanced but a little way towards solving the physiological problems as to the working of the vital machine. The gross absurdities of the preceding centuries had, however, been finally disposed of, such as that fluids passed down the windpipe into the lungs,[918] or that the arteries contained air.[919] Ordinary operations were performed freely; and the surgeon was conscious that it was more creditable to save a limb than to amputate it.[920] Three centuries before the Christian era Theophrastus had laid the foundations of systematic botany, as had his master Aristotle those of zoology and comparative anatomy.[921] The resources of therapeutics were extensive and varied, but the action of drugs was not well understood. Remedies were compounded not only from the vegetable kingdom, but also with animal substances[922] to an extent which seems likely to be equalled by the more precise medication with the principles of living tissues gaining ground at the present day. Knowledge of minerals, however, was too deficient for such bodies to take a prominent place in pharmacology.[923]

3. The arts of Greece, after having flourished in perfection from the time of Pericles to that of Alexander in the various departments of architecture, sculpture, painting, and literature, remained dormant for some centuries until the establishment of universal peace under the dominion of Rome provided a new theatre for their exercise. Fostered in the Augustan age by the indolence and luxury of the Imperial city, which offered the prospect of fortune to every artist of ambition and talent, they were communicated to the Latins, who strove earnestly to imitate and equal their masters. The exotic art bloomed on the foreign soil to which it had been transplanted; and the Italians, if they never displayed creative genius or originality of conception, at least learned to reproduce with consummate skill and novelty of investment the emanations of Hellenic inspiration. But the elements of permanency were wanting to such factitious aptitudes, as they were in fact to the fabric of the Empire itself; and the wave of political stability was closely followed in its rise and fall by the advance or decline of the arts. After the reign of Augustus the tide of prosperity ebbed for about half a century until it reached its lowest level during the Civil Wars which heralded the settlement of Vespasian on the throne. It rose again, and for more than fifty years

maintained an active flow during the reigns of Trajan and Hadrian, subsequent to which its course is marked by a gently descending line, under the benign rule of the Antonines, until it sinks somewhat abruptly in the temporary dissolution of the Empire, which preceded the triumph of Severus. Thenceforward, but two centuries from its foundation,[924] the sovereignty of Rome entered on shoals and quicksands, calamity succeeded calamity, and a position of stable equilibrium was never afterwards regained; but in the vicissitudes of fortune before the final catastrophe, an illusive glow appeared to signalize more than once a return of the supremacy of the Caesars.[925]

By the time of Constantine the neglect and degradation of art had become so pronounced that artists could scarcely be found competent to execute, even in an inferior style, any monumental record of the events of the age; or for the construction of the public buildings so lavishly planned by that monarch in his attempted renovation of the Empire.[926] To meet the difficulty he promulgated decrees, which were kept in force and multiplied by his successors, with the view of stimulating his subjects to devote themselves to arts and the allied handicrafts. Immunity from all civil burdens was guaranteed; and salaries, with the free occupation of suitable premises in public places, were offered to those who would undertake to teach.[927] These measures undoubtedly tended to the elevation of taste and the maintenance of civilization, although they could not infuse a new genius into the people of a decadent age.

At the opening of the sixth century Constantinople was the focus of civilization not only in the East, but also with respect to those western countries which had until lately been united as members of the same political system. The suzerainty of the eastern Emperor was still tacitly allowed, or, at least, upheld; and the prestige of his capital was felt actively throughout the ruder West as a refining influence which only waned after the period of the Renaissance. The main characteristic of art at this epoch is an unskilled imitation of ancient models; and the conventional style regarded as typically Byzantine, which at one time prevailed so widely in Europe, was not to become apparent for many centuries to come.[928] But by the fifth century certain modifications of design, betraying the infiltration of Oriental tastes, also began to be observable.[929]

a. Architecture at Constantinople remained essentially Greek, or, at least, Graeco-Roman; and the constant demand for new buildings, especially churches, ordained that it should still be zealously studied. In the provinces, however, particularly on the Asiatic side, some transitional examples would have enabled an observer to forecast already an era of cupolar construction.[930]

b. On the other hand, statuary almost threatened to become a lost art. The devotion to athletic contests, which prevailed among the Greeks, caused them to lay great stress on physical culture; and at the public games, as well as in the preparatory gymnasia, they were constantly familiarized with the aspect of the human figure undraped in every phase of action and repose.[931] The eye of the artist thus acquired a precision which enabled him to execute works in marble with a perfection unapproached in any later age. To the anthropomorphic spirit of polytheism it was necessary that the images of the gods should be multiplied in temples and even in public places; and the Greeks essayed to express the ideal beauty of their divinities under those corporeal forms which appeared most exquisite to the human senses. Received as being of both sexes and as fulfilling the conception of faultless excellence in a variety of spheres, a boundless field lay open before the artist in which to represent them according to their diverse attributes of sovereignty, of intellect, or of grace.[932] But the traditions of Hebrew monotheism sternly forbid any material presentation of the Deity, and sculpture in the round was almost abolished at the advent of Christianity. In one minor department, however, that of ivory carving, a school of artists was constantly exercised in order to provide the annual batch of consular diptychs, which it was customary to distribute throughout the provinces every new year.[933] On each set of these plates, figured in low relief, appeared generally duplicate likenesses of the consul of the day, clad in his state robes and surrounded by subsidiary designs. The style of these productions, perfunctorily executed it may be, suggests that the average artist of the period was incapable of portraiture or of tracing correctly the lines of any living form.[934]

c. Less unfortunate with reference to religion were the pictorial arts at this date. The decoration of churches, in brilliant colour and appropriate iconography, was gradually carried to a degree of elaboration which has never since been surpassed. The intrinsic nature of popular devotion insensibly established the convention that images in the flat did not contravene the divine prohibitions; and ecclesiastical prejudice yielded to expediency. On the iconostasis and around the walls of the sacred edifice, in proximity to the worshippers, Christ, the Virgin, the Apostles, and the Saints, with many a scene of Gospel history, were depicted in glowing tints on a blue or a golden ground. On every available space of the ceiling similar subjects, but of larger dimensions, were executed in a brilliant glass mosaic, and the mass of colour overhead completed the gorgeous effect of the interior.[935] Accordingly it was considered that reverence for the holy scriptures was fittingly shown by the reproduction of copies in the most costly form; and hence the painting of manuscripts in miniature revived and endured as one of the staple industries of the age. But in all these cases defective drawing and perspective are often painfully conspicuous, and a meretricious display of colour seems to be regarded by the artist as the highest expression of his skill.[936]

d. By the end of the fifth century we are on the verge of that new era in literature, introduced by the Byzantines, when to make a transcript of some previous writer was to become an author.[937] In other branches of art from time to time some obvious merit becomes visible on the surface, but in the domain of poetry, during nearly fourteen centuries previous to the fall of the Empire, a single name only, that of Claudian, survives to remind us that both Greeks and Latins once possessed the faculty of expressing themselves in verse with nobility of thought and felicity of diction. Poetasters existed in abundance, but without exception their compositions exemplify the futility of striving after an object which in that age had resolved itself into the unattainable. The usefulness of prose as a medium of information, however low may be its literary level, often compensates us for lack of talent in an author; and the bald chronicler, who plagiarized his predecessors in the same field and presented their work as his own, is sometimes as welcome to the investigator as a writer of more ambitious aims. In these barren centuries, however, history and theology are occasionally illustrated by some work of original power.

In the foregoing paragraphs I have dealt with education in relation only to the male sex, and it remains for me to say a few words respecting the mental training of the female. In keeping with the rule as to their social seclusion, the instruction of girls was conducted in the privacy of the family circle. There they received, in addition to the usual rudiments, a certain tincture of polite learning, which implied the methodical reading of Homer and a limited acquaintance with some of the other Greek poets and the dramatists.[938] Music, as being an elegant accomplishment, was also taught to them.[939] They were not, however, debarred from extending the scope of their studies, and instances of learned ladies are not altogether wanting to this age, for example, the Empress Athenais or Eudocia[940] and the celebrated Hypatia.[941]

A glance at the slight structure of knowledge, the leading lines of which I have just lightly traced, may enable the modern reader to appreciate the conditions of intellectual life among the ancients, and to perceive within how narrow an area was confined the exercise of their reasoning faculties. Viewed in comparison with the vast body of contemporary science, all the information acquired by the Greeks must appear as an inconsiderable residue scarcely capable of conveying a perceptible tinge to the whole mass. For fully eighteen hundred years, from the age of Aristotle to that of Columbus and Copernicus, no advance was made in the elucidation of natural phenomena or even towards exploring the surface of the globe. The same globe has been surveyed and delineated in its widest extent by the industry of our cartographers, has been seamed with a labyrinth of railways for the conveyance of substance, and invested in a network of wire for the transmission of thought. In the universe of suns our solar system appears to us as a minute and isolated disc, the earth a speck within that disc; to the ancients the revelations of telescopic astronomy were undreamt of, and the world they inhabited (all but a tithe of which was concealed from them, and whose form they only mistily realized) seemed to them to be the heart of the universe, of which the rest of the celestial bodies were assumed to be merely subordinate appendages. Geological investigation has penetrated the past history of the earth through a million of centuries to those primeval times when meteorological conditions first favoured the existence of organic life; the people of antiquity were blinded by unfounded legends which antedated the origin of things to a few thousand years before their own age. Spectroscopic observation has assimilated the composition of the most distant stars to that of our own planet. Chemical analysis has achieved the dissolution of the numberless varieties of matter presented to our notice, and proved them to arise merely from diverse combinations of a few simple elements; and electrical research has almost visually approached that primordial substance in which is conceived to exist the ultimate unity of all things.[942] Synthetical chemistry has acquired the skill to control the inherent affinities of nature, and to compel her energies to the production of myriads of hitherto unknown compounds.[943] By the aid of the microscope we can survey the activities of those otherwise invisible protoplasmic cells which lie at the foundation of every vital process; and the possibility is foreshadowed that, in the alliance of biology and chemistry, we may one day succeed in crossing the bridge which links the organic to the inorganic world and command the beginnings of life.[944] In all these departments of objective knowledge the speculations and researches of the Greek philosophers had not even broken the ground. For these primitive observers, without history and without science, the world was a thing of yesterday, a novel appearance of which almost anything might be affirmed or denied. Magnetism was known merely as an interesting property of the lodestone; electricity, as yet unnamed, had barely arrested attention as a peculiarity of amber, when excited by friction, to attract light substances. Nor had the mechanical arts been developed so as to admit of any practical application and stimulate the industries of civilization. Although automatic toys were sometimes constructed with considerable ingenuity,[945] the simplest labour-saving machine was as yet uninvented.[946] In the early centuries of our era knowledge had become stagnant, and further progress was not conceived of. One half of the world lived on frivolity; the individuality of the other half was sunk in metaphysical illusion. The people of this age contemplated nature without comprehending her operations; her forces were displayed before their eyes, but it never entered into their heads to master them and make them subservient to the needs of human life; they moved within a narrow cage unconscious of the barriers which confined them, without a thought of emerging to the freedom of the beyond; and an ordinary citizen of the present day is in the possession of information which would surprise and instruct the greatest sage of ancient Greece.

III. Religious.

The increase of knowledge in the nineteenth century has stripped every shred of supernaturalism from our conception of popular religions. The studies and inventions of modern science have illuminated every corner of the universe; and our discovery of the origins has cleared the greatest stumbling-block from the path of philosophy and removed the last prop which sustained the fabric of organized superstition. The world will one day have to face the truth about religion; and it may then become necessary to restrain by legal enactment those who would draw away the masses to some old historical, or to some new-born superstition.[947]

In primitive times the curiosity and impatience of mankind demanded an immediate explanation of the activities of nature; and by a simple analogy they soon conceived the existence of a demiurge or maker of worlds who, in his loftier sphere, disposed of the materials of the universe by methods comparable to those of their own constructive operations.[948] Or, perchance, by even less speculative reasoning they were led to accept the phenomenal world as the result of a perpetual generation and growth which accorded closely with their everyday experience of nature; whilst a divinity of some kind seemed to lurk in every obscurity and all visible objects to be instinct with a life and intelligence of their own.[949] In either case they believed themselves to be in the presence of beings of superior attributes whom it was desirable or necessary to conciliate by some form of address adapted to gain their favour or to avert their enmity. Hence worship, the parent of some system of ritual likely to become more elaborate in the lapse of time; and the ultimate establishment of a priestly caste who would soon profess to an intercourse with the unseen not vouchsafed to ordinary mortals. Gradually the first vague notions of a celestial hierarchy grew more realistic by imaginative or expedient accretions; and in a later age the sense of a less ignorant community would not be revolted by incredible details as to the personal intervention of divinities in the history of their progenitors when such events were relegated to a dimly realized past. But, although a belief in revelation as seen through the mists of antiquity prevails readily at all times among the unthinking masses, a spirit of scepticism and inquiry arises with the advent of civilization and increases concurrently with the vigour of its growth. Then the national mythology is submitted to the test of a dispassionate logic, and its crude constituents become more and more rejected by the sagacity of a cultured class. They, however, always hitherto an inconsiderable minority, feel constrained to an indulgence more or less qualified of the superstitions of the vulgar for fear of disturbing the political harmony of the state.

The early Greek philosophers awoke into life to find themselves endowed with vast intelligence in a world of which they knew nothing. No record of the past, no forecast of the future disturbed the serenity of their intellectual horizon. In a more aesthetic environment they renewed the impulse to interpret nature with a finer sense of congruity than was possessed by their rude ancestors, but their methods were identical, and they believed they could advance beyond the bounds of experience by the exercise of a vivid imagination. The coarse myths of polytheism were thrust aside, and the void was filled with fantastic cosmogonies, some of which included, whilst others dispensed with, the agency of a Deity.[950] The truth and finality of such speculations was shortly assumed, and schools of philosophy, representing every variety of doctrine, were formed, except that in which it was foreseen that knowledge would be attained only by the long and laborious path of experimental investigation. But whilst disciples were attracted to different sects by the personal influence of a teacher, by the novelty of his tenets, or by their own mental bias, the general sense of the community remained unconvinced; and the independent thinkers of the next generation perceived the futility of inquiries which evolved nothing coherent and revealed no new facts. Scientific research, for the deliberate striving after deeper insight ranked as such in the unpractised mind of the period, was discredited, and an impression that the limits of human knowledge had already been reached began to prevail universally. A reign of scepticism was inaugurated, the evidence of the senses in respect even of the most patent facts was doubted, and the study of nature was virtually abandoned.[951] Then philosophy became synonymous with ethics, but by ethics was understood merely the rule of expediency in public life, a subject which was debated with much sophistry. The inspiration of Socrates impelled him to combat this tendency, to search earnestly after truth, and to inculcate an elevated sense of duty. His mind was pervaded by an intense philanthropy which affected his associates so profoundly that his teaching did not lose its influence for centuries after his death. From the time of Socrates the fruits of experience began to be gathered, and new schools of philosophy were organized on the sounder basis of divulging to their votaries how to make the best use of their lives. The views entertained on this question were as various as the divergences of human temperament, and adapted to countenance the serious or the frivolous proclivities of mankind.[952] A theological or cosmical theory was a usual part of the equipment of these schools, but in outward demeanour they conformed, more or less strictly, with the religion of the state. The intellectual movement among the Greeks culminated after about two centuries of activity in the career of Aristotle, who undertook to sift, to harmonize, and to codify all the knowledge of his age.[953] A great work had been accomplished; all that wild outgrowth with which savage intellection is wont to encumber the domain of reason had been swept away, and the ground had been subjected to an orderly, though unproductive planting. The conception that nature would yield a harvest as the reward of rational study had been awakened, but the efforts lapsed because the method had yet to be discovered of fertilizing the vacant soil.[954]

The conception of social ethics or of mutual obligation among the members of a community appears to have been one of those influences which presided at the birth of civilization, and to have attained theoretical perfection far back in the prehistoric past; whilst the perpetual conflict between duty and individual advantage has always inhibited altruism from being accepted as an invariable guide to conduct without the artificial support of penal law. In Homer and Hesiod we find almost every rule for living uprightly adequately expressed. A man should honour his parents, love and be generous to his friends, be a good neighbour, and succour strangers and suppliants. He should be truthful, honest, continent, and industrious; and should consider sloth to be a disgrace.[955] In the next age Hellenic refinement could add little more than fuller expression to these simple precepts. But from Pythagoras to Socrates, from Aristotle to Cicero, from Seneca to Marcus Aurelius, a constant emission of ethical doctrine was maintained. Amid the wealth of disquisition, innumerable striking aphorisms might be selected, but only a few such can be recorded here: We should scan the actions of each day before resigning ourselves to sleep;[956] We have contracted with the government under which we live to submit ourselves to its laws, even should they condemn us to death unjustly;[957] We should pity the man who inflicts an injury more than him who suffers it, for the one is harmed only in his body, the other in his more precious soul;[958] Do not unto others what it angers you to suffer yourself;[959] Even should we be able to conceal our conduct from gods and men, we are not the less bound to act uprightly;[960] The judge, as well as the criminal, is on his trial that he may deliver just decisions;[961] Do not revile the malefactor, but commiserate him as one who knows not right from wrong;[962] Blame none, for men only do evil involuntarily.[963] By the first century slaves had begun to be considered in a more humane light; and masters were enjoined to look on them as humble friends, as brothers with whom it was no disgrace to sit at meat.[964] The iniquity of the gladiatorial shows was beginning to be felt in the time of Cicero,[965] and they were denounced in no measured terms by Seneca.[966] Such exhibitions had never been proper to the Greek communities and, when an attempt was made to introduce them at Athens in the second century, the cynic philosopher Demonax restrained his fellow citizens by declaring that before doing so they should first demolish the altar of Pity.[967] The exposure of new-born infants was one of the besetting sins of antiquity, and the practice was universal among the Latins and Greeks.[968] The inhumanity of it was, however, perceived early in our era; yet not until the reign of Severus do we find a legal pronouncement against it.[969] Constantine discountenanced it, but no comprehensive enactment for its suppression was promulgated till the end of the fourth century.[970] Charity towards the needy was a recognized duty from the earliest times, and Homer voices the general sentiment when he writes that strangers and the poor are to be treated as emissaries from the gods.[971] At Athens, in its palmy days, an allowance was made to indigent citizens;[972] and the lavish system of outdoor relief denoted by the trite phrase, *Panem et circenses*, as introduced by the Caesars, threatened to pauperize the urban population of the Empire.[973] The origin of charitable asylums is not well ascertained, but there is evidence that in the first century at least the foundation of such institutions was already being promoted by the rulers of the state.[974] The Roman Empire entered the Christian era equipped with a civilization scarcely at all inferior to that of the present day in relation to art, literature, and social ethics, but a sustaining principle, which could endow the splendid fabric with quality of permanency, was wanting. It was vulnerable within and without; and two powerful enemies, superstition and the barbarian, were awaiting the opportune moment to prey upon it. The dissolution commenced within; ignorance of natural science allowed the first to work havoc in its vital parts; the barbarian assaulted the infected mass from without, and the ruin became complete.

The political unification of the most civilized portion of the globe was begun by the conquests of Alexander and completed by those of Rome. Sociological homogeneity was attendant on centralization of government. From Britain to North Africa and from Spain to Asia Minor thought flowed through the same channels. Rome and Greece dominated the world between them; while the former assumed the physical control of the nations, the latter held their mental faculties in subjection. Progressively, however, influences began to permeate the Empire which were foreign to both Latins and Hellenes. East and west confronted each other on the Asiatic frontier; Egyptians and Jews were commingled with the Latin and Greek races in the great mart of Alexandria. Oriental mysticism became rife, and gods of every nationality were received into the bosom of Rome.[975] In the first century of the Christian era the times were ripe for new religious beliefs. By the expansion of the Roman dominions the classes had become cosmopolitan, and a wide experience of men and manners had dissipated the rustic simplicity of the Republic. The society of the Empire was enlightened by the speculations of Greek philosophy; it became versed in metaphysical discussion, and soon conceived an irreverence for the divinities of a ruder age.[976] Everywhere the same level of mental apprehension was ultimately reached. Then the inanity of earthly existence began to be acutely felt. The thoughtful looked through the void and saw nowhere for the mind to rest. Zeal for public distinction had been suppressed by military despotism, and the pride which animates the strenuous virtues of a rising commonwealth was extinct. Levity pervaded the aimless crowd who lived only for the diversion of the hour. Nature had been interrogated repeatedly with an invariably negative result; her secret, if she possessed one, seemed to be impenetrable and destined to remain for ever unknown. No discovery in science had opened up the vista of a path which led through inexhaustible fields of knowledge. The psychical unrest longed for new ideals and was willing to be appeased by the slightest semblance of a revelation. Religion-making became a craft which was followed by more than one practitioner in all the chief cities of the Empire. A host of charlatans arose and made many victims by pretending to theurgic powers.[977] Agitated by vague impulses the social units drifted with indeterminable currents, for more than a century before the heterogeneous elements which were in commotion showed a tendency to group themselves under any concrete forms. At length the appearances of a settlement became visible, and three distinct forms emerged successively from the previously existing chaos, each of which claimed to have sounded the abysmal depths and to have brought to the surface the inestimable balm which was to salve the bruised souls of humanity. But they beheld each other with horror and contempt, and a contest was initiated between them on the theatre of the Empire for the spiritual dominion of mankind.

I. In the year 28 A.D., the fifteenth of the reign of Tiberius, Pontius Pilate was governor of Judaea, the subordinate officer of Aelius Lamia, the Imperial legate of Syria.[978] At that point of time a man, previously unknown among the Jews, assumed the rôle of a public teacher of religion and ethics and devoted himself to an itinerant mission throughout the cities and districts of Palestine. He seemed to be about thirty years old and it was soon realized that he was a certain Jesus who had hitherto worked as a carpenter, his father's trade, in his native village of Nazareth. He preached a reformation of manners among the people generally, and rebuked with a penetrating bitterness the pride and hypocrisy of the chief men of his own race. At the outset of his career he summoned to his assistance twelve men of the same humble rank as himself and enjoined them to follow his example. He did not confine himself to hortatory discourses, but proved on numerous occasions that he had the gift of working miracles. At his command the sick were healed and even the dead returned to life. Those who were possessed with devils he immediately released from their baleful thraldom.[979] The laws of nature appeared to be subject to his will and were reversed whenever he thought fit to exert his power over them. Finally he declared himself to be the Messiah or Christ, a more than mortal being whom the Jews expected to rescue them from their political abasement and raise them to a position of national supremacy. Israel as a body rejected his claims with scorn and derision; his ministry of peace afforded no prospect of the rehabilitation they aspired to.[980] He met them in the temple at Jerusalem and they demanded of him a sign that he was an emissary sent from heaven. In reply he assailed them with vituperation and hurried from the precincts. Amongst his own following he explained himself; his design had been entirely misconceived; he was the son of Jehovah and his kingdom was not of this world. He had been sent to reconcile his own nation to his father, the ruler of the universe, whom they had offended by their moral laxity and corruption. He would shortly depart from the earth, but he would soon return with all the powers of heaven to judge the inhabitants of this lower sphere. Then the just would be received into a state of bliss without end, whilst the wicked should be consigned to everlasting torment. He persisted in his didactic work, which tended to make the chief priests and elders odious in the eyes of the people, until they determined to compass his destruction. Ultimately he was seized and brought before the Roman governor as a mover of sedition, but Pilate was unconcerned and wished to release him. His accusers insisted, he yielded and, after suffering every indignity, Jesus was crucified between two thieves on mount Calvary during the Paschal festival of A.D. 29, under the consulship of the two Gemini.[981] But his disciples had been forewarned by their master that his death in the guise of a malefactor was preordained as an atonement to effect the redemption of the world from sin. Had it been otherwise legions of angels would descend to discomfort his impious antagonists. At the same time he predicted that he would rise from the dead on the third day after the burial of his body. This promise was fulfilled, his sepulchre was found empty, and Jesus appeared again to his disciples. He discoursed with them for forty days, constituted them apostles to preach his Gospel not only to the Jews, but also to the Gentiles, and in their presence ascended into the heavens until the clouds received him out of their sight.

Such was the astounding relation elicited with some difficulty from a sect of new religionists called Christians, who, as early as the reign of Nero, were sufficiently numerous at Rome to have incurred the hatred of the populace through their austere disposition and their stern abjuration of the national gods.[982] In the year 64 the city was devastated by an appalling conflagration of which the insensate emperor was himself accused, but he shifted the odium to the already discredited recusants, and condemned many of them to perish in the flames by a peculiarly atrocious method.[983] Nevertheless the Christians maintained their ground and thirty years later were regarded with hostility by the tyrant Domitian as a body of proselytizing Jews in the capital.[984] At the dawn of the second century the younger Pliny found them so numerous in his province of Bithynia as almost to have subverted the established religion. In great concern he wrote to the Emperor Trajan questioning whether he should proceed to extremities in his efforts to suppress them. This epistle is extant, and through it some details were first made public as to their tenets and mode of worship. Before daybreak on a certain day they met and recited an address to Christ as to a god; bound themselves by oath to commit no crime against society, and partook together of a common meal. The cultured Roman, imbued with literature and philosophy, estimated the Christian belief as a depraved and extravagant superstition, the eradication of which was dictated by state policy, but his master counselled him to disregard it unless popular animosity should in particular instances compel him to drag its devotees from their obscurity.[985] The Christian missionaries pursued their labours unremittingly and were especially active among the proletariat, from whom during the first centuries their converts were almost exclusively drawn.[986] Throughout the length and breadth of the Empire they persistently undermined the existing order of things by teaching doctrines which were at variance with the received conception of Roman citizenship. Not only did they revile the pagan deities, whom they classed as demons instead of gods, and shun their festivals,[987] but they evinced an utter aversion for military service.[988] The polytheists were incensed at the pretensions of a deity who would not share the theocracy, but claimed to oust all other divinities from their seats and occupy the celestial throne alone,[989] whilst statesmen became alarmed at the prospect of political defection, and began to second the vulgar prejudice by systematic efforts at exterminating the spreading sect. The benignant Marcus Aurelius was induced to believe that the Christians were a danger to the state and he issued a decree (*c.* 177) that they should be sought out and put to death unless willing to abandon their faith.[990] This was the first decided persecution, but, although many perished, it proved ineffective, as no means available were strong enough to extinguish the flames of fanaticism. On the contrary, those who stood firm before the tribunals and were allowed to escape with their lives ranked afterwards as "Confessors," a title more glorious in the eyes of their fellows than any temporal dignity; whilst constancy to the death became the essential qualification of Martyrs or witnesses to the truth, Saints who were admitted forthwith among the heavenly host as mediators between God and man.[991] As soon as the repressive measures were relaxed all the weaker brethren, who had abjured in the face of danger, prayed for readmission to the conventicles, and were usually received after the infliction of a term of penance. Once and again during the next century and a half widespread persecution was had recourse to by Decius and by Diocletian, but the Christians throve and prospered in the intervals despite of fitful and local hostility.[992] The memorable battle of the Milvian bridge in 312 proved to be a turning-point in the history of Rome and of Christianity; and the state religion of the ancient world was involved in the fall of the dissolute Maxentius. The victorious Constantine, as sole Emperor of the West, immediately concerted a measure with his colleague of the East, Licinius, for the establishment of religious toleration throughout their dominions.[993] Thenceforward Christianity was free to expand in obedience to the charge she had received at her origin and to apply herself to the task of supplanting every other belief.

The acceptance of all religions is pressed by an appeal to the supernatural sub-structure on which they profess to be based; and this claim is substantiated by the presentment of some miraculous circumstances from which they are asserted to have derived their birth. Evidential obscurity has always been the soul of such pretensions; and the truth of the most improbable occurrences has been resolutely maintained because assured witnesses could not be produced in order to prove a negative. But the time for historical discussion or sifting of evidence in relation to such matters has long gone by; and in the twentieth century the philosopher is enabled without examination to dismiss with a smile the mere suggestion that such events have occurred.[994] That any narrative, which in its essential statements consists largely of the marvellous, should be rejected as false in its entirety has almost risen to the dignity of a canon of historical criticism. The principle, however, has often been unduly strained in its application; and no judicious investigator would refuse to allow that a slender thread of fact may sometimes be extricated from a mass of incredible legend. The awe-inspiring life of Jesus emanates from authors of unascertainable date and repute. No neutral scribe, no adverse critic, has furnished us with any personal impressions of his career bearing the intrinsic marks of truth and simplicity. Nor can it be affirmed that any character fairly discernible on the stage of history ever knew an apostle. The Twelve who are credited with having disseminated the faith of the Gospel from east to west lie buried in a more than prehistoric obscurity, the writings ascribed to them doubted, denied, or clearly disproved.[995] It can scarcely be a matter of surprise, therefore, if some serious scholars of modern times have committed themselves to an absolute denial that the nominal founder of Christianity has had any real existence.[996] Yet the cause of mysticism was well served by the impenetrable cloud which hung over the mundane activity of Jesus. No common inquiry enabled the diligent adversaries of Christianity to strip the veil from the idealized figure, and expose its features to the gaze of vulgar observation. The philosophic critic was reduced to mere expressions of incredulity; and the despair of historians became the firmest pillar of belief in the church.[997]

II. In an idle hour Plato applied himself to shadowing forth a theological doctrine which should account for the origin and guidance of the objective universe.[998] A supreme god, the One or the Good,[999] at a certain moment conceived a creative design and fashioned the material world out of pre-existing elements.[1000] This task completed, he created intellect and soul; and by combining the two together produced living intelligence.[1001] He was now provided with all the requisite ingredients for peopling the world he had made; and his next step was to form a primal race of spiritual beings or daemons whom he endowed with immortality. From these by generation issued the whole progeny of gods worshipped by the Greeks, for whom their pedigrees and actions were recorded by Orpheus, Homer, and Hesiod. Among the divine existences were also to be reckoned the stars. At this stage the creative work of the One came to an end. He addressed the daemons and said: "You have observed my method of procedure when engaged in moulding yourselves. Follow my example and set about the production of mortal natures to inhabit the air, the water, and the earth." They obeyed his behests, and the whole animal kingdom was the result of their labours. But the grosser matter with which mortal souls are weighed down is the essence of evil, and the just man will, therefore, desire to escape from the body in order to be free from its impure passions.[1002] For the Creator had appointed that each soul should be associated with a particular star, to whose blissful abode it might return as the reward of a life well spent on earth. The unrighteous soul, however, must first be chastened by an ordeal of transmigration through descending grades of lower animal natures, the least abased being that of a woman.

This cosmological phantasy of Plato was destined, after lying dormant for more than five centuries, to breathe a new spirit into the almost inanimate body of polytheism. The higher social caste, still adhering languidly to the old belief, counted among them many elevated minds devoted to the traditions of the past, who apprehended with dismay the dissolution of all they prized in the ebbing tide of Paganism. The effete superstition could only be sustained by some process of depuration capable of reconciling it with the more refined perceptions of the age. The required influence was at hand. From Alexandria, where an international fusion of philosophies and religions had been in progress almost since the foundation of the city, a new dispensation proceeded before the middle of the third century. In that capital, the Greek was penetrated by the spirit of Oriental mysticism, and the Jew was fascinated by the intellectual ascendancy of the schools of Athens. The ancient rivalry of sects had almost died out, and a later generation of inquirers adopted freely whatever they could assimilate from various systems of philosophy.[1003] After passing tentatively through several stages from the first years of our era, a theological doctrine under the name of Platonism was elaborated by the Egyptian, Plotinus,[1004] with sufficient completeness to be presented to the devout polytheist as a rule of life. In general conception, the new faith did not differ essentially from the scheme advanced by the founder of the Academy, but, with its deficiencies supplied from exotic sources, it was propounded solemnly as a theosophy which revealed the whole purport of human existence. As a practical religion, this revival, Neoplatonism by name, enjoined a purity of life which should free the soul from defilement by contact with the world, and allow it to coalesce with the divine potential whence it had emanated.[1005] The crowning allurement of the system was that this blissful conjunction might be attained by the fervid votary even during life. Those who had subjugated all their natural, and, therefore, evil passions, might rise by contemplation to an ecstatic union with the Deity, the transcendant One; or, to express it irreverently in modern language, might acquire the faculty of passing into a hypnotic trance.[1006] As soon as Plotinus had perfected his invention, he proceeded to Rome (*c.* 244), with the view of professing his doctrine to the mystically inclined on the most extended theatre in the Empire. Here his success was very considerable, and he gained numerous adherents, especially as he conceded that all forms of Pagan worship availed as a real approach to the Deity and enshrined germs of truth derived from some primitive revelation. He became influential at Court and was about to organize a Utopian community on the lines of Plato's ideal republic under the auspices of Gallienus when the fall of that Emperor frustrated his design.

Plotinus died in 270, leaving many disciples to continue the work of his school, the foremost of whom was Porphyry, known as a keen assailant of Christianity.[1007] To him succeeded the Syrian, Iamblichus, a contemporary of Constantine, who gave the final form to Neoplatonism and adapted it for widest acceptance. The religion of Plotinus was an ineffable creed which avowedly excluded vulgar participation, and was addressed only to cultured aspirants;[1008] but a descent was made by his successors who, with the object of amplifying their influence, embraced gradually all the crass superstitions of the multitude. A mystical signification was read into the sacred books of the Greeks, as the poems of Orpheus, Homer, and Hesiod may appropriately be termed, by an allegorical interpretation of every phrase or incident in the text. All trivial circumstances or immoral pictures were thus disclosed to be fraught with spiritual or ethical meaning for the pious reader.[1009] The endless procession of invisible beings with which Eastern fancy had peopled space, angels, demons, archons, and demigods, were accepted by the latter school and associated to the theocracy as mediators who could be summoned and suborned to human purposes by magic rites, incantations, and sacrifices.[1010] By the time this stage had been reached, Neoplatonism appeared to be fully equipped for satisfying the occult proclivities of all classes, and asserting its right to become the prevailing religion of the state.

III. The most distinctive and irrepressible theological principle which entered Western civilization from the East, was the dualistic conception of nature inherent in the old Babylonian religions. The seers of that ancient people could not resolve the problem as to the providential government of the world, without postulating a perpetual strife between two opposed powers, who were engaged in determining the course of events. The spectacle of suffering humanity enforced the belief that a potent spirit of evil shared the control of the existing order of things to an equal extent with the benign Deity from whom all blessings flowed. The eastern provinces of the Empire became saturated with these views, and the prime mover in diffusing them was said to be that Simon Magus who, although he makes but a brief and insignificant appearance in Gospel history, occupies a very considerable space in extra-biblical literature.[1011] Under the name of Gnostics, recipients of a special enlightenment or *gnosis*, his reputed progeny swarmed about the early Christian Church, whose presence seemed to rouse them into vitality; for, in the doctrine of redemption by Jesus, they found, as they imagined, the key to much that was unexplained in their own system.[1012] Diversity in the apprehension of detail was an innate characteristic of the Gnostic brood; whence it followed that they became apparent in small sects only, computed at some scores, and, though numerous, never attained the weight of union as a religious body. Gradually they were dissolved by the preponderance of the Catholic Church, which absorbed their members and proscribed their peculiar tenets.[1013]

There was, however, one form of dualism which arose beyond the borders of the Empire, and, from its centre in Persia, spread with great rapidity eastwards to the frontiers of China, and westwards as far as the Atlantic ocean. This international faith, for such it became in less than a century, was called Manichaeism from its founder Mani, of whom little certain is known; but he was probably a native of Ecbatana, the Median capital.[1014] As the prophet of a new dispensation, Mani belongs to the second class of makers of religion, that is, he did not claim to be himself a god, but only an apostle commissioned by the Deity. His life extended to upwards of sixty years, and he was countenanced by more than one of the Sassanian kings. At length, however, he fell a victim to the jealousy of the Magi, the exponents of the established belief of Zarathushtra, at whose instigation he was crucified and flayed by Bahram I. In the system of Mani the fundamental conception is the antithesis of light and darkness, by which the opposition between good and evil is vividly denoted; and the present world originates in the accident of a war breaking out between the respective powers. Satan, the Prince of Darkness, discovers by chance the kingdom of light, the existence of which was previously unknown to him, and, with his army of demons, makes an incursion into it. The God of Light, sustained by his pure spirits, engages and defeats him, but during the campaign a commingling has occurred of elements of the two realms. The contest now resolves into the efforts of the Deity to regain, and of Satan to retain, the portions of light which were lost in the darkness. The first step is the formation by the former of this world, but the latter creates man as a secure receptacle for the light he had acquired. Hence this creature is animated by two souls, an evil one as well as a soul of light; and Satan enslaves him by exciting his bad passions.[1015] The process of restoring the light goes on continually, and the sun and moon are great reservoirs into which it is poured by the active agents of the superior Deity. The human race is placed in possession of the clue to paradise by having this gnosis imparted to it. A rigid asceticism must be practised according to prescribed rules. There were, however, two ranks of Manichaeans, the Elect and the Auditors. The earnest votaries joined the first, and on them celibacy and a vegetarian diet were imposed. Membership of the second was adapted to the masses, from whom only moderate abstinence was required. They ministered religiously to the Elect, whom they thus enlisted as redeemers on their behalf, so that with the addition of a term of purgatory after death, they also became fitted for paradise. Mani utilized some of the ideas of Christianity in order to connect his religion practically with mankind, but his transferences are rather imitations than acceptances of anything really Christian. Thus he acknowledged a Jesus Christ, who abides in the son, as the "primal man" or first-born of the Deity.[1016] He had visited the earth as a prophet, and from him Mani had received his apostolic mission, whence he usurped the title of the Paraclete, whose advent was promised in the Gospels. He also instructed twelve disciples to preach his doctrine. The success and prevalence of Manichaeism was at one time very great, for it arose as the revivifying force of more than one aspect of dualism in the East and West. It fostered the time-honoured traditions of the inhabitants of the Euphrates valley, and drew to itself the disintegrating coteries of Gnostics within the Roman Empire. A Manichaean popedom was established, which had its seat for several centuries in Babylon. As early as 287 Diocletian denounced the propagation of the religion as a capital offence, on the grounds that the "execrable customs and cruel laws" of the Persians might thereby gain a footing among his "mild and peaceful" subjects.[1017]

From the foregoing summary it will be seen that in the first years of the fourth century polytheism, as resuscitated by Neoplatonism, held the field against its rivals with the support and approval of the government. We cannot attempt here to fathom the motives, so prolific as a literary theme, which induced Constantine first to favour Christianity, then to embrace it for himself and his family, and finally to raise it into the safe position of being the only religion recognized by the state. In the blank outlook of the times some definite belief was a necessity, and, whether from policy or conviction, he steered his course in the direction where the tide seemed to set most strongly. Pure Neoplatonism was congenial only to persons of a meditative temperament; to the sober-minded it was artificial and unconvincing. Its loftier heights were inaccessible to the masses, and in its later development it threatened to make common cause with the jugglers and charlatans who risked a conflict with the law.[1018] Manichaeism had only begun to rear its head, and at the best contained much that was fantastic and incomprehensible to a non-Semitic people.[1019] Christianity was simple, positive, socialistic, a leveller of class distinctions, for the slave as well as for the free man, and absolutely intolerant of every other religion. Its emissaries believed implicitly in their mission, and worked incessantly among the lower stratum of the population, to whom they delivered the message of their Gospel in clear and precise terms. By their vehement assertion there was no escape from, and no alternative to the acceptance of their creed. The Day of Judgment was at hand; at any moment Jesus might return to inaugurate a golden age of one thousand years upon the earth; and all those who had been regenerated by baptism would participate in His glory.[1020] The primitive church was communistic in principle, and exceptional solicitude was shown in the administration of charity to its indigent members. Liberality in this sense was doubtless the means of winning over many converts, for its bounty was not withheld from the poor on account of any difference in religion.[1021]

The Christian Church from its inception gradually unfolded itself as an anarchical association, consisting of affiliated branches scattered throughout the Empire. At first all members possessed equal rank, and the status of each one as a presbyter or propagandist was limited only by his natural capacity for the work. Enthusiasm prevailed in the secret assemblies, and the excitable, whether male or female, relieved themselves by impassioned utterances which were accepted by the listeners as prophetic inspiration.[1022] Subsequent history relates the development of a hierarchy with the consequent formation of two parties in the Church, clergy and laity, and the ultimate suppression of all spiritual assumption by the latter.[1023] Rites and ceremonies of increasing complexity were instituted, rules of discipline were elaborated, and proselytes were no longer admitted hastily to the congregations, but were previously relegated for a course of instruction to the class of *catechumens* or probationers. About the end of the second century Christianity assumed some importance in the eyes of the educated and wealthy,[1024] so that its doctrines began to be scrutinized in the spirit of Greek philosophy. A catechetical school was founded at Alexandria (*c.* 170) for the training of converts of higher mental capacity; and learned teachers, notably Clement and Origen, essayed to prove that the new religion could be substantiated theologically by reference to Plato and Aristotle.[1025] At the same time the Church began to discard the policy of stealthiness under which it had grown up, and to indulge the expansive vigour which pervaded its constitution. Soon the conventicles ceased to meet under the cloak of secrecy; and by a few decades public edifices were erected with an architectural ostentation and a treasure of ornaments rubric which roused the indignation of those who frequented the Pagan temples in the vicinity.[1026] From that moment the encroaching temper of Christianity and its uncompromising antagonism to polytheism became manifest to the government, and zealous officials prepared themselves for a determined effort to overthrow the upstart power which was undermining the old order of society.[1027] The futile struggle of Paganism against Christianity was terminated by Theodosius the Great, who promulgated edicts both in the East and in the West for the abolition of the pristine religion of the Empire.[1028] During more than half a century previously the battle between the two faiths had been open and violent; and the mild Christians of earlier times often appeared in the light of ruthless fanatics more conspicuously than had their heathen adversaries in the heat of a legalized persecution.[1029] The Church triumphant now entered on its career of quasi-political predominance; wealth and honours were showered on those who attained to its highest offices; and the precepts of the poor carpenter, whose constant theme was humility, were inculcated by a succession of haughty prelates who equalled the magnificence and exceeded the arrogance of kings.[1030]

From the day of its birth almost to the present hour the Church has been agitated by internal dissensions generated by the efforts of reason to understand and to define those inscrutable mysteries, to a belief in which every supernatural religion must owe its existence. The primitive religion of the ancients was a natural growth, accepted insensibly during a state of savagery and maintained politically long after it had been repudiated by philosophy, but Christianity was offered to a world already advanced in civilization, and had to pass through a process of intellectual digestion before it could take its place as an unassailable national belief. The Church, before it stands clearly revealed in the light of history, had been inspired with the conception of a Trinity by a contemplation of the Platonic philosophy; and the problem as to how this doctrine could be expounded as not inconsistent with monotheism occasioned the first of those great councils called Oecumenical. It met in 325 at Nicaea of Bithynia, and there formulated the Nicene creed, which branded as heretics the presbyter Arius and his supporters for asserting that the Word, the Son, the man Jesus, had not eternally existed as of one substance with the Father, but had been created out of nothing at some date of an inconceivably remote past. Under the emperors who succeeded Constantine, however, the Arians returned to power in the East, and for long oppressed their opponents, the Catholics, until they were finally reduced to impotence by the orthodox Theodosius I.[1031] But centuries were yet to elapse before the Church could desist from weaving those subtleties of dogma as to the inexpressible nature of the Godhead, in the study of which later theologians discover an exercise for their memory rather than for their understanding.[1032] Numerous other councils were convened before the opening of the sixth century, but of these only three were allowed to rank as Oecumenical, that of Constantinople in 381, that of Ephesus in 431, and that of Chalcedon in 451. The first of these did little more than to confirm the decisions of Nicaea, but it won from Theodosius a tacit permission to proceed to extremities against Paganism.[1033] The second anathematized the heresy of Nestorius, Patriarch of the Eastern capital, who wished to deprive the Virgin Mary of the title of Theotokos, or Mother of God. The bishops who assembled at the Asiatic suburb of Chalcedon, under the supervision of the Emperor Marcian, were less successful in producing concord in the Church than those who composed any of the previous councils; and their resolutions were debated for long afterwards by dissentient ecclesiastics throughout the East. On this occasion the orthodox party delivered their last word as the mystic junction of the divine and human in the Incarnate Christ, and repudiated for ever the error of the Monophysites that the Saviour was animated only by a celestial essence.[1034] This was the first instance in which the new Rome triumphed over her great rival in the East, Alexandria, which had previously trampled on her Patriarchs, Chrysostom, Nestorius, Flavian; as the doctrine of the one nature was peculiarly dear to the Egyptian Church. But the spiritual peace of the Asiatic and African provinces had been too rudely disturbed for an immediate settlement to ensue; and more than thirty years later the Emperor Zeno was forced to issue a *Henoticon*, or Act of Union, in which he sought to induce unanimity among the prelates of his dominions by effacing the harsher expressions of the Chalcedonian canons.[1035] The measure, however, was ineffectual; the conflict of doctrine could not be quelled; and even Anastasius was branded as a heretic by the Byzantines for not adopting a hostile attitude towards the Monophysites.[1036] The state of religious parties under that Emperor may be summarized briefly as follows: Europe was firmly attached to the Council of Chalcedon, Egypt was bitterly opposed to it, whilst in Asia its adversaries and adherents were almost equally divided. Of Arians there were not a few, but they were everywhere severely repressed. Nevertheless, in the capital itself a handsome church was reserved for those addicted to that heresy, St. Mocius in the Exokionion. But this was an indulgence conceded exclusively to the Gothic soldiery, all bigoted Arians, with whose faith no emperor ever dared to tamper.[1037] At the same time polytheism appeared to be extinct; the Pagan temples were everywhere evacuated, and for the most part purposely ruined.[1038] After the murder of Hypatia the Neoplatonists deserted Alexandria and betook themselves to Athens, where they were disregarded as a merely philosophical association without the privilege of public worship.[1039] Manichaeans were numerous within the Empire, but could only exist in secret as a proscribed sect subject to severe penalties, confiscation, loss of civil rights, and relegation to the mines, if convicted.[1040] Relics of minor denominations, more or less obscure and impotent, need not be more particularly alluded to in this place.

Nothing in this age accelerated the social descent towards barbarism so much as the illusion that bliss in a future state was most positively assured to those Christians who denied themselves every natural gratification whilst on earth. By the end of the fourth century the passion for the mortification of the flesh had risen to such a height that almost one half of the population of the Empire, male and female, had abandoned civilized life and devoted themselves to celibacy and ascetic practices.[1041] By choice, and even by legal prescription,[1042] they sought desert places and vast solitudes to pass their lives in sordid discomfort, at one time grazing like wild beasts, at another immured in noisome cells too narrow to admit of any restful position of the body or limbs.[1043] Some joined the class of stylites, or pillar saints, who lived in the air at a considerable altitude from the ground on the bare top of a slender column.[1044] Such were the anchorites or hermits, who arose first in order of time and claimed for their founder an illiterate though well-born youth of Alexandria,[1045] Anthony, the subject of familiar legends. A little later, however, Pachomius,[1046] also an Egyptian, instituted the coenobites, or gregarious fraternity of ascetics, whose assemblage of cells, called a *laura*, was generally disposed in a circle around their common chapel and refectory. The extensive waste lands of Egypt greatly favoured the development of monachism; and within half a century the isle of Tabenna in the Nile, the Nitrian mountain, and the wilderness of Sketis, became densely populated with these fanatic recluses.[1047] From Egypt the mania for leading a monastic life spread in all directions, and religious houses, on the initiative of Basil, began to invade the towns and suburban districts.[1048] One of the most remarkable of these foundations was the monastery of Studius, erected at Constantinople (in 460) for the *Acoemeti*, or sleepless monks, whose devotional vigils were ceaseless both night and day.[1049] After the promotion of Christianity to be the state religion, one emperor only, the ordinarily ineffective Valens, assumed a hostile attitude towards the monks.[1050] He denounced them as slothful renegades from their social duties and dispatched companies of soldiers to expel them from their retreats and reclaim them for civil and military life. A considerable number were massacred for attempting resistance to the decree; but under the successors of Valens monachism flourished as before with the Imperial countenance and the popular regard.[1051]

The supersession of dogmatic religions founded on prehistoric mythologies by the success of modern research, confers the right of free speculation on contemporary philosophers, and urges them to construct, from the ample materials at their command, an intellectual theory of the universe. In proportion as experimental physics teaches us to apprehend more profoundly the constitution of matter, reason advances impulsively from the outposts of knowledge to suspend itself over the abyss in those dimly-lighted regions where science and mysticism seem to hold each other by the hand.

The atomic conception of nature, first broached as a phantasy by the Greeks, derives an actuality from the growth of chemical and electrical discoveries at the present day, which goes far to establish it as an immediate, if not the ultimate, explanation of phenomena. Our mind has thus been prepared to realize the vision of swarms of atoms in the possession of limitless space, each one of which is instinct in the prime degree with all the attributes of life: with consciousness, will, motion, the bias of habit, and an unquenchable desire for association and aggregation.[1052] They become conjoined, numerically and morphologically, in progressive grades of complexity, originating by one kind of alliance the chemical elements which constitute the organic world, and by another the vital elements, which form the protoplasmic basis of animal and plant life.[1053] The organic kingdom rests upon the inorganic, and preys upon it, evolving itself throughout endless time into more highly differentiated forms by its incessant appetite for material acquisition and sensuous stimulation in its environment.[1054]

Whilst the records of ages assiduously collated from every quarter of the globe exhibit the irrepressible folly of undisciplined human thought and the immeasurable credulity of ignorance, the boundless expansion of our intellectual horizon compels us to reject as irrational, the belief in an almighty and intelligent Father, who regards with equanimity the disruption of worlds, but is capable of being delighted by a choir of fulsome praise emanating from their ephemeral inhabitants.[1055] From the earliest times the infertile efforts to approach and win the favour of such a being have constituted the heaviest drag on civilization and progress; and, as man rises in the sphere of rationality, the highest lesson he can learn is to discard definitively all such dreams. He must convince himself that there is nothing divine, nothing supernatural, no providence but his own, that prayer is futile, piety impossible; and the sage may postulate that humanity is God until some higher divinity be discovered. The mythological terrors of antiquity are effete in the world of to-day, and any citizen who has learned to live uprightly should be above all religion, and free from the bondage of every superstition. By self-reliance and his own exertions alone can man be led upwards; his advancement depends on the extent to which he can penetrate the mystery of, and subdue the forces which surround him; and to preach the dominion of man over nature is the work of the modern prophet or apostle.[1056] By a retrospect of the past he is justified in cherishing the hope of a brighter future for his descendants; no obstacle appears in view to bar their journey along the upward path; the illimitable capacity of protoplasm for physiological elevation may triumph over the universal cycle of birth, maturity, and decay; and in humanity as it exists we may see the progenitors of an infinitely superior, perhaps of an immortal race, the ultimate expression and end of evolution and generation.[1057]

The student of European civilization cannot fail to wonder what sociological manifestation would have taken the place of Christianity had that religion never seen the light, or failed to win a predominant position in the Graeco-Roman world. Was the disintegration of the Empire, he must ask, and the retreat of its inhabitants almost to the threshold of barbarism a result of the prevalence of the Gospel creed? or was the new faith merely a fortuitous phenomenon which became conspicuous on the surface of an uncontrollable social cataclysm? No decision could be accepted as incontestable when dealing with such far-reaching questions, but with the wisdom which follows the event we may recognize that contingencies not very remote might have altered materially the course of history. The dissolution of powerful political organizations was no new feature in the ancient world; in Egypt, in Asia, dynasties with their dominions had periodically collapsed, but in Europe the Roman supremacy was the first to consolidate the principal countries into a compact and homogeneous state. Civil wars, however, had been waged on several occasions; princes unfit to reign had been the cause of serious administrative perturbation. Did these vicissitudes, we may inquire, herald the break-up of the Empire, unassailable as it was by any civilized adversary? Had the national genius and vigour so declined that armies could not be recruited to repeat the successes of Marius, of Trajan, of Diocletian, against hordes of barbarians ill-disciplined and ill-armed? The proposition cannot be entertained; the individuals were as capable as ever, but the purview of life had changed. Religious dissension had engendered personal rancour, neighbour distrusted neighbour, and the name of Roman no longer denoted a community with kindred feelings and aspirations. The Persian and the Teuton beyond the border were not more hostile to the subjects of the Empire than were they among themselves when viewed as separate groups of Pagans, of Manichaeans, of Arians, and of Catholics. This disseverance was not, however, quite permanent; after a couple of generations had passed away a partial reunion was effected by the submission of all classes to Christianity; and strife was limited to controversies between differing sects of the same church. But in the process mankind were led to break with all past traditions; the world became effete in their eyes; and to be released from it in order to gain admission to the celestial sphere was preached as the sole object of human existence. Civilization succumbed to the despotic influence of religion, a new field of effort was opened to the race of mortals, and all the genius of the age was exhausted in the attempt to advance the pseudo-science of theology. That genius was as brilliant as any which has hitherto been seen upon the earth. The administrative and literary powers of a Tertullian, an Origen, a Cyprian, a Eusebius, an Athanasius, of the Gregories, of Basil, Ambrose, Augustine, Chrysostom, and many others might have raised the Empire above the level of the most glorious period of the past. It is scarcely an exaggeration to say that these ecclesiastics founded a dominion which surpassed that of Rome in its widest extent; but it was a dominion over men's minds which precipitated material progress into a gulf out of which it was not to rise again for more than a thousand years. Their success was facilitated by the confirmation of despotism and the abolition of free institutions under the first Caesars; but without Christianity there would probably have been no exacerbation of religious fervour more intense than was involved in Neoplatonism. That new departure in polytheism was not likely to have caused a serious drain upon the energies of the state. Julian, its most impassioned votary, was not less imbued with the spirit of a conqueror than were Alexander and Trajan.[1058] Neoplatonism, and especially Manichaeism, borrowed Christian elements and might not have aspired to more than a passive influence but for their rivalry with that religion. From these considerations we may draw the inference that only for the Palestinian capture of the psychical yearnings of the age history might never have had to record the lapse of social Europe into the slough of mediaevalism; and the experience of a terrestrial hierarch who should give laws to kings and incite the masses to rebel against their political rulers would have been lost to Western civilization. That the Empire would have subsisted until modern times is inconceivable; the tendency to disruption of the vast fabric soon became apparent, and its unity was only restored by reconquest on several occasions; notably by Severus, by Constantine, by Theodosius. Under Diocletian it was virtually transformed into a number of federated states; and by the sixth or seventh century a somewhat similar partition might have become definite and permanent. With the maintenance of sociological institutions at the original level, barbarism would have been repelled and civilization would have penetrated more rapidly the forests of Scythia and Germany. The spirit of scientific inquiry which was manifest in Strabo, in Pliny, in Ptolemy, in Galen, might have been fostered and extended; and many a leading mind, whose vigour was absorbed by the arid waste of theology, might have taken up the work of Aristotle and carried his researches into the heart of contemporary science.[1059] The condition of the proletariat was not elevated by the diffusion of the Gospel after their wholesale acceptance of it had been assured by coercion. Whatever ethical purity may have adorned the lives of the first converts, Christianity as an established religion was not less of a grovelling superstition than Paganism in its worst forms. The worship of martyrs, of saints, the factitious miracles wrought at their graves, the veneration of their relics and images, were but a travesty of polytheism under another name without the saving graces of the old belief.[1060] A large section of the community were encouraged to fritter away their lives in the sloth of the cloister; and the ecclesiastical murder, disguised under the charge of heresy, of opponents who dared to think and speak became a social terror in grim contrast with the easy tolerance of Pagan times.[1061] At length the night of superstition began to wane and the unexpected advent of a brighter era was announced by a great social upheaval. Again the tide of cosmopolitanism began to flow between the Atlantic and the Euphrates, and a new unification of the detached fragments of the Roman Empire was brought about. Amid the turmoil of two centuries of barren Crusades[1062] the active intercourse of numerous peoples taught Europe to think and judge; and she began to appraise the harvest which had been reaped during so long a period of blind devotion to a creed. The result of the scrutiny was disheartening; the store of gold was found to have turned to dross; and, while one type of man struggled to break the chains which bound them in spiritual subjection, another bent their minds to discover whether through nature and art they could not reach some goal worthy of human ambition. The Renaissance and the Reformation were almost contemporary movements.[1063] From that period to the present, more than five centuries, the history of the world has been one of continued advancement. Since Dante composed his great poem and Copernicus elaborated his theory of the heavens, the well of literature has not run dry nor has the lamp of science been extinguished. Yet in all these years while the rising light has been breaking continuously over the mountain tops the spacious valleys beneath have lain buried in the gloom of unenlightened ages. The peace of society has never ceased to be disturbed by the discord of religious factions; and the task of a modern statesman is still to reconcile conflicting prejudices in a world of ignorance and folly.[1064]

CHAPTER III
BIRTH AND FORTUNES OF THE ELDER JUSTIN: THE ORIGINS OF JUSTINIAN

THE function of a government is to administer the affairs of mankind in accordance with the spirit of the age. Not from the political arena, but from the laboratory emanates that expansion of knowledge which surely, though fitfully, changes the aspect and methods of civilization both in peace and war. An impulse which controls the passions of millions may originate with some obscure investigator who reveals a more immediate means to individual or national advantage; and the executive of government is called on to create legislative facilities for the utilization of the new discovery. During the modern period such influences have been continuous and paramount. In the course of a single century a transformation of the world has been achieved by fruitful research, greater than in all previously recorded time. The Georgian era contrasts less strongly with the times of Aristotle and Cicero than with the present day; and the rapid progress of the nineteenth century almost throws the age of Johnson and Gibbon into the shadow of mediaevalism.

Far back in the prehistoric past a bridge was thrown across the chasm which separates savage from civilized life by the discovery of a process for the smelting of metallic ore; and the birth of all the arts may be dated from the time when some primitive race passed from the age of stone into that of bronze or iron. To the ancient world that first step in science must have appeared also to be the last; and ages rolled away during which man learned no more than to employ effectively the materials thus acquired. If the expectation that diligent research may be rewarded by some signal increase of knowledge be excluded from the sphere of human activity, individual aspirations must be restricted to whatever is social and national; and those desirous of distinction have no choice but to devote themselves to art or politics. Within these channels were confined the energies of the people of antiquity; in some states the leading characteristic was civic adornment; in others the cultivation of martial efficiency; to rise to despotic power was the usual ambition of a democratic statesman; to attain to an imperial position that of a flourishing state. Wars of aggression were constantly undertaken, and defensive wars uniformly became so whenever superiority was manifested. Such conflicts in the past have had no permanent influence on the advancement of mankind; and from time to time have been equally conducive to the spread of civilization or barbarism. During the classical period the arts and learning of Athens were attendant on the success of the Grecian or the Roman arms; in the Middle Ages the Goth, the Hun, the Saracen, and the Tartar closed in on the Roman Empire and nullified the work of those enlightened nations. At the present day the advance of civilization, though independent of conquest, is often hastened by aggression;[1065] and there seems no likelihood that it will ever again recede from a territory where it has once been established. At all times scarcity of the necessaries of life, real or conventional, tends to initiate a contest; nor is it possible to foresee an age when, in the absence of a struggle for existence, the world will subside into a condition of perpetual peace.

In the sixth century, among the Byzantines, the public mind was still oppressed with a sense of the supreme importance of religion. That orthodox Christianity must prevail remained the passion of the day; and in the view of each dissentient sect their creed alone was orthodox. Hence government became an instrument of hierarchy, politics synonymous with sectarianism, and the chief business of the state was to eradicate heresy. Mediaevalism was created by this spirit; in the East the Emperor became a pope;[1066] in the West the Pope was to become a sovereign. The conception of being ruled from the steps of an altar was foreign to the genius of classical antiquity, and Christianity almost effected a reversal of the political spirit of the ancient world.

In the midsummer of 518 occurred the death of Anastasius,[1067] one of the few capable and moderate Emperors whom the Byzantines produced. Although imbued with a heresy by his mother,[1068] and zealous for its acceptance,[1069] he refrained from persecution, and declared that he would not shed a drop of blood to effect the removal of his ecclesiastical opponents.[1070] All his efforts were conciliatory, and he would have obliterated disunion in the Church if his influence could have induced fanaticism to accord in the Henoticon of Zeno.[1071] He dealt impartially with the Demes, but inclined slightly to one faction, the Green, in formal compliance with traditional usage in the Circus.[1072] He relieved oppressive taxation,[1073] restrained extravagance, and, though practising thrift,[1074] responded liberally to every genuine application.[1075] His administration was much admired by those who were free from sectarian prejudice;[1076] and even the bigoted adherents of the Chalcedonian synod cannot avoid being eulogistic when recounting some of his measures.[1077]

Within the Byzantine province of Dardania, to the south of modern Servia, was situated the municipal town of Scupi,[1078] in a plain almost contained by a mountainous amphitheatre, consisting of the Scardus chain, and its connections with the greater ranges of Pindus and Haemus.[1079] Among its dependent villages, lying along the banks of the Axius or Vardar, the river of the plain, were the hamlets of Bederiana and Tauresium.[1080] Under Roman rule the language and manners of Latium became indigenous to this region; and, although the barbarians in their periodical inroads poured through the passes of Scardus on the north-west to spread themselves over Thrace and

Macedonia,[1081] the Latinized stock still maintained its ground in the fifth century.[1082] Throughout the Empire it was a usual practice for sons of the free peasantry to abandon agricultural penury, and, without a change of clothing, provided only with a wallet containing a few days provisions, to betake themselves on foot to the capital, in the hope of chancing on better fortune.[1083] About the year 470, when Leo the Thracian occupied the throne, a young herdsman of Bederiana, bearing the classical name of Justin, resolved on this enterprise, and arrived at Constantinople with two companions whose lot had been similar to his own.[1084] There they presented themselves for enlistment in the army, and, as the three youths were distinguished by a fine physique, they were gladly accepted, and enrolled among the palace guards.[1085] Two of them are lost to our view for ever afterwards in the obscurity of a private soldier's life,[1086] but Justin, though wholly illiterate, entered on a successful military career. At the end of a score of years he reappears under Anastasius, with the rank of a general, and intrusted with a subordinate command in the Isaurian war.[1087] A decade later he is again heard of among those who prosecuted the siege of Amida, which led to its recovery from the Persians;[1088] and before the death of the Emperor he becomes conspicuous at head-quarters, with the dignities of a Patrician, a Senator, and of Commander of the household troops.[1089] While holding this office he was also deputed to a command at sea, and took an active part in repelling the naval attack of Vitalian.[1090]

During the vicissitudes of his life in the camp, Justin remained unmarried and childless, but he became the purchaser of a barbarian captive, named Lupicina, whom he retained as a concubine, and never afterwards repudiated.[1091] While, however, he was rising to a position of importance and affluence, he was not unmindful of those relatives from whom he had separated at his native place. At Tauresium dwelt a sister,[1092] the wife of one Sabbatius,[1093] and the mother of two children, a son and a daughter.[1094] As soon as young Sabbatius,[1095] for the nephew of Justin bore his father's name, had arrived at a suitable age, he was invited to the capital by his uncle, who became his guardian, and had him educated in a manner befitting a youth of high rank.[1096] On the completion of his studies, it was natural that Sabbatius should be claimed for military service, wherein his guardian's influence was centred, and he was drafted forthwith into the ranks of the Candidati or bodyguards of the Emperor.[1097] Finally Justin legally adopted Sabbatius;[1098] and in token of the fact the latter assumed the derivative name of Justinian.[1099]

On the death of Anastasius, as at his accession, the Grand Chamberlain appeared to be master of the situation.[1100] But the chief eunuch of the day, Amantius, was less influential than his predecessor, Urbicius, who, with the Empress Ariadne as an ally, had invested the popular silentiary with the purple; and the means he devised to ensure the acceptance of his candidate were the actual cause of his rejection. He decided to bribe the palace guards to proclaim his favourite, Count Theocritus, and placed a large sum of money in the hands of Justin for that purpose; but the procedure only served to render those soldiers conscious of their power to elect an emperor, and they immediately acclaimed their own commandant as the fittest occupant of the throne.[1101] The venerable Justin, for he was now long past three score, did not decline; the Senate bowed to the nomination of the guards, and the former herdsman took his place in line with the successors of Augustus.[1102]

The Emperor Justin was a rude soldier, devoid of administrative capacity except in relation to military affairs, and so illiterate that he could only append his sign-manual to a document by passing his pen through the openings in a plate perforated so as to indicate the first four letters of his name.[1103] After his coronation he married Lupicina; and the populace, while accepting her as his consort, renamed her Euphemia.[1104] On his accession Justin promoted his nephew to the rank of Patrician[1105] and Nobilissimus;[1106] and Justinian became so closely associated with his uncle that he was generally regarded as the predominant partner in ruling the state.[1107] But the Emperor was jealous of his authority, and when the Senate petitioned that the younger man should be formally recognized as his colleague, he grasped his robe and answered, "Be on your guard against any young man having the right to wear this garment."[1108] Owing to the suddenness of their elevation both princes were ignorant of the routine of government, a circumstance which rendered the position of Proclus, the Quaestor or private adviser of the crown, peculiarly influential during this reign.[1109]

The first act of Justin, who adhered to the orthodox creed, was to reverse the temporizing religious policy of Anastasius; and he at once prepared an edict to render the Council of Chalcedon compulsory in all the churches. Amantius, Theocritus, and their party saw in this measure an opportunity of disputing the unforeseen succession, the overthrow of which they were eager to accomplish. A conspiracy was hastily organized, and the malcontents assembled in one of the principal churches, where they entered on a public denunciation of the new dynasty. The movement, however, was ill supported, and Justin with military promptness seized the chiefs of the opposition, executed several, including the eunuch and his satellite, and banished the others to some distant part.[1110] The edict was then issued and a ruthless persecution instituted against all recalcitrants throughout the Asiatic provinces, where ecclesiastics of every grade professing the monophysite heresy were put to death in great numbers.[1111] At the same time the Emperor recalled those extremists whom Anastasius had been unable to mollify and restored them to their former or to similar appointments.[1112] One danger still remained which might at any moment subvert the newly erected throne; the powerful Vitalian was at large, apparently, if not in reality, master of the forces in Thrace and Illyria. Emissaries were therefore dispatched to him with an invitation to reside at Constantinople as the chief military supporter of the government.[1113] He accepted the proposals, stipulating that an assurance of good faith should previously be given with religious formalities. The parties met in the church of St. Euphemia, at Chalcedon,[1114] and there Justin, Justinian, and Vitalian pledged themselves to each other with solemn oaths while they partook of the Christian sacraments.[1115] The rebel general was, however, too weighty a personage to subside into the position of a tame subordinate, and his masterful presence threatened to nullify the authority of the Emperor and his nephew.[1116] His ascendancy was endured for more than a twelvemonth, and the consulship of 520 was conceded to him. But while he celebrated the games in the Hippodrome popular enthusiasm in his favour rose to a dangerous height.[1117] The Court became alarmed, and a hasty resolution was arrived at to do away with him. In the interval of the display he repaired to the palace with two of his lieutenants to be entertained at a collation, and on entering the banqueting hall they were attacked by a company of Justinian's satellites,[1118] and Vitalian fell pierced with a multitude of wounds.[1119] Shortly afterwards Justinian succeeded to his place and was created a Master of Soldiers, with the virtual rank of commander-in-chief of the Imperial forces.[1120] The next year he was raised to the consulship[1121] and, in order to consolidate his popularity, he determined to signalize the occasion by those lavish festivities which were recorded from time to time among the wonders of the age. But times had changed since the Roman public might be edified or disgraced by those spectacles in which human and animal combatants fought to the death, in mimic land and sea warfare or hunting encounters, to the number of many thousands; and the chronicler, in referring to a half-hundred of lions and pards, evolutions of mail-clad horses, and an increased largess of scattered coin, in addition to the usual races, bear-baiting, and theatrical shows, thinks he indicates sufficiently how far the Consul of the day surpassed the ordinary expectations of the Byzantine populace.[1122] Having finally won over the capital by these gratifications, Justinian in his military capacity departed on a tour for the inspection of garrisons and fortresses throughout the East.[1123] During this period he made the palace of Hormisdas his official residence.[1124]

The reign of Justin was uneventful politically, the age of the Autocrator and his incapacity for state affairs precluding the initiation of any reforms of importance; whilst, although the foreign relations of the Empire were often in a state of tension, no considerable hostilities were undertaken.[1125] At home official activity was chiefly engrossed with the planning of police precautions for the repression of sedition. During three or four years all the chief cities were agitated by the turbulence of the Blue faction, which sought to suppress their rivals of the Green by stoning, assassination, and wrecking of their dwellings. At length, in 523, the rioters were subdued by the appointment of special Praefects, whose severity of character did not shrink from making the culprits pay the extreme penalty of the law.[1126] With its neighbours of the East and West the Empire might have existed at this period on terms of perfect amity but for the disturbing influence of religion. Incensed at Justin's oppressive treatment of the Arians, Theodoric, the Gothic king, declared that he would exterminate the Catholics in Italy[1127] if freedom of belief were not granted to his co-religionists; and he compelled Pope John I to lead an embassy to Constantinople with the object of pleading the cause of those heretics at the Byzantine court. John, the first of his line to visit New Rome, was received with enthusiasm by the orthodox Emperor;[1128] but, if the head of the Western Church urged his appeal with sincerity, Justin at least proved obdurate, and no concession to the Arians could be extorted from his bigotry. The Pope returned to Ravenna, the regal seat of the barbarian king, to expiate his abortive mission by being incarcerated for the last few months of his life; and the death of Theodoric shortly afterwards, before he had time to execute his threats, saved Italy from becoming the scene of brutal reprisals.[1129]

The interspace between the Caspian Sea and the Euxine, the modern Transcaucasia, was inhabited by semi-savage races, over whom Rome and Persia preferred almost equal claims to suzerainty. A perpetual source of friction between the two powers in this region arose from the necessity of guarding the Caspian Gates,[1130] now the Pass of Darial,[1131] a practicable gorge through the Caucasus, often traversed by the Scythian hordes when carrying their devastations to the south. Alexander is said to have blocked the entry with an iron barrier,[1132] and subsequently the pass was kept by the Romans until the Sassanian dynasty became predominant in those parts. The utility to both nations, however, of maintaining the defence, caused the Persians, after the collapse of Julian's expedition, to demand that the Romans should share the expense.[1133] Theodosius I bought off the claims, but by the time of Anastasius a Hunnish king, in friendly league with that emperor, had obtained possession of the forts.[1134] On his death they passed to the Persians, with the consent of Anastasius, who engaged vaguely to contribute annually.[1135] Justin tried to evade this payment, but the Persian monarch declined to be put off, and, as often as the Emperor fell into arrears, proceeded to recover the amount by distraint.[1136] His chosen bailiff, whenever he put in an execution, was a ferocious sheik of the Saracens, named Alamundar,[1137] who raided Syria up to the walls of Antioch, massacring the population indiscriminately, and holding captives of substance against their being replevied by the Romans.[1138] On one occasion he burst into the city of Emesa, and finding there four hundred virgins congregated in a church, he sacrificed them all on the same day to Al Uzzâ, the Arabian Venus.[1139]

In two states of the Caucasian region, both under kingly rule, Christianity had gained a footing about the time of Constantine.[1140] Lazica, previously Colchis, the subject of heroic legends, and now Mingrelia, occupied the coast of the Black Sea north and south of the river Phasis. On its eastern border, watered by the Cyrus, lay Iberia, at present known as Georgia.[1141] In 522 the young king of the Lazi, alarmed lest the Persian religion should be forced on him, fled to Constantinople, and prayed for Christian baptism under the immediate countenance of the Emperor. Justin assented, and not only sustained him at the sacred font, but afterwards united him to a Roman wife, the daughter of one of the patricians of his court. Before his departure Tzathus was formally invested with ornaments and robes of state, expressly designed to denote the closeness of his relationship to Justin and to Rome.[1142] A letter of remonstrance against surreptitiously tampering with the allegiance of Persian subjects soon resulted from these proceedings; but Justin denied their political significance, and dwelt with fanatical insistence on the exigences of the faith, and the urgency of resisting heathen error.[1143] The throne of Persia was still occupied by Cavades,[1144] and that monarch now began to think seriously of going to war with Rome. On reviewing his resources he decided to enlist the Hunnish tribes, who dwelt beyond the Caucasus, as allies against the Empire. One of the most powerful chiefs agreed to his proposals, and met him by prearrangement with a large following of his nation, but during the conference messengers arrived who protested that a short time previously the Hun had been induced by a large subsidy to pledge his support to the Byzantines. "We are at peace," said Justin, "and should not allow ourselves to be duped by these dogs." In reply to an amicable inquiry the barbarian boasted shamelessly of the circumstance, whereupon Cavades, convinced of his treachery, at once ordered him to be cut down by his guards. Forthwith a night attack was secretly planned against his forces, who, without becoming aware of the author of the calamity, were dispersed and slain to the number of many thousands.[1145] More friendly counsels now began to prevail with the Persian, as it occurred to him that he might compose his differences with the Emperor to his own advantage. He was extremely anxious to secure the succession to his favourite son Chosroes,[1146] to the exclusion of his two elder brothers. There was reason to fear, however, that on his decease, by the intervention of the Court or the populace, one of the senior princes might be raised to the throne. Cavades, therefore, proposed to Justin that he should adopt Chosroes, considering that no party would have the temerity to dispute the tiara with a ward of the Empire. Justin and Justinian were elated at the prospect of exercising a controlling influence in Persian affairs, but the Quaestor Proclus quickly intervened, and by specious arguments, led them to see the matter in a totally different light. The adoption of the Sassanian prince, he urged with heat, would convey to him a title to inherit the crown of the Empire, Justinian might be ousted from the succession, and Justin would live in dread of being the last of the Roman emperors.[1147] An evasive course was resolved on, and a commission was dispatched to meet the Persian delegates in the vicinity of Nisibis. Chosroes himself advanced to the Tigris in the expectation of being escorted to Constantinople by the Roman envoys. The representatives of the two nations met without cordiality, and the Persians, contrary to their instructions, began by taunting the Byzantines with having usurped their rights in Lazica. The Romans then announced that the Emperor could not adopt a foreigner with legal formalities, but only by an act of arms, such as was customary among barbarians. The suggestion was taken as a deliberate insult by the Persians; the colloquy came to an end abruptly, and Chosroes returned to his father, vowing vengeance against the Romans.[1148]

It was now evident that war at no distant date could scarcely be averted, but a further embroilment with respect to religion provoked overt hostilities, which rendered a positive conflict inevitable. Having experienced that defection to Rome was a natural sequence of Christianity being promulgated in his dependencies, Cavades determined to enforce Magism among the Iberians. But, at the first intimation, the king of that people made an earnest appeal to Justin, and prepared to take up arms in defence of his faith. The Emperor responded by sending two of his generals,[1149] provided with a large sum of money, to levy auxiliaries for the Iberians, among the Huns who inhabited the northern shores of the Euxine.[1150] Such was the practical overture to a war with Persia, which was to last for several years, without any appreciable gain to either side. During the reign of Justin, however, hostilities were carried on in a desultory manner, and no battle of any magnitude was fought. Military detachments were told off to ravage Persian territory to the north, in the vicinity of the frontier. They were opposed by similar bands of the enemy, and from time to time indecisive skirmishes took place. As to Iberia, that country was abandoned for the time being, the forces raised being insufficient to withstand the Persian host, and the king with all the native magnates retreated into Lazica by a narrow pass, called the Iberian Gates, which was then fortified by a Byzantine garrison.[1151] During these operations the first mention occurs of some names which became associated later on with the most notable events in the annals of the age. An advance into Persarmenia was conducted by two young officers, specially deputed by Justinian, named Sittas and Belisarius. After the lapse of a few months (in 527) the latter was transferred to a more important command at Daras. There, among the civil members of his staff, he received the future historian Procopius as his legal adviser or assessor.[1152] About the same time occurred the death of Justin, whose reign lasted for nine years and a few weeks.

If the sea of politics remained comparatively unruffled in Justin's time, nature made amends for the lack of excitement by showing herself physically in her most active mode. His reign opened with the appearance of a remarkable comet, the most dreaded portent of impending disaster.[1153] Nor were the forebodings belied, as the provinces on both continents were afflicted progressively with violent earthquakes, intensified by volcanic phenomena.[1154] In Europe, Dyrrachium, the birthplace of Anastasius, recently adorned by him at great cost, was overthrown; and Corinth shortly after experienced a similar fate. In Asia, Anazarbus, the capital of Cilicia, suffered; the central half of Pompeiopolis sunk into the earth;[1155] and Edessa was ruined by a flood of the river Scirtus.[1156] The withdrawal of large sums from the Imperial treasury was entailed by the restoration of these cities. This series of calamities culminated in the almost total destruction of Antioch, where the seismological disturbances persisted for more than a year, the eighth of Justin's reign, and upwards of a quarter of a million of the inhabitants perished.[1157] The ground was rifted in all directions with great gaps which ejected flames; the houses caught fire or collapsed with their occupants into the yawning chasms; and a hill of considerable size, overhanging the city, was shattered with such violence that the streets and buildings in that quarter lay buried beneath a uniform surface formed by the debris.[1158] The preliminary shocks were generally disregarded, and the climax, which occurred during the dinner hour,[1159] was so sudden and widespread, that the bulk of the population was overwhelmed before they had a chance to escape. Then only the residue of the citizens made a rush for the open country, carrying with them whatever valuables they could seize on in their hasty flight. As soon, however, as they had arrived at a safe distance, they found themselves beset by bands of rustics, who had gathered together from every side in order to plunder the fugitives. Conspicuous among the despoilers was a certain Thomas, a man with the rank of a silentiary, and wealthy enough to keep a private guard. Posting himself daily in a convenient position, he directed his retainers in the operation of stripping systematically all who came in their way. It is satisfactory to learn from the contemporary historian that all these wretches were soon overtaken by a miserable death, as the penalty of their inhumanity; but as we are assured that, without legal intervention, their retribution emanated from an indignant providence, which had impelled, or, at least, lain dormant during the catastrophe, we must conclude that the Nemesis was desiderated rather than real. The assertion, however, need not be questioned that the said Thomas died suddenly, to the great joy of the survivors, on the fourth day of his nefarious enterprise. Great consolation was also derived from the preternatural appearance of a cross in the clouds; and all burst into tears and supplications at this signal proof of the compassion felt for them by a beneficent Deity. In two or three weeks after the crisis, nature assumed her wonted quiescence, and the deserted city began to be re-peopled by the returning inhabitants. The work of restoration at once commenced; and it is recorded that many persons were then rescued by being dug out of the ruins, under which they had been buried; among them numbers of women, who in the meantime had passed safely through the pangs of childbirth.[1160] As soon as the news of the downfall of Antioch was carried to Constantinople, the capital was thrown into a state of consternation, and all public festivities for the season of Whitsuntide, which was at hand, were renounced. The Emperor, discarding all regal pomp, debased himself in sackcloth and ashes,[1161] and led a suppliant procession of the Senate, wearing mourning garments, to the church of St. John at the Hebdomon. Commissioners were immediately dispatched with ample funds for reparation, and the ruined city again became visible on the face of the earth with a rapidity which, in the words of a writer of the period, gave the impression that it had reappeared suddenly out of the infernal regions.[1162] But the earthquakes continued and ultimately, as a safeguard against further visitations of the kind, Antioch was demised to the special care of the Deity by being renamed Theopolis, or the City of God.[1163]

The desultory war with Persia was maintained all the time under the chief command of Licelarius, a Thracian. But that general, while pushing hostilities over the border into the vicinity of Nisibis, managed so unskilfully that his whole forces were seized with a panic and fled back to Roman territory without ever having sighted an enemy. As an immediate result Licelarius was disgraced and Belisarius promoted to fill his place. The youth, as he must be called, fulfilled the expectations he inspired and thenceforward entered on that career of achievement which was to render him the military hero of his age.

On the 1st of April, 527, Justin formally associated his nephew to the throne, with the rank of Augustus. He lived exactly four months afterwards,[1164] and on the 1st of August in the same year the sole reign of Justinian began.[1165]

CHAPTER IV
PRE-IMPERIAL CAREER OF THEODORA: THE CONSORT OF JUSTINIAN

THE influence of women in antiquity varied extremely according to circumstances of time and place. During the mythical age they are celebrated as the heroines of many a legend; and in the epics of Homer the free woman seems to live on terms of equality with her male relations.[1166] Down to the historical period the same consideration was continued to them at Sparta, where the mental and physical integrity of the females was cultivated as essential to the designed superiority of the race;[1167] but among the Athenians we find the women of the community ignored as factors in the state to such an extent, that they rank little higher than domesticated animals.[1168] In neither of these states, however, were they ever invested with any political office; and their power could only be felt indirectly by the executive as the result of their activity as wives and mothers in the family circle.[1169] But outside Greece, in those wider territories more or less permeated by Hellenes, women sometimes attained to a full share of government, inherited or assumed a sovereignty on the death of their husbands, commanded armies, and even appeared in martial attire at the head of their troops. Two Ionian princesses, both of whom bore the name of Artemisia, reigned in Caria: the elder distinguished herself at sea as an ally of Xerxes in the naval battle of Salamis (480 B.C.);[1170] her successor erected the magnificent monument at Halicarnassus in memory of her husband Mausolus, hence called the Mausoleum, which was admired as one of the seven wonders of the world.[1171] Cynane, a daughter of Philip of Macedon, led an expedition into Illyria, and is said to have killed the queen of that country, in an engagement which ensued, with her own hand.[1172] This lady had applied herself vigorously to military exercises, and similarly trained up her daughter Eurydice in the school of arms. As the wife of the imbecile Arrhidaeus, one of the successors of Alexander, Eurydice advanced into Asia to meet Olympias, the mother of that monarch, in a contest which was to decide the fate of Macedonia. While the young queen, as we are told, displayed herself with all the attributes of a female warrior, the dowager chose to accompany her forces with a train of attendants, who seemed rather to be acting their part in a Bacchanalian procession.[1173] This war, however, proved ultimately fatal to all three women, who were merely moved as puppets by the firmer hands of Alexander's generals in their rivalry for shares at the dissolution of his empire.[1174] After the partition of the extensive dominions of Alexander among his numerous heirs, the number of Grecian women who enjoyed, or were allied to, sovereign power, was proportionately increased; and the names of many princesses of varied distinction in that age have been recorded historically, and even perpetuated popularly to the present day by towns designated in their honour, and spread over the three continents.[1175] While some of these ladies won an unusual share of marital respect and affection, not only by the graces of their person, but by their capacity for taking part in the councils of state,[1176] there were not a few who signalized themselves by a cruelty or criminality hardly exceeded by the male tyrants of that semi-lawless and contentious epoch. Two Egyptian princesses, sisters named Cleopatra, were ambitious of occupying the thrones of Egypt and Syria, respectively, to the exclusion of their own sons. The Syrian queen, having murdered one of her sons, was obliged to accept his brother as a colleague, but being unable to nullify his authority, resolved to make away with him also. On his return from military drill one day, she presented him with a poisoned cup, which, however, he declined to empty, having had an intimation of her design, and bade her swallow the draught herself. She refused, while denying her guilt, but he insisted that in no other way could she clear herself, and she thus fell a victim to her intended treachery.[1177] Her sister, who reigned in Egypt, under almost similar circumstances was not more fortunate; for, having expelled one of her sons and committed various cruelties, she raised another to a partnership in the kingdom. Finding still that her ascendancy could not be maintained, she planned to assassinate him, but, being forestalled, perished herself in the attempt.[1178] Precocious in guilt, but, perhaps, more excusable, was the Cyrenean princess Berenice, who caused her intended husband to be murdered in the arms of her own mother, as the penalty of his having slighted her for this adulterous intercourse.[1179] Her name has been preserved to us in the nomenclature of science, and through an astronomical compliment a cluster of stars is still distinguished as the Coma Berenices.[1180] From these few examples the reader may derive some notion of the social relations of the ruling families in that extended Greek realm which came into being as the result of the conquests of Alexander. One by one the separate autonomies succumbed to the force of the Latin arms, and before the beginning of the Christian era all of them which lay to the west of the Euphrates had become merged in the provincial system of the Roman Empire.

When we turn our attention to the Roman Republic, we find that the females, although in law subjected absolutely to the will of their male relatives,[1181] were virtually as influential in the state as were the women at Sparta. From Cloelia[1182] to Portia[1183] the maidens and matrons of that community displayed the spirit and resolution which we should assume to be characteristic of the wives and sisters of the men who made themselves gradually the masters of the earth. Nor were they backward in applying themselves to intellectual pursuits when the rusticity of the Republic began to be dissipated by the infiltration of Hellenic culture; and by their assiduous studies in philosophy, geometry, literature, and music, they kept pace determinedly with the mental development of the sterner sex.[1184] With the establishment of the Empire, a greatly enhanced authority became the permanent endowment of a limited class. It followed naturally that the female connections of the emperors and their chief ministers could aspire to participate in the despotic government, but the throne itself always remained debarred to women, and to the last days of the Empire the Romans never acquiesced in a female reign. When Agrippina, presuming on her power over a son whom her intrigues had raised to the throne, pressed forward amid general amazement to preside as of equal authority with him at a reception of ambassadors, the philosopher Seneca hastily impelled the young Emperor to arrest his mother with a respectful greeting, and thus, in the words of Tacitus, "under the semblance of filial devotion the impending disgrace was obviated."[1185] Yet, in several instances, as the guardian of an immature heir to the crown, or as the associate of an incapable husband or brother, a woman was able to retain for a considerable time all the attributes of monarchy. The Syrian Soaemias, the equal in profligacy of her son Elagabalus, assumed the reigns of government, and took her seat in the Senate, which then beheld for the first time a female assisting at its deliberations.[1186] Her career speedily terminated in disaster,[1187] but during the break-up of the Western Empire, two centuries later, no opposition was offered to the predominance of her sex by a dejected people. The Empress Placidia Galla, after enduring many misfortunes, exercised a regency scarcely distinguishable from absolutism for more than a decade, in the name of her son Valentinian III.[1188] In the East the rule of Pulcheria, as the adviser of her brother Theodosius II, and afterwards of her nominal husband Marcian, extended almost to half a century.[1189] The importance of an Augusta in disposing of the crown on the decease of her husband has been indicated in the description of the elevation of Anastasius;[1190] and the official who records the election of Justin, ascribes the turbulence of the populace on that occasion to the absence of control by a princess of that rank.[1191] But the power of a dowager empress was most signally exemplified in the case of Verina, widow of Leo I, who, in her dissatisfaction with the policy of her son-in-law Zeno, succeeded in provoking a revolution, placed the chief of her party on the throne for more than a twelvemonth, and continued to involve the Empire in bloodshed for a series of years.[1192] Below the Imperial dignity the feminine element was perpetually active and widely exerted, especially throughout the provinces. The wives of legates, of proconsuls or governors, accompanied their husbands on their missions to distant parts, and were often responsible, both in peace and war, for the complexion assumed by the local administration.[1193] They displayed themselves ostentatiously in public, addressed themselves authoritatively to the army, and instigated measures of finance, to such an extent that they were sometimes regarded as the moving spirit in whatever was transacted.[1194]

Agrippina shared the hardships of Germanicus in his campaign against the Germans, opposed herself to the disorder of the troops when retreating through fear of the enemy, preserved the bridge over the Rhine, which in their panic they were about to demolish, and, combining the duties of a general with those of the intendant of an ambulance, restored confidence to the legions.[1195] Yet Germanicus, in his Asiatic command, fell a victim to the machinations of Plancina, the wife of a colleague; and Agrippina strove ineffectively to withstand the malignant arts of another woman.[1196] In some instances oppression of the provincials was clearly traceable to female arrogance and intrigue; and at length it was seriously proposed in the Senate that no official should be accompanied by his consort, when deputed to the government of a province. The motion was hotly debated, but was ultimately lost through the vehemency of opposition.[1197]

Nothing in antiquity is more remarkable than the diversity of sentiment as to prostitution among the Greeks. Considering the deification of amorous passion and fecundity expressed by polytheism in the cult of Aphrodite, and the ethics of social order which instilled a reverence for chastity, the popular mind continually wavered as to whether the *hetaira* or courtesan should be contemned as an outcast, or adored as the priestess of a goddess. Among the Semites who dwelt along the Oriental borders of the Grecian dominions an act of prostitution at the temple of the goddess of concupiscence was enjoined on every woman at least once in her life as a religious rite;[1198] but the nicer ethical discrimination of the Greeks debarred this custom from ever establishing itself in Hellenic religion. At Corinth, however, one of the most distinguished art centres of Greece, it obtained a footing in a modified form; and in that city a thousand female slaves sacred to Aphrodite were maintained as public courtesans attached to her temple.[1199] At Athens, Solon regarded the state regulation of prostitution as an essential safeguard to public morality, whence he constituted a number of brothels under definite rules throughout the town, thus providing, in his opinion, an outlet for irrepressible passions which might otherwise be manifested in a more unseemly manner.[1200] As in all ages there were two grades of females who led a life of incontinence for the sake of gain; and of these the higher class, the hetairas, filled a place not devoid of a certain distinction in most of the Grecian cities. This class relied not on their personal attractions only, but also on their mental accomplishments, aspiring to become the intellectual companions of their lovers by applying themselves to the study of literature and philosophy.[1201] Hence they ranked as the best educated women of the community, and exerted more influence in the state than the usually dull and secluded housewives. The majority and the most noted of such courtesans flourished, of course, in Athenian society, the ascendancy of the women which obtained at Sparta being altogether adverse to their pretensions. Thus it happened that the hetairas of Athens were generally regarded as persons of some consequence; and several writers of the period thought it no unworthy task to compose their biographies, as might be done at the present day in the case of eminent women.[1202] To the connection of Aspasia with Pericles and her position as the leader of Athenian society during his tenure of power, an important page is devoted in all histories of Greece; and it appears that even matrons were permitted to frequent her salon in order to improve themselves mentally by listening to the elevated discourses held there.[1203] Socrates visited Theodote for the purpose of augmenting his sociological insight, and Xenophon has included an account of his debate with her in his memoirs of that father of philosophers.[1204] Leontium was a conspicuous figure in the garden of Epicurus, where he convened his disciples; and she penned a treatise against the Peripatetics, which deserved the commendation of Cicero.[1205] Scarcely, indeed, can a man of note in this age, whether potentate, orator, philosopher, or poet, be found whose name does not occur in anecdote or more serious record as the associate of some hetaira. It follows that courtesans should appear not rarely as the mothers of persons of distinction. Themistocles, the younger Pericles, Timotheus, and Nicomachus, the son of Aristotle, are mentioned in this connection;[1206] and more than one sovereign prince is allowed to have been the offspring of some hetaira, namely, Arrhidaeus, king of Macedonia, alluded to above, and Philetaerus, the founder of the kingdom of Pergamus.[1207] Many of these hetairas realized wealth, and some had the faculty of keeping it; nor were they disinclined to spend it patriotically if an opportunity offered. Lamia erected a splendid portico at Sicyon;[1208] and Phryne proposed to rebuild the walls of Thebes, which had been levelled by Alexander, provided that the fact should be commemorated by a suitable inscription. The Thebans, however, were too proud to owe the restoration of their town to such a source.[1209] As the result of their notoriety and the consideration accorded to them, some courtesans won the distinction of living in metal or marble; and it was remarked that, whilst no wife had been honoured by a public monument, the memory of hetairas had often been perpetuated by the statuary.[1210] The reasons, however, why courtesans happened to be thus distinguished were in many instances totally dissimilar: some for actual merit, others merely through the caprice of passionate lovers, challenged the popular eye from a pedestal. Leaena was represented at Athens under the form of a tongueless lioness, because she preferred to die by the torture rather than disclose the conspiracy of Harmodius and Aristogeiton against the tyrants of the day.[1211] Even at Sparta the image of Cottina was a familiar object, standing beside a brazen cow which she had consecrated to Athena.[1212] A sculptured tomb to Lais was set up at Corinth,[1213] and a golden statue of Phryne was dedicated at Delphi,[1214] to express the admiration of their townsmen for their pre-eminence as venal beauties. A magnificent cenotaph on the Sacred Way from Athens to Eleusis surprised a wayfarer into the belief that he was approaching the tomb of some great general or statesman; it was no more than the fantasy of Harpalus, an extravagant viceroy of Alexander's, constructed in glorification of his deceased mistress, Pythionice.[1215] At Abydos, a temple to Aphrodite, styled the Prostitute, recorded the patriotic treachery of a band of loose women, which conduced to the slaughter of an alien garrison;[1216] but when the degradation of Greece was already far advanced, both Athens and Thebes descended to flatter Demetrius Poliorcetes by rearing fanes in honour of his favourite concubine, Lamia.[1217]

In the earlier centuries of the Republic the strict censorship upheld at Rome kept the city purged of dissoluteness; and prostitution, regularly supervised and licensed,[1218] was reduced to the inevitable minimum; but in proportion as Hellenic manners permeated the community, the courtesan established herself on the same footing as in Greece. We are told that a fortune gained by her harlotry was willed to Sulla by Nicopolis;[1219] and the relations of Flora with the great Pompey are given in detail by Plutarch. Captivated by the beauty of the latter, Caecilius Metellus included her portrait among the adornments of the temple of Castor and Pollux.[1220] Precia, a notorious strumpet, won the devotion of Cethegus, one of the abettors of Sulla, and the heritor of a large share of his power. At Rome he carried all before him for some years, whilst he surrendered himself absolutely to the caprices of his mistress. The provinces were distributed to her nominees; and the command against Mithridates, in which Lucullus acquired such extensive territories for the Republic, was obtained by courting her favour by costly presents and blandishments.[1221] It is needless to inquire how far illicit sexual connections were politically operative during the rule of insensate emperors, for in these times every excess had its parallel;[1222] but it may be noted that the stern and sordid Vespasian abandoned the patronage of the Empire to a mistress, into whose lap riches were poured by governors, generals, and pontiffs, in the form of bribes for securing coveted appointments.[1223] Concurrently with the decline of the Empire, municipal institutions decayed, especially in the West, and the sense of public decency became blunted. When Theodosius visited Rome in , he found prostitution in league with crime and administrative measures more offensive than the moral laxity they were intended to correct.[1224] Nor was the balance of public morality redressed until Europe had passed through mediaevalism, and advanced for two or three centuries into the modern period.[1225]

During the greater part of the reign of Justinian the fortunes of the Empire were influenced to an unusual extent by two women, the Empress Theodora and Antonina, the wife of Belisarius, whom chance had raised from a base origin to the highest rank in the state. In the early years of the reign of Anastasius, a man named Acacius filled the post of bear-keeper to the Green faction. Dying somewhat unexpectedly, he left his wife and three daughters,

Comito, Theodora, and Anastasia, totally unprovided for. The eldest child was but seven years old, and the widow immediately attempted to provide for the future by uniting herself with the man who was expected to become her late husband's successor. Another candidate, however, presented himself, and by bribing the master of the shows, whose decision was final, despoiled them of the situation. The family was now destitute, but the mother resolved on a last effort to enlist the sympathy of the faction. Binding the heads and hands of her little girls with wreaths of flowers, according to ancient custom, she displayed herself with them in the crowded Hippodrome in the posture of suppliants. These tactics proved successful, for, although the Greens rejected her prayer, it happened that the Blue faction were at the moment in want of a bear-keeper, and they at once preferred the stepfather to the vacant place. In course of time the daughters developed into handsome young women, and one by one were consigned to the theatre, as the sphere most congenial to the associations in which they had been reared. The eldest, Comito, was the first to make her appearance, and she soon became a person of some consequence, if not as an actress, at least as a hetaira, a career indissolubly linked with that of a female performer on the stage. At the same time her younger sister Theodora became a familiar object to the public. Dressed in a short tunic, such as was worn by young slaves, she was always to be seen in the wake of Comito, bearing on her shoulder the folding seat[1226] without which no one of any pretensions could stir abroad. Thrown into the haunts of vice thus prematurely, she became initiated objectively, before she attained the age of womanhood, in all the excesses of lasciviousness.[1227] In her turn, as soon as she was old enough, she was pushed to the front to play a part upon the scene, where she soon captivated the audience by her special gifts. Theodora was short of stature, of slight physique and pale,[1228] whence she became possessed with the procacity and insistence peculiar to those who fear to be slighted on account of some physical defect. Her accomplishments included neither singing nor dancing, but she proved herself to be a burlesque comédienne of singular aptitudes. She was quick-witted and full of repartee, and her air in coming on the stage was at once provocative of mirth. She excelled particularly in the comic piteousness with which she resented a mock chastisement delivered, according to a trick of the day, on her puffed-out cheeks, which seemed to resound with the severity of the infliction.[1229] But she was far from trusting to merely histrionic art to gain the notoriety she craved for, and she applied herself sedulously to charm that considerable section of humanity for whom the salt of life is indecency. On the scene, or at private reunions, she distinguished herself by her impudicity above any of her companions. Her ingenuity was inexhaustible in inventing occasions for the exposition of her nudities, and in sexual vice she became a mistress of everything fantastic and unnatural. She dispensed with drapery as far as was permissible by law, and one of her favourite devices was to prostrate herself on the stage, with grains of corn distributed about her person, so that a number of geese, in searching for their food, might throw her scanty clothing into obscene disorder.[1230] At orgies of the dissolute she was the life and soul of the festivities; and she assumed the rôle of instructress in depravity among her compeers of the theatre.[1231] Yet with respect to the latter, she also achieved a reputation for being quarrelsome and spiteful beyond the usual measure of her tribe. By her habitual and flagrant excesses, she became universally known in the capital, and she was shunned by all worthy citizens to such an extent, that they shrunk from being sullied by her touch, should they chance to meet her in the street.[1232] If a merchant encountered her in the morning he was as much scared at the sight as at that of a bird of ill-omen.[1233] Animated by a genius so restless and aspiring, it is evident that such a woman needed only transference to a field of higher potential, to become one of the most notable characters of the age. Such a place had been prepared for her by fate, and she was destined to renew on the throne of the Empire the triumphs she had won on the boards of the theatre.[1234]

By a mischance, which she had always practised every expedient to avert,[1235] Theodora became the mother of a son while at Constantinople. His father christened him John and, fearing that the repugnance evinced towards the boy by his mother might endanger his life, he carried him off into Arabia, the province of his permanent residence.[1236] Soon afterwards Theodora was induced to quit the capital by a Tyrian named Hecebolus, who was proceeding to North Africa to occupy the seat of government in the Pentapolis. In a short time, however, she alienated this lover by her petulant temper until, provoked by her insolence, he expelled her from his establishment without making any provision for her future. This consummation was assuredly a valuable lesson by which she did not fail to profit at a later date. Devoid of resources, she betook herself from Cyrene to Alexandria, where she attempted to live by prostitution; but in a strange city, without the entry of a congenial circle, she discovered that her talents or her attractions were unavailing to procure a livelihood. From city to city of the East she proceeded, repeating always the same experience in a state of incurable distress.[1237] She directed her steps constantly northwards in her wanderings, keeping her mind fixed on the capital, to which she longed to return, and at length she found herself on the southern shores of the Euxine, within the limits of Paphlagonia.[1238] In that austere province, where the circus and the theatre were eschewed, and fornication and adultery were looked on as the most abominable crimes,[1239] it is possible that she may have been affected by the puritanism of the inhabitants, certain that she must have felt chastened by the trials she had undergone. It is probable also that she remained there for some time in the receipt of hospitality, whilst being exhorted and encouraged to live a life of continence. Ultimately, however, she found means to regain Constantinople, where she arrived in a sober frame of mind and with the resolution not to relapse into her former habits. She sought out a humble tenement in a portico near the district of Hormisdas,[1240] where she resigned herself to earn a modest living by feminine industry.[1241] A veil of obscurity hangs over the circumstances which preceded the social elevation of Theodora, which can only be partly dissipated by surmise. It appears that after the accession of Justin she was discovered by Justinian sitting demurely at her spinning-wheel, and that he was fascinated by her at once with a force which he was unable to resist.[1242] It is allowed that she was not devoid of beauty,[1243] but if she captivated him by that quality, it was one which she possessed in common with a thousand others of her class. Rather must we conclude that she won her dominion over him by her distinction of mind and character, by her wit, vivacity, insight, and social address.[1244] He was now verging on his fortieth year, and, as we shall recognize more fully hereafter, must always have been of a staid disposition, as free as possible from the wildness of youth. How far he was acquainted with her past is altogether unknown; if her travels had extended to a few years her former intimates might now for the most part be scattered, her person might be half forgotten, and her meretricious enormities but faintly remembered. Her scenic extravagances may never have been witnessed by Justinian, but it is certain that before long her former mode of life was at least partially revealed to him. Their intercourse soon ripened into familiarity; he made her his mistress, but without concealment, and with the fixed intention of marrying her; and as the first step towards that end he raised her to the rank of a patrician.[1245] Theodora was now removed from her sordid surroundings and housed in a style suitable to her enhanced fortunes.[1246] At the same time her sisters, Comito and Anastasia, were rescued from their degrading vocation and maintained in a manner befitting their semi-royal relationship.[1247] Her influence with Justinian became unbounded, and, as the favourite of the virtual master of the Empire, she was courted by all aspirants to the emoluments of state.[1248] Her age was now more mature; she had been taught discretion and self-restraint in the school of adversity, and she was wise enough for the future not to hazard her ascendancy by yielding intemperately to her passions. Her physical mould was not that of a sensual woman, her amazing immorality resulted merely from an inordinate desire to outrun all competition in the career on which she had been launched, and we may believe that, after every incentive to sexual excess had been removed from her path, she found no difficulty in leading a life of the strictest chastity. Her energies were now directed into other channels; she did not deny herself the indulgence of using the exceptional power with which she was invested to gratify her ambition to the full; she accumulated wealth by every means possible to an official of the highest authority, and she seldom allowed the machinery of government to escape altogether from her control.

Two obstacles stood in the way of Justinian when he proposed to make Theodora his wife. In the first place he was confronted by the old law of Constantine which aimed at preserving the aristocratic families of the Empire free from any taint in their blood. It was enacted thereby that no woman of vicious life, actress or courtesan, or even of lowly birth, could become the legal spouse of a man who had attained to the rank of Clarissimus or Senator, the third grade of nobility.[1249] To abrogate this statute was therefore a necessity before he could carry out his design, but he easily prevailed on Justin to give the Imperial sanction to a Constitution which recites at length the expediency of granting to such women, who have repented and abjured their errors, an equality of civil privileges with their unblemished sisters.[1250] A further impediment arose from the opposition of the Empress Euphemia, who withstood the marriage with an obstinacy which neither argument nor entreaty could overcome.[1251] Although her relationship to Justin had until recently been abased, the quondam slave had never deviated from the path of virtue and had imbibed all the prejudices of the strictest matron against women who made a traffic of their persons. A critical delay thus became inevitable, but Theodora passed through it triumphantly, and in 524, by the death of Euphemia, Justinian was freed from all restraint. Their nuptials were then celebrated with official acquiescence and without even popular protest. The Church, the Senate, and the Army at once accepted the former actress as their mistress, and the populace, who had contemplated her extravagances on the theatre, now implored her protection with outstretched hands.[1252] The crown with the title of Augusta was bestowed on her by Justinian at the time of his own coronation;[1253] and she acquired an authority in the Empire almost superior to that of her husband. After her elevation Theodora became a zealous churchwoman, and extended her protection far and wide to ecclesiastics and monks who had fallen into distress or disrepute through being worsted in the theological feuds which were characteristic of the age. But she was always bitterly hostile to those who opposed her particular religious views or political plans, and proceeded to the last extremity to subject them to her will.[1254]

Antonina sprang from the same coterie as Theodora, but her birth was more disreputable. Her father was a charioteer of the Circus at Thessalonica, and her mother a stage-strumpet.[1255] The two women were not, however, companions, perhaps not even acquainted, as the wife of Belisarius was almost a score of years senior to the Empress, and she also exceeded the age of her husband by an even greater amount. It appears, therefore, that whilst Justinian was probably twenty years older than Theodora, Belisarius was at least as much junior to Antonina. The latter was, in fact, the mother of several illegitimate children before being married, and a son of hers named Photius, not more than eight or ten years junior to his stepfather, is an observable figure in the historic panorama.[1256] We have no details as to the career of Antonina previous to her becoming involved in the current of political affairs, nor can we regret the loss of another story of moral obliquity, but there is evidence to prove that she was a woman of a totally different stamp from the Empress, one disposed by natural propensity to debauchery, and at no time inclined to deny herself the pleasures of incontinency. At the outset of Justinian's reign Theodora regarded her with the greatest aversion, but whether because the character of Antonina was at variance with her own or that she loathed the presence of one too well informed as to her own antecedents cannot now be determined. In the political vortex they were unavoidably thrown much together, and it will often be necessary to inquire as to how far the course of history may have been modified by their respective activities and temperaments.[1257]

END OF VOL. I.

FOOTNOTES

[1] To these must now be added Diehl's beautifully illustrated work, *Justinien et la civilization Byzantine au VIe siècle*, Paris, 1901. The leading motive is that of art, and it is replete with interesting details, but the conception is too narrow to allow of its fully representing the age to a modern reader.

[2] Radium was unknown in 1901 when the above was written.

[3] In presenting this history to the modern reader I shall not imitate the example of those mediaeval stage-managers, who, in order to indicate the scenery of the play, were content to exhibit a placard such as "This is a street," "This is a wood," etc. On the contrary, on each occasion that the scene shifts in this drama of real life, I shall describe the locality of the events at a length proportionate to their importance.

[4] Schliemann found neolithic remains at Hissarlik, not far off (Ilios, p. 236, 1880).

[5] In the sixteenth century, as we are told by Gyllius (Top. CP., iv, 11), the Greeks of Stamboul were utterly oblivious of the history of their country and of the suggestiveness of the remains which lay around them. But an awakening has now taken place and the modern Greeks are among the most ardent in the pursuit of archaeological knowledge. They have even revived the language of Attica for literary purposes, and it may be said that an Athenian of the age of Pericles could read with facility the works now issued from the Greek press of Athens or of Constantinople—a unique example, I should think, in the history of philology. Through Paspates (Βυζαντινὰ Ἀνάκτορα, pp. 95, 140), we are made aware of the difficulties the topographical student has to encounter in the Ottoman capital, where an intruding Giaour is sure to be assailed in the more sequestered Turkish quarters with abuse and missiles on the part of men, women, and children.

[6] Alluded to by both Homer and Hesiod (Odyss., xii, 69; Theog., 992). It was one of those unknown countries which, as Plutarch remarks (Theseus, 1), were looked on as a fitting scene for mythical events.

[7] Pindar, Pythia, iv, 362; P. Mela, i, 19, etc.

[8] Of these Sinope claimed to be the eldest, and honoured the Argonauts as its founders (Strabo, xii, 3).

[9] *Ibid.*, vii, 6.

[10] Herodotus, iv, 144.

[11] Pliny, Hist. Nat., iv, 18 [11]. Ausonius compares Lygos to the Byrsa of Carthage (De Clar. Urb., 2).

[12] Not a Greek name; most likely that of a local chief.

[13] According to the Chronicon of Eusebius, Chalcedon was founded in Olymp. 26, 4, and Byzantium in Olymp. 30, 2, or 673, 659 B.C. In modern works of reference the dates 684, 667 seem to be most generally accepted. I pass over the legends associated with this foundation—the divine birth of Byzas; the oracle telling the emigrants to build opposite the city of the blind; another, which led the Argives (who were also concerned in the early history of Byzantium) to choose the confluence of the Cydarus and Barbyses, at the extremity of the Golden Horn, whence they were directed to the right spot by birds, who flew away with parts of their sacrifice—inventions or hearsay of later times, when the real circumstances were forgotten (see Strabo, vii, 6; Hesychius Miles, De Orig. CP., and others), all authors of comparatively late date. Herodotus (iv, 144), the nearest to the events (*c.* 450 B.C.), makes the plain statement that the Persian general Megabyzus said the Chalcedonians must have been blind when they overlooked the site of Byzantium.

[14] The remains of a "cyclopean" wall (Paspates, Βυζαντινὰ Ἀνάκτορα, p. 24), built with blocks of stone (some ten feet long?) probably belonged to old Byzantium, respecting which it is only certainly known that it stood at the north-east extremity of the promontory (Zosimus, ii, 30; Codinus, p. 24; with Mordtmann's Map, etc.). It can scarcely be doubted that the site of the Hippodrome was outside the original walls, and thus we have a limit on the land side. It may be assumed that the so-called first hill formed an acropolis, round which there was an external wall inclosing the main part of the town (Xenophon, Anabasis, vii, 1, etc.). Doubtless the citadel covered no great area, and the city walls were kept close to the water for as long a distance as possible to limit the extent of investment in a siege.

[15] Polybius, iv, 38, 45, etc. It was abolished after a war with Rhodes, 219 B.C.

[16] Tacitus, Annal., xii, 63, and commentators. Strabo, ii, 6; Pliny, Hist. Nat., ix, 20 [15]. They are mostly tunny fish, a large kind of mackerel. In the time of Gyllius, women and children caught them simply by letting down baskets into the water (De Top. CP. pref.; so also Busbecq). Grosvenor, a resident, mentions that seventy sorts of fish are found in the sea about the city (Constantinople, 1895, ii, p. 576).

[17] Strabo proves that the gulf was called the Horn, Pliny that the Horn was Golden (the promontory in his view), Dionysius Byzant. (Gyllius, De Bosp. Thrac., i, 5), that in the second century the inlet was named Golden Horn. Hesychius (*loc. cit.*) and Procopius (De Aedific., i, 5) say that Ceras was from Ceroessa, mother of Byzas.

[18] Dionys. Byz. in Gyllius, De Top. CP., i, 2. The statement is vague and can only be accepted with some modification in view of other descriptions.

[19] Livy, xxxii, 33.

[20] Phylarchus in Athenaeus, vi, 101.

[21] See Müller's Dorians, ii, 177.

[22] Hesychius, *loc. cit.*; Diodorus Sic., xvi, 77, etc.

[23] Polybius, iv, 46, etc.

[24] Cicero, Orat. de Prov. Consular., 3.

[25] Tacitus, *loc. cit.*; Pliny, Epist. to Trajan, 52.

[26] Suetonius, Vespasian, 8.

[27] Dion Cassius, 10, 14. I have combined and condensed the separate passages dealing with the subject.

[28] Herodian, iii, 1; Pausanias, iv, 31. Walls of this kind were built without cement, so that the joinings were hardly perceptible.

[29] At an earlier period it seems that there was only one harbour (Xenophon, Anabasis, vii, 1; Plutarch, Alcibiades, 31).

[30] A not uncommon acoustic phenomenon, such as occurs in the so-called "Ear [prison] of Dionysius" at Syracuse, etc. It can be credited without seeking for a mythical explanation.

[31] Suidas, *sb.* Severus; Herodian, iii, 7.

[32] The general details are from Dion Cassius, lxxiv, 12-14.

[33] Suidas, *loc. cit.*; Jn. Malala, xii, p. 291; Chron. Paschale, i, p. 495.

[34] Eustathius *ad* Dionys., Perieg. 804; Codinus, p. 13.

[35] Hist. August. Caracalla, 1. He is represented as a boy interceding with his father.

[36] Hist. August. Gallienus, 6, 13, etc.; Claudius, 9; Zosimus, i, 34, etc.; Aurelius Victor, De Caesar., xxxiii, etc. There is much to support the views in the text, which reconcile the somewhat discrepant statements of Dion and Herodian with those of later writers. The Goths seem to have been in possession of Byzantium—therefore it was unfortified (Zosimus, i, 34; Syncellus, i, p. 717). More than a century later, Fritigern was "at peace with stone walls" (Ammianus, xxxi, 6). I apply the description of Zosimus (ii, 30) to this wall of Gallienus (so to call it), which probably included a larger area, taking in the Hippodrome and other buildings of Severus.

[37] The tops of the various hills can now be distinguished by the presence of the following well-known buildings: 1. St. Sophia; 2. Burnt Pillar; 3. Seraskier's Tower; 4. Mosque of Mohammed II; 5. Mosque of Selim; 6. Mosque of Mihrimah (Gate of Adrianople); 7. Seven Towers (south-west extremity). The highest point in the city is the summit of the sixth hill, 291 ft. (Grosvenor).

[38] The last reach of the Barbyses runs through a Turkish pleasure ground and is well known locally as the "Sweet Waters of Europe."

[39] Procopius, De Aedific., i, 11.

[40] Notwithstanding the southerliness of these regions, natives of the Levant have always been well acquainted with frost and snow. Thus wintry weather is a favourite theme with Homer:

ἤματι χειμερίῳ. ..

κοιμήσας δ' ἀνέμους χέει ἔμπεδον, ὄφρα καλύψῃ

ὑψηλῶν ὀρέων κορυφὰς καὶ πρώονας ἄκρους,

καὶ πεδία λωτεῦντα καὶ ἀνδρῶν πίονα ἔργα,

καί τ' ἐφ' ἁλὸς πολιῆς κέχυται λιμέσιν τε καὶ ἀκταῖς,

κῦμα δέ μιν προσπλάζον ἐρύκεται· ἄλλα τε πάντα

εἴλυαται καθύπερθ' ὅτ ἐπιβρίσῃ Διὸς ὕμβρας.

Iliad, xii, 279, κ.τ.λ.

[41] His reasons for this step can only be surmised. A political motive is scarcely suggested. A second capital cannot have been required to maintain what Rome had conquered, and was soon made an excuse for dissolving the unity of the Empire. His nascent zeal for Christianity, by which he incurred unpopularity at pagan Rome, has been supposed to have prejudiced him against the old capital, and moved him to build another in which the new religion should reign supreme, but these opinions emanate only from writers actuated more or less by bigotry. Although he virtually presided at the Council of Nice and accepted baptism on his death-bed, that he was ever a Christian by conviction is altogether doubtful. For a *résumé* see Boissier, Revue des Deux Mondes, July, 1886; also Burchardt's Constantine.

[42] For the founding of Constantinople see Gyllius (De Topogr. CP., i, 3), but especially Ducange (CP. Christiana, i, p. 23 *et seq.*), who has brought together a large number of passages from early and late writers. According to a nameless author (Muller, Frag. Hist., iv, p. 199), Constantine was at one

time in the habit of exclaiming: "My Rome is Sardica." He was born and bred in the East, and hence all his tastes would naturally lead him to settle on that side of the Empire.

[43] It may have been earlier. Petavius (in Ducange) fixes this date, Baronius makes it 325 (*c.* 95).

[44] Plutarch, De Defect. Orac. He explains it by the death of the daemons who managed them. These semi-divinities, though long-lived, were not immortal.

[45] See Ducange, *loc. cit.*, p. 24.

[46] Philostorgius, ii, 9. Copied or repeated with embellishment, but not corroborated, by later writers, as Nicephorus Cal., viii, 4; Anon. (Banduri), p. 15; Codinus, p. 75. Eusebius is silent where we should expect him to be explicit. The allusion in Cod. Theod., XIII, v, 7, seems to be merely a pious expression.

[47] The result of Diocletian's persecution must have shown every penetrating spirit that Christianity had "come to stay": the numerous converts of the better classes were nearly all fanatics compared with Pagans of the same class, who were languid and indifferent about religion. He indulged both parties from time to time.

[48] Zosimus, ii, 30, Anon. Patria (Banduri, p. 4), and indications in Notitia Utriusque Imperii, etc., in which the length of Constantine's city is put down at 14,705 Roman feet. From Un Kapani on the Golden Horn (near old bridge) it swept round the mosque of Mohammed II, passed that of Exi Mermer, and turned south-east so as to strike the sea near Et Jemes, north-east of Sand-gate. I am describing the imaginary line drawn by Mordtmann (Esquisses topogr. de CP., 1891), who has given us a critical map without a scale to measure it by. It was not finished till after Constantine's death, Julian, Orat., i, p. 41, 1696.

[49] Anon. (Banduri) and Codinus *passim*; Eusebius, Vit. Constant., iii, 54, etc.; Jerome, Chron., viii, p. 678 (Migne).

[50] Zosimus, ii, 31.

[51] Or Florentia (blooming). Jn. Malala, xiii, p. 320, etc. Everything was done in imitation of Rome, which, as John Lydus tells us (De Mens., iv, 50), had three names, mystic, sacerdotal, and political—Amor, Flora, Rome.

[52] Cedrenus, i, p. 495; Zonaras, xiii, 3. Eusebius knows nothing of it. See Ducange's collection of authorities (CP. Christ., i, p. 24), all late, *e.g.,* Phrantzes, iii, 6.

[53] Anon. (Banduri), p. 5; Codinus, p. 20. The stories of these writers do not deserve much credit. Glycas, however, accepts the tale and is a sounder authority, iv, p. 463. "It is well known that the flower of your nobility was translated to the royal city of the East," said Frederic Barbarossa, addressing the Roman Senate in 1155 (Otto Frising. Muratori, Rer. Ital. Script., vi, 721).

[54] Eunapius in Aedesius. Burchardt jeers at C. and his new citizens.

[55] Idatius, Descript. Consul. (Migne, S. L., li, 908). The accepted date.

[56] Jn. Lydus, De Mensibus, iv, 2. "A bloodless sacrifice" (Jn. Malala, p. 320). According to later writers (Anon., Banduri, etc.) the "Kyrie Eleison" was sung, a statement we can easily disbelieve.

[57] Jn. Malala, xiii, p. 321; Chron. Paschal., i, p. 529.

[58] Anon. (Banduri), p. 4. *Ibid.* (Papias), p. 84.

[59] In cloaks and Byzantine buskins, "chlaenis et campagis" (Κάμπαγος or κομβαῶν). For the latter see Daremberg and Saglio, Dict. Antiq., *sb. voc.* They covered the toe and heel, leaving the instep bare to the ground.

[60] Jn. Malala and Chron. Paschal., *loc. cit.*, etc.

[61] M. Glycas, iv, p. 463. Eusebius does not describe the founding of CP., doubtless because he saw nothing in it pertinent to Christian piety, of which only he professes to treat (τὰ πρὸς τὸν θεοφιλῆ), Vit. Const., i, 11.

[62] The name occurs in Cod. Theod. from 323 onwards, but also as a palpable error at an earlier date. See Haenel's Chronological Index. It is thought coins stamped CP. were issued as early as 325 (Smith, Dict. Christ. Biog., i, p. 631). Had Constantine fixed on any other place it is probable that "New Rome" would have passed into currency as easily as "New York." But the Greeks did not call their city Constantinople till later centuries. Thus with Procopius, the chief writer of the sixth century, it is always still Byzantium.

[63] Socrates, i, 16; Sozomen, ii, 3; Cod. Theod., XIV, xiii, etc.

[64] Socrates, *loc. cit.*

[65] Anon. Valesii, 30.

[66] The last Roman emperor, in name only, Romulus Augustulus, abdicated in 476, but long before that date the Empire had been gradually falling to pieces. In 410 Alaric sacked Rome; by 419 the Goths had settled in the south of France and the Vandals had appropriated Spain; in 439 Genseric took possession of Africa; in 446 Britain was abandoned; in 455 Rome was again sacked (by Genseric), etc.

[67] Ciampini (De Sacr. Aedific., a C. Mag., etc., Rome, 1693), enumerates twenty-seven. Eusebius says many (Vit. C., iii, 48). It is curious, however, that the dialogue Philopatris (in Lucian) gives an impression that in or after 363 (Gesner's date, formerly accepted) churches were so few and inconspicuous that the bulk of the population knew nothing about them. The Notitia, again, half a century later, reckons only fourteen within the city proper, including Sycae (Galata). Probably, therefore, these twenty-seven churches attributed to Constantine are mostly suppositious, for even in the reign of Arcadius it would seem that there were not many more than half that number.

[68] Socrates, i, 16. Two only, as if Constantine had built no more.

[69] Chron. Paschal., i, p. 531.

[70] Eusebius, iv, 58. *Op. cit.*

[71] Anon. (Banduri), p. 45; Codinus, p. 72.

[72] Hesychius, *op. cit.*, 15 (Codinus, p. 6).

[73] Cicero (Orat. De Prov. Consul., 4) says that Byzantium was "refertissimam atque ornatissimam signis," a statement which doubtless applies chiefly to works of art preserved in temples. The buildings would remain and be restored, notwithstanding the many vicissitudes through which the town passed. The Anon. (Banduri, p. 2) says that ruins of a temple of Zeus, columns and arches, were still seen on the Acropolis (first hill) in the twelfth century.

[74] Eunapius, *loc. cit.*, Themistius, Orats., Paris, 1684, pp. 182, 223, "equal to Rome"; Sozomen, "more populous than Rome"; Novel lxxx forbids the crowding of provincials to CP.

[75] Cod. Theod., XV, i. 51; Socrates, vii, 1, etc.

[76] Marcellinus, Chron. (Migne, li, 927). See also Evagrius, i, 17, and Ducange, *op. cit.*, i, p. 38.

[77] Priscus, Hist. Goth., p. 168. In 433.

[78] The work of Cyrus is not precisely defined by the Byzantine historians, but Déthier (Der Bosph. u. CP., 1873, pp. 12, 50) and Mordtmann (*op. cit.*, p. 11) take this view. The words of one inscription, "he built a wall to a wall" (ἐδείματο τείχεϊ τεῖχος), support the theory. The walls of Theodosius were afterwards called the "new walls" (Cod. Just., I, ii, 18; Novel lix, 5, etc.).

[79] On the Porta Rhegii or Melandesia, about halfway across. See Paspates (Βυζαντιναὶ Μελέται, pp. 47, 50). They are preserved in the Anthol. Graec.

(Planudes), iv. 28. The gate called Xylocercus, with its inscription, has disappeared.

[80] Marcellinus, *loc. cit.*; Zonaras, xiii, 22; Nicephorus Cal., xiv, 1, confuses the work of the two men. The Anon. Patria (Banduri), p. 20, says that the two factions of the circus, each containing eight thousand men, were employed on the work. Beginning at either end, they met centrally at a gate hence called "of many men" (Polyandra). Mordtmann (*op. cit.*, p. 28) wholly rejects this tale, as it does not fit in with some of his identifications. It would, however, be well suited to the P. Rhegii, where the existing inscriptions are found. Some local knowledge must be conceded to an author of the twelfth century, who probably lived on the spot. Wall-building was a *duty* of the factions.

[81] Dionysius caused the Syracusans to build the wall of Epipolae, of about the same length, in twenty days (Diod. Sic., xiv, 18). The Peloponnesians built a wall across the isthmus against Xerxes in a short time (Herodotus, viii, 71, etc.). There was much extemporary wall-building at Syracuse during the siege by Nicias (Thucydides, vi, 97, etc.). The wall of Crassus against Spartacus was nearly forty miles long (Plutarch, Crassus). Except the first, however, these were more or less temporary structures. Very substantial extempore walls are frequently mentioned by both Greek and Latin historians as having been erected during sieges, etc. See especially Caesar (i, 8) and Thucydides (iii, 21, Siege of Plataea).

[82] The earliest and most reliable source is the Notitia Dignitatis utriusque Imperii, etc., which dates from the time of Arcadius. To this work is prefixed a short description of Rome and CP., which enumerates the chief buildings, the number of streets, etc., in each division of those cities. Next we have the Aedificia of Procopius, the matter of which, however, does not come within the scope of the present chapter. A gap of six centuries now occurs, which can only be filled by allusions to be found in general and church historians, patristic literature, etc. We then come to a considerable work, the Anonymous, edited by A. Banduri (Venice, 1729), a medley of semi-historical and topographical information, often erroneous, ascribed to the twelfth century. A second edition of this work, introduced by the Byzantine fragment of Hesychius of Miletus, passes under the name of Geo. Codinus, who wrote about 1460. Here we draw the line between mediaeval and modern authors, and we have next the Topography of CP., by P. Gyllius, a Frenchman, who wrote on the spot about a century after the Turkish conquest. His Thracian Bosphorus, which preserves much of the lost Dionysius of Byzantium, is also valuable. Later still comes the monumental CP. Christiana of Ducange (Paris, 1680), a mine of research, by one of those almost mediaeval scholars, who spent their lives in a library. Of contemporary treatises, which are numerous and bulky, I will only mention

the following, from which I have derived most assistance: J. Labarte, Le Palais Impériale de CP., Paris, 1871; A. G. Paspates, Βυζαντιναὶ Μελέται, CP., 1877, and Βυζαντινα Ἀνάκτορα, Athens, 1885; W. Mordtmann, Esquisses topographiques de CP., Lille, 1891. Among books intended less for the archaeologist than for popular perusal, the only one worthy of special mention is Constantinople, Lond., 1895, by E. A. Grosvenor, a fine work, admirably illustrated, but the author relies too implicitly on Paspates, and he has emasculated his book for literary purposes by omitting references to authorities. The book also contains several absurd mistakes, *e.g.*, "The careful historian who ... wrote under the name of Anonymos," etc., p. 313. To the above must now be added the important, Byzantine CP., the Walls, by Van Millingen, Lond., 1899, a sound and critical work. Another beautiful work has also been recently issued, viz., Beylié, L'Habitation byzantine, Grenoble, 1902. A wealth of authentic illustrations renders it extremely valuable for the study of the subject. This chapter was begun in 1896, and in the meantime scholars have not been idle. As the Bonn Codinus gives inter-textually all the passages of the anonymous Patria which differ, as well as an appendix of anonymous archaeological tracts, I shall in future, for the sake of brevity, refer to the whole as Codinus simply in that edition.

[83] That is the pierced dome elevated to a great height on pendentives. The splendid dome of the Pantheon dates, of course, from Hadrian, but the invention of the modern cupola may fairly be assigned to the Byzantines. The conception, however, had to be completed by raising it still higher on a *tour de dome*, the first example of which is St. Augustine's, Rome (1483); see Agincourt, Hist. of Art, i, 67.

[84] Procopius, De Aedific., i, 3; Nicephorus Cal., xv, 25.

[85] Κυκλόβιον or στρογγύλον; Procopius, *ibid.*, iv, 8. Theophanes, an. 6165, p. 541, etc. Possibly it looked like the tomb of Caecilia Metella or a Martello Tower and was the prototype of the castle shown on the old maps as the "Grand Turk's Treasure-house," built in 1458 by Mohammed II within his fortress of the Seven Towers; Map by Caedicius, CP., 1889; Ducas, p. 317; Laonicus, x, p. 529. Most likely, however, it was a wall uniting five towers in a round. The Cyclobion is attributed to Zeno, about 480; Byzantios, Κωνσταντινούπολις, i, 312; Grosvenor, *op. cit.*, p. 596.

[86] Grosvenor calls the existing road the remains of Justinian's "once well-paved triumphal way," I have found no corroboration of this assertion. From Constant. Porph. (De Cer. Aul. Byz., i, 18, 96, etc.), I conclude there was no continuous road here for many centuries afterwards. Paspates (*op. cit.*, p. 13) thinks the last passage alludes to it as πλακωτῆ, but this is evidently the highway to Rhegium, etc. (Procop., De Aedific., iv, 8).

[87] Cod. VIII, x, 10; Procopius, De Bel. Pers., i, 25; Cinnamus, ii, 14; Anthol. (Planudes), iv, 15, etc.

[88] This fount is still extant and accessible beneath the Greek church of Baloukli (Grosvenor, *op. cit.*, p. 485, etc.).

[89] Gyllius (Dionys. Byz.), De Bosp. Thrac., ii, 2; De Topog. CP., iv, 5.

[90] Suidas, *sub* Anast. Mordtmann (*op. cit.*, p. 33), thinks the ruins existing at Tekfur Serai may represent the original Palace of Blachernae, the basement, at least. It is commonly called the palace of Constantine, etc., but Van Millingen proves it to be a late erection.

[91] Zonaras, xiii, 24; Codin., p. 95, etc.

[92] Const. Porph., De Cer. Aul. Byz., ii, 12. Still frequented (Paspates, *op. cit.*, p. 390, etc.).

[93] To "a man's height" (Paspates).

[94] Paspates has all the credit of solving the problem of this moat (*op. cit.*, p. 7, etc.). It has been maintained that it was a dry moat, owing to the physical impossibility of the sea flowing into it. The words of Chrysoloras (Migne, Ser. Grk., vol. 156, etc.) are alone sufficient to dispose of this error.

[95] This space seems to have been called the παρατείχιον; Const. Porph., *loc. cit.*; or rather, perhaps, the πρωτείχισμα; see the Anon., Στρατηγική (Koechly, etc.), 12 (*c.* 550). Paspates calls it the προτείχιον, "because," says he, "I have found no name for it in the Byzantine historians."

[96] Ducas, 39, etc.; Paspates, *op. cit.*, p. 6. It is, however, the usual word for the walls of a city. Μεσοτείχιον and σταύρωμα are more definite; Critobulos, i, 60. Paspates states that the ground here has been raised six feet above its ancient level.

[97] Déthier, Nouv. recherch. à CP., 1867, p. 20; cf. Vegetius, iv, 1, 2, 3, etc. These walls have much similarity to the *agger* of Servius Tullius, but in the latter case the great wall forms the inner boundary of the trench and the lesser wall, retaining the excavated earth, was about fifty feet behind in the city. See Middleton's Ancient Rome, etc.

[98] Paspates, *op. cit.*, p. 17.

[99] *Ibid.*, Grosvenor, *op. cit.*, p. 584.

[100] Paspates, *op. cit.*, p. 10. See also Texier and Pullan, Architect. Byzant., Lond., 1864, pp. 24, 56, for diagrams illustrating walls of the period. Some, unlike the wall of CP., had continuous galleries in the interior. The towers were also used for quartering soldiers when troops were massed in the vicinity of the city (Cod. Theod., VII, viii, 13). There were about one hundred

and two of the great, and ninety of the small ones. Owners of land through which the new wall passed had also reversionary rights to make use of the towers (*Ibid.*, XV, i, 51).

[101] The Roman plan of filling an outer shell with rubble and concrete was adopted (Grosvenor, *loc. cit.*). At present the walls appear as a heterogeneous mass of stone and brick, showing that they have been repaired hurriedly numbers of times. But little is left of the fifth century structure. Some parts, better preserved, exhibit alternate courses of stone and brick, a favourite style of building with the Byzantines, but not dating further back than the seventh century (Texier and Pullan, *op. cit.*, p. 165).

[102] Paspates (*op. cit.*, p. 14), to whom much more than to historical indications we are indebted for our knowledge of these walls.

[103] Those who have a topographical acquaintance with Stamboul are aware that at about three-quarters of a mile from the Golden Horn the wall turns abruptly to the west and makes a circuit as if to include a supplementary area of ground. It is well understood that this part, which is single for the most part and without a moat, but by compensation on a still more colossal scale, is the work of later emperors—Heraclius, Leo Armenius, Manuel Comnenus, and Isaac Angelus (600 to 1200). All traces of the wall of Theodosius, which ran inside, have disappeared, according to Paspates, but Mordtmann thinks he can recognize certain ruined portions (*op. cit.*, p. 11 and Map).

[104] Or from Charisius, one of the masters of the works (Codin., p. 110).

[105] It appears that Anthemius in 413 (Cod. Theod., XV, i, 51) only raised the great wall, and that in 447, when fifty-seven towers collapsed (Marcellin. Com., A.D. 447; Chron. Pasch., 447, 450 A.D.), Cyrus repaired the damage and added the lesser wall (Theophanes, an. 5937; Cedrenus, i, p. 598, and the words ἐδείματο τείχεϊ τεῖχος of the inscription). Cedrenus states virtually that he demolished the wall and replaced it by three others, alluding perhaps to the moat, but Cedrenus is often wrong. All seven (or nine) chronographists relate more or less exactly that Cyrus gained such popularity by his works that the public acclamations offended the Emperor, who forced the tonsure on him and sent him to Smyrna as bishop in the hope that the turbulent populace, who had already killed four of their bishops, would speedily add him to the number. By his ready wit, however, he diverted their evil designs and won their respect. Zonaras, xiii, 22, and Nicephorus Cal., xiv, 1, have an incorrect idea of the wall-building. According to the latter, Anthemius was the man of speed. Malala mentions Cyrus, but not the wall.

[106] The Greek verses are given in the Anthology (Planudes, iv, 28). The Latin I may reproduce here:

Theudosii jussis gemino nec mense peracto

Constantinus ovans haec moenia firma locavit.

Tam cito tam stabilem Pallas vix conderet arcem.

This epigram and its companion in Greek are still legible on the stone of the Rhegium Gate (now of Melandesia). See Paspates, *op. cit.*, pp. 47, 50. The Porta Xylocerci has practically disappeared.

[107] Mordtmann's exposition of these gates is the most convincing (*op. cit.*, p. 16, etc.). I have omitted the Gate of the Seven Towers as it has always been claimed as a Turkish innovation, a view, however, which he rejects. In any case it was but a postern—there may have been others such in the extinct section of the wall.

[108] That is an S, which at this period was formed roughly like our C.

[109] Cedrenus, ii, p. 173; or a personification of the city; Codin., p. 47.

[110] Zonaras, xv, 4.

[111] A fragment still exists on the northern tower. See Grosvenor, *op. cit.*, p. 591.

[112] Chrysoloras, *loc. cit.*, Gyllius, De Top. CP., iv, 9.

[113] *Ibid.* Gyllius would seem to have been inside when making these observations, but that would be within the fortress of Yedi Koulé, rigorously guarded at that time. Doubtless the city side was adorned, but no description of the gate as a whole is left to us. The ornaments are only mentioned incidentally when recording damage done by earthquakes (in their frequency often the best friends of the modern archaeologist) and their arrangement can only be guessed at. Most likely they were of gilded bronze, a common kind of statue among the Byzantines. See Codinus, *passim*. The idea that the Golden Gate opened into a fortress should be abandoned. The conception of the Seven Towers seems to have originated with the Palaeologi in 1390, but Bajazet ordered the demolition of the unfinished works (Ducas, 13), and it was left to the Turkish conqueror to carry out the idea in 1458. See p. 26. I may remark here that Mordtmann's map has not been brought up to date as regards his own text.

[114] Cedrenus, i, p. 675.

[115] *Ibid.*, i, p. 567; Codin., pp. 26, 47; said to have been brought from the temple of Mars at Athens.

[116] The first Golden Gate was erected, or rather transformed, by Theodosius I, as the following epigram, inscribed on the gate, shows (Corp. Inscript. Lat., Berlin, 1873, No. 735):

Haec loca Theudosius decorat post fata tyranni,

Aurea secla gerit, qui portam construit auro.

It was, of course, in the wall of Constantine (Codin., p. 122) and seems to have remained to a late date—Map of Buondelmonte, Ducange, CP. Christ., etc. For a probable representation see Banduri, Imp. Orient., ii, pl. xi. But Van Millingen (*op. cit.*), having found traces of the inscription on the remaining structure, considers there never was any other. In that case it was at first a triumphal arch outside the walls.

[117] The remarkable structure known as the Marble Tower, rising from the waters of the Marmora to the height of a hundred feet, near the junction of the sea-and land-wall is of later date, but its founder is unknown and it has no clear history in Byzantine times. See Mordtmann, *op. cit.*, p. 13.

[118] Glycas, iv; Codin., p. 128. A legend, perhaps, owing to *débris* of walls ruined by earthquakes collecting there in the course of centuries.

[119] See Mordtmann, *op. cit.*, p. 60; Codin., p. 109.

[120] Codin., p. 101. Great hulks of timber were built to float obelisks and marble columns over the Mediterranean; Ammianus, xvii, 4.

[121] *Ibid.*, p. 102.

[122] Codin., pp. 49, 104.

[123] Notitia, Reg. 12.

[124] Codin., *loc. cit.*

[125] Gyllius, De Top. CP., iv, 8.

[126] Mordtmann, *op. cit.*, p. 59.

[127] Zosimus, iii, 11; Codin., p. 87.

[128] Notitia, Reg. 3. We hear of a trumpet-tower (βύκινον, Codin., p. 86; βύκανον, Nicetas Chon., p. 733) by this harbour fitted with a "siren" formed of brass pipes, whose mouths protruding outside resounded when they caught the wind blowing off the sea. Ducange, i, p. 13, thinks a later fable has risen out of the vocal towers of Byzantium. "Sic nugas nugantur Graeculi nugigeruli," says Banduri (ii, p. 487). There was certainly a watch-tower here, but of origin and date unknown. Mordtmann, *op. cit.*, p. 55.

[129] Codin., *loc. cit.*

[130] Marcel. Com., an. 409.

[131] Suidas, *sb.*, Anast. In a later age this port was enlarged and defended by an iron grill. Anton. Novog. in Mordtmann, *op. cit.*, p. 55.

[132] About fifty feet above it; for a photograph of the existing ruins see Grosvenor, *op. cit.*, p. 388. Also Van Millingen's work and others.

[133] William of Tyre, xx, 25.

[134] Anna Comn., iii, 1.

[135] Zonaras, xv, 25, etc.; Const. Porph., i, 19, etc.

[136] Codin., p. 100, says the palace was founded by Theodosius II. The group was probably ravished from some classic site at an early period when the mania for decorating CP. was still rife. The existence of the harbour at this date may be darkly inferred from Socrates, ii, 16; Sozomen, iii, 9; Procopius, De Bel. Pers., i, 24; Theophanes, an. 6003. Τὰς πύλας τοῦ βασιλείου πανταχόθεν ἀπέκλεισεν, καί πλοῖα εἰς τὸ φυγεῖν, τῷ παλατίῳ παρέστησεν; Theodore Lect., ii, 26. All these passages prove the existence of a harbour approachable only from the palace, which probably was then, or afterwards became, the Boukoleon. Van Millingen (*op. cit.*) gives good reasons for placing the Boukoleon on this site, the only likely one (see Appendix). The name Boukoleon is not found in literature before 800; Theoph., Cont., i, 11. From *ibid.*, vi, 15, it may be inferred that the main group of statuary had long been in position.

[137] For his story see Zosimus, ii, 27; Ammianus, xvi, 10. He was a Christian who escaped from prison to the court of Constantine; see Appendix.

[138] Nicephorus Cal., xiv, 2, etc.

[139] *Ibid.*, Niceph. Greg., iv, 2, etc.; Codin., De Offic. CP., 12.

[140] Ἡ Ὁδηγός. The place was called Ὁδηγήτρια; Codin., p. 80.

[141] *Ibid.*

[142] Or a monastery for blind monks, perhaps; Niceph. Greg., xi, 9, etc.

[143] Probably the Master of the Infantry under Theodosius I; Zosimus, iv, 45, etc.

[144] It is said that those going from Byzantium to Chalcedon, at the mouth of the Bosphorus on the Asiatic side, were obliged to start from here and make a peculiar circuit to avoid adverse currents. See Gyllius, *op. cit.*, iii, 1.

[145] That is, the fig-region, Codin. (Hesych.), p. 6. Now Galata and Pera.

[146] The Constantinopolitans generally confounded this name with the legendary Phosphoros (see p. 5), and the geographical Bosporos. The Notitia (Reg. 5) proves its real form and significance; also Evagrius, ii, 13.

[147] Codin., pp. 52, 60, 188. This ox was believed to bellow once a year to warn the city of the advent of some calamity (*ibid.*, p. 60).

[148] *Ibid.*, p. 113. The wall here formed another Sigma to surround the inner sweep of the port. These two harbours we may suppose to be those of Byzantium as known to Dion Cassius (see p. 7).

[149] A patrician, who came from Rome with Constantine and took a share in adorning the city (Glycas, iv, p. 463), or another, who lived under Theodosius I (Codin., p. 77).

[150] Codin., p. 114; Cedrenus, ii, p. 80; Leo Diac., p. 78. This tower was standing up to 1817; see Κωνσταντινιαδε, Venice, 1824, p. 14, by Constantius, Archbishop of CP. This appears to be the first attempt by a modern Greek to investigate the antiquities of CP. He had to disguise himself as a dervish to explore Stamboul, for which he was banished to the Prince's Islands, and his book was publicly burnt.

[151] Leo Diac. (*loc. cit.*) explains how the chain was supported at intervals on piles. It seems to have been first used in 717 by Leo Isaurus; Theophanes, i, p. 609; Manuel Comn. even drew a chain across the Bosphorus from CP. to the tower called Arcula (Maiden's T., etc.), which he constructed for the purpose (Nicetas Chon., vii, 3).

[152] Theophanes, an. 6024; Codin., p. 93. The "junction," that of the mules to the vehicle containing the relics of St. Stephen newly arrived from Alexandria!

[153] Xenophon notices the plenty of timber on these coasts (Anab., vi, 2).

[154] Strabo, vii, 6; Gyllius, *op. cit.*, iii, 9.

[155] Zosimus, ii, 35. This circumstance, and the fact that almost all the towers along here bear the name of Theophilus (Paspates, *op. cit.*, p. 4), suggest that this side was not walled till the ninth century. Chron. Paschal. (an. 439) doubtless refers only to the completion of the wall on the Propontis. Grosvenor (p. 570) adopts this view, but as usual without giving reasons or references. He is wrong in saying that the chain was first broken in 1203 by the Crusaders; it was broken in 823 (Cedrenus, p. 80; Zonaras, xv, 23). I do not credit the statement of Sidonius Ap. (Laus Anthemii) that houses were raised in the Propontis on foundations formed of hydraulic cement from Puteoli. In any case, such could have been obtained much nearer, viz., across the water at Cyzicus (Pliny, Hist. Nat., xxxv, 47). The Bp. of Clermont never visited CP.

[156] Notitia, Reg. 14. There was a populous suburb at Blachernae, which had walls of its own before Theodosius included it within the city proper.

[157] Codin., pp. 30, 120; Suidas, *sb*. Mamante (St. Mamas, however, appears to have been outside the walls; Theophanes, an. 6304, etc.); Glycas, iv. Versions of the same story, probably. Gyllius' memory fails him on this occasion.

[158] Ἀργυρολίμνη; see Paspates, *op. cit.*, p. 68.

[159] Chrysoloras, *loc. cit*. The Notitia enumerates fifty-two, which we may understand to be pairs, before the enlargement by Theodosius.

[160] Codin., p. 22. In this account the patricians, who accompanied Constantine, are represented as undertaking many of the public buildings at their own expense. See also Nonius Marc. (in Pancirolo ad Notit.). In this case a testator wills that a portico with silver and marble statues be erected in his native town.

[161] Cod. Theod., XV, i, 44; iv; vii, 12, etc., with Godfrey's commentary. The imperial portraits were painted in white on a blue ground; Chrysostom, 1 Cor., x, 1 (in Migne, iii, 247). "The countenance of the Emperor must be set up in courts, market-places, assemblies, theatres, and wherever business is transacted, that he may safeguard the proceedings"; Severianus, De Mund. Creat., vi, 5 (apud. Chrysost., Migne, vi, 489).

[162] Cod. Theod., *loc. cit.*; Philostorgius, ii, 17.

[163] *Ibid.*, IX, xliv; Institut., i, 8. On proof the master could be compelled to sell the slave on the chance of his acquiring more congenial service, but the privilege was often abused.

[164] *Ibid.*, XV, vii, 12.

[165] *Ibid.*, XV, i, 52.

[166] *Ibid.*, 53; Vitruvius, v, 11, etc.

[167] Cod., VIII, x, 12. A Greek Constitution of Zeno of considerable length, and uniquely instructive on some points. These οἰκήματα were limited to six feet of length and seven of height.

[168] Novel cxxxvi; Plato, Apol., 17, etc.

[169] Whence called *emboliariae* (ἱμβολος being Byzantine for portico). So say Alemannus *ad* Procop. (Hist. Arcan., p. 381) and his copyist Byzantios (*op. cit.*, i, p. 113), but Pliny seems to use the word for an actress in interludes (H. N., vii, 49), an occupation not, however, very different.

[170] Theophanes, Cont., p. 417. In the severe winter of 933, Romanus Lecapenus blocked the interspaces and fitted them with windows and doors.

[171] They are, in fact, called the "narrows" in the Greek στενωποί.

[172] Παρακύπτικος, Cod., *loc. cit.*

[173] Texier and Pullan, *op. cit.*, p. 4; Agincourt, Hist. of Art, i, pl. 25. Mica or talc (*lapis specularis*) was commonly used at Rome for windows (Pliny, H. N., xxxvi, 45). Gibbon rather carelessly says that Firmus (*c.* 272) had glass windows; they were vitreous squares for wall decoration (Hist. August., *sb.* Firmo). Half a century later Lactantius is clear enough—"fenestras lucente vitro aut speculari lapide obductas" (De Opif. Dei, 8). Pliny tells us that clear glass was most expensive, and, six centuries later, Isidore of Seville makes the same remark (Hist. Nat., xxxvi, 67; Etymologies, xvi, 16).

[174] The climate of the East requires that windows shall generally be kept open; even shutters are often dispensed with.

[175] See Cod. Theod., XV, i, De Op. Pub., *passim*. This legislation was initiated by Leo Thrax, probably after the great fire of 469 (Jn. Malala; Chron. Pasch., etc.).

[176] Zosimus, ii, 35.

[177] Cod., *loc. cit.*

[178] Agathias, v, 3.

[179] A century earlier there were 322 according to the Notitia.

[180] Zeno, Cod., *loc. cit.*

[181] We know little of the *insulae* or συνοικίαι of CP., but we can conceive of no other kind of private house requiring such an elevation. Besides, *insulae* are the subject of an argument in Cod., VIII, xxxviii, 15 (enacted at CP. about this time).

[182] Chrysostom, In Psal. xlviii, 8 (Migne, v, 510); Agathias, *loc. cit.*; Texier and Pullan, *loc. cit.*

[183] Niceph. Greg., viii, 5. Merely a tradition in his time; it is commonly called the column of Theodosius. Grosvenor absurdly places on it an equestrian statue of Theodosius I, with an epigram which belongs to another place; *op. cit.*, p. 386; see *infra*. Founded on a rock, it has withstood the commotions of seventeen centuries.

[184] Hist. August., *sb.* Gallieno. Much more likely than Claudius II; everything points to its being a local civic memorial. "Pugnatum est circa

Pontum, et a Byzantiis ducibus victi sunt barbari. Veneriano item duce, navali bello Gothi superati sunt, tum ipse militari periit morte" (*c*. 266).

[185] "Fortunae reduci ob devictos Gothos." The Goths had been in possession of Byzantium and the adjacent country on both sides of the water; G. Syncell., i, p. 717, etc.; Zosimus, i, 34, etc. There was a temple to Gallienus at Byzantium; Codinus, p. 179. He was evidently popular here.

[186] Jn. Lydus, De Mens., iii, 48.

[187] Codin., p. 74; Glycas, iv, p. 468.

[188] *Ibid.*

[189] Codin., p. 31; Notitia, Reg. 2.

[190] Zosimus, ii, 31.

[191] Jn. Lydus, De Mens., iv, 86; Codinus, pp. 15, 28.

[192] See the plates in Banduri, *op. cit.*, ii; repeated in Agincourt on a small scale, *op. cit.*, ii, 11; i, 27. Déthier (*op. cit.*) throws some doubt on the accuracy of these delineations, the foundation of which the reader can see for himself in Agincourt without resorting to the athleticism imposed on himself by Déthier. The Erechtheum shows that the design could be varied, the Pantheon that the dome was in use long before this date; see Texier and Pullan, etc.

[193] Leo Gram., p. 126, etc.

[194] Codin., p. 60; Theophanes, i, p. 439.

[195] His architect was named Aetherius; Cedrenus, i, p. 563. Probably a short but wide colonnade flanked by double ranges of pillars; Anthol. (Plan.), iv. 23.

[196] Several names are given to these palatines or palace guards, but it is not always certain which are collective and which special. Procopius mentions the above; the Scholars were originally Armenians (Anecdot. 24, 26, etc.). Four distinct bodies can be collected from Const. Porph. De Cer. Aul. Codinus (p. 18) attributes the founding of their quarters to Constantine; see Cod. Theod., VI, and Cod., XII. All the household troops were termed Domestics, horse and foot; Notit. Dig.

[197] See Const. Porph., De Cer. Aul., *passim*, with Reiske's note on the Candidati.

[198] Codin., p. 18; Chron. Pasch. (an. 532) calls them porticoes.

[199] See an illustration in Gori, Thesaur. Vet. Diptych.; reduced in Agincourt, *op. cit.*, ii, 12, also another in Montfaucon containing a female

figure supposed to be the Empress Placidia Galla; III, i, p. 46 (but Gori makes it a male figure!). The *kiborion* (a cup), also called *kamelaukion* (literally a sort of head covering), was sometimes fixed, in which case the columns might be of marble. Silver pillars are mentioned in Const. Porph., *op. cit.*, i, 1; cf. Texier and Pullan, *op. cit.*, p. 135, a cut of an elaborate silver *kiborion*. From Gori it may be seen that the design of these state chairs is almost always that of a seat supported at each of the front corners by a lion's head and claw, etc.

[200] Built by Constantine; Codin., p. 18.

[201] Another foundation of Constantine, clearly enough from Chron. Pasch. (an. 328, p. 528), as Labarte remarks (*op. cit.*, p. 137).

[202] Codin., p. 100; it had been brought from Rome. I prefer this indigenous explanation to the surmise of Reiske (Const. Porph., *op. cit.*, ii, p. 49), that it was here that the victors in the games received their crowns of laurel (Δάφνη):

Nay, lady, sit; if I but wave this wand,

Your nerves are all bound up in alabaster,

And you a statue, or, as Daphne was,

Root-bound that fled Apollo.

MILTON'S Comus.

[203] Codin., p. 101; the most likely position, as a surmise.

[204] Jn. Malala, xvi; Zonaras, xiv, 3, etc.

[205] Procopius, De Bel. Pers., ii, 21, etc. "Three decurions marshalled the thirty brilliantly armed Silentiaries who paced backwards and forwards before the purple veil guarding the slumber of the sovereign"; Hodgkin, Cassiodorus, p. 88.

[206] Codin., p. 101; see the plans of Labarte and Paspates.

[207] Built by Constantine according to Codinus (p. 19) as emended by Lambecius. The original palace extended eastward to the district called Τόποι (*ibid.*, p. 79), on the shore near the Bucoleon.

[208] The conception of the sanctity of the Emperor's person, which originated in the adulation of the proconsuls of the eastern provinces by the Orientals and in the subservience of the Senate to Augustus, attained its height under Diocletian (*c.* 300), who first introduced at Court the Oriental forms of adoration and prostration (Eutropius, ix, etc.). It was probably even increased under the Christian emperors, and Theodosius I was enabled to

promulgate a law that merely to doubt the correctness of the Emperor's opinion or judgement constituted a sacrilege (Cod., IX, xxix, 3, etc.).

[209] Cod. Theod., VI, viii; Cod., XII, v.

[210] Theophanes, Cont., iv, 35; cf. Symeon, Mag., p. 681, where the invention is ascribed to Bp. Leo of Thessalonica under Theophilus. The stations by which an inroad of the Saracens was reported *c. 800* are here given. Its use for signalling at this date cannot be asserted definitely, but it was a relic of old Byzantium erected as a nautical light-house; Ammianus, xxii, 8.

[211] Codin., p. 81; the particular area to which this name was applied seems to have been a polo ground; Theoph., Cont., v, 86, and Reiske's note to Const. Porph., ii, p. 362. It was encompassed by flower gardens.

[212] Marrast has given us his notion of these gardens at some length: "Entre des haies de phyllyrea taillées de façon de figurer des lettres grecques et orientales, des sentiers dallés de marbre aboutissaient à un phialée entourée de douze dragons de bronze.... Une eau parfumée en jaillissait et ruisselait par dessus les branches des palmiers et des cedres dorés jusqu'à hauteur d'homme. Des paons de la Chine, des faisans et des ibis, volaient en liberté dans les arbres ou s'abattaient sur le sol, semé d'un sable d'or apporté d'Asie à grands frais." La vie byzantine au VIe siècle, Paris, 1881, p. 67.

[213] Labarte gives these walls, towers, etc. Doubtless the palace was well protected from the first, but did not assume the appearance of an actual fortress till the tenth century under Nicephorus Phocas; Leo Diac., iv, 6.

[214] Codin., p. 95 (?); Const. Porph., i, 21, etc. Probably a structure like the elevated portico at Antioch mentioned by Theodoret, iv, 26.

[215] Luitprand, Antapodosis, i, 6. A legend of a later age, no doubt, which may be quietly interred with Constantine's gift to Pope Sylvester. We hear nothing of it in connection with Arcadius, Theodosius II, etc., and it is only foreshadowed in 797 by a late writer (Cedrenus, ii, p. 27), who would assume anything. The epithet became fashionable in the tenth century. One writer thinks the name arose from a ceremonial gift of purple robes to the wives of the court dignitaries at the beginning of each winter by the empress; Theoph., Cont., iii, 44.

[216] Anna Comn., vii, 2.

[217] The archaeological student may refer to the elaborate reconstructions by Labarte and Paspates of the palace as it existed in the tenth century. Their conceptions differ considerably, the former writer being generally in close accord with the literary indications. Paspates is too Procrustean in his methods, and unduly desirous of identifying every recoverable fragment of

masonry. Their works are based almost entirely on the Book of Ceremonies of Constantine VII, but even if such a manual existed for the date under consideration the historical reader would soon tire of an exposition setting forth the order and decoration of a hundred chambers.

[218] Codin., pp. 16, 130.

[219] This name is understood to refer, not to a female saint, but to the Holy Wisdom (Ἅγια Σοφία), the Λόγος, the Word, *i.e.*, Christ; Procopius, De Bel. Vand., i, 6, etc.

[220] Lethaby and Swainson give good reasons for supposing that this early church opened to the east; St. Sophia, etc., Lond., 1894, p. 17. It was burnt in the time of Chrysostom, but apparently repaired without alteration of design.

[221] Ambo, plainly from ἀναβαίνω, to ascend, not, as some imagine, from the double approach; Reiske, Const. Porph., ii, p. 112; Letheby and S., *op. cit.*, p. 53.

[222] The gift of Pulcheria, presented as a token of the perpetual virginity to which she devoted herself and her sisters; Sozomen, ix, 1; Glycas, iv, p. 495. The Emperor used to sit in the *Bema*, but St. Ambrose vindicated its sanctity to the priestly caste by expelling Theodosius I; Sozomen, vii, 25, etc.

[223] Socrates, vi, 5; Sozomen, viii, 5.

[224] Codin., pp. 16, 64. There is no systematic description of this church, but the numerous references to it and an examination of ecclesiastical remains of the period show clearly enough what it was; see Texier and Fullan, *op. cit.*, p. 134, etc.; Agincourt, *op. cit.*, i, pl. iv, xvi; Eusebius, Vit. Const., iv, 46, etc. It may have been founded by Constantine, but was certainly dedicated by his son Constantius in 360; Socrates, ii, 16.

[225] *Ibid.*

[226] Procopius, De Aedific., i, 2, etc.

[227] Codin., p. 83; cf. Mordtmann, *op. cit.*, p. 4.

[228] We know little of the Magnaura or Great Hall (*magna aula*) at this date, but its existence is certain; Chron. Paschal., an. 532. Codinus says it was built by Constantine (p. 19).

[229] Theophanes, Cont., v, 92, etc.

[230] Const. Porph., ii, 15. The author professes to draw his precepts from the ancients, but his "antiquity" sometimes does not extend backwards for more than half a century.

[231] Codin., pp. 14, 36; Zonaras, xiv, 6, etc. Zeuxippus is either a cognomen of Zeus or of the sun, or the name of a king of Megara; Chron. Paschal., an. 197, etc.; Jn. Lydus, De Magist., iii, 70.

[232] Sozomen, iii, 9.

[233] Anthology (Planudes), v.

[234] Cedrenus, i, p. 648; cf. Anthol. (Plan.), v, 61.

[235] The vast baths of the Empire, as is well known, were evolved into a kind of polytechnic institutes for study and recreation.

[236] Chron. Pasch., an. 450. Artificial lighting was first introduced by Alex. Severus; Hist. August.; Cod. Theod., XV, i, 52; Cod., XI, i, 1, etc.

[237] Cedrenus, i, p. 648.

[238] Codin., p. 83; cf. Mordtmann, *op. cit.*, p. 66.

[239] Zosimus, iii, 11. It contained 120,000 volumes, the pride of the library being a copy of Homer inscribed on the intestine of a serpent 120 feet long. The building, however, was gutted by fire in the reign of Zeno; Zonaras, xiv, 2, etc.

[240] Suidas, *sb.* Menandro; Agathias, iii, 1; Procop., De Aedific., i, 11.

[241] Zonaras, xiv, 6; Marcellinus, Com., an. 390, etc.

[242] Socrates, vi, 18; Theophanes, an. 398; Sozomen (viii, 20) says merely an inaugural festival. The pedestal, with a bilingual inscription, was uncovered of late years, precisely where we should expect it to have stood, and yet Paspates (Βυζαντινὰ Ἀνάκτορα, p. 95) in his map removes it a quarter of a mile southwards to meet his reconstructive views, cf. Mordtmann, *op. cit.*, p. 64.

[243] Codin., p. 35.

[244] *Ibid.*, p. 19. There is now an Ottoman fountain on the same site. In the case of doubtful identifications, I usually adopt the conclusions of Mordtmann (*op. cit.*, p. 64).

[245] *Milliarium Aureum* (Notitia, Reg. 4). In imitation of that set up by Augustus in the Roman Forum; Tacitus, Hist., i, 27, etc.

[246] Cedrenus, i, p. 564; Codin., pp. 28, 35, 168, etc. Byzantios and Paspates speak of an upper storey supported by seven pillars, on the strength of some remains unearthed in 1848, but the situation does not seem to apply to this monument as at present located; see also Grosvenor (*op. cit.*, p. 298) for an illustration of the figures.

[247] Codin., p. 40. Removed to Hippodrome, perhaps, at this date. In any case the scrappy and contradictory records only allow of a tentative restoration of the Milion. Close by was the death-place of Arius, in respect of whom, with Sabellius and other heretics, Theodosius I set up a sculptured tablet devoting the spot to public defilement with excrement, etc. (*ibid.*). Such were the manners and fanaticism of the age.

[248] Zosimus, iii, 11.

[249] Gyllius, De Topog. CP., ii, 13.

[250] The method of construction can be seen in the sketch of the ruins (*c. 1350*) brought to light by Panvinius (De Ludis Circens., Verona, 1600) and reproduced by Banduri and Montfaucon. As to whether the intercolumnar spaces were adorned with statues we have no information. The wealth of such works of art at Constantinople would render it extremely likely. Cassiodorus says the statues at Rome were as numerous as the living inhabitants (Var. Ep., xv, 7). We know from existing coins that the Coliseum was so ornamented (see Maffei, Degl' Amfiteatri, Verona, 1728; Panvinius, *op. cit.*, etc.). High up there appears to have been a range of balconies all round (Cod. Theod., XV, i, 45).

[251] They were of wood till 498, when they were burnt, but what time restored in marble is unknown; Chron. Pasch., an. 498; Buondelmonte, Descript. Urb. CP., 1423.

[252] Codin., p. 14, etc. These substructions still exist; Grosvenor, *op. cit.*, p. 303.

[253] Const. Porph., *op. cit.*, ii, 20; Nicetas Chon., De Man. Com., iii, 5. Eight, or perhaps twelve, open-barred gates separated the Manganon (more often in the plural, Mangana) from the arena; see the remains in the engraving of Panvinius.

[254] Const. Porph., i, 68, 92, etc.; Agincourt, *op. cit.*, ii, pl. 10. The latter gives copies of bas-reliefs in which the Emperor is shown sitting in his place in the Circus (see below). Procopius calls it simply the throne; De Bel. Pers., i, 24; cf. Jn. Malala, p. 320; Chron. Pasch., an. 498. Originally, it appears, merely the seat or throne, but afterwards the whole tribunal or edifice.

[255] Const. Porph., i, 9, 92. It was also called the Pi (Π) from its shape; *ibid.*, i, 69.

[256] Named the Cochlea or snail-shell; it seems to have been a favourite gangway for assassinating obnoxious courtiers; Jn. Malala, p. 344; Chron. Pasch., an. 380; Theophanes, an. 5969; Codin., p. 112, etc.

[257] Const. Porph., i, 68; cf. Procop., De Bel. Pers., i, 24.

[258] Const. Porph., i, 63; Codin., p. 100. The Circus, begun by Severus, was finished by Constantine; Codin., pp. 14, 19; see Ducange, *sb. nom.*

[259] Euripus (Εὔριπος). I. The narrow strait at Chalcis, said to ebb and flow seven times a day; Strabo, x, 2; Suidas, *sb. v.* II. Tr. Any artificial ornamental pool or channel, partic. if oblong; see refs. in Latin Dicts., esp. Lewis and S. III. A canal round the area of the Roman Circus, to shield the spectators from the attack of infuriated beasts; devised apparently by Tarquinius Priscus; Dionysius Hal., iii, 68; rather by Julius Caesar, and abolished by Nero; Pliny, H. N., viii, 7, etc. IV. Restored by, or in existence under, Elagabalus as a pool in the centre; Hist. Aug., 23; so Cassiodorus, Var. Ep., iii, 51; Jn. Malala, vii, p. 175 (whence Chron. Pasch., Olymp., vii, p. 208; Cedrenus, i, p. 258); Lyons and Barcelona mosaics (see Daremberg and S. Dict. Antiq.). V. The name tr. to whole Spine by Byzantines; Jn. Lydus, De Mens., i, 12, Εὔριπος ὠνομάσθη ἡ μέσον τοῦ ἱπποδρόμου κρηπίς; Const. Porph., *op. cit.*, pp. 338, 345; Cedrenus, ii, p. 343, etc. Labarte seems strangely to have missed all but one of the numerous allusions to the Euripus; *op. cit.*, p. 53. This note is necessary, as no one seems to have caught the later application of the name.

[260] This monument still exists; see Agincourt, *loc. cit.*, for reproduction of the sculptures, etc.

[261] Notitia, Col. Civ. This name was not bestowed on it by Gyllius, as Labarte thinks (p. 50). It remains in position in a dilapidated condition; see Grosvenor, *op. cit.*, p. 320, etc.

[262] Also in evidence at the present day; see Grosvenor's photographs of the three, pp. 320, 380. It is mentioned by Herodotus (ix, 80); and by Pausanias (x, 13), who says the golden tripod was made away with before his time. Some of the Byzantines, however, seem to aver that Constantine had regained possession of that memorial; Eusebius, Vit. Const., iii, 54; Codin., p. 55; Zosimus, ii, 31, etc. It appears that the defacement of this monument was carried out methodically during a nocturnal incantation under Michael III, *c. 835*. At the dead of night "three strong men," each armed with a sledge-hammer, stood over it (Ἐν τοῖς εἰς τὸν εὔριπον (see p. 62) τοῦ ἱπποδρομίου χαλκοῖς ἀνδριᾶσιν ἐλέγετό τις εἶναι ἀνδριὰς τρισὶ διαμορφούμενος κεφαλαῖς) prepared to knock off the respective heads on the signal being given by an unfrocked abbot. The hammers fell, two of the heads rolled to the ground, but the third was only partly severed, the lower jaw, of course, remaining; Theoph., Cont., p. 650; Cedrenus, ii, p. 145. On the capture of the city in 1453 the fragment left was demolished by Mahomet II with a stroke of his battle-axe to prove the strength of his arm on what was reputed to be a talisman of the Greeks; Thévenot, Voyage au Levant, etc., 1664, i, 17, "la maschoire d'embas." So history, as it seems, has given itself the trouble to

account for the mutilation of this antique. I must note, however, that neither Buondelmonte, Gyllius, Busbecq, Thévenot, nor Spon, has described the damages it had sustained at the time they are supposed to have contemplated the relic. See also Grosvenor, *op. cit.*, p. 381, whose account is scarcely intelligible and is not based on references to any authorities.

[263] Nicetas Chon., De Signis CP. This figure appears to be delineated in the plate of Panvinius, which, however, is not very reliable, as both the Colossus and the Serpent-pillar are absent from it.

[264] Codin., p. 124. Probably, and supplanted at a later date by one of Irene Attica. This is the literal Euripus.

[265] Theophanes, an. 699. That the Empress sat in this lodge to view the races (Buondelmonte) is beyond all credence, nor is there any authority for placing it to one side among the public seats (Grosvenor's diagram), where her presence would be equally absurd. Her bust may have appeared in it beside that of her husband. It is clearly indicated in its true place on the engineering sculptures of the Theodosian column (see above).

[266] Nicetas Chon., De Alexio, iii, 4; De Signis; Codin., p. 39. First at Tarentum; Plutarch, in Fabius Max., etc. To the knee it measured the height of an ordinary man.

[267] Nicetas Chon., De Signis; also celebrated by Christodorus, Anthology, *loc. cit.*

[268] The eggs in honour of Castor and Pollux; Tertullian, De Spectaculis, 8:

Κάστορά θ' ἱππόδαμον καὶ πὺξ ἀγαθὸν Πολυδεύκεα.

Iliad, iii.

The dolphins probably referred to Neptune, to whom the horse was sacred.

[269] See Lyons and Barcelona mosaics as referred to above.

[270] See the coins, etc., in Panvinius, which show that these cones with their stands were about fifteen to twenty feet high. Sometimes they rested on the ends of the Spina, at others on separate foundations three or four feet off it.

[271] Nicetas Chon., De Man. Comn., iii, 5; Codin., pp. 53, 192. They were brought to Venice by the Crusaders in 1204, and now stand before the cathedral of St. Mark; Buondelmonte, *loc. cit.* A much longer pedigree is given by some accounts (Byzantios, *op. cit.*, i, p. 234), from Corinth to Rome by Mummius, and thence to CP. by Constantine. They even had a journey to Paris under Napoleon.

[272] Grosvenor, *op. cit.*, p. 351. Some remains of it are still visible.

[273] Codin., p. 54.

[274] Nicetas Chon., *loc. cit.*

[275] *Ibid.*, Codin., p. 54.

[276] *Ibid.*, p. 31.

[277] Nicetas Chon., De Signis: Καλοῦμαι Νίκων καὶ ὁ ὄνος Νίκανδρος, κ.τ.λ. Cf. Plutarch, Antony.

[278] *Ibid.*

[279] *Ibid.*

[280] Codin., p. 53.

[281] Jerome, Chronicon, an. 325. CP. "dedicatur pene omnium urbium nuditate." This Saint, however, is somewhat given to hyperbole.

[282] See the various illustrations in Panvinius.

[283] We hear nothing of *vomitoria*, approaches beneath the seats to the various positions, nor do we know how the large space under the incline of benches was occupied. At Rome, in the Circus Maximus, there were "dark archways" in this situation, which were let out to brothel-keepers; Hist. August. *sb.* Heliogabalo, 26, etc. In the time of Valens, however, a record office was established here; Jn. Lydus, De Magistr., iii, 19.

[284] Procopius, De Bel. Pers., i, 24.

[285] Ducange, *op. cit.*, i, p. 104; a collection of instances.

[286] Const. Porph., *loc. cit.* At Rome such awnings were decorated to resemble the sky with stars, etc.

[287] Codin., pp. 20, 22; part previously by Severus; Zosimus, ii, 30.

[288] Codin., p. 39.

[289] *Ibid.*, p. 37.

[290] Cedrenus, p. 564.

[291] *Ibid.*, p. 616; Zonaras, xiv, 2.

[292] Resembling, if not the prototype of, the Venus dei Medici; see Lucian, Amores.

[293] See Pausanias, v, 12.

[294] Cedrenus, *loc. cit.*

[295] Theophanes, an. 6024.

[296] Zosimus, ii, 30; Codin., p. 41. Said to have been designed to the size and shape of Constantine's tent, which was pitched here when he took Byzantium from Licinius.

[297] *Ibid.*; Jn. Malala, p. 320; Zonaras, xiii, 3, etc. Really a statue of Apollo taken from Heliopolis in Phrygia and refurbished.

[298] *Ibid.*; Cedrenus, i, p. 565. The blending of Paganism and Christianity is an interesting phase in the evolution of Constantine's theology. The crosses of the two thieves were also reputed to have been stowed here till removed to a safer place by Theodosius I; also a part of the true cross; Socrates, i, 17; Codin., p. 30. Curiously enough, this Forum has been confounded with the Augusteum both by Labarte and Paspates, a mistake almost incredible in the latter, a resident, considering that the pillar of Constantine still exists in a scarred and mutilated condition; hence known as the "Burnt Pillar," and called by the Turks "Djemberli Tash," or Hooped Stone; see Grosvenor, *op. cit.*, p. 374, etc.

[299] Jn. Malala, *loc. cit.*; Codin., pp. 44, 180.

[300] *Ibid.*, pp. 28, 68; Cedrenus, ii, p. 564.

[301] Notitia, Reg. 6; Cedrenus, i, p. 565. It had been burnt down previous to this date, but seems to have been restored.

[302] Codin., p. 48.

[303] Notitia, Reg. 5; Gyllius, De Top. CP., iii, 1.

[304] Socrates, i, 16.

[305] Codin., p. 48.

[306] Jn. Malala, p. 292.

[307] Codin., p. 76.

[308] Codin., pp. 41, 170. It fell into decay and was, perhaps, removed before this date; cf. Mordtmann, p. 69; one of the Gorgons was dug up in 1870.

[309] Codin., p. 40.

[310] See Mordtmann, *op. cit.*, p. 69, and Map.

[311] Evidenced by the discovery of a swarm of leaden *bullae*, or seals for official documents, about 1877; *ibid.*, p. 70. But in the sixth century the legal records from the time of Valens were kept in the basement of the Hippodrome; Jn. Lydus, De Magistr., iii, 19.

[312] Cod. Theod., XIV, ix, 3, with Godfrey's commentary. The Turkish Seraskierat has taken the place of Taurus.

[313] Cedrenus, i, p. 566; Codin., p. 42, etc. The chronographists think it particularly necessary to mention that this pillar was pervious by means of a winding stair. In a later age, when the inscriptions on the base became illegible, they were supposed to be prophecies of the future conquest of Constantinople by the Russians.

[314] Marcell., Com., an. 480, 506; Zonaras, xiv, 4.

[315] Déthier, *op. cit.*, p. 14; he discovered a few letters of the epigram (Anthology, Plan., iv, 4) on a fragment of an arch; cf. Cedrenus, i, p. 566.

[316] The favourite Byzantine appellation for Joshua the son of Nun.

[317] *Ibid.*; Nicetas Chon., De Signis, 4.

[318] Codin., p. 42.

[319] *Ibid.*, p. 124.

[320] *Ibid.*, pp. 42, 74; see Anthology (Plan.), iv, 22, for two epigrams which give some idea of the scope of these *Xenodochia*.

[321] Notitia, Reg. 10.

[322] Cedrenus, i, p. 610; Zonaras, xiv, 1; sufficiently corroborated by Cod., VIII, xii, 21, and not a mere assumption arising out of the similarity of νυμφαῖον to νύμφη, a bride, as argued by some commentators. Fountains were sacred to the Nymphs; see Ducange, CP. Christ, *sb. voc.*

[323] See the title *De Aqueductu* in both Codes and Godfrey's commentary.

[324] This aqueduct seems to have been built originally by Hadrian, restored by Valens, who used for the purpose the walls of Chalcedon as a punishment for that town having taken the part of the usurper Procopius, and again restored by Theodosius I. Hence it is denoted by the names of each of these emperors at different times; Socrates, iv, 8; Zonaras, xiii, 16; and the Codes, *loc. cit.*

[325] Chrysoloras, *loc. cit.*, etc.

[326] Codin., p. 14.

[327] *Ibid.*, p. 21; Byzantios, *op. cit.*, i, p. 262. Still existing in a dry state, and occupied by silk weavers. Most probably the name arises from its having been founded by a patrician Philoxenus; the Turks call it *Bin ber derek*, meaning 1,001 columns; see Grosvenor, *op. cit.*, p. 366.

[328] Cod., XI, xlii, 7: "It would be execrable," remarks Theodosius II, "if the houses of this benign city had to pay for their water." By a constitution of Zeno every new patrician was to pay 100 lb. of gold towards the maintenance of the aqueducts; Cod., XLI, iii, 3.

[329] Codin., p. 9.

[330] Forty of these at Rome; Notitia (Romae), Col. Civ.

[331] Codin., p. 50; cf. Cedrenus, ii, p. 107. "Hypnotic suggestion" might account for some displays of this kind, and create a popular belief in the test, which in most instances, however, would be more likely to prove a convenient method of varnishing a sullied reputation. Near the Neorium was a shelter called the Cornuted Porch, in which St. Andrew, the apostle assigned by tradition to these regions, was supposed to have taught. It took its name from a four-horned statue in the vicinity, which had the credit of evincing its disapproval of an incontinent wife by turning three times round on its pedestal if such a one were brought into its presence; Codin., p. 119.

[332] Cedrenus (i, p. 565) attributes it to Theodosius I, Codinus (p. 108) to Leo Isaurus; Nicetas Chon. (De Signis) laments its destruction without mentioning the founder.

[333] Legendary apparently. They really met in Pannonia; Julian, Orat.

[334] Codin., pp. 43, 44, 182, 188. The Philadelphium was considered to be the μεσόμφαλος or middle of the city. The numerous crosses set up by Constantine are supposed to refer to the cross which he is said to have seen in the sky near Rome before his victory over Maxentius—a fiction, or an afterthought, but whose?

[335] Codin., pp. 45, 65.

[336] Cedrenus, i, p. 566.

[337] *Ibid.*; Anna Comn., xii, 6.

[338] Codin., p. 45. Unless the course of the brook has altered, the Amastrianum should be more to the south or west than shown on Mordtmann's map.

[339] Codin., pp. 45, 172; forming some kind of boundary or inclosure perhaps.

[340] Cedrenus, i, p. 566.

[341] *Ibid.*; Codin., pp. 44, 173.

[342] Theophanes, an. 5895, etc.; cf. Chron. Paschal., an. 421.

[343] Cedrenus, i, p. 567.

[344] Zonaras, xiii, 20; the base still remains in *Avret Bazaar*; the pillar was still intact in the time of Gyllius, who ascended it; *op. cit.*, iv, 7. The sketches supposed to have been taken of the figures on the spiral and published by Banduri and Agincourt have already been alluded to; see p. 49.

[345] Notitia, Reg. 12, etc.

[346] Buondelmonte's map; a "very handsome gate"; Codin., p. 122. I have noted Van Millingen's opinion that this was not the original "Golden Gate"; see p. 34. But its mention in Notitia, Reg. 12, seems fatal to his view.

[347] Codin., p. 46.

[348] *Ibid.*, pp. 102, 121; see Paspates for an illustration of the structure still on this site; Βυζαντιναὶ Μελεταί, p. 343.

[349] Codin., p. 72; the Arians, chiefly Goths, were hence called Exokionites; Jn. Malala, p. 325; Chron. Pasch., an. 485.

[350] Codinus, p. 47.

[351] *Ibid.*

[352] Gregory Nazianz., De Somn. Anast., ix.

[353] Eusebius, Vit. Constant., iv, 58, *et seq.*; a later hand has evidently embellished this description.

[354] Const. Porph., De Cer. Aul. Byz., ii, 43; Codin., p. 203.

[355] Corp. Inscript. Lat., Berlin, 1873, no. 738; still existing and called by the Turks the "Girls' Pillar," from two angels bearing up a shield figured on the pedestal; see Grosvenor, *op. cit.*, p. 385; there is an engraving of it in Miss Pardoe's "Bosphorus," etc. The "girls" are utilized by Texier and P. in their frontispiece.

[356] Notitia, Reg. 13; Procopius, De Bel. Pers., ii, 23, etc. Perhaps not walled till later; Jn. Malala, xiii, p. 430.

[357] Suetonius, in Augusto, 30.

[358] Notitia, Reg. 1, with Pancirolus's notes; Pand., I, xv; cf. Gallus by Becker-Göll, Sc. i, note 1.

[359] Ammianus, xiv, 1, with note by Valesius.

[360] Cod. Theod., XIV, xvii; Suidas *sb.* Παλατῖνοι; we do not know the exact form of these *Gradus,* but only that they were high, the design being doubtless such as would prevent a crush. This state-feeding of the people was begun at Rome by Julius Caesar, and of course imitated by Constantine; Socrates, ii, 13, etc. The tickets were checked by a brass plate for each person fixed at the Step; Cod. Theod., XIV, xvii, 5.

[361] Cod. Theod., IV, v, 7; always with Godfrey's commentary; Eunapius, Vit. Aedesii.

[362] Notitia, Urb. CP., *passim.*

[363] See Cod., I, iii, 32, 35, 42, 46, etc. Cf. Schlumberger's work on the Byzantine *bullae*.

[364] Cod. Theod., XIII, iii, 8; Cod., X, lii, 9.

[365] Codin., p. 22; cf. Pandect., XLIII, xxiii, 1. It appears probable that neither middens nor cesspools existed within the walls.

[366] See Minucius, Octavius, 10.

[367] Paspates, Βυζαντιναὶ Μελεταί, p. 381, etc. There were, perhaps, over one hundred churches and monasteries in Constantinople at this time, but the Notitia, a century earlier, reckons only fourteen churches; see Ducange's list.

[368] Western scholars since the Renaissance have fallen into the habit of applying the diminutive *Graeculi* to the Byzantines, thereby distinguishing them from the *Graeci*, their pre-eminent ancestors, who established the fame of the Dorians and Ionians. The Romans, after their conquest of the country, began to apply it to all Greeks. Cicero, De Orat., i, 22, etc.

[369] Suidas, *sb. nom.*; Tertullian, Apologia, 39; Athenaeus, xiii, 25. There was, however, a minor school of philosophy at Megara.

[370] Aristotle, Politica, iv, 4. As late as the sixteenth century the housewives residing next the water habitually took the fish by simple devices, which are described by Gyllius; De Top. CP. Praef.

[371] See the statements by Theopompus, Phylarchus, etc., in Müller, Fragm. Hist. Graec., i, pp. 287, 336; ii, p. 154; iv, p. 377. Having obtained an ascendancy over the frugal and industrious Chalcedonians they are said to have corrupted them by their vices; cf. Müller's Dorians, ii, pp. 177, 418, etc.

[372] Sextus Empir., Adversus Rhetor., 39. A demagogue, being asked what laws were in force, replied, "Anything I like"—a frivolous or a pregnant answer?

[373] Aristotle in the doubtful Economica (ii, 4) describes some of their makeshifts to maintain the exchequer. According to Cicero (De Prov. Consular.) the city was full of art treasures, an evidence, perhaps, of wasteful extravagance.

[374] See p. 17. His daily grant of 80,000 measures of wheat, together with the other allowances, to those who were served at the Steps, would seem to indicate as many families, but there is no doubt that the distribution was at first indiscriminate, and many were supplied who could afford to keep up considerable establishments. Constantius reduced the amount by one half; Socrates, ii, 13; Sozomen, iii, 7. Heraclius abolished the free doles altogether; Chron. Paschal., an. 618.

[375] "Matronae nostrae, ne adulteris quidem plus sui in cubiculo, quam in publico ostendant"; see Seneca, De Beneficiis, vii, 9; cf. Horace, Sat., I, ii, 102:

Cois tibi paene videre est

Ut nudam, etc.

[376] By a law of Honorius the Romans were forbidden to wear long hair (in 416), or garments of fur (in 397), such being characteristic of the Goths who were then devastating Italy; Cod. Theod., XIV, x, 4, 3, 2.

[377] See the lowest bas-reliefs on the Theodosian obelisk (Banduri, ii, p. 499; Agincourt, ii, pi. x); Cod. Theod., XIV, x, 1; Hefner-Altenek, Trachten des Mittelalters, pl. 91, 92.

[378] Chrysostom, the pulpit declaimer against the abuses of his time, was so enraged at seeing the young men delicately picking their steps for fear of spoiling their fine shoes that he exclaims: "If you cannot bear to use them for their proper purpose, why not hang them about your neck or stick them on your head!"; In Matt. Hom. xlix, 4 (in Migne, vii, 501).

[379] "You bore the lobes of your ears," says Chrysostom, "and fasten in them enough gold to feed ten thousand poor persons"; In Matt. Hom. lxxxix, 4 (in Migne, vii, 786); cf. Sozomen, viii, 23.

[380] Chrysostom, In Ps. xlviii, 3 (in Migne, v, 515); Sozomen, *loc. cit.*, etc. Women's girdles were worn under the breasts.

[381] See Bingham's Christian Antiquities, vii, 1, and Racinet, Costume historique, iii, pl. 21. Read Lucian's Cynicus for a defence of a somewhat similar life on a different plane.

[382] Chrysostom, In Epist. Tim. II, viii, 2 (in Migne, xi, 541). Even these he rates for coquetry; cf. Bingham, *op. cit.*, vii, 4, etc. See also Viollet-le-Duc (Dict. du mobil. fr., i, pl. 1) for a coloured figure which, though of the thirteenth century, corresponds very closely with Chrysostom's description. Formal costume, however, of the present day, political, legal, ecclesiastical, is for the most part merely a survival of the ordinary dress of past ages.

[383] Basil Presbyt. ad Gregor. Naz., Steliteut. Const. Porph., *op. cit.*, ii, 52, p. 753, with Reiske's notes, p. 460.

[384] Cod. Theod., XV, vii, 11, 12; Cod., I, iv, 4(5); actresses (*mimae = meretrices*, no doubt) are forbidden to use this and other styles of dress which might bring women of repute into ridicule.

[385] Cod. Theod., XIV, xii; Chrysostom, De Perf. Carit., 6 (in Migne, vi, 286).

[386] Chrysostom, *loc. cit.* (in Migne, v, 515).

[387] A *quadriga*.

[388] Chrysostom, In Epist. ad Cor. Hom. xi, 5 (in Migne, x, 353). "Do not be afraid," says the Saint, "you are not among wild beasts; no one will bite you. You do not mind the contact of your horse, but a man must be driven a thousand miles away from you."

[389] Cod. Theod., XV, xiii, and Godefroy *ad loc.*

[390] Chrysostom, In Epist. I ad Thess., v, Hom. xi, 2 (in Migne, xi, 465).

[391] The laws and restrictions relating to the use of purple and the collection of the *murex*, which was allowed only to certain families or guilds, are contained in Cod. Theod., X, xx, xxi; Cod., XI, viii, ix. Julius Caesar first assumed a full purple toga (Cicero, Philip, ii, 34, probably from); Nero first made a sweeping enactment against the use of the colour (Suetonius, in Nero, 32; cf. Julius, 43). Women, however, were generally permitted some latitude and not obliged to banish it altogether from their dress.

[392] The globe as a symbol of the universal sway of Rome came into use at or about the end of the Republic. It was not merely ideographic, but was sometimes exhibited in bulk, and hollow globes have been found with three chambers in which are contained samples of earth from the three continents; see Sabatier, Mon. Byzant., Paris, 1862, p. 33. The cross came in under the Christian emperors, and is said to be first seen on a small coin of Jovian (363); *ibid.*

[393] Cod., XII, iii, 5; Inst. i, 12. "Imperatoris autem celsitudinem non valere eum quem sibi patrem elegerit," etc. This new order of patricians seems to have been instituted by Constantine, their title being coined directly from *pater*; Zosimus, ii, 40; cf. Cedrenus, i, p. 573. They were not lineally connected with the patrician caste of ancient Rome (see Reiske, *ad* Const. Porph., *sb. voc.*), but were turned out of the Imperial workshop as peers are created by an English premier; see Leo Gram., p. 301.

[394] These crowns have given rise to much discussion, for a clue to which see Ludewig, *op. cit.*, p. 658. Probably most emperors designed a new crown.

[395] Some of the large coloured stones worn by the ancients were not very valuable according to modern ideas, *i.e.*, cairngorms, topazes, agates, etc.; see Pliny, H. N., xxxvii.

[396] Ἡ πατρικία ζωστὴ: Codin., pp. 108, 125; cf. Reiske, *op. cit., sb. voc.*

[397] It would be tedious, if not impossible, to put into words the details of these costumes. They are represented in the great mosaics of S. Vitale at Ravenna, dating from the sixth century. They have been beautifully restored in colour by Heffner-Altenek, *op. cit.*—too well perhaps. There are also full-sized paper casts at South Kensington. There are many engravings of the same, but in all of them the details have been partly omitted, partly misrepresented. The device on the tables of the Emperor's robe consists of green ducks (!) in red circles; that on the Empress's skirt of *magi* in short tunics and Phrygian caps, bearing presents. The men's shoes, or rather slippers, are fitted with toe and heel pieces only, and are held on by latchets. The ladies' shoes are red, and have nearly the modern shape, but are not laced at the division. Their gowns and shawls are of all colours, and much resemble diagonal printed calico, but in such cases it is the richness of the fabric which tells. The materials for illustrating the costume of this period are very scanty; we have neither the countless sculptures, wall-paintings, fictile vases, etc., of earlier times, nor the wealth of illuminated MSS., which teach so much objectively respecting the later Middle Ages.

[398] The *Curopalates* at this date probably, a place not beneath the first prince of the blood.

[399] The Byzantine logothetes are first mentioned by Procopius, De Bel. Goth., iii, 1, etc. At this date they were the Imperial accountants.

[400] Procopius, Anecd. 30. Hence it appears that the abject prostration introduced by Diocletian was abandoned by his successors; see p. 52.

[401] Magister Scriniorum; Notitia, Or., xvii.

[402] Cod., I, xxiii, 6; a law of Leo Macella in 470.

[403] Cryptograms to modern readers if we are to follow the perplexities of Pancirolus and Böcking, who, misled by the nonsense of Cedrenus as to CONOB (i, p. 563), cannot realize the obvious as it lies before their eyes. Godefroy expanded the legends to their full complement with no difficulty; that of the Spectabiles is FeLiciter INTer ALLectos COMites ORDinis PRimi; Cod. Theod., VI, xiii; cf. Böcking's Notitia, F. ii, pp. 283, 515, 528.

[404] As the illustrations of the Notitia are not accompanied by any explanation, considerable uncertainty prevails in respect of their point and intention; it appears almost incontestable, however, that the coloured figures were depicted in the codicils as they are seen in the MSS. of the work; otherwise only verbal descriptions of the insignia would be given; cf. Novel xxv, *et seq.*; Const. Porph., ii, 52.

[405] Cod. Theod., VI, xxii; a title omitted from the Code.

[406] *Principes Officii* and *Cornicularii*; Notitia, *passim*; Cod., XII, liii, etc.

[407] Const. Porph., ii, 1, 2; cf. Valesius ad Ammianum, xxii, 7. These early visitations were habitual in the Roman republic, as when the whole Senate waited on the newly-elected consuls on the Calends of January; Dion Cass., lviii, 5, etc.; and especially in the regular matutinal calls of clients on their patrons *re* the *sportula*; cf. Sidonius Ap. Epist., i, 2. His description of the routine of a court *c. 450* corresponds closely with the above. It must have been copied from Rome.

[408] Chrysostom, De Perf. Carit., 6 (in Migne, vi, 286); Theophanes, an. 6094, 6291, etc.; cf. Suetonius, in Nero, 25, etc.; Ducange, *sb. eq. alb.*

[409] These state carriages, open and closed, painted in gaudy colours, with gilded pilasters, mouldings, and various figures in relief, resembled certain vehicles used in the last century and some circus cars of the present day; see Banduri, ii, pl. 4, *sup. cit.*; the work of Panvinius on Triumphs, etc.

[410] Const. Porph., i, 1, and Append., p. 498, with Reiske's Notes; Dion Cass., lxiii, 4; lxxiv, 1, etc.

[411] Theophanes, an. 6019, 6050, etc.; Menologium Graec., i, p. 67; Cedrenus, i, p. 599; ii, p. 536.

[412] Theophanes, an. 6030, 6042, etc.

[413] See Reiske *ad* Const. Porph., p. 434, *et seq.*

[414] See Zosimus, ii, 39; Alemannus ad Procop., iii, p. 390; Ducange, *sb. voc.*

[415] See Godfrey's Notitia Dignitatum, *ad calc.* Cod. Theod.; Selden's Titles of Honour, p. 886; the epilogues to the Novels, etc. Minor dignities, entitled *Perfectissimi, Egregii*, are also mentioned, but are obsolete at this date; *Superillustres* were not unknown; see Ducange, *sb. voc.*

[416] Const. Porph., i, 68; see Labarte, *op. cit.*, pp. 16, 140, etc.

[417] Const. Porph., i, 92, with Reiske's Notes.

[418] Const. Porph., i, 68, *et seq.* This open-air hymn-singing was an early feature in Byzantine life; Socrates, vii, 23; Jn. Lydus, De Magistr., iii, 76. Later, at least, each Deme used an organ as well; Const. Porph., *loc. cit.*

[419] Procopius, De Bel. Pers., i, 25.

[420] *Ibid.*, 24.

[421] Doubtless according to Cod. Theod., XIV, ii; Cod., XI, xiv-xvii. These Corporations had certain privileges and immunities, such as exemption from military conscription, but they were bound to defend the walls on occasion; Novel, Theod. (Valent. I), xl. Naturally, therefore, after the earthquake of 447 they were sent by Theod. II to rebuild the walls (see p. 22), and also in

other emergencies they were sent to guard the Long Walls; Theophanes, an. 6051, 6076. Of course, in view of such appointed work, they had some military training. Building of forts was a regular part of a soldier's duties; Cod. Theod., XV, i, 13, and Godfrey, *ad loc.* The Demes were probably a later expression of the parties in the old Greek democracies, who associated themselves with the colours of the Roman Circus, when imported into the East, as the most effective outlet for their political feelings.

[422] These four colours, which date from the first century of the Empire, are supposed to represent the seasons of the year (Tertullian, De Spectaculis, 9); or the different hues of the sea and land (blue and green); see Chron. Pasch., Olymp., vii, p. 205; Alemannus, *ad* Procop., p. 372; Banduri, *op. cit.*, ii, p. 376, etc. Originally there were but two divisions. The leading and subsidiary colours are said to distinguish urban from suburban members of the factions; cf. Jn. Lydus, De Mens., iv, 25.

[423] Const. Porph., i, 6, with Reiske's Notes.

[424] Procopius, *loc. cit.*, ii, 11.

[425] Jn. Malala, xiv, p. 351.

[426] *Ibid.*, xvii, p. 416; cf. Procopius, De Bel. Pers., ii, 11.

[427] Chrysostom, De Anna, iv, 1 (in Migne, iv, 660); an almost identical passage; Gregory Naz., Laus Basil., 15.

[428] The Decennalia represented the ten years for which Augustus originally "accepted" the supreme power; the Quinquennalia are said to have been instituted by Nero, but may have become obsolete at this date; see the Classical Dicts. There were also Tricennalia.

[429] Novel cv; Const. Porph., *loc. cit.*, Codin., p. 17; Procop., De Bel. Vand., ii, 9, etc.

[430] Cod. Theod., VI, iv, 5, 26, etc. By a law of 384, eight praetors were appointed to spend between them 3,150 lb. of silver, equal to about £10,000 at that date, a credible sum; but the common belief that three annual praetors used to be enjoined to disburse more than a quarter of a million sterling in games is, I make no doubt, rank nonsense. Large amounts were, no doubt, expended by some praetors (Maximus, *c. 400-420, for his sons'* 4,000 lb. of gold, over £150,000, yet, only half the sum; Olympiodorus, p. 470), but these were intended to be great historic occasions, and are recorded as such, bearing doubtless the same relation to routine celebrations as the late Queen's Jubilees did to the Lord Mayor's shows, on which a few thousands are annually squandered. Maximus was then bidding for the purple, in which he was afterwards buried. The question turns on the enigma of the word *follis*, which in some positions has never been solved. But Cod. Theod., XII,

i, 159, makes it as clear as daylight that 25,000 *folles* in *ibid.*, VI, iv, 5, means just about fifty guineas of our money (he had also to scatter £125 in silver as largess), a sum exactly suited to *ibid.*, VII, xx, 3, by which the same amount is granted to a superannuated soldier to stock a little farm. The first law publishes the munificence of the Emperor in presenting the sum of 600 *solidi* (£335) to the people of Antioch that they may not run short of cash for, and so be depressed at the time of, the public games. And so the colossal sum doubted by Gibbon, accepted by Milman, advocated by Smith, and asserted by Bury may be dissipated like a puff of smoke in the wind. The office of *praetor ludorum* seems to have been falling into abeyance at this time.

[431] Jn. Lydus, De Mens., i, 12. Twenty-four races were the full number, but they were gradually reduced to eight; Const. Porph., i, 68, p. 307.

[432] Anastasius put a stop to this part of the performance—for the time; Procop. Gaz. Panegyr., 15, etc.

[433] H. A. Charisius, 19, etc. A favourite exhibition was that of a man balancing on his forehead a pole up which two urchins ran and postured at the top; Chrysostom, Ad Pop. Ant., xix, 4 (De Stat.; in Migne, ii, 195). Luitprand (Legatio, etc.) six centuries later was entertained with the same spectacle, an instance of the changeless nature of these times over long periods.

[434] Novel cv; Socrates, vii, 22; Cod. Theod., XV, xi, etc.

[435] Aulus Gell., iii, 10, etc.

[436] Sueton., Nero, 22; Novel cv, 1, etc.

[437] Chrysostom, In Illud, Vidi Dominum, etc. (in Migne, vi, 113); Ad Pop. Ant., xv, 4 (in Migne, ii, 158); In Illud, Pater Meus, etc., Hom. ix, 1 (in Migne, xii, 512); a particular instance of a youth killed in the chariot race the day before his intended wedding.

[438] Chrysostom, In Illud, Vidi Dominum, etc., Hom. iii, 2 (in Migne, vi, 113); In Genes. Hom. v, 6 (in Migne, iv, 54).

[439] Const. Porph., *op. cit.*, i, 69; Theophanes, an. 5969, etc. The winners usually received about two or three pounds in money, also a laurel crown and a cloak of a peculiar pattern (Pellenian, perhaps; Strabo, VIII, vii, 5); Chrysostom, In Matth. Hom. liv, 6 (in Migne, vii, 539); but under some of the insensate emperors immense prizes, small fortunes in fact, were often given; see Reiske's Notes, *ad op. cit.*, p. 325. I have not met in Byzantine history with any allusion to the seven circuits of the races (except Jn. Lydus, De Mens., i, 12), the eggs or the dolphins; these are assumed from the Latin writers of old Rome and from the sculptured marbles. It appears from Cod. Theod. (XV, ix, etc.), that the successful horses, when past their prime, were

carefully nurtured through their old age by the state. The choicest breeds of these animals came from Spain and Cappadocia; Claudian, De Equis Hon., etc. All the technical details of the Roman Circus will be found in the Dicts. of Clas. Antiqs., especially Daremberg and Saglio's; see also Rambaud, De Byzant. Hip., Paris, 1870.

[440] Of epilepsy (Evagrius, etc.). This is not a fatal disease, and hence a fiction arose that he had been buried alive in a fit. A sentry on guard at the sepulchre heard moanings for two days, and at length a voice, "Have pity, and let me out!" "But there is another emperor." "Never mind; take me to a monastery." His wife, however, would not disturb the *status quo*; but ultimately an inspection was made, when he was found to have eaten his arms and boots; Cedrenus, Zonaras, Glycas, etc.

[441] Theoph., an. 5983; Cedrenus, i, p. 626, etc. He was a Manichaean according to Evagrius, iii, 32; cf. Theoph., an. 5999.

[442] Julian seems to have been the first Roman emperor who was hoisted on a buckler and crowned with a necklet; Ammianus, xx, 4. By Jn. Lydus, however, the use of the collar instead of a diadem would appear to be a vestige of some archaic custom traceable back to Augustus or, perhaps, even to the times of Manlius Torquatus; De Magistr., ii, 3. The Germans originated the custom of elevating a new ruler on a shield; Tacitus, Hist., iv, 15.

[443] See the full details of this election and coronation in Const. Porph., *op. cit.*, i, 92. It is to be noted that twelve chapters of this work (i, 84-95) are extracted bodily from Petrus Magister, a writer of the sixth century.

[444] Jn. Malala, xvi, p. 394; Chron. Pasch., an. 498.

[445] Sc., "Holy God, Holy Mighty, Holy Immortal, pity us!" said to have been the song of the angels as heard by a boy who was drawn up to heaven and let down again in the reign of the younger Theodosius; Menologion Graec., i, p. 67, etc.

[446] Evagrius, iii, 32; Jn. Malala, xvi, p. 407; Theoph., an. 6005, etc. The date is uncertain; as recounted by some of the chronographists only 518 would suit the incident. As soon as the government felt again on a stable footing numerous executions were decreed.

[447] In 425 theatres and other amusements were forbidden on Sundays; Cod. Theod., XV, v, 5. In the time of Chrysostom people coming out of church were liable to encounter bands of roisterers leaving the theatre.

[448] Procopius, Anecdot., ix; Chrysostom, In Coloss., iii, Hom. ix (in Migne, xi, 362), "Satanical Songs" is his favourite expression; also "diabolical display"; In Act. Apost. Hom. xlii, 4 (in Migne, ix, 301); "naked limbs" of

[448] actresses; In Epist. I Thess., iv, Hom. v, 4 (in Migne, xi, 428); cf. Ammianus, xiv, 6; Lucian, De Saltatione.

[449] By a sumptuary law, however, the most precious gems and the richest fabrics were forbidden to the stage (Cod. Theod., XV, vii, 11); but the restriction seems to have been relaxed, as this law has been omitted from the Code. The intention was to prevent mummers from bringing into disrepute the adornments of the higher social sphere.

[450] Chrysostom, In Matth. Hom. vii, 5 (in Migne, vii, 79); cf. Cod., V, xxii, 9. A trick, doubtless, to evade the law, which forbade absolute nakedness on the stage; Procop., Anecdot., ix.

[451] Cod. Theod., XV, vii, 12, etc.

[452] *Ibid.*, 5.

[453] *Ibid.*, 6; Cod., XI, xl, 3.

[454] Cod. Theod., XV, vi, 8, etc.

[455] The immorality of the stage is the constant theme of Chrysostom. The fact that he draws no ethical illustrations from the drama seems to prove that no plays were exhibited in which virtue and vice were represented as receiving their due award. Fornication and adultery were the staple allurements of the stage; Act. Apost. Hom. xlii, 3 (in Migne, ix, 301). From the culminating scene of "The Ass" in the versions both of Apuleius and of Lucian it would seem that practical acts of fornication were possible incidents in public performances. It must be remembered, however, that women did not frequent the Greek or, at least, the Byzantine theatre. Sathas labours vainly to prove the existence of a legitimate Byzantine drama; Ἱστορ. δοκ. περὶ τ. θεάτρ. καὶ τ. μουσικ. τ. Βυζαντίων, Ven., 1878; cf. Krumbacher, Byzant. Literaturgesch., Munich, 1897, p. 644, *et seq.*

[456] Haenel, Cod. Theod., IV, vi, 3; Cod., V, xxvii, 1. By the first draft, due to Constantine, the prohibition might apply to any poor but virtuous girl. This defect was remedied by Pulcheria; Nov. Mart. iv. Here we may discern a result of Athenais, the dowerless but well educated Athenian girl being chosen (by Pulcheria) for her brother's consort; or, perhaps, of her own union with Martian, at first a private soldier.

[457] Called *trabea* or *toga palmata*; Claudian, Cons. Olyb. et Prob., 178; Cassiodorus, Var. Ep., vi, 1.

[458] *Ibid.*

[459] Ammianus, xxii, 7. Julian, when at CP., in his enthusiasm for democratic institutions, followed the consul on foot, but, forgetting himself,

he performed the act of emancipation, an inadvertence for which he at once fined himself 10 lb. of gold (£400).

[460] Procopius, De Bel. Pers., i, 25; Jn. Lydus, De Magistr., ii, 8, etc.

[461] Even under the barbarian kings in Italy, Odovacar the Herule and Theodoric the Goth, a consul was appointed annually at Rome in accordance with the arrangement made when Constantine decreed that the metropolitan honours should be divided between the old and the new capital.

[462] Nov. cv, 1, where they are enumerated. The regular cost of the display was 2,000 lb. of gold (£80,000), which, with the exception of a small amount by the consul himself, came from the Imperial treasury; Procopius, Anecdot., 26; cf. Jn. Lydus, *loc. cit.* Hence it appears that even the consulship need not be held by a millionaire; see p. 100.

[463] Cod. Theod., XV, v, 2. No lower dignitary was allowed to distribute anything more precious than silver.

[464] Cod. Theod., VIII, xi; Cod., XII, lxiv.

[465] Cod. Theod., XV, ix. Numbers of these diptychs are still preserved. There is a specimen at South Kensington of those of Anastasius Sabinianus, Com. Domest., who was consul in 518. Each plate was usually about twelve by six inches, and they were hinged so as to close up together. The designs on each face were practically duplicates. Generally as to the position of consuls at this time see Godefroy ad Cod. Theod., VI, vi, and the numerous cross references he has supplied.

[466] Constantine instituted a regular observance of Sunday as the Dominica or Lord's Day in 321; Cod. Theod., III, viii, with Godfrey's Com.; Cod., III, xii, 3. Towards the end of the ninth century, however, Leo Sapiens prohibited even farmers from working on Sundays; Novel. Leo. VI, liv. Daily service was only instituted about 1050 by Constant. Monom.; Cedrenus, ii, p. 609.

[467] See Ducange, *sb.* Σήμαντρον; Reiske's Notes, *op. cit.*, p. 235. The instrument is still in use in the Greek Church, but literary notices of it seem to be unknown before the seventh century.

[468] Chrysostom, Habentes eundem, etc., 11 (in Migne, iii, 299).

[469] *Ibid.* The well-known palindrome, ΝΙΨΟΝΑΝΟΜΗΜΑΤΑΜΗΜΟΝΑΝΟΨΙΝ (Wash away your sins not only your face), was at one time inscribed on the basin in front of St. Sophia; Texier and Pullan, *op. cit.*, p. 10. This composition is, however, attributed to Leo Sap.

[470] Sozomen, vii, 16; Gieseler, Eccles. Hist., i, 71, etc.

[471] Procopius, De Aedific., i, 1, p. 178; Paul Silent., 389, 541. At this time, however, men and women seem to have been in view of each other in the nave as well, though separated by a wooden partition; Chrysostom, In Matth. Hom. lxxiii, 3 (in Migne, vii, 677), but in earlier times they were allowed to mix indiscriminately; *ibid.*

[472] Socrates, vi, 8, etc.

[473] Sozomen, viii, 5; not invariably perhaps. Part of the present description applies, of course, to St. Sophia.

[474] Cantacuzenus, i, 41; this could easily be done, as the clerical staff of each church was very numerous—over five hundred in St. Sophia; Novel iii, 1.

[475] Chrysostom, In Epist. I Tim., ii, Hom. viii, 1 (in Migne, xi, 541); In Psal. xlviii, 5 (in Migne, vi, 507).

[476] Chrysostom, De Virgin., 61 (in Migne, i, 581).

[477] Chrysostom, In Matth. Hom. lxxiii, 3 (in Migne, vii, 677). "In the temple of God," says he, "you commit fornication and adultery at the very time you are admonished against such sins."

[478] Chrysostom, In Epist. I Tim., ii, Hom. viii, 9 (in Migne, xi, 543).

[479] Chrysostom, Epist. ad Innocent., Bishop of Rome, 3 (in Migne, iii, 533). He here describes how the women had to fly naked from the Baptistery during the riots connected with his deposition from the see of Constantinople. It must be noted, however, that the severe modesty of modern times had scarcely been developed amid the simplicity of the ancient world, as it has not among some fairly civilized peoples even at the present day.

[480] I had almost said *piety*, one of the words destined, with the extinction of the thing, to become obsolete in the future, or to be applied to some other mental conception.

[481] Chrysostom, In Matth. Hom. xvii, 2 (in Migne, vii, 256). He inveighs against the farce of ascetics taking virgins to live with them, who are supposed to remain intact; cf. De Virginitate (in Migne, i, 533); also Cod. Theod., XVI, ii, 20, to which Godefroy supplies practical illustrations.

[482] Chrysostom, In Epist. ad Coloss., iii, Hom. vii, 5 (in Migne, xi, 350); in Matth. Hom. lxxxiii, 4 (in Migne, vii, 750). Or even of more costly materials, gold, crystal; Plutarch, Adv. Stoic., 22; Clement Alex. Paedag., ii, 3. The notion of unparalleled luxury has been associated with the Theodosian age, but without sufficient reason. It was rather the age of a man of genius who denounced it persistently and strenuously, and whose diatribes have come

down to us in great bulk, viz., Chrysostom. The period of greatest extravagance was, in fact, during the last century of the Republic and the first of the Empire, and the names of Crassus, Lucullus, Nero, Vitellius, etc., are specially connected with it.

[483] Chrysostom, In Epist. ad Coloss., i, Hom. 4 (in Migne, xi, 304).

[484] As late as the tenth century, according to Luitprand, Antapodosis, vi, 8. In the Vienna Genesis (*c. 400*) a miniature shows banqueters reclining at a table of this sort. I will not attempt to enlarge on the courses at table and the multifarious viands that were consumed, as there are but few hints on this subject. We may opine, however, that gastronomics indulged themselves very similarly to what is represented in the pages of Petronius and Athenaeus, etc., cf. Ammianus, xvi, 5; xxviii, 4.

[485] Chrysostom, In Psalm xlviii, 8 (in Migne, v, 510). Most of the eunuchs were of the nation of the Abasgi, who dwelt between the Caspian and Euxine; Procopius, De Bel. Goth., iv, 3.

[486] Chrysostom, In Epist. ad Corinth. Hom. xl, 5 (in Migne, x, 353); In Matth. Hom. lxiii, 4 (in Migne, vii, 608).

[487] See below.

[488] Constantine enacted that families—husbands and wives, parents and children, brothers and sisters—should not be separated; Cod. Theod., II, xxv, 1; cf. XVI, v, 40, etc. But there was little practical philanthropy in the world until the Middle Ages had long been left behind. Thus by the Assize of Jerusalem, promulgated by Crusaders in the twelfth century, a war-horse was valued at three slaves! Tolerance, the toning-down of fanaticism, doubt as to whether religious beliefs are really of any validity, appears to be the foster-mother of humane sentiment. A slave could be trained to any trade, art, or profession, and their price varied accordingly. Thus common slaves were worth about £12, eunuchs £30; before ten years of age, half-price. Physicians sold for £35, and skilled artificers for £40; Cod., VII, vii. The modern reader will smile at the naïveté of Aristotle when he states that some nations are intended by Nature for slavery, but, as they do not see it, war must be made to reduce them to their proper level; Politics, i, 8.

[489] The following directions of a mother to her daughter how to shine as a society *hetaira* emanate from a Greek of the second century: "Dress yourself with taste, carry yourself stylishly, and be courteous to every one. Never break into a guffaw, as you often do, but smile sweetly and seductively. Do not throw yourself at a man's head, but behave with tact, cultivate sincerity, and maintain an amiable reserve. If you are asked to dinner be careful not to drink too much; do not grab the viands that are offered to you, but help yourself gracefully with the tips of your fingers. Masticate your food

noiselessly, and avoid grinding your jaws loudly whilst eating. Sip your wine delicately, and do not gulp down anything you drink. Above all things do not talk too much, addressing the whole company, but pay attention chiefly to your own friends. By acting in this way you will be most likely to excite love and admiration"; adapted from Lucian, Dial. Meretr., vi.

[490] Chrysostom, In Matth. Hom. xxx, 5 (in Migne, vii, 368); In I: Tim., i, 3 (in Migne, xi, 524); In Epist. ad Hebr., xxix, 3 (in Migne, xii, 206). "A country wench," says he, "is stronger than our city men."

[491] Chrysostom, De non Iterat. Conj., 4 (in Migne, i, 618). At all times there were ladies of such lubricity as to court the opportunity of bathing before men in the public baths; prohibited by Marcus (Hist. Aug., 23), this commerce of the sexes was encouraged by Elagabalus, and again forbidden by Alexander (Hist. Aug., 24, 34). Hadrian, however, seems to have been the first to declare against this promiscuous bathing (Hist. Aug., 18): "Olim viri foeminaeque mixtim lavabant, nullo pudore nuditatis," says Casaubon, commenting on the passage; cf. Aulus Gell., x, 3; Cod. Theod., IX, iii, 3; Cod., V, xvii, 11; Novel, xxii, 16, etc. Clement Alex. (*c. 200*) complains that ladies were to be seen in the baths at Alexandria like slaves exposed for sale; Paedag., iii, 5. Far different was the conduct of the Byzantine matrons a thousand years later; they then fell into the ways of Oriental exclusiveness as seen amongst the dominant Turks; see Filelfo, Epistolae, ix, Sphortiae Sec., 1451. A native of Ancona, who lived at CP. for several years in the half century preceding the capture of the city.

[492] Chrysostom, In Epist. ad Ephes., iv, Hom. xv, 3 (in Migne, xi, 109). The cries of the girl, often tied to a bedpost, might even be heard in the street, and if she stripped herself in a public bath the weals on her back were sometimes the subject of public remark. Whilst counselling mercy he considers that the whipping is generally deserved.

[493] Chrysostom, Quales duc. sint Uxores, 7 (in Migne, iii, 236); In Epist. I ad Corinth., Hom. xii, 5 (in Migne, x, 103).

[494] Fifteen for males and thirteen for females were the marriageable ages as legally recognized; Leo, Novel., lxxiv.

[495] Chrysostom, Quales duc. sint Uxores, 5 (in Migne, iii, 233); γραΐδια μυθεύοντα, κ. τ. λ.

[496] Even Arcadius had to be content with a portrait and a verbal description of the charms of Eudoxia, the daughter of a subject and a townsman; Zosimus, v, 3.

[497] The early Christians gradually inclined to the custom of asking a formal benediction from the clergy as an essential part of the marriage ceremony,

but about the time of Chrysostom the practice began to be disregarded. With the disuse also of pagan rites it began to be doubted whether nuptials could be legal unless accompanied at least by an orgiastic festival. To dispel this misgiving Theodosius II in 428 decreed that no sort of formal contract was required, but merely fair evidence that the parties had agreed to enter the connubial state; Cod. Theod., III, vii, 3. The Christian rite was not made compulsory till the end of the ninth century; Leo Sap. Novel., lxxxix.

[498] Chrysostom, In Matth. Hom. xxxvii, 5 (in Migne, vii, 425); In Act. Apost., xlii, 3 (in Migne, ix, 300); In Epist. I ad Corinth, Hom. xii, 5 (in Migne, x, 102), etc. His favourite theme for objurgation. He complains especially: "And worse, virgins are present at these orgies, having laid aside all shame; to do honour to the bride? rather disgrace," etc. These must be *ancillae*, or girls of a lower class, as it is evident from the above account that young ladies of any family could not be seen even at church by intending suitors; possibly they were kept closely veiled. On this point see further Puech's Chrysostom, Paris, 1891, p. 133. An introduction of this kind had always been considered necessary, as is shown by the equitation of the phallus (Mutinus) imposed on Roman brides the first night. These old customs were a constant mark for gibe among the early Christian Fathers; Lactantius, Div. Inst., l, 20; Augustine, De Civ. Dei, iv, 11; Arnobius, iv, *et passim*, etc.

[499] Chrysostom, In Joann. Hom. xxxii, 3 (in Migne, vii, 186).

[500] *Ibid.*, In Epist. ad Corinth. Hom. xii, 7 (in Migne, x, 105).

[501] Chrysostom, In Epist. ad Corinth. Hom. xii, 7 (in Migne, x, 105).

[502] *Ibid.*, In Matth. Hom. lxxii, 2 (in Migne, vii, 669); Ad Pop. Antioch., xix, 4 (in Migne, ii, 196).

[503] *Ibid.*, Ad Illum. Catech., ii, 5 (in Migne, ii, 240).

[504] *Ibid.*, In Epist. I ad Corinth., xii, 7 (in Migne, x, 105).

[505] *Ibid.*, De Consol. Mort. 6 (in Migne, vi, 303).

[506] *Ibid.*, Expos. in Psalm cxi, 4 (in Migne, v, 297), etc. He often protests against this form of luxury. At Rome especially, when the ownership of these costly piles had passed into oblivion, it was the habit of builders to pillage them in order to use their architectural adornments and materials for new erections; Cod. Theod., IX, xvii. Apparently the sepulchres were sometimes violated for the supply of false relics.

[507] Chrysostom. Habentes autem eumdem, etc. Hom. ii, 9 (in Migne, iii, 284).

[508] See Plato's Phaedrus, Symposium, etc.; Plutarch, Pelopidas, 19. A modern Democritus might smile at the conclusion of Lucian that, whilst the commerce of the sexes is necessary for the propagation of the race, paederasty is the ideal sphere for the love of philosophers; Amores. According to Aristotle, Minos introduced the practice into Crete as an antidote against over-population; Politics, ii, 10; vii, 16. In this respect the Greeks, perhaps, corrupted on the one hand and on the other Romans and Persians alike; Herodotus, i, 135. It was indigenous, however, among the Etruscans; Athenaeus, xii, 14, etc.

[509] The shadowy Scantinian law was enacted against it, but remained a dead letter; Cicero, Ad Famil., viii, 12, 14, etc.; cf. Plutarch, Marcellus, 2.

[510] I have not, however, fallen in with any account of the dedication of a temple to *Amor Virilis*. Such a shrine would have been quite worthy of Nero or Elagabalus, indeed of Hadrian.

[511] Suetonius, Nero, 28; Hist. Aug. Hadrian, 14; Heliogabalus, 6, 15, etc.; Statius, Silvae, iii, 4, etc. The adulation of this vice pervaded even the golden age of Latin poetry:

But Virgil's songs are pure except that horrid one

Beginning with "Formosum pastor Corydon."

Byron, Don Juan, i, 42.

For the estimation in which paederasty was held in Crete see Strabo, X, iv, 21; Athenaeus, xi, 20. Old men even wore a robe of "honour" to indicate that in youth they had been chosen to act the part of a pathic. The epigram on Julius Caesar is well known—"omnium mulierum vir, omnium virorum mulier"; Suetonius, in Vit. 52. Anastasius, who seems to have been somewhat of a purist for his time, abolished a theatrical spectacle addressed particularly to the paederasts, against which Chrysostom had vainly launched his declamations; In Psalm xli, 2 (in Migne, v, 157). "Boys, assuming the dress and manners of women, with a mincing gait and erotic gestures, ravished the senses of the observers so that men raged against each other in their impassioned fury. This stain on our manners you obliterated," etc.; Procopius, Gaz. Panegyr., 16. The saint is much warmer and more analytical in his invective.

[512] Hist. Aug. Alexander, 24.

[513] Tertullian, De Monogam., 12; Lactantius, Divin. Instit., v, 9; Salvian, De Gubern. Dei, vii, 17, etc.

[514] Cod. Theod., IX, vii, with Godefroy's duplex commentary. The peculiar wording of the law of Constantius almost suggests that it was enacted in a spirit of mocking complacency; *ibid.*, Cod., IX, ix, 31.

[515] Chrysostom, Adv. Op. Vit. Mon., 8 (in Migne, i, 361). There was probably a stronger tincture of Greek manners at Antioch, of Roman at Constantinople, but the difference does not seem to have been material. We here take leave of Chrysostom. The saint fumes so much that we must generally suspect him of exaggeration, but doubtless this was the style which drew large crowds of auditors and won him popularity.

[516] Procopius, Anecdot., 9, 11; Novel., lxxvii, etc. The first glimpse of Byzantine sociology is due to Montfaucon, who, at the end of his edition of Chrysostom brought together a selection of the most striking passages he had met with. These excerpts were the germ and foundation of a larger and more systematized work by P. Mueller, Bishop of Zealand; De Luxu, Moribus, etc., Aevi Theod., 1794. An article in the Quarterly Review, vol. lxxviii, deals briefly with the same materials. I have derived assistance from all three, but, as a rule, my instances are taken directly from the text of Chrysostom.

[517] Twelve ounces, rather less than the English ounce. The difficulty in obtaining a just equivalent for ancient money in modern values is almost insuperable. After various researches I have decided, as the safest approximation, to reckon the *solidus* at 11*s.* 2*d.* and the lb. Byz. of gold at £40.

[518] This appears to have been merely a "coin of account," but there were at one time large silver coins, value, perhaps, about six shillings, also pieces of alloyed silver. For some reason all these were called in and made obsolete at the beginning of the fifth century; Cod. Theod., IX, xxi, xxii, xxiii. No silver coins larger than a shilling seem to have been preserved to our time.

[519] As the price of copper was fixed at 25 lb. for a *solidus*, these coins might have been very bulky; "dumps," as such are called by English sailors abroad, above an ounce in weight, but nothing near so heavy has come down to us; Cod. Theod., XI, xxi.

[520] Other emperors, however, struck single *nummia*, and these may have remained in use. They are known to collectors and weigh 5 grs. and upwards.

[521] See the specimens figured by Ducange, CP. Christ., or in other works on numismatics.

[522] The Macedonian kings in the fifth century B.C. were the first princes to put their names and portraits on their coinage, but the practice did not become common till after Alexander the Great; cf. Procopius, De Bel. Goth.,

iii, 33. Very large gold medals were minted by most of the Roman emperors, weighing even one or two lb. Hist. Aug., Alexander, 39. This imposing coinage appears to have been used for paying subsidies or tribute to barbarian nations. They were carried slung over the backs of horses in those leathern bags, which we see in the Notitia among the insignia of the Counts of the Treasury; Cod., XII, li, 12; Paulus Diac., De Gest. Langob., iii, 13.

[523] The value of money in relation to the necessaries of life, always a shifting quantity, was not very different in these ages to what it is at present. To give a few examples: bread was about the same price, common shoes cost 1*s.* 6*d.* to 5*s.* a pair; a workman, according to skill, earned 1*s.* 6*d.* to 4*s.* a day; see Dureau de la Malle, Econ. polit. des Romains, Paris, 1840; also Waddington's Edict of Diocletian; an ordinary horse fetched £10 or £12; Cod. Theod., XI, i, 29, etc. On the Byzantine coinage see Sabatier, Monnaies Byzant., etc., Paris, 1862, i, p. 25, *et seq.* An imperfect, but so far the only comprehensive work; cf. Finlay, Hist. Greece, i, p. 432, *et seq.* Mommsen's work also gives some space to the subject. False coining and money-clipping were of course prevalent in this age and punishable capitally, but there was also a class of magnates who arrogated to themselves the right of coining, a privilege conceded in earlier times, and who maintained private mints for the purpose. In spite of legal enactments some of them persisted in the practice, and their penalty was to be aggregated with all their apparatus and operatives to the Imperial mints, there to exert their skill indefinitely for the government; Cod. Theod., IX, xxi, xxii. Their lot suggests the Miltonic fate of Mulciber:

Nor aught availed him now

To have built in heaven high towers; nor did he 'scape

By all his engines, but was headlong sent

With his industrious crew to build in hell.

Paradise Lost, I.

[524] In 1885, a "guess" census taken by the Turkish authorities put it at 873,565, but the modern city is much shrunk within the ancient walls; Grosvenor, *op. cit.*, p. 8.

[525] The Avars, during an incursion made in 616, carried off 270,000 captives of both sexes from the vicinity of the city; Nicephorus CP., p. 16.

[526] The largest reservoir, now called the "Bendt of Belgrade," about ten miles N.W. of CP. is more than a mile long. The water is conveyed, as a rule, through subterranean pipes, and there is no visible aqueduct within six miles

of the city. The so-called "Long Aqueduct" is about three-quarters of a mile in length.

[527] Evagrius, iii, 38; Procopius, De Aedific., iv, 9; Chron. Paschal., an. 512, etc.

[528] In modern Hindostan somewhat of a parallel might be traced, but very imperfectly. After the third century Gothic must also have become a familiar language at CP.

[529] The partial survival of the Latin language in the East during these centuries is proved, not merely by the body of law, inscriptions, numismatics, etc., but by the fact that some authors who must have expected to be read generally at Constantinople, chose to write in that tongue, especially Ammianus ("Graecus et miles," his own words), Marcellinus Comes, and Corippus.

[530] This vulgar dialect has probably never been committed to writing. Specimens crop up occasionally, particularly in Jn. Malala, also in Theophanes, i, p. 283 (De Boor). See Krumbacher, *op. cit.*, p. 770, *et seq.* The cultured Greeks, however, even to the end of the Empire, always held fast to the language of literary Hellas in her prime; see Filelfo, *loc. cit.*

[531] It is worthy of remark that assumption of the aspirate was in the period of best Latinity a vulgar fault decried by Romans of refined speech:

Chommoda dicebat, si quando commoda vellet

Dicere, et hinsidias Arrius insidias....

Ionios fluctus, post quam illuc Arrius isset,

Jam non Ionios esse, sed Hionios.

Catullus, lxxxii.

[532] Jn. Lydus, De Magistr., iii, 27, 68.

[533] In the absence of full contemporary evidence for a complete picture of Byzantine life at the point of time dealt with, it has often been necessary to have recourse to writers both of earlier and later date; an exigency, however, almost confined to Chrysostom and Constantine Porphyrogennetos. In taking this liberty I have exercised great caution so as to avoid anachronisms; and if such exist I may fairly hope them to be of a kind which will not easily be detected. I have always tried to obtain some presumptive proof in previous or subsequent periods that the scene as represented may be shifted backwards and forwards through the centuries without marring its truth as a picture of the times. In these unprogressive ages, wherever civilization was

maintained, it often had practically the same aspect even for thousands of years.

[534] It is generally conceded that iconoclastic zeal in respect of primitive Roman history, under the impulse given by Lewis and Niebuhr, has been carried too far. Even now archaeological researches with the spade on the site of the Forum, etc., are producing confirmation of some traditional beliefs already proclaimed as mythical by too astute critics; see Lanciani, *The Athenaeum*, 1899. In any case the legends and hearsay as to their origin, current among various races, have a psychological interest, and may afford valuable indications as to national proclivities, which must rescue them from the neglect of every judicious historian.

[535] Livy, iv, 52, etc.

[536] The favourite title of Augustus was *Princeps* or "First citizen," but the more martial emperors, such as Galba and Trajan, preferred the military *Imperator*, which after their time became distinctive of the monarch. By the end of the third century, under the administration of Aurelian and Diocletian, the emperor became an undisguised despot, and henceforward was regarded as the *Dominus*, a term which originally expressed the relation between a master and his slaves; see Jn. Lydus, De Magistr., i, 5; the series of coins in Cohen's Numismatics of the Empire, etc.

[537] Strabo says it was full of Tarsians and Alexandrians; xiv, 5. Athenaeus calls it "an epitome of the world"; i, 17; cf. Tacitus, Ann., xv, 44; "The city which attracts and applauds all things villainous and shameful."

[538] Tiberius made an end of the *comitia* or popular elections, and after his time the offices of state were conferred in the Senate, a body which in its elements was constituted at the fiat of the emperor; Tacitus, Ann., i, 15, etc.

[539] Under Diocletian (*c.* 300) the legislative individualism of the emperor attained maturity; see Muirhead, Private Law of Rome, Edin., 1899, P. 353.

[540] The choice of Galba by the soldiers in Spain (68 A.D.) first "revealed the political secret that emperors could be created elsewhere than at Rome"; Tacitus, Hist., i, 4. Trajan, if actually a Spaniard, was the first emperor of foreign extraction.

[541] In the quadripartite allotment by Diocletian, he himself fixed his residence at Nicomedia, his associate Augustus chose Milan, whilst the scarcely subordinated Caesars, Galerius and Constantius, made Sirmium and Treves their respective stations; Aurelius Vict., Diocletian.

[542] Arcadius, as the elder, reigned in the East, a proof that it was esteemed to be the most brilliant position. The Notitia also, a contemporary work, places the East first as the superior dominion. No doubt the new tyrants

found themselves in an uncongenial atmosphere at Rome, and the sterner stuff of the Western nations would not tolerate their sublime affectations. They could stand the follies of Nero, but not the vain-glory of Constantine, who soon fled from the covert sneers of the capital and merely paid it a couple of perfunctory visits afterwards. It is significant that the forms of adoration are omitted from the Notitia of the West; cf., however, Cassiodorus, Var. Ep., xii, 18, 20.

[543] About a year, but sometimes prolonged; he could be indicted afterwards for misconduct, unless like Sulla, Caesar, etc., and the aspirants to the purple later, he found himself strong enough to seize on the supremacy.

[544] See Mommsen, Das röm. Militärwesen, etc. Hermes, xxiv, 1889.

[545] Aurelius Vict., Diocletian, etc. After Elagabalus Aurelian was the pioneer in this departure, but in their case it seems to have been not a policy so much as a love of pompous display. It is worth noting that these emperors were men of low origin; Aurelian was a peasant, Diocletian the son of a slave. Yet Aurelian would not let his wife wear silk; Hist. Aug. Aurelian, 45.

[546] The brood of eunuchs (bed-keepers) flows to us from prehistoric times. Ammianus (xiv, 6) attributes the invention to Semiramis, whose date, if any, is about 2000 B.C. They appear to be engendered naturally by polygamy. Isidore of Seville characterizes them as follows: "Horum quidam coeunt, sed tamen virtus in semine nulla est. Liquorem enim habent, et emittunt, sed ad gignendum inanem et invalidum"; Etymolog., x, *sb. voc.* Hence the demand for such an enactment as that of Leo, Novel., xcviii, against their marrying, which, however, would be unnecessary in the case of the καρξιμάδες.

[547] The names of Eusebius, Eutropius, Chrysaphius, etc., are well known as despots of the Court and Empire. "Apud quem [si vere dici debeat] Constantius multum potuit," is the sarcasm of Ammianus on the masterful favourite Eutropius; xviii, 4. Ultimately members of the royal family were castrated to allow of their being intrusted with the office of Chamberlain, practically the premiership, whilst unfitting them to usurp the throne; see Schlumberger, L'épopée byzant. au dix. siècle, 1896, p. 6.

[548] See Const. Porph., *passim*. The emperor cannot even uncover his head without the castrates closing round him to intercept the gaze of rude mankind; Reiske, ii, p. 259.

[549] The use of numerical affixes to the names of monarchs did not exist among the ancients, and hence many cruxes arise for antiquarians to distinguish those of the same name. Popularly they were often differentiated by nicknames. Thus we read of Artaxerxes the Longhanded, Ptolemy the Bloated, the Flute-player; Charles the Bald, the Fat; Philip the Fair, Frederic

Barbarossa, etc. The grandson of the last, Frederic II, seems to have been the first who assumed a number as part of his regal title; see Ludewig, Vita Justin., VIII, viii, 53.

[550] CP. fell to Mahomet II in 1453, and the kingdom of Trebizond, a fragment which still existed under a Comnenian dynasty, in 1461. Bosnia, Herzegovina, Roumania, Armenia proper, Georgia, and the lower part of Mesopotamia did not, however, belong to the Eastern Empire, but there was suzerainty over most of the adjacent territory except Persia.

[551] The town itself was in the hands of the Bulgarians till 504, when it was won by Theodoric for Italy; Cassiodorus, Chron.

[552] This frontier was delimited by Diocletian, *c. 295*; Eutropius, ix; Procopius, De Bel. Pers., i, 19.

[553] At this time Western Armenia, about one-third of the whole, was called Roman, the rest Persian. It was divided at the end of the fourth century, but no taxes were collected there by the Byzantines; see below.

[554] Neither the north-eastern nor the north-western boundaries can now be precisely defined. According to Theodoret, the north-eastern verge of the Empire was Pityus, about seventy miles farther north; Hist. Eccles., v, 34. After the reign of Trajan the Euxine was virtually a Roman lake, and a garrisoned fort was kept at Sebastopol, considerably north of the Phasis, Bosphorus (Crimea) under its Greek kings being still allowed a nominal autonomy; Arrian, Periplus Pont. Euxin. After 250, however, under Gallienus, etc., these regions were overrun by the Goths. In 275 Trajan's great province of Dacia was abandoned by Aurelian, but he preserved the remembrance of it by forming a small province with the same name south of the Danube; Hist. Aug., Aurelian, 39, etc.

[555] This geographical sketch is based chiefly on the Notitia, the Synecdemus of Hierocles, and Spruner's maps.

[556] Less than the present population of England, which has barely a tenth of the area of the Empire.

[557] To take a few instances: Thessalonica and Hadrianople, former population not less than 300,000 each, now about 70,000 each; Antioch, formerly 500,000 (Chrysostom mentions 200,000, doubtless only freemen), now 7,500; Alexandria, formerly 750,000, now again growing into prosperity, 230,000; on the other hand, Ephesus, Palmyra, Baalbec, etc., once great cities, have entirely disappeared. Nor have any modern towns sprung up to replace those mentioned; Cairo alone, with its 371,000, is an apparent exception, but it is almost on the site of Memphis, still a busy town in the sixth century. For these and many similar examples the modern gazetteers,

etc., are a sufficient reference. Taking all things into consideration, to give a hundred millions to the countries forming the Eastern Empire, in their palmy days, might not be an overestimate; and even then the density of population would be only about one-third of what it is in England at the present day.

[558] Institut. Just., Prooem., etc.

[559] Here, however, seems to have been the tract first known to the Greeks as Asia, but the name was extended to the whole continent fully ten centuries before this time.

[560] Hierocles, *op. cit.* By the Notitia the civil and military government of Isauria and Arabia are in each case vested in the same person.

[561] Now the Dobrudscha.

[562]

The birds their choir apply; airs, vernal airs,

Breathing the smell of field and grove, attune

The trembling leaves, while universal Pan,

Knit with the Graces and the Hours in dance,

Led on the eternal Spring.

Paradise Lost, IV.

[563] Including the small province of that name.

[564] On the roll of precedence the Vicars and Proconsuls were Spectabiles, the ordinary governors Clarissimi. The intendant of the Long Walls was also called a Vicar; Novel., viii.

[565] See the Notitia.

[566] The independence of proconsular Asia has already been mentioned.

[567] "Yielding only to the sceptre"; Jn. Lydus, De Magistr., ii, 5. On the roll of precedence, however, he came after consuls and patricians, but he was usually an ex-consul and patrician as well; see Godefroy *ad* Cod. Theod., VI, vi.

[568] The most noted of these roads, the Via Appia, ran from Rome to Brindisi. It was about fifteen feet wide, with raised footpaths proportionately narrow. The only road in the Eastern Empire with a special name was the Via Egnatia, leading from the coast of the Adriatic through Thessalonica to Cypsela (Ipsala, about forty miles north of Gallipoli). The Antonine Itinerary

shows the distance between most of the towns and ports in the Empire (*c. 300*). The Tabula Peutingeriana is a sort of panoramic chart on which towns, roads, mountains, forests, etc., are marked without any approach to delineating the outline of the countries, except in the vicinity of the Bosphorus and CP. (third century, but brought up to a later date; about 15 feet × 1). There is a photographic reproduction, Vienna, 1888. Strabo (IV, iii, 8) notes how careless the Greeks were, as compared with the Romans, in the matter of public works of ordinary utility.

[569] Cod. Theod., XV, iii. By the absence of this title from the Code and from Procopius (De Bel. Goth., i, 14; De Aedific., iv, 8; v, 5) we can discern that the roads in the East were generally in bad condition. No rubbish or filth or obstructive matter of any kind was allowed to be discharged into the roads or rivers. All roads or canals, that is, by-paths, were to be maintained in their primary condition, whether paved or unpaved; Pand., XLIII, x-xv. Soldiers were enjoined not to shock the public decency by bathing shamelessly in the rivers; Cod. Theod., VII, i; 13.

[570] The modern caravanserai, a great square building with open central court and chambers on two floors (see Texier and Pullan, *op. cit.*, p. 142, for a description and plans of one attributed to the times of the Empire), is supposed to represent not only these mansions, but even the pattern of the original Persian *angari* of the classic period. Travellers could stop at them gratuitously and obtain provender, etc. Cicero, Atticus, v, 16, etc.

[571] About forty animals were kept at each station; Procopius, Anecd., 30.

[572] Cod. Theod., VIII, v, 28, etc. 22½ lb. avd. seems absurdly little for a horse to carry; a parhippus, an extra-strong horse, was kept, and might take 100 lb. (75 avd.), but even that is only half the weight of an average man; Cassiodorous, Var. Epist., iv, 47; v, 5. C. remarks, however, that it is absurd to load an animal who has to travel at a high speed. I think, therefore, that the load is in addition to a rider (*hippocomus*).

[573] Cod. Theod., VIII, v, 2.

[574] The Jerusalem Itinerary (*c.* 350) shows the mansions and mutations from Bordeaux to J., etc. The former seem to have been in or near large towns, the latter by the wayside.

[575] Cod. Theod., VIII, v, with Godefroy's paratitlon.

[576] Cod. Theod., VI, xxvii; called *Agentes in rebus*.

[577] They appear to have originated in the *Frumentarii* (corn-collectors), who were sent into the provinces to purvey for the wants of the capital. Encouraged on their return to tattle about what they had seen, signs of disaffection, etc., their secondary vocation became paramount; and under

Diocletian they were reconstituted with a more consonant title, whilst their license was restrained; Aurelius Vict., Diocletian; Hist. Aug. Commodus, 4, etc.

[578] Libanius, Epitaph. Juliani (R., I, p. 568); cf. Xenophon, Cyropaedia, viii, 2. The Persian king was the original begetter of "eyes and ears" of this description; Herodotus, i, 114.

[579] Liban., Adv. eos qui suam Docendi Rat., etc. At this time they were generally called *Veredarii, veredus* being the name of the post-horses they always rode; Procopius, De Bel. Vand., i, 16; De Bel. Pers., ii, 20.

[580] Vetus Glossarium, *sb. Vered. eq.* (Godefroy *ad* Cod. Theod., VI, xxix, 1).

[581] *Curiosi*; Cod. Theod., VI, xxix.

[582] *Irenarchi*; *ibid.*, XII, xiv; Cod., X, lxxv.

[583] In no instance better exemplified than in that of Anastasius.

[584] Galba, Pertinax, Alexander, Probus, Maurice, etc.

[585] See their insignia and appointments in the Notitia; there was a separate set for the East and West even after the extinction of the Roman dynasty of the latter division.

[586] Or more briefly, Masters of Soldiers, of Troops, or of the Forces; in the Notitia the five military magnates are placed before the Counts of the Treasury.

[587] *In praesenti*, in the Presence; to be with the Emperor travelling was to be *in sacro Comitatu*; to send anything to Court was to send it *ad Comitatum*, etc.

[588] For the probable daily order of the Consistorium see p. 92; Cod. Theod., XI, xxxix, 5, 8; the materials at this date are too scanty to fill an objective picture; cf. Schiller, Gesch. d. röm. Kaiserzeit, Gotha, 1887, ii, p. 66.

[589] Cod. Theod., VI, xii, and Godefroy *ad loc.*

[590] *Ibid.*, I, i, ii, with Godefroy's paratitla.

[591] They had much the force of a decree nisi, to be made absolute only in the quarter where all the circumstances were known. The Codes are full of warnings against acting too hastily on the Emperor's rescript; thus Constantine says, "Contra jus Rescripta non valeant," but his son on the same page, "Multabuntur Judices qui Rescripta contempserint." They had to

steer between Scylla and Charybdis; in most cases, however, an easy task enough in Byzantine administration; Cod. Theod., I, i, 1, 5.

[592] Julian, in his zeal for constitutional government, tried to make it a real power in the state, but his effort was quietly ignored after his short career by his successors; Zosimus, iii, 11.

[593] In theory the Consul (Cod. Theod., VI, vi), but practically the P.U.; *ibid.*, ii, and Godefroy's paratitlon; cf. Cassiodorus, Var. Epist., i, 42, 43, etc.

[594] Cod. Theod., VI, xxiii, 1; XII, i, 122; IX, ii, 1, etc.

[595] Ammianus, xxviii, 1; Cod., I, xiv. Thus even Theodosius based himself on a decree of the Senate before embarking on the war with Maximus; Zosimus, v, 43, 44.

[596] When there was no emperor in the East, after the death of Valens, Julius, the Master of the Forces, applied for sanction to the Senate before ordering the massacre of all the Gothic youth detained as hostages throughout Asia; Zosimus, iv, 26.

[597] As in the case of Anastasius himself; Marcellinus Com., an. 515, etc.

[598] Ammianus, xxviii, 1; Procopius, De Bel. Goth., iii, 32.

[599] Cod. Theod., VI, ii, 4; XV, ix; Cod., I, xiv. Leo Sap. at last abolished the Senatusconsulta; Nov. Leo., lxxviii.

[600] References to, and a *résumé* of, modern authorities who have tried to work out the political significance of the Senate at this epoch will be found in Schiller, *op. cit.* p. 31. I may add that fifty members formed a quorum (Cod. Theod., VI, iv, 9), but a couple of thousand may have borne the title of Senator; Themistius, xxxiv, p. 456 (Dind.). Many of these, however, had merely the "naked" honour by purchase (Cod. Theod., XII, i, 48, *et passim*), or received it on being superannuated from the public service, but the potential Senators inherited the office or assimilated it naturally on account of their rank. Many of the titular Senators lived on their estates in the provinces; Cod. Theod., VI, ii, 2; cf. Cassiodorus, Var. Epist., iii, 6, etc.

[601] Cod. Theod., XII, i; Godefroy reckons seventy-nine Curiae in the Eastern Empire, but there must have been many more not definitely indicated; paratitlon *ad loc.*

[602] Cod. Theod., I, xxix.

[603] *Ibid.*, XII, i, 151; Novel., xv; see Savigny, Hist. Roman Law, I, ii. They seem to have been created by Valentinian I; Cod., I, lv, 1, etc.

[604] Cod. Theod., I, vii, 3; the first book contains most of Haenel's additions, and his numbers often differ from Godefroy's, to which I always refer on account of the commentary.

[605] Jn. Lydus, De Magistr., iii, 37; cf. Cassiodorus, Var. Ep., xi, 6. *Cancellarius*, from the *cancelli* or grille, within which they sat or stood.

[606] Plutarch, Cato Min., 23, etc.; cf. Savigny, *loc. cit.*

[607] Generally about 400 in number; the Count of the East was allowed 600; Cod., XII, lvi, lvii, etc. A sort of constabulary lower in rank than ordinary soldiers; Cod., XII, lviii, 12, etc.

[608] *Ibid.*, I, xii.

[609] *Ibid.*, IV, xvii.

[610] Cod. Theod., I, vii, 2; Cod., III, iii. Notwithstanding a long article by Bethmann-Hollweg (Civilprozessen, Bonn, 1864, iii, p. 116), nothing is known as to how they held their court, etc.

[611] Cod. Theod., XI, xxx.

[612] *Ibid.*, I, v.

[613] *Ibid.*, I, vii, 5, 6.

[614] Thus the first, the fifteenth, indiction were the first and last years of the round of fifteen. This method of reckoning mostly superseded all other dates, both in speaking and writing. The first Indiction is usually calculated from 1st September, 312. Fundamentally, indiction means rating or assessment.

[615] Hyginus, de Limitibus, etc., is our chief source of knowledge as to Roman land-surveying. Permanent maps were engraved on brass plates and copies were made on linen, etc. See Godefroy *ad* Cod. Theod., XI, xxvii.

[616] Pand., L, xv, 4; Cod. Theod., IX, xlii, 7; Cod., IX, xlix, 7.

[617] From a Syriac MS. in the British Museum, it appears that to every *caput* or *jugum* of 1,000 solidi (£560) were reckoned 5 *jugera* (about ⅝ acre) of vineyard, 20, 40, or 60 of arable land, according to quality, 250 olive trees, 1st cl., and 450 2nd cl.; see Mommsen on this document, Hermes, iii, 1868, p. 429; cf. Nov. Majorian, i. The amount exacted for each head varied with time and place. When Julian was in Gaul (*c. 356*), the inhabitants were paying 25 solidi (£14) *per caput* or *jugum*, which he managed to reduce to 7 solidi (£4); Ammianus, xvi, 5.

[618] Cod. Theod., XI, i, 10; XIII, xi, 12; Cod., XI, lviii, etc. Deserted lands were mostly near the borders, from which the occupiers had been driven by hostile incursions. Barren lands presumably were put in the worst class.

[619] The duties of these officials are nowhere precisely defined, and a consistent account must be presumed from the scattered indications contained in the Codes, Cassiodorus, etc.; see Cod. Theod., XIII, xi; Cod., XI, lvii, etc.

[620] Cod. Theod., XIII, x, 5; xi, 4, etc.

[621] Ibid., XIII, x, 8.

[622] For this assessment the adult age was in general 18, but in Syria, males 14, females 12; Pand., L, xv, 3.

[623] "Capitatio humana atque animalium"; Cod. Theod., XI, xx, 6; cf. Cedrenus, i, p. 627; Zonaras, xiv, 3; Glykas, iv, p. 493, etc. Owing to the use in the Codes of the words *caput* and *capitatio* with respect to both land-tax and poll-tax, these were generally confounded together, till Savigny made the distinction clear in his monograph, Ueber d. röm. Steuerverfassung, pub. 1823 in the Transact. of the Berlin Acad. of Science. The poll-tax is usually distinguished as *plebeia capitatio*. The epigram of Sidonius Ap. is always quoted, and has often misled the expositors of the Codes, in this connection. To the Emperor Majorian he says:

Geryones nos esse puta, monstrumque tributum,

Hic capita, ut vivam, tu mihi tolle tria.

The taxes must have been again very high for him to anticipate so much relief from the remission of only three heads (*c.* 460).

[624] Cod. Theod., XI, i, 14; "quantulacumque terrarum possessio."

[625] Ibid., XIII, x, 2.

[626] Ibid., XIII, x, 4, 6.

[627] Ibid., XIII, iii, iv. A list of thirty-five handicrafts exempted is given, including professionals, such as physicians, painters, architects, and geometers. I find no relief, however, in the case of lawyers.

[628] Cod. Theod., IV, xii; Godefroy could only recover one Constitution of this title, but Haenel has been able to collect nine; thirteen are contained in the corresponding title of the Code, IV, lxi. On imported eunuchs $1/8$ was paid; Cod., IV, xlii, 2.

[629] Ibid., X, xix, 3, 12.

[630] *Ibid.*, IV, xii.

[631] Cod., IV, lxiii, 2; "subtili auferatur ingenio."

[632] Cod. Theod., XIII, i; Cod., XI, i. Evagrius (iii, 39), one of the nearest in time, is most copious on the subject of this tax. Cedrenus, Glykas, Zonaras ("an annual tribute!") evidently confused it with the poll-tax, but their remarks show that every animal useful to the farmer returned something to the revenue; a horse or an ox one shilling, an ass or a dog fourpence, etc.

[633] Evagrius alone mentions these; cf. Hist. August. Alexander, 34.

[634] According to an old Biblical commentator, it was called the *penalizing gold*, "the price of sorrow," as we might say (aurum poenosum or pannosum, the *gold of rags*, levied even on beggars); see Valesius ad Evagr. *loc. cit.*; Quaest. Vet. et Nov. Test. 75, *ad calc.* St. August, (in Migne, iii, 2269). He also is thinking of a poll-tax, *didrachma*, less than two shillings a head. The Theodosian Code in twenty-one Constitutions is clear and precise as to the incidence of the chrysargyron, and nothing can be interjected extraneous to the definitions there constituted. The quadriennial contribution of Edessa was 140 lb. of gold (£5,600); Joshua Stylites (Wright), Camb. 1882, 31.

[635] Zosimus, ii, 38. He is severe on Constantine for inflicting it, but there must have been something like it before; see Godefroy *ad* Cod. Theod., XIII, i, 1.

[636] Cod. Theod., XVI, ii, 8, 14, 15; XIII, i, 11, etc.; VII, xx, 3, 9, etc. (also some Court officers; XI, xii, 3); XIII, iv; i, 10.

[637] It is the signal action of Anastasius respecting it which has caused so much notice to be taken of the impost; see esp. Procopius, Gaz. Panegyric., 13. One Timotheus of Gaza is said to have aimed a tragedy at the harshness of it; Cedrenus; Suidas, *sb.* Timoth. By Code, XI, i, 1, it seems that traces of it remained permanently. Evagrius alludes vaguely to some compensating financial measures of Anastasius; iii, 42; cf. Jn. Malala, p. 394.

[638] This was the regular procedure when state debtors were officially forgiven—a ceremonial burning of the accounts; Cod. Theod., XI, xxviii, 2, 3, etc.

[639] Cod. Theod., VI, ii, 1, 4, 13, etc. The idea of abolishing these senatorial taxes was entertained in the time of Arcadius, but the scheme fell through; Cod., XII, ii. Senatorial estates were kept distinct from all others during peraequation at the quindecennial survey; Cod. Theod., VI, iii, 2, 3.

[640] Cod. Theod., VI, xxiv, 8, 9; XIII, iii, 15, 17, etc., see Godefroy's paratitlon to VI, ii.

[641] *Ibid.*, VI, ii, 5, 9; VII, xxiv, etc.

[642] Cod., XII, iii, 3.

[643] Cod. Theod., VII, xxiii.

[644] *Ibid.*, XII, xiii, and Godefroy's commentaries. Cod., X, lxxiv.

[645] Cod. Theod., VI, xxx, 2; Nov., xxx, etc.

[646] Cod. Theod., X, vi; XV, x, and Godefroy *ad loc.*

[647] *Ibid.*, X, xix; Cod., XI, vi; see Dureau de la Malle (*op. cit.*, iv, 17), who summarizes with refs. our scanty information on the subject. It seems that the ancient methods of working the ore were very defective, and the *scoriae* of the famous silver mines at Laurium have been treated for the third time in recent years with good results; see Cordella, Berg u. hüttenmän. Zeitung, xlii, 1883, p. 21; Strabo, IX, 1.

[648] Cod. Theod., I, v, 1, etc. Chrysostom alludes to the severity of the miner's existence; Stagirium, 13; Mart. Aegypt., 2 (in Migne, i, 490; ii, 697). During the Gothic revolt of 376 the Thracian miners joined the insurgents; Ammianus, xxxi, 6.

[649] Cod. Theod., XI, i, 1, 34; v, 3, 4; xvi, 8, etc.

[650] Cod. Theod., XI, i, 15, 16; xxv; XII, vi, 15, etc.

[651] *Ibid.*, XII, vi, 2, etc.

[652] *Ibid.*, XI, vii, 14, 16, etc.

[653] *Ibid.*, XI, vii, 1, etc.

[654] *Ibid.*, XI, vii, 10, 13; VIII, viii, 1, 3; this privilege was extended to the Jews' Sabbath; II, viii, 3.

[655] *Ibid.*, XI, vii, 16, etc.

[656] *Ibid.*, XI, i, 34, 35; xxii, 4, etc.

[657] *Ibid.*, XI, vii, 3, etc.

[658] *Ibid.*, X, xvii; XI, ix; that is by auction.

[659] *Ibid.*, [?] xxviii; cf. Cassiodorus, Var. Epist., xi, 7.

[660] *Ibid.*, XI, vii, 2, 6, etc., cf. Cassiodorus, *op. cit.*, iv, 14.

[661] Cod. Theod., XI, i, 9, 21; XII, vi, 19, and Godefroy *ad loc.*; *ibid.*, XII, vii, 2, etc.

[662] *Ibid.*, XII, vi, 19, 21, etc.

[663] *Ibid.*, XI, vii, 1; XIII, x, 1, etc. The demand notes had to be signed by the Rector; XI, i, 3.

[664] *Ibid.*, XI, i, 19; xxvi, 2; XII, vi, 18, 23, 27. The Defender of the City was generally present to act as referee on these occasions. A single annone was valued at 4 *sol.* (£2 5*s.*) per annum; Novel., Theod., xxiii. It appears that the precious metals were accepted by weight only to guard against adulteration, clipping, etc. Thus, in 321, Constantine enacted that 7 *sol.* should be paid for an ounce by tale instead of six, indicating $\frac{1}{7}$ alloy in his own gold coin at that period; see Dureau de la Malle, *op. cit.*, i, 10; Cod. Theod., XII, vii, 1; cf. vi, 13.

[665] *Ibid.*, VII, vi; xxiii; XI, i, 9; cf. Cassiodorus, *op. cit.*, xi, 39. When it was found that sheep and oxen fell into poor condition after being driven a long way the estimated price was exacted instead.

[666] Cod. Theod., I, xv; one law only in Godefroy, 17 in Haenel.

[667] Cod. Theod., VIII, v, 13, 18; X, xx, 4, 11, etc.

[668] *Ibid.*, XIII, v, 28; ix; Cod., XI, iii, 2, etc. In an emergency any one possessing a ship of sufficient size was liable to be impressed. The prescribed least capacity seems to have been about ten measured tons according to the modern system (100 cub. ft. per ton register), that is, cargo space for 2,000 *modii*, about 650 cub. ft.

[669] There were three grand treasuries at CP., viz., that of the Praefect of the East, of the Count Sacrarum Largitionum, and of the Count Rerum Privatarum (his local agents were called *Rationales*, but seem from the Notitia to have become extinct in the East), but the Praefect was the chief minister of finance and ruled both the returns and the disbursements; see Godefroy's Notitia, *ad calc.*; Cod. Theod.; Jn. Lydus, De Magistr., ii, 27; Cassiodorus, Var. Epist., vi, 3, etc. The Rectors and the Curiae could levy local rates for public works, to which purpose a third of the revenue from the customs in each district and from national estates (mostly property of abolished temples) was regularly devoted; see Cod. Theod., XV, i, with Godefroy's paratitlon and commentaries. The Emperor indulged his fancy in building out of the public funds or granted sums in the form of largess, as when Anastasius bestowed a considerable amount on the island of Rhodes to repair the damage done by an earthquake; Jn. Malala, xvi. There were some small taxes I have not noticed, such as the *siliquaticum*, pay for the army, by which each party to a sale gave a ½ siliqua (3*d.*). This was devised by Valentinian III (Novel., Theodos., xlviii; Do. Valent., xviii) and existed in the time of Cassiodorus (*op. cit.*, iv, 19, etc.), but does not seem to have been adopted in the East.

[670] Antioch also had an allowance of free provisions, but there is no precise evidence in this case.

[671] Cod. Theod., VIII, iv, 6; XI, i, 11, etc.

[672] *Ibid.*, XI, xxvi.

[673] Considerable obscurity envelops the office of *protostasia*. I conjecture it to have been a supervision imposed on local nobles, chiefly residential Senators, who had to serve for two years; Cod. Theod., XI, xxiii. In theory all the superior offices had to be vacated on the expiration of a year, but they were often prolonged. Thus a trustworthy and efficient *Susceptor* retained his post for five years; *ibid.*, XII, vi, 24. The latter were mostly elected by the Curiae, who were liable for their defalcations; *ibid.*, 1, etc.

[674] Cod. Theod., VIII, viii; x; XI, vii, 17, etc. These palatine emissaries, coming as *Compulsors* or otherwise, were detested by the Rectors, etc., who could scarcely show them the deference due to their brevet-rank, which was high: doubtless they gave themselves airs; *ibid.*, VI, xxiv, 4; xxvi, 5, etc. They were entitled to be greeted with a kiss and to sit with the Judge on his bench.

[675] 320,000 lb. of gold; Procopius, Anecdot., 19. In the time of Pompey it was thought a considerable achievement when that general raised the income of the Republic to the trifling sum, according to modern ideas, of £3,500,000; Plutarch, Pompey, 45. On the other hand we have the statement of Vespasian, a century later, that he needed close on £400,000,000 to keep the Empire on its legs, a sum almost equal to the requirements of modern Europe, but the scope of his remark is not plain; Suetonius, Vespas., 16. Antoninus Pius, again, with the finances of the whole Empire under his hand during his reign of twenty-three years saved £22,000,000, nearly the same amount per annum as Anastasius for a similar extent of territory; Dion Cass., lxxiii, 8. Such small savings by the most thrifty emperors do not argue a large income. In our own best years a surplus may reach about five per cent. of the receipts. This gives us grounds for a guess that the revenue of Rome after Augustus was something like £20,000,000.

[676] See p. 131 for the names of those hordes who shared the Western Empire between them. Overflow of population and pressure by the most powerful nomads, the Huns and Alani, were the general causes which precipitated the barbarian hosts on the Empire.

[677] About this time the Bulgarians made their first appearance on the Danube as the foes of civilization. They were lured into a treaty by Zeno; Müller, Fr. Hist. Graec., iv, p. 619 (Jn. Antioch.); cf. Zonaras, xiv, 3, etc.

[678] See p. 124.

[679] The capitation tax was remitted in Thrace; Cod., XI, li. In fact, hardly any taxes were drawn from that Diocese, for, as Anastasius himself remarks, the inhabitants were ruined by barbarian irruptions; *ibid.*, X, xxvii, 2. How irrepressible were the wild tribes across the Danube can best be appreciated by a perusal of Ammianus, xxxi, etc., and Jordanes *passim*.

[680] The new Persian Empire which dissolved the Parthian sovereignty was founded, *c. 218*, by Ardashir (Artaxerxes); see Agathias, ii, 26, etc.

[681] See Godefroy *ad* Cod. Theod., VII, xiv, xv, xvii; Hist. Aug. Hadrian, 11, 12; Probus, 13, 14; Ammianus, xxviii, 2, etc. The walls of Hadrian and Antonine in North Britain are well known, and have been exhaustively described. The camps are represented as military cities. See Bruce's Handbook to the Roman Wall, 1885, etc.

[682] Cod. Theod., VII, xv, etc.

[683] Arrian, Peripl. Pont. Eux. This force was reduced by Constantine; Zosimus, ii, 34.

[684] In the Notitia Or., there are two Counts and thirteen Dukes. All of the latter, however, were Counts of the First Order, as evidenced by their insignia. In rank they were *Spectabiles*, that is, a step higher than the Rectors and ordinary Senators.

[685] Evidently from the Notitia.

[686] See Godefroy *ad* Cod. Theod., VII, i, 18; Mommsen, *op. cit.*, Hermes, 1889. In Agathias (v, 13) we have the vague statement that the whole forces of the Empire amounted to 645,000 men at the period of highest military efficiency. More than half of these would be assigned to the East. But John of Antioch, in making a similar statement, seems to have the Eastern Empire only in his mind; Müller, Fr. Hist. Graec., iv, p. 622.

[687] See p. 50.

[688] Procopius, Anecdot., 24, 26; Agathias, v, 15.

[689] See Godefroy *ad* Cod. Theod., VI, xxiv; XIV, xvii, 8, 9, 10. On the Candidati see Reiske *ad* Const. Porph., p. 77. In the field they seem to have been the closest bodyguard of the Emperor, as were the eunuchs on civil occasions; Ammianus, xxxi, 13.

[690] See the Notitia and Mommsen, *op. cit.*

[691] These are all given in the Notitia, some copies of which are coloured.

[692] The general appearance was probably: "The tuft of the helmet, the lance pennon, and the surcoat were all of a fixed colour for each band;" Oman, Art of War, p. 186.

[693] For the ensign see Ammianus, xvi, 10; Vegetius, ii, 7, 13, 14, etc.; Cod., I, xxvii, 1 (8); Jn. Lydus, De Magistr., i, 46; Maurice, Strategikon, ii, 9, 13, 14, 19; Cedrenus, i, p. 298. The dragons were hollow so as to become inflated with the wind; Gregory Naz., Adv. Julian, i, 66.

[694] The cavalry with mail-clad horses were called *cataphractarii* or *clibanarii*; Ammianus, xvi, 10; Cod. Theod., XIV, xxvii, 9.

[695] Ammianus, xx, 11; xxix, 5; Procopius, De Bel. Pers., i, 1; Maurice, *op. cit.*, XII, viii, 2, 4, 11, etc. There were fifteen factories for the forging of arms; Notitia; see below.

[696] Vegetius, i, 4, 5, 6; Cod. Theod., VII, xiii, 3; xx, 12, etc.

[697] Cod. Theod., VII, xiii, 8; Pand., XLIX, xvi, 11, etc.

[698] Vegetius, i, 7; Cod. Theod., VII, xiii, etc.; eighteen was the usual age for the recruit, 5 ft. 8 in. the height. They were branded in a conspicuous part of the body; Cod. Theod., X, xxi, 4, and Godefroy *ad loc.*

[699] Provided they were physically fit; Cod. Theod., VII, xxii.

[700] Ammianus, xxi, 6; Cod. Theod., VII, xiii. An officer called a *temonarius* collected the quittance money for the recruits, which varied from £14 to £20 apiece.

[701] Ammianus, xvii, 13; xix, 11; xxviii, 5, etc.; Zosimus, iv, 12, etc. Barbarians of this class were called *Dedititii*.

[702] Cod. Theod., VII, xiii, 16, and Godefroy *ad loc.*

[703] Jordanes, De Reb. Get., 21, 28. The enlistment of barbarians seems to have reached its height under Justin II, when Tiberius led 150,000 mercenaries against the Persians (*c.* 576); Evagrius, v, 14; cf. Theophanes, an. 6072, etc.

[704] Godefroy *ad* Cod. Theod., VII, xvii; Vegetius, v (the Liburnian galleys); Marcellinus Com., an. 508 ("centum armatis navibus totidemque dromonibus." By "armed ships" I presume he means bulky transports laden with soldiers and munitions of war); Procopius, De Bel. Vand., i, 11, etc.

[705] Cod. Theod., VII, xx.

[706] Evidently from Agathias, v, 15, and the following.

[707] Rescript of Anastasius, Mommsen, *op. cit.*, pp. 199, 256.

[708] The *Limitanei* and *Comitatenses* are mentioned in the Code (I, xxvii, 2 (8), etc.), but the Palatine troops do not occur by name in the literature of the sixth century (?).

[709] The term was used long before the word legion dropped out; Cod. Theod., VII, i, 18, etc. By the Greeks the *Numeri* were called the *Catalogues*; Procopius, *passim* (also in previous use).

[710] Cod. Theod., [?] vii, 16, 17, etc.; Procopius, De Bel. Goth., iii, 39; iv, 26. Applicants of all soils were on occasion attracted by the offer of a bounty called *pulveraticum*.

[711] Cod., XII, xxxiv, 6, 7.

[712] Olympiodorus, p. 450; Novel., Theod., xx; Procopius, De Bel. Vand., i, 11; De Bel. Goth., iv, 5, etc.

[713] Cod., IV, lxv, 35; Novel., cxvii, 11; cf. Benjamin, Berlin Dissert., 1892.

[714] Procopius, De Bel. Vand., i, 2, 3; Agathias, ii, 7, 9, etc. There were no true allies of the Empire at this time, although all those who fought for her may not have been technically *Foederati*; cf. Mommsen, *op. cit.*, pp. 217, 272.

[715] The name defines them as "biscuit-eaters," in allusion to their being maintained at the table of their lord.

[716] Benjamin's essay is written to oppose this view which is favoured by Mommsen; *op. cit.*, in both cases.

[717] Procopius, De Bel. Vand., ii, 18.

[718] *Ibid.*, De Bel. Pers., i, 25; De Bel. Goth., iii, 1, etc.

[719] *Ibid.*, De Bel. Vand., i, 17; ii, 19, etc.

[720] Cod., IX, xii, 10.

[721] Ammianus, xiv, 2; xxvii, 9, etc.

[722] Cassiodorus, Var. Epist., v, 16, 17. An order for 1,000 *dromons* was executed for Theodoric in an incredibly short time. "Renuntias completum quod vix credi potest inchoatum."

[723] The general character given to Byzantine soldiers is exceptionally bad: "The vile and contemptible military class"; Isidore Pelus., Epist., i, 390: "as free from crime as you might say the sea is free from waves"; Chrysostom, In Matth. Hom. LXI, 2 (in Migne, vii, 590). These, of course, are priests, but cf. Ammianus, xxii, 4; Zosimus, ii, 34, etc. Thus a century earlier the army had already fallen into a wretched condition; see also Synesius, De Regno.

[724] Maurice, *op. cit.*, XII, viii, 16.

[725] From the anonymous Strategike it would seem that the phalanx was restored on occasion during the sixth century (Köchly and Rüslow).

[726] See Arrian's Tactica *v.* Alanos. For an interesting exposition of the vicissitudes of warfare by means of cavalry, infantry, and missiles pure, see Oman's Art of War, but the author's selection of the battle of Adrianople (378) as marking a sharp turn in the evolution of Roman cavalry is quite

arbitrary and could not be historically maintained. That disaster made no demonstrable difference in the constitution of the armies of the Empire. The forces of Rome were consumed to a greater extent at the battle of Mursa less than thirty years previously (351), when the army of the victor contained, perhaps, 40,000 cavalry, half of the whole amount; Julian, Orat. I, ii (p. 98, etc., Hertlein); Zonaras, xiii, 8, etc.

[727] Constantine, according to Zosimus (ii, 33), first appointed a Magister Equitum in the new sense; cf. Cod. Theod., XI, i, 1 (315).

[728] Notitia Or.

[729] Procopius, De Bel. Pers., i, 13, etc.

[730] Procop., De Bel. Pers., i, 13, etc.

[731] Ibid., De Bel. Vand., i, 19.

[732] Ibid., Anecdot., 24; Agathias, v, 15. Under Leo Macella the Scholars consisted of selected Armenians, but Zeno introduced a rabble of Isaurians, his own countrymen; these, of course, were chased by Anastasius; Theodore Lect., ii, 9, etc. Leo also levied the Excubitors to be a genuine fighting corps of the Domestics; Jn. Lydus, De Magist., i, 16.

[733] Longinus, brother of Zeno, expected to succeed him, but he was seized promptly, shaved, and banished as a presbyter to Alexandria; Theophanes, an. 5984, etc.

[734] Ibid., an. 5985. To his power among the Isaurians Zeno owed his elevation, being taken up by Leo as a counterpoise to Aspar and his Goths, the authors of his own fortune, of whom he was in danger of becoming the tool; Candidus, Excerpt., p. 473, etc.

[735] Marcellinus Com., an. 498.

[736] This was the end of the war according to Theophanes (an. 5988), who gives it only three years; cf. Jn. Malala, xvi.

[737] These brigands had been subsidized to the amount of 5,000 lb. of gold annually (Jn. Antioch., Müller, v, p. 30, says only 1,500 lb.), which was henceforth saved to the treasury; Evagrius, iii, 35. All the most troublesome characters were captured and settled permanently in Thrace; Procopius, Gaz. Paneg., 10. For a monograph on this war see Brooks, Eng. Hist. Rev., 1893.

[738] Kavádh in recent transliteration. Persian history has been greatly advanced by modern Orientalists; see especially Nöldeke, Geschichte der Perser, Leyden, 1887. But the history of Tabari is absurdly wrong in nearly all statements respecting the Romans and the translations of Nöldeke and Zotenberg vary so much that we often seem to be reading different works.

[739] Theodore Lect., ii; Procopius, De Bel. Pers., i, 7, *et seq.*; De Aedific., iii, 2, *et seq.*

[740] *Ibid.*; De Bel. Pers., ii, 3.

[741] Procopius, De Bel. Pers., i, 7; cf. his parallel story of Attila and the storks at Aquileia; De Bel. Vand., i, 4 (copied, perhaps, by Jordanes). While such anecdotes may enliven the page of history, their effectivity must always be accepted with suspicion.

[742] If the statements of Zacharias Myt. and Michael Melit. can be accepted, the town must have been very populous, as the number of citizens slain is put by them at eighty thousand.

[743] The Nephthalites or White Huns who occupied Bactria, previously the seat of a powerful Greek kingdom under a dynasty of Alexander's successors.

[744] Ammianus, xxv, 7.

[745] Procopius, De Aedific., ii, 1; cf. Jn. Malala, xvi, etc.

[746] Jordanes, 58. I am putting it, perhaps, too mildly in the text if Theodoric, who was a vassal of the Empire, knew beforehand of the course taken by his general. Sabinianus was chiefly supported by Bulgarians in consequence of Zeno's treaty with them; cf. Ennodius, Panegyr. Theodor. Petza had only 2,000 foot and 500 horse.

[747] Marcellinus Com., an. 505; Ennodius, *loc. cit.*

[748] Marcellinus Com., an. 508. Doubtless this was the event which caused Theodoric to build a large fleet; Cassiodorus, Var. Epist., v, 15, 16.

[749] Cassiodorus, Var. Epist., i, 1, might apply here; in any case the sentiments of Theodoric are clearly expressed by Jordanes, 59; cf. 57.

[750] Jn. Antioch. and Jn. Malala, Hermes, vi (Mommsen), pp. 344, 389.

[751] Marcellinus Com., an. 514; Jn. Malala, xvi; Theophanes, an. 6005, etc.

[752] Marcellinus Com., an. 514; Theophanes, an. 6005. The texts merely imply, perhaps, that they deserted to Vitalian. Hypatius, the Byzantine general, and nephew to Anastasius, was taken prisoner, deliberately given up in fact. A second engagement, however, under Cyril, was undoubtedly bloody; Jn. Malala, xvi.

[753] Jn. Malala, xvi; Zonaras (xiv, 3) says the fleet was inflamed by burning (concave) mirrors.

[754] As a ransom for their captives; Marcellinus Com., an. 515; Theophanes, an. 6006. The Senate negotiated for Anastasius.

[755] Marcellinus Com., an. 515.

[756] See, besides the above authorities, the correspondence between Emperor and Pope (in Migne, S.L., lxiii, also Concil. and Baronius).

[757] Theophanes, an. 6006; Cedrenus, i, p. 632.

[758] All the chronographists relate the vision of Anastasius, to whom, just before his death, a figure with a book appeared, saying: "For your insatiable avarice I erase fourteen years." Every one must regret the inherent defect of character which deprived us of a centenarian emperor.

[759] That of Anastasius is the last life written by Tillemont, which, as usual, he has illustrated by his wide erudition in ecclesiastical literature. But the infantile credulity of the man in theological matters abates much of the critical value of his work. Thus he gravely questions if the action of the Deity was correct when, for the benefit of the Persian king, he allowed a Christian bishop to release a treasure guarded by demons whom the Magi had failed to exorcise. He believes implicitly that an orthodox bishop emerged from the flames intact so as to convince an Arian congener of his error, etc. Rose's thesis (Halle, 1886) on these wars is of some value.

[760] Strabo, II, i, 30, etc.; Pliny, Hist. Nat., ii, 112. The earth was thought to be about 9,000 miles long and half that width, north to south.

[761] Cosmas Indicopleustes, a merchant who eventually turned monk, in his Christian Topography is our chief authority for popular cosmogony and trade in the sixth century (in Migne, S.G.). The theories of philosophers jar with his Biblical convictions and excite his antagonism. He writes to prove that the world is flat, that the sun rounds a great mountain in the north to cause night, etc. Being something of a draughtsman he explains his views by cosmographical diagrams, and figures many objects seen in his travels. There is an annotated translation by McCrindle, Lond., 1899 (Hakluyt Soc.).

[762] Diodorus, Sic., v, 19, 22, etc. For tin to the Scilly Is., etc.

[763] Phoenician trade is summarized with considerable detail by Ezekiel, xxvii; cf. Genesis, xxxvii, 25. But a couple of centuries earlier the race was well known to Homer, who often adverts to their skill in manufactures, as also to their knavery and chicanery:

Αὐτὴ δ' ἐς θάλαμον κατεβήσατο κηώεντα,

Ἔνθ' ἔσαν οἱ πέπλοι παμποίκιλοι, ἔργα γυναικῶν

Σιδονίων. κ.τ.λ.

Iliad, vi, 288.

Ἔνθα δὲ Φοίνικες ναυσίκλυτοι ἤλυθον ἄνδρες

Τρῶκται, μυρί' ἄγοντες ἀθύρματα νηΐ μελαίνῃ ...

Τὴν δ' ἄρα Φοίνικες πολυπαίπαλοι ἠπερόπευον. κ.τ.λ.

Odyssey, xv, 415.

The recently discovered ruins in Mashonaland (Rhodesia) prove, perhaps, that their unrecorded expeditions reached to S. Africa; see works by Bent, Neal and Hall, Keane, etc.

[764] 326 B.C. In Arrian's Indica, 18, *et seq.*

[765] Strabo, XVII, i, 13.

[766] Pliny, Hist. Nat., vi, 26; Pseud-Arrian, Peripl. Mar. Erythr., 57. For a discussion as to the date of Hippalus see Vincent, Commerce of the Ancients, ii, p. 47, etc. The S.W. monsoon blows from April to October, the N.E. in the interval.

[767] Very small, however, according to modern ideas; Pliny (*op. cit.*, vi, 24) gives them 3,000 *amphorae*, not more than 40 or 50 tons register. Arrian (*op. cit.*, 19) marks the distinction between "long, narrow war-galleys and round, capacious trading ships." A few great ships—floating palaces rather—were built by the Ptolemies and Hiero of Syracuse, but they were never seriously employed in navigation; Athenaeus, v, 36, *et seq.* Yet ships of at least 250 tons register were in common use by 170; Pand., L, v, 3.

[768] Pliny, *op. cit.*, vi, 26, *et seq.*; Pseud-Arrian, *op. cit.*, 57. The vessels had to be armed lest they should fall in with pirates. "The merchant floating down the stream; the caravan crossing the desert, mounting the defile, looking out upon the sea and its harbours; the ferry passing the river; the mariners in their little ship—they are real figures, yet they are nameless, all but a few; they suffer and they succumb without ever finding a voice for their story. On the desert, perhaps, a cloud of robber horse burst upon them; on the river the boat sinks, overladen; in the mountain passes they drop with cold; in the dirty lanes of the mart they die of disease. Commerce is not organized, safeguarded, universalized, as at present, but, such as it is, it reaches wide, and its life is never quite extinct." Beazley, Dawn of Modern Geography, i, p. 177.

[769] Pliny, *op. cit.*, vi, 19. He remarks that Pompey, during the Mithridatic war, first made the existence of this trade known to the Romans; cf. Strabo, XI, ii, 16; the geographer notes that Dioscurias, about 50 miles north of Phasis, was a great barbarian mart frequented by 70, or even, as some said, by 300 different nations; see also Ammianus, xxiii, 6.

[770] Cosmas, *op. cit.*, ii; cf. Procopius, De Bel. Pers., i, 20.

[771] So called from a sophist who was murdered there; Libanius, Epist., 20. Previously Nicephorium.

[772] Cod. Theod., VII, xvi, 2, 3, and Godfrey *ad loc.*; Cod., IV, lxiii, 4.

[773] The inhabitants were a mixed race, containing Semitic and Hellenic elements, etc. Greek inscriptions were common there; Cosmas, *op. cit.*, ii; cf. Philostorgius, iii, 6, etc.

[774] For the transport of an army to the opposite coast the king was able to collect 120 Roman, Persian, and native vessels; Act. Sanct. (Boll.), lviii, p. 747 (not 1,300 as Finlay, i, p. 264, which comes from adding a cipher to the figures in Surius).

[775] Called Taprobane by the Greek and Roman writers. It was distinguished by the possession of an immense lustrous jewel (ruby perhaps) which scintillated from the top of a temple; Cosmas, *op. cit.*, xi.

[776] The junks from Annam, as it appears, ploughed round the Malay peninsula to Galle; Hirth, China and the Roman Orient, 1885, p. 178. The Cingalese took no active part in the trade!; Tennant, Ceylon, i, p. 568 (*ibid.*).

[777] Cosmas, *op. cit.*, xi. His own trade seems to have lain chiefly between Adule and Malabar. In this age all the southern regions eastward of the Nile were commonly referred to as India; and that river was often named as the boundary between Africa and Asia. Hence the Nile was said to rise in India; Procopius, De Aedific., vi, 1, etc.

[778] Now Somaliland.

[779] Cosmas, *op. cit.*, xi; cf. Strabo, XVI, iv, 14. When Nonnosus went to Axume, *c.* 330, he saw 5,000 elephants grazing in a vast plain; Excerpt., p. 480.

[780] Cosmas, *op. cit.*, ii. This kind of wordless barter was also the mode of trading with the Serae or Chinese on the higher reaches of the Brahmaputra (?); Pliny, Hist. Nat., vi, 24; Ammianus, xxiii, 6; cf. Herodotus, iv, 196.

[781] Pliny, *op. cit.*, xii, 30. This district was also called the land of Frankincense; cf. Strabo, XVI, iv, 25; Pseud-Arrian, *op. cit.*, 29. There was also a port called Arabia Felix on or near the site of modern Aden.

[782] Cosmas, *op. cit.*, xi. White slaves, especially beautiful females for concubinage, were among the most important exports to India; Pseud-Arrian, *op. cit.*, 49. One Eudoxus tried to reach that country by rounding West Africa with a cargo of choir girls, physicians, and artisans, but twice failed; Strabo, II, iii, 4. In the time of Pliny the Empire was drained by the East

yearly to the amount of £800,000 in specie; Hist. Nat., xii, 41. Statues and paintings were also exported from the Empire; Strabo, XVI, iv, 26; Pseud-Arrian, *op. cit.*, 48; Philostratus, Vit. Apol., v, 20. The import of precious stones, etc., may be conceived from the statement that Lollia Paulina appeared in the theatre wearing emeralds and pearls to the value of £304,000; Pliny, *op. cit.*, ix, 58.

[783] Cosmas, *op. cit.*, ii.

[784] Malchus, p. 234; Theophanes, an. 5990. The island was taken by the Scenite (tent-dwelling) Arabs under Theodosius II, but was recovered by Anastasius.

[785] *Ibid.*

[786] Antoninus Martyr, Perambulatio, etc., 38, 41 (trans. in Pal. Pilgr. Text Soc., ii). The martyr, however, is a liar, as he professes to have produced wine from water at Cana, unless some brother monk in copying has been anxious to enhance his reputation. Clysma is now Suez.

[787] Rhinocolura, near Gaza, was the depôt for this trade in the time of Strabo (XVI, iv, 24).

[788] Strabo, XVII, i, 45; Pliny, Hist. Nat., vi, 26; Pseud-Arrian, *op. cit., passim.* Cosmas does not mention Berenice, but it was flourishing in the time of Procopius (De Aedific., vi, 2).

[789] Strabo, XVII, i, 45; Pliny, *op. cit.*, vi, 26.

[790] Strabo, XVI, iv, 24; XVII, iv, 10, *et seq*. There was a canal from the Red Sea to the Nile, but it silted up too rapidly to be permanently used. In Roman times Trajan last reopened it; see Lethaby and S., *op. cit.*, p. 236, for monographs on this subject.

[791] Notitia Or., X, XII; Cod. Theod., X, xx, xxi, xxii, and Godefroy's commentaries; Cod., XI, viii, ix, x.

[792] Strabo, XVI, iv, 24; Pliny, *op. cit.*, v, 16. There were different shades of purple and only the imperial shade was prohibited; Pliny, *op. cit.*, xxi, 22. The murex was gathered in several other places, especially Laconia, where it was inferior only to that of Tyre; Pausanias, iii, 21, etc.

[793] Sozomen, v, 15. Much money was also coined at Cyzicus.

[794] Cod. Theod., X, xx, 8.

[795] Cod., IV, lxxxiii, 6. This doubtless applied only to great houses, not to petty retail dealers and shopkeepers (to the ἔμπορος not the κάπηλος); the number seems too large to understand it of the capital alone.

[796] Pliny, *op. cit.*, viii, 73; Athenaeus, i, 50; xv, 17, etc.

[797] Strabo, XII, viii, 16; Pliny, *op. cit.*, 73, etc.

[798] Athenaeus, ii, 30; vi, 67.

[799] Pliny, *op. cit.*, xi, 27, etc. It is a question whether the transparent Coan fabrics were of silk, linen, or cotton, or a mixture.

[800] Procopius, Anecdot., 25.

[801] *Ibid.*

[802] Athenaeus, i, 50.

[803] Pliny, *op. cit.*, xxxv, 46.

[804] Strabo, XVI, ii, 25; Pliny, *op. cit.*, xxxvi, 65. False stones were plentifully manufactured; *ibid.*, xxxvii, 78, etc.

[805] Strabo, XIII, iv, 17.

[806] Athenaeus, i, 50; xiii, 24.

[807] Pliny, *op. cit.*, xiii, 21.

[808] Strabo, XVII, i, 15; Pliny, *op. cit.*, xiii, 22; Hist. August. Firmus, etc.

[809] Pausanias, v, 5; vii, 21.

[810] Strabo, XIII, iv, 14.

[811] Cod. Theod., XV, xi; Cod., XI, xliv. Indigenously called Mabog. It was a mart of venal beauty as well as of beasts; Lucian, De Syria Dea.

[812] Ammianus, xxix, 4; Procopius, Anecdot. 21.

[813] Pliny, *op. cit.*, iv, 27; xxxvii, 11.

[814] Pliny, *op. cit.*, xiv, *passim*; Athenaeus, i, 52, 55; x, *passim*.

[815] Strabo, XVII, iii, 23; Pliny, xxiv, 48; measuring more than 100 by 30 miles. What silphium really was is now indeterminate, but it was economically akin to garlic and asafoetida. It seems to have been indispensable in ordinary cooking.

[816] Totius Orb. Descript. (Müller, Geog. Graec. Min., Paris, 1861) 36; Procopius, De Aedific., v, 1.

[817] Tot. Orb. Descr., 51, 53. This tract from a Greek original (*c.* 350) summarizes the productions of the whole Empire, and for the most part confirms the continuance of the industries adverted to by the earlier and more copious writers.

[818] Athenaeus, i, 49.

[819] *Ibid.*

[820] Strabo, VII, vi, 2; Pliny, ix, 17, *et seq.*

[821] Cosmas, *op. cit.*, ii.

[822] Several "embassies" from Rome are mentioned in the Chinese annals, but nothing seems to have been known of them in the West. Stray merchants sometimes penetrated very far; Strabo, XV, i, 4. At first Rome is disguised as *Ta-thsin*, but later (643) the Byzantine power figures as *Fou-lin*; see Pauthier, Relat. polit. de la Chine avec les puiss. occid., 1859; cf. Hirth, *op. cit.*, who was without books to pursue the inquiry; Florus, iv, 12, etc.

[823] Aristotle, Hist. Animal., v, 19; Pliny, *op. cit.*, xi, 26; Pausanias, vi, 26.

[824] Cosmas, *op. cit.*, ii.

[825] Procopius, De Bel. Pers., i, 30.

[826] A serf was called *colonus, inquilinus,* or *adscriptus glebae*, terms fairly synonymous; Cod., XI, xlvii, 13. Godefroy's paratitlon to Cod. Theod., V, ix, x, is an epitome of everything relating to the serfs of antiquity; cf. Savigny, Römische Colonat u.s.w. Berlin Acad., 1822-3. The name of modern works on slavery and serfdom is legion.

[827] Cod., XI, xlvii, 21.

[828] *Ibid.*, 18, 23.

[829] Cod. Theod., X, xv, and Godefroy *ad loc.*; Pand., XLVII, vi; Novel., xvii, 17; lxxxv, 4, etc. This general disarmament of the industrial classes often left them defenceless against the barbarian raiders, as is instanced practically by Synesius, Epist. 107. Yet in an age of non-explosives peasants armed only with agricultural implements could become terrible, as was shown in Paphlagonia (359), when the incensed Novatian sectaries routed the legionaries sent against them with their hatchets, reaping-hooks, etc.; Socrates, ii, 30; Sozomen, iv, 21.

[830] Cod. Theod., X, xx, 16.

[831] *Ibid.*, X, xx, xxi, xxii; Cod., XI, viii, ix, x. To be a public baker (*manceps*) was a particular sort of punishment; Cod. Theod., XIV, lii, 22, etc.

[832] *Ibid.*, X, xx, 3, 5, 10, 15. Male and female alike, as well as their offspring, became bound to the sodality into which they married. The *addicti* were branded on the arm like recruits; *ibid.*, X, xxi, 4; cf. IX, xl, 2; Cod., XI, ix, 2. Scarcely less stringent were the rules by which even the private guilds or colleges were governed. All the trades were incorporated in such associations

under an official charter; Cod. Theod., XIV, ii-viii. But the note of personal liberty had already been sounded, and the more coercive restrictions were omitted from the later Code; cf. Choisy, L'art de batir chez les Byzantins, Paris, 1883, p. 200, etc. (Mommsen's pioneer work on guilds is well known).

[833] Cod. Theod., XIII, v, vi, ix; Cod., X, ii, etc. (and Godefroy).

[834] Procopius, De Aedfiic., v, 1.

[835] Although their property was held in lien by the state as security for the maintenance of ships, it appears that they could grow rich through the facilities they enjoyed for private commerce and possess an independent fortune; Cod. Theod., XIII, vi; cf. Pand., L, iv, 5. Hence some joined voluntarily.

[836] Cod. Theod., XII, i. This title, the longest of all (192 laws), provides us with a plummet with which we may sound the depths of their misery, and exemplifies their eagerness to escape to any other mode of existence as well as the stringency with which they were reclaimed.

[837] Hence their property was always in chancery, as we may say, and the Curia to which they belonged was their reversionary heir, necessarily to a fourth; Cod., X, xxxiv. In the Code the laws relating to them are reduced to about seventy; X, xxxi, *et seq.* Their duties and liabilities are indexed in Godefroy's paratitlon. Libanius had seen people of substance reduced to beggary by these obligations; Epitaph. Juliani (R., I., p. 571). Majorian (457-61) attempted reforms in the West.

[838] See Libanius, Epist., 248, 339, 825, 1079, 1143, etc. The sophist had much interest owing to the number of pupils he had trained to succeed in advocacy, etc., and could often beg off one old disciple by appealing to another. A Rector's nod in such cases was more potent than an Imperial rescript; Cod. Theod., XII, i, 17; *ibid*, 1, notwithstanding. Zeno enacted that even some Illustrious officials should not be exempt after vacating their office; Cod., X, xxxi, 64, 65.

[839] Fathers of a dozen children were released or not called upon; Cod. Theod., XII, i, 55; Cod., X, xxxi, 24. Otherwise disease or decrepit old age seem to have the only effective claims for relief, apart from interest, bribery, etc. The general result of this political economy was that the Empire resembled a great factory, in which each one had a special place, and was excluded from everywhere else. "In England a resident of Leeds is at home in Manchester, and has judicially the same position as a citizen of Manchester, whereas in the Roman Empire a citizen of Thessalonica was an alien in Dyrrachium; a citizen of Corinth an alien in Patras"; Bury, Later Rom. Emp., i, p. 38.

[840] The Verrine sequence of Cicero's speeches remains a picture up to this date of the usual tyranny of a Roman governor. Few went to the provinces with any other idea but that of rapine. "Cessent jam nunc rapaces officialium manus," says Constantine, "cessent inquam: nam si moniti non cessaverint, gladiis praecidentur," etc.; Cod. Theod., I, vii, 1. The revolution of two centuries brings no improvement: "Confluunt huc (Constantinople) omnes ingemiscentes, sacerdotes, et curiales, et officiales, et possessores, et populi, et agricolae, judicum furta merito et injustitias accusantes," etc.; Novel., viii, Pro. For this law, ineffective as ever, all are enjoined to return thanks to God! a vain parade of legislation.

[841] Cod. Theod., X, xxiv; XII, ix; Salvian, De Gubern. Dei, v, 4, *et passim*. Titles x, xi, xii, xiii, xiv (of X) deal with the self-seekers who, in the guise of delators or informers, infested the Court in unsettled times and tried to oust people from their possessions by accusing them of treason; cf. Ammianus, xix, 12, etc.

[842] Cod. Theod., XI, vi; Ammianus, xvii, 3; Salvian, *op. cit.*, v, 7, etc.

[843] So Verres, ii, 38, etc.

[844] Cod. Theod., XII, vi, 27, etc.

[845] *Ibid.*, XI, vi, viii; XV, i; and Godefroy's commentaries. The Defenders of the Cities seem to have been in general too cowed to exercise their prerogative or were gained over.

[846] *Ibid.*, VIII, xv. In this, as in other instances, I refer to the laws against the offences which were committed in disregard of them. Godefroy usually supplies exemplifications.

[847] *Ibid.*, XI, xxx, 4; xxxiv.

[848] Cod. Theod., X, ix, 1, and Godefroy *ad loc.*; cf. *ibid.*, i, 2; Novel. xvii, 15; Agathias, v, 4. They even attempted to invalidate Imperial grants. Notices on purple cloth were suspended to denote confiscation of estates to the crown.

[849] Cassiodorus, Var. Epist., v, 34; ix, 14, etc.

[850] Palladius, Vit. Paphnutii; Hist. Lausiaca, 63 (not by Jerome, as Godefroy *ad* Cod. Theod., III, iii).

[851] Synesius, Epist., 79, 96, etc. These may have been isolated devices of Andronicus at Ptolemais. One of his subordinates used to seize objects of art *à la* Verres. Yet these men were only reached by the happy thought of excommunicating them. In this the great Athanasius had set the example.

[852] Cod. Theod., IX, xxxv, and Godefroy. This was the regular method of scourging, but illegal as a means of enforcing payment of taxes; *ibid.*, XI, vii, 7. The Egyptians were particularly obstinate, and even proud to show the weals they had suffered sooner than pay; Ammianus, xxii, 6, 16.

[853] Cod. Theod., XI, xxviii, 10, 14; cf. vii, 20.

[854] Evagrius, iii, 39. He pretended to have made a sad mistake, and spread a report that he would promptly reimpose it were he not without documentary evidence to enable the books to be reopened. Enticed by this ruse the knavish collectors brought in the accounts they had kept back and a second conflagration was made with them.

[855] Under Arcadius the traffic was barefaced by Eutropius, and probably little less so in the succeeding reign by Chrysaphius:

Vestibulo pretiis distinguit regula gentes.

Tot Galatae, tot Pontus, eat, tot Lydia nummis.

Si Lyciam tenuisse velis, tot millia ponas, etc.

Claudian, In Eutropium, i, 202.

Afterwards it was more underhand; see Novel. viii.

[856] As Bury well observes; Gibbon, v, p. 533.

[857] Cod., I, xlviii.

[858] Novel. viii; xcv; clxi.

[859] Cod. Theod., III, iii; V, viii; XI, xxvii, and Godefroy's illustrations. Sold in this way, Roman citizens were not held in perpetual bondage, but regained their liberty after serving for a term; cf. Cassiodorus, Var. Ep., viii, 33. Constantine was shocked to find that deaths from starvation were frequent in his dominions, and so advertised a measure of outdoor relief, which Rectors were instructed to exhibit conspicuously in all parts; cf. Lactantius, Divin. Inst., vi, 20. The same Constantine is the author of an extravagant law by which lovers who elope together are subjected to capital (?) punishment without any suffrance of accommodation, whilst even persons who may have counselled them to the step are condemned to perish by having molten lead poured down their throats. By such frantic whims could legislation be travestied in those days; Cod. Theod., IX, xxiv.

[860] Cod. Theod., II, xiv; Cod., II, xvi; Augustine, Enarr. in Psalm. XXI, etc.

[861] Cod., IX, xii, 10. See Priscus for a general outline of some of the grievances dealt with in this article; Hist. Goth. Excerpt., p. 190; cf. Nov. xxxiii, etc.

[862] Cod. Theod., XI, xxiv; Cod., XI, liii; cf. liv. Libanius in the East and Salvian in the West, at the distance of nearly a century, complain in analogous terms of the manner in which the wealthy residents turned the tribulations of their poorer neighbours to their own profit; De Prostasiis (ii, p. 493 R.); De Gubern. Dei, v, 8, 9; cf. Nov. xxxiii, etc.

[863] Cod. Theod., XIII, i, 16; XVI, ii, 10, etc. "Distincta enim stipendia sunt religionis et calliditatis" is the caustic taunt put into the mouth of Arcadius. The concessions were withdrawn by Valentinian III (Novel. II, xii), ineffectively we may safely assume from Nov. xliii; 1,100 duty-free shops at CP. belonging to St. Sophia alone.

[864] Cod. Theod., XII, xiv.

[865] *Ibid.*, IX, xxx, 2, 5; xxxi. A further hardship was the quartering of soldiers on private persons, but this, of course, was only local and temporary. The Goths and other barbarians were especially harsh and grasping among those who had to receive them when in transit through the country; see Jos. Stylites, *op. cit.*, 86. Generally the military were arrogant towards, and contemned the civil population; Zosimus, ii, 34.

[866] There seems to be no good reason why children should not now be taught from a primer of scientific cosmology, and have a catechism of ethics as well to the exclusion of everything mythological. The human brain is a weak organ of mind, and requires, above all things, a tonic treatment. Nothing can be more enfeebling than any teaching which causes children to imagine that they are surrounded by unseen intelligences having the power to affect them for good or evil. In most instances, a mind so subdued never recovers its resiliency; liberty of thought is always hampered by dread of the invisible; and many of our greatest men have been unable in after life to free themselves from this fatuity. There should, however, be places of public assembly where people could resort for ethical direction and encouragement, without the lessons taught being vitiated or nullified by being made to depend on mythology. But the objectionable name "agnostic" should be discarded, as if to be properly educated were to belong to a peculiar sect. It suggests a country in which a special designation has to be given to all who are neither diseased nor deformed.

[867] Even Cicero affects to think it *infra dig.* for him to show any correct knowledge of the most famous Greek sculptors; Verres, II, iv.

[868] Suetonius, De Ill. Gram., 2; De Clar. Rhet., 1; Aul. Gell., xv, 11. Crates Mallotes has the credit of being the first Greek Grammarian who taught at

Rome, c. 157 B.C. The Rhetoricians had migrated earlier, and in 161 a SC. was launched against them, and again a few years later.

[869] When the system was fully organized under Ant. Pius (138-161), the largest communities were allowed ten Physicians, five Rhetoricians (or Sophists), and three Grammarians; the smallest recognized under the scheme, five Physicians, three Rhetoricians, and three Grammarians; Pand., XXVII, i, 6; Hist. August. Ant. Pius, 11. Antonius Musa, physician to Augustus, seems to have been the first learned man to whom public honours were decreed at Rome, viz., a statue of brass on the recovery of the Emperor, 23 B.C.; Suetonius, August., 59, 81. He was even the cause of privileges being conferred on his profession generally; Dion Cass., liii, 30. Vespasian was the first to give regular salaries to Rhetoricians; he also gave handsome presents to poets, artists, and architects, and granted relief from public burdens to physicians and philosophers; Suetonius in Vita, 18; Pand., L, iv, 18(30). But the idea of remitting their taxes to learned men was old; Diogenes Laert., Pyrrho, 5. That of selling philosophers for slaves when they could not pay them, was also old; *ibid.*, Xenocrates; Bion. Hadrian, called *Graeculus* from his pedantry, also did much for the cause of learning; Hist. August. in Vita, 1, 17, and commentators. The Athenaeum at Rome was his foundation, an educational college of which no details are known; Aurel. Victor, in Vita. Alexander Sev. went further than any of his predecessors in granting an allowance to poor students; Hist. August. in Vita, 44.

[870] Cod. Theod., XV, i, 53, and Godefroy *ad loc.*

[871] Zacharias, De Opific., Mund., 40, *et seq.* (in Migne, S. G., lxxxv, 1011); See Hasaeus, De Acad. Beryt., etc. Halae Magd., 1716. The humblest school was adorned with figures of the Muses; Athenaeus, viii, 41; Diogenes Laert., Diog., 6. A lecture hall was generally called a "Theatre of the Muses"; Himerius, Or., xxii; Themistius, Or., xxi.

[872] Diogenes Laert., Theophrastus, 14; Eumenius, De Schol. Instaur.; Themistius, Or., xxvi, etc.

[873] Gregory Naz., Laud. Basil, 14, *et seq.* In Julian, ii; Zosimus, v, 5. Synesius pictures the schools as deserted when he visited Athens (*c. 410*); no philosophers, no painted porches, nothing in evidence but the jars of honey from Hymettus. Hypatia, in fact, was attracting every one to Alexandria. After her murder, however, it doubtless began to recuperate (*c.* 415). Themistius inveighs against those parents who sent their sons to a *place* on account of its repute, instead of looking out for the *best man*. He mentions that pupils came to him at CP. from Greece and Ionia; Or., xxvii; xxiii. The students of this age are described as extremely fractious. At Athens, a great commotion greeted the arrival of a freshman, who was put through a rude ordeal until they had passed him into the public bath, whence he issued again

as an accepted comrade; Gregory Naz., Laud. Basil., 16. There also they fought duels, and Libanius reprobates their presenting themselves to him slashed with knives; Epist., 627; Himerius, Or., xxii. Practical jokes amongst themselves, or played on the professors, were often pushed by the students to the verge of criminality; Pand. praef., 2(9). At Carthage St. Augustine found his class for rhetoric so unruly that he threw it up and migrated to Rome. There, indeed, they were more orderly, but indulged in the galling practice of flocking in a body to a certain teacher, whom they suddenly abandoned after a time, forgetting to pay their fees. Sick of it all, he eagerly closed with an offer of the P. U. to take up a salaried post at Milan; Confess., v, 8, 12, 13.

[874] Cod. Theod., XIV, ix, 3; Cod., XI, xviii.

[875] *Ibid.*

[876] Cod. Theod., XIV, ix, 2. Constantius seems to have founded the first great library (*c.* 351), and another was originated by Julian; Themistius, Or., iv; see p. 88. Themistius says that he spent twenty years in studying the "old treasures" of literature at CP.; Or., xxxiii (p. 359, Dind.).

[877] Themistius, Or., xxiii; xxviii, etc. Chrysostom, Ad Pop. Ant. Hom. xvii, 2 (in Migne, ii, 173).

[878] See p. 58; Themistius, Or., xxiv; cf. Cresollius, Theatr. Vet. Rhet., Paris, 1620, a huge repertory of details relating to this class.

[879] Themistius, Or., xxviii, etc.

[880] Themistius, Or., xiii; Chrysostom, In Epist. ad Ephes. Hom. xxi, 3 (in Migne, xi, 153); Eunapius, Proaeresius. These popular lectures were often merely colloquial entertainments, such as used to be associated with the name of Corney Grain, without the music. See the correspondence of Basil Mag. with Libanius, Epist., 351 (Migne), *et seq.*, L.'s most effective piece, a dialogue in which he mimicked the fretfulness of a morose man.

[881] Cod. Theod., XIII, iii, 1, and Godefroy *ad loc.* At this time, however, pagan professors were often much persecuted by Christian fanatics, and Themistius complains that they were even officially muzzled; Or., xxvi, and *ibid.* Professors were naturally the last to become converts. As to the general esteem in which the class was held, see the poetical commemoration of the Bordeaux professors by Ausonius. Lucian deals satirically with philosophers in his Eunuch, De Merc. Cond., Hermotimus, etc.

[882] Cod. Theod., XIII, iii, 7, and Godefroy *ad loc.*; Cod., X, lii, 8; Themistius, Or., xxi, etc. Chrysostom, *loc. cit.* (note 4 *supra*).

[883] Cod. Theod., XIII, iii, 5. A law of Julian to facilitate his ousting Christian professors, but retained for its literal application.

[884] Themistius fairly covers the ground as to this question; Or., xxi; xxiii. The inferior teachers were exacting, and even extortionate. They accused him of requiring a talent (£240?), but he asked nothing at CP. where he was subsidized; on the contrary, he assisted needy pupils. Still, he received a great deal of money as presents. At Antioch, where it was the custom, he took fees like the rest. For more ancient times and generally, see Cresollius, *op. cit.*, v, 3, 4, etc. What the government paid is uncertain. Augustus gave V. Flaccus £800 a year for acting exclusively as tutor to his nephews; Suetonius, De Ill. Gram., 17. £1,040 has been conjectured as the salary of Eumenius (600,000 *nummi*, *op. cit.*). In Diocletian's Act for fixing prices, ordinary schoolmasters are allowed only about 4*s.* a month, professors 12*s.*; for each pupil in a class, of course. The case of M. Aurelius bestowing £400 per ann. on the professors at Athens is also to be noted; Dion Cass., lxxxi, 31.

[885] Chrysostom, Genesis, i, Hom. iii, 3 (in Migne, iv, 29); In Epist. ad Coloss. Hom. iv, 3 (in Migne, xi, 328); Paulus Aegin., i, 14; cf. Quintilian, i, 1, etc. Youths from the provinces studying at Rome were packed home again at twenty, but this order seems to have been dropped later on; Cod. Theod., XIV, ix, 1 (not retained in Code).

[886] On first methods with children, see Quintilian, i; Jerome, Epist., 107; Chrysostom, Ad Pop. Ant. Hom. xvi, 14 (in Migne, ii, 168); De Mut. Nom. ii, 1 (in Migne, iii, 125); Genesis, i, Hom. iii, 3; Epist. Coloss. i, Hom. iv, 3 (in Migne, xi, 329), etc. Libanius, In Chriis (Reiske, ii, p. 868). The first book of Augustine's Confessions gives many particulars as to his own bringing up in childhood. Greek nursemaids were hired at Rome so that young children might learn the language; Tacitus, De Caus. Cor. Eloq., 29. Wooden or ivory letters were used as playthings. These schoolmasters are represented as very harsh instructors, who cowed the spirit of their pupils. The rod was freely used, and chiefly by the paedagogue. Even scholars of maturer age were corrected by whipping. Libanius used to "wake up the lazy ones with a strap, the incorrigible he expelled." Epist., 1119. Chrysostom himself accepts as axiomatic that nothing can be done with boys without beating; Act. Apost. Hom. xlii, 4 (in Migne, ix, 308). Quintilian and Paul of Aegina, however, advise going on the opposite tack; *loc. cit.*

[887] Pand., L, v, 2, etc.

[888] Martianus Capella, an African who lived in the fifth century, is the author of the only self-contained manual of liberal education which has come down to us. His treatise seems to contain all the book-work a student was expected to do while under oral teaching by the professors. Cassiodorus has left a slight tract, but he recommends other volumes to supplement his own

merely tentative work. Isidore of Seville, a century later, has also included an epitome of the seven liberal arts in the first three books of his Etymologies, but his exposition is almost as thin as that of Cassiodorus. The remaining seventeen books are a sort of encyclopaedic dictionary with explanatory jottings on almost every subject, well worth dipping into.

[889] Introduced, perhaps, by Boethius; De Arith., i, 1. Τετρακτὺς is found in Greek; Anna Comn.; i, pref.; see Ducange, *sb. voc.* The latter word is really the original and goes back to Pythagorean times.

[890] See Priscian, Partitiones, xii, Vers. Aen., etc.

[891] After Rome had produced good writers, such as Virgil, Horace, Livy, etc., they were added to the course of literature in the West; Quintilian, i, 8; x.

[892] There is some obscurity about his date, which suggests that he was a centenarian. Ordericus Vit. says he died in 425; cf. Cassiodorus, De Orthograph., 12, etc.

[893] "One father," says Chrysostom, "points out to his son how some one of low birth by learning eloquence obtained promotion to high office, won a rich wife, and became possessed of wealth with a fine house, etc., or how another through a mastery of Latin achieved a great position at Court"; Adv. Oppug. Vit. Mon., iii, 5 (in Migne, i, 357).

[894] The details of teaching are presented most circumstantially in the rhetorical catechism of Fortunatianus (*c. 450*).

[895] Cresollius has brought together an immense amount of information on this branch of the art in his Vacationes Autumnales, Paris, 1620; cf. Kayser in his introduction to the lives of Philostratus (Teubner). Blandness of voice was sedulously pursued by professional sophists, and *plasmata*, or emollient medicaments were much resorted to. There was a *phonascus*, or voice-trainer, who paid special attention to such matters.

[896] Libanius has outlined very clearly the course of instruction through which he put his class; Epist., 407.

[897] Nothing could be more meagre than the allusions to this subject; even the treatise on geometry by Boethius, which seems to have been the only one current, contains little more than enunciations of propositions.

[898] I have already referred to the geography of this period, see p. 182.

[899]

Altera pars orbis sub aquis jacet invia nobis,

Ignotaeque hominum gentes, nec transita regna,

Commune ex uno lumen ducentia sole, etc.

Manilius (Weber), i, 375.

The Christian fathers ridicule the antipodes severely. "More rational to say that black was white"; Lactantius, Div. Inst., iii, 24; Epitome, 39. "The earth stands firm on water [going back to Thales] and does not turn"; Chrysostom, Genesis, Hom. xii, 3, 4 (in Migne, iv, 101); In Titum Hom. iii, 3 (in Migne, xi, 680); cf. Cosmas Ind., *op. cit.*, x, for other theological authorities on cosmology.

[900] Such as that five represents the world, being made up of three and two, which typify male and female respectively; or that seven equates Minerva, the virgin, neither contained or containing; and other Pythagorean notions; see M. Capella, vii, and the arithmetic of Boethius.

[901] Such is the well-known system elaborated by Hipparchus and Ptolemy, but the Pythagoreans put the sun at the centre, though without definite reasons and with imaginative details; see Diogenes Laert. and Delambre's Hist. Astron. Ant. Although Democritus, Epicurus, and others held that there were an infinite number of worlds (κόσμοι), they regarded the objective universe as only one of them, and had no idea that myriads of systems similar to that in which they lived lay before their eyes.

[902] Thus M. Capella states that Mercury and Venus revolve round the sun; and Isidore of Seville says the crystalline sphere runs so fast that did not the stars retard it by running the opposite way the universe would fall to pieces; Etymolog., iii, 35.

[903] See Themistius, Or., xxvi (p. 327 Dind.); cf. Boethius (?), De Discipl. Scholar., iii.

[904] Graduated from about A below treble stave to E in fourth space (A to E" = La_2 to Mi_4), but there seems to have been great variety in pitch.

[905] Cassiodorus often alludes to the organ of his time, especially in Exposit. Psal. CL, where he describes many instruments. See Daremberg and Saglio, *sb. voc.*

[906] See M. Capella, ix; Boethius on Music, etc., and Hadow's Oxford History of Music, 1901.

[907] See Plato, Protagoras, 43, etc. Even in the time of Homer the Greek warriors were practical musicians, but the Romans were not so originally. I can make no definite statement as to how far the Byzantine upper classes were performers on instruments at this date, but see Jerome, Ep., 107.

Further remarks on Greek education, with references to an earlier stratum of authors, will be found in Hatch, Hibbert Lectures, 1888, ii, *et seq*. There is a great compilation by Conringius (De Antiq. Academ., Helmstadt, 1651), which I have found extremely useful. From the observations of Chrysostom (see p. 118), it appears that little advantage was taken of educational facilities in his day, but it may be assumed that the foundation of the Auditorium caused mental culture to be fashionable, at least for a time.

[908] Themistius, Or., xxvi, *loc. cit*. Theodosius II was the first Christian emperor who systematically fostered philosophy by creating a faculty at CP. and extending clearly to philosophers the immunities granted to other professors; Cod. Theod., XIII, iii, 16; XIV, ix, 3; Cod., X, lii, 14, etc. We are continually reminded that Socrates brought down the sophists of his time from star-gazing and speculation as to the origin of things to the ethics of common life. Thence arose a succession of dialogues in which Utopian republics were discussed, where wives should be in common so that everybody might be the supposititious brother, etc., of every one else. A more harmonious community could not be engendered by such a device; cf. Herodotus, iv, 104.

[909] See the elogium of Berytus in Nonnus, Dionysiacs, xli. From 389, etc., Hasacus (*op. cit.*) thinks that the school was founded by Augustus after the battle of Actium, but it is first distinctly noted as flourishing *c. 231*; Gregory Thaum., Panegyric. in Origen, 1, 5 (in Migne, S. G., 1051).

[910] Pand. praef., 2 [7]; Totius Orb. Descript.; Gotlefroy *ad* Cod. Theod., XI, i, 19, etc.

[911] Nowhere definitely expressed, but inferred from Pand. praef., 2 (superscription), with confirmative evidence; see Hasaeus, *op. cit.*, viii, 2, *et seq*.

[912] The freshmen rejoiced in the "frivolous and ridiculous cognomen" of *Dupondii* (equivalent to "Tuppennies," apparently); in the second year they became *Edictionaries* (students of Hadrian's Perpetual Edict); thirdly, *Papinianistae* (engaged on the works of Papinian); fourthly, Αὐται (when reading Paulus); fifthly, the last year, *Prolytae* (mainly given up to reviewing previous studies); Pand. praef., 2. The last two terms are not explained; the idea is evidently that of being *loosed* or dismissed from the courses. Cf. Macarius Aegypt. Hom. xv, 42 (in Migne, S. G., xxxiv, 604), who presents a different scheme, perhaps, from the Alexandrian law-school.

[913] The first attempt at consolidating the laws was the Perpetual Edict of Hadrian, *c. 120*.

[914] Pand., *loc. cit*. And many more were probably dragged up in court from time to time, which it would be the bent of despotism to taboo. Cod. Theod.,

I, iv, gives the rule as to deciding knotty points by the collation of legal experts.

[915] It was specially decreed by Diocletian that students might remain at B. to the age of twenty-five; Cod., X, xlix, 1. This law could doubtless be pleaded even against a call to their native Curia. We need not suppose that the periods allotted to the various branches of education were always rigidly adhered to in spite of circumstances. Thus Libanius complains that his pupils used to run off to the study of law before he had put them through the proper routine of rhetorical training, the moment they had mastered a little Latin in fact; iii, p. 441-2 (Reiske).

[916] Sufficiat medico ad commendandam artis auctoritatem, si Alexandriae se dixerit eruditum; Ammianus, xxii, 16. This celebrity was won *c. 300* B.C. through the distinction acquired by Erasistratus and Herophilus. See Conringius, *op. cit.*, i, 26.

[917] Cod., I, ii, 19, 22; this and the next title for charities *passim*.

[918] Even Plato held this notion (Timaeus, 72), but it was flouted at once by Chrysippus; Plutarch, De Stoic. Repug., 29.

[919] Galen gives very correct descriptions of the action of the larynx; Oribasius, xxiv, 9; and tells us how he satisfied himself by various vivisections that the blood actually flowed in the arteries; An Sanguis in Arter. Nat. Cont.; De Placit., i, 5; vi, 7, 8, etc.

[920] Themistius, Or., i.

[921] What appears to be an epitome of current knowledge of natural history and botany is given by Cicero in De Nat. Deor., ii, 47, etc.

[922] See especially Dioscorides, ii. Tinctures and ointments made from toads, scorpions, bugs, woodlice, centipedes, cockroaches, testes of stag and horse, etc., were staple preparations. The realistic coloured illustrations in the great edition published by Lonicerus in 1563 with a colossal commentary, are worth looking at. The pills of seminal fluid (*à la* Brown-Séquard) decried in the *Pistis Sophia* appear to have been merely a mystic remedy.

[923] The profession did not yet stand apart from the lay community as pronouncedly as at present. Thus Celsus, author of a noted medical treatise, was an amateur, a Roman patrician in fact; and the precious MS. of Dioscorides, with coloured miniatures, preserved at Vienna, was executed (*c. 500*) for a Byzantine princess, Julia Anicia, daughter of Olybrius, one of the fleeting emperors of the West.

[924] Less than a century previously Plutarch had declared the common opinion that Fortune, having divested herself of her pinions and winged

shoes, had settled down as a permanent inhabitant of the Palatine Hill; De Fortuna Rom.

[925] Art in the time of Augustus and Tiberius has to be judged mainly by the wall-paintings recovered at Rome and Pompeii, many of which are highly meritorious. For succeeding centuries a series of sculptures remain which allow us to keep the retreat of art in constant view. The chief landmarks are: 1. The arch of Titus and the column of Trajan; 2. The Antonine column and the arch of Severus; 3. The arch of Constantine, remarkable for its crudity and for some spaces being filled by figures ravished from that of Titus; 4. The Theodosian column at CP.; though much defaced, the incapacity of the executant is still recognizable. The reproduction of the Arcadian pillar published by Banduri (see p. 49) cannot be regarded as a faithful copy, it being evident that the artist has elevated the bas-reliefs to his own standard. In Agincourt, *op. cit.*, and Mau's Pompeii these subjects are pictorially represented, as well as in many other works.

[926] Cod. Theod., XIII, iv, 1. Architectis plurimis opus est, sed quia non sunt, etc. (334). His buildings were so hastily run up that they soon went to ruin; Zosimus, ii, 32. Hence, perhaps, C.'s opinion that there were no proper architects.

[927] Cod. Theod., XIII, iv, 1, 4. Few, however, of these regulations, if any, were new; they were mostly in force before the reign of Commodus; Pand., L, vi, 9.

[928] In the eleventh century, after a flush of splendour in the already greatly contracted Empire, owing to the conquests of the Saracens, this particular form of degeneracy began to be manifested. "Les personnages sont trop longs, leur bras trop maigres, leur gestes et leur mouvements plein d'affectation; une rigidité cadavérique est repandue sur l'ensemble"; Kondakoff, Hist. de l'art byz., Paris, 1886, ii, p. 138.

[929] This was not altogether new to the Greeks; for in the juxtaposition of Athenian and Assyrian bas-reliefs at the British Museum it can be seen that even the school of Phidias adhered to some types which had originated in the East, drawing of horses, etc.

[930] See Lethaby and Swainson for arguments on this head. Certain churches in the domical style at Antioch, Salonica, etc., are maintained by some authorities to be anterior to the sixth century; *op. cit.*, x. For illustrations see Vogüé, Archit. de la Syrie cent., Paris, 1865-77.

[931] Thus even maidens in a state of nudity engaged publicly in the athletic games at Sparta and Chios; Plutarch, Lycurgus; Athenaeus, xiii, 20. The parade of virgins before Zeuxis at Agrigentum in order that he might select models for his great picture of the birth of Venus, as related by Pliny, has

often been quoted; Hist. Nat., xxxv, 36. Yet even among the Greeks a squeamish modesty existed in some quarters, as is evidenced by the famous statue of Venus by Praxiteles having been rejected by the Coans in favour of a draped one, previous to its being set up at Cnidus; *ibid.*, xxxvi, 4; cf. Lucian, Amores.

[932] Thus Shakespeare:

See what a grace was seated on this brow:

Hyperion's curls; the front of Jove himself;

An eye like Mars, to threaten and command;

A station like the herald Mercury,

New-lighted on a heaven-kissing hill.

Hamlet, III, 4.

[933] See p. 109.

[934] They vary in merit considerably; see some reproductions of the better ones in Bayet, L'art byz., Paris, 1892, ii, 3, and other similar works, especially Gori, *op. cit.* Specimens at South Kensington.

[935] Choricius of Gaza (*c.* 520) has left us an elaborate description of such a church interior and also of the frescoes in a palace. The whole has been republished by Bertrand in his work, Un art crit. dans l'antiq., Paris, 1882. Modern Greek churches are precisely similar, and those belonging to the monasteries of Mt. Athos are especially noteworthy; see Bayet, *op. cit.*, iv, 2. Two can be inspected in London. That in Bayswater is a "Kutchuk Aya Sofia." Walsh's CP., Lond., 1838, has a good engraving; ii, p. 31. See also the striking mosaics of St. George's, Salonica (Texier and P., *op. cit.*), the Pompeiesque style of which suggest an early date in church building—vistas of superimposed arcades raised on a forest of fantastically graceful, but impossible columns, architecture run wild in fact.

[936] "Du moment qu'il avait exécuté une composition dans la manière antique et qu'il y avait mis toute la splendeur de sa palette, il ne se demandait pas si le dessin de ses personnages était correct ou non, s'ils se trainaient bien sur leur jambes, s'ils étaient réellement assis sur une chaise ou un fauteuil, ou simplement appuyés contre ces meubles"; Kondakoff, *op. cit.*, i, 108. Of existing MSS. with coloured miniatures, only some six or eight date back to these early centuries. Labarte's Hist. des arts indust., Paris, 1892, with coloured facsimiles is the most satisfying work in which to study mediaeval art objectively. At South Kensington a variety of specimens are to be found,

including ivories, enamels, paper casts of mosaics, reproductions of frescoes, etc., many of which go as far back as the sixth century.

[937] Oribasius, physician to Julian, seems to be the genuine father of bookmaking, the real prototype of the "scissors and paste" author, but he foreran the swarming of the brood by a couple of centuries.

[938] Gregory Nys., De Vit. S. Macrinae (in Migne, iii, 960). Whence it appears that it was unusual for them to be taught to apply themselves to the distaff or the needle. Maidenhood was mostly passed in luxury and adornment; Chrysostom, Qual. Duc. Sint Uxores, 9 (in Migne, iii, 239); in Epist. ad Ephes., iv, Hom. xiii, 3 (in Migne, xi, 97); cf. Jerome, Epist., 128, 130. The latter sets forth his ideas as to the training of a girl at some length. As soon as she has imbibed the first rudiments she is to begin psalm-singing and reading of prophets, apostles, etc. Later she should proceed to the study of the fathers, especially Cyprian, Athanasius, and Hilarius. She should spend much time in church with her parents, and must be guarded circumspectly from the attentions of the curled youth (*cincinatti, calamistrati*). She rises betimes to sing hymns, and employs herself generally in weaving plain textures. Silks and jewellery are to be rigorously eschewed; and the saint cannot reconcile himself to the idea of an adult virgin making use of the bath, as she should blush to see herself naked; Epist., 107. His remarks, of course, apply directly to life at Rome.

[939] From Jerome's letter just quoted it appears that it was usual for girls to play on the lyre, pipe, and organ.

[940] See her life by Gregorovius, 1892. Her cento of Homeric verses applied to Christ is extant. To her inspiration most probably is due the foundation of the Auditorium at CP., and the prominence given to philosophy. Pulcheria was occupied in building churches and in disinterring the relics of martyrs.

[941] She is best known from the epistles of Synesius. Nothing of hers is extant. Murdered 415, wife or maid uncertain; see Suidas, *sb. nom.* She was scraped to pieces with shells, a mode of official torture peculiar to the Thebais, which may have been inflicted often on Christian ladies during Pagan persecutions. In other districts an iron scraper was used; Eusebius, Hist. Eccles., viii, 9; 3, etc.

[942] I need not refer more particularly to the phenomena of radio-activity and cathode rays, information concerning which has been exploited by every popular periodical. The atoms (electrons) which become visible in the low-pressure tube have been calculated to be of but 1/800 the magnitude of the hydrogen atom, and many physicists are inclined to regard them as the first state of matter on its way to resolution into the formless protyle or ether.

[943] A great part of modern books on chemistry is now devoted to synthesis. Not only have such well-known organic substances as indigo, vanilla, citric acid, etc., been prepared artificially, but also those new articles of commerce, the aniline dyes, saccharine, etc. Numbers of new drugs for therapeutic experiment are synthetized annually in the great German laboratories of Bayer, Merck, etc.

[944] Especially suggestive are the ingenious experiments with ferments, which tend to show that the anabolic and katabolic activities of living matter may soon be imitated in the laboratory; see Buchner, Bericht d. deutsch. chem. Gesel., xxx, xxxi, xxxii; also recent physiological treatises in which are contained the speculations of Pflüger and others as to the "biogens" of protoplasm, etc. Most important of all is Loeb's discovery of the possibility of chemical fertilization; see Boveri, Das Problem der Befruchtung, Jena, 1902.

[945] Archytas, with his flying wooden dove, was the most noted mechanician in this line; A. Gellius, x, 12, etc.

[946] Even windmills were unknown until they were introduced into Europe by the Saracens in the twelfth century.

[947] It appears that of late years a dearth of candidates for orders in every religious denomination of Christendom has been experienced, but this may be due merely to the usual poverty of the career. The Church should fall to principle not to poverty. And here we may catch a glimpse of the process by which the various Protestant sects may ultimately die out naturally: that young men of high character, ambitious of honourable distinction, will avoid a profession which entails an attitude of disingenuous reserve towards those whom they are deputed to instruct. On the other hand it may be foreseen that the Romish and Orthodox churches, upholding as they do a gross superstition and instituting the members of their priesthood almost from childhood, will retain their power over the masses for a much longer period, until at last they have to face suppression by force. Those who at the present time are engaged in impressing a belief in obsolete mythologies on the community should realize that they are doing an evil service to their generation instead of exerting themselves for the liberation and elevation of thought. However brilliant their temporary position, they deserve, much more than the oblivious patriot, to go down

To the vile dust from whence they sprung,

Unwept, unhonoured, and unsung.

[948] Grotius has made a large collection of those passages in classical and other ancient writers, which seem to support the creation-myth of Genesis;

De Veritate Relig. Christ., i, 16. For the Chaldaean or Babylonian variations, and some earlier associations of Adam, see King's Seven Tablets of Creation, Lond., 1903. It appears that the protoplast in the original account was created by Marduk, the tutelary deity of Babylonia, out of his own blood, a circumstance which the "priestly" redactor of Genesis has suppressed, together with many other interesting details; cf. Radau, Creation Story of Genesis i, Chicago, 1903. Margoliouth's attempt to show that Abraham's Jehovah was the male moon-god of Ur is interesting; Contemporary Review, 1896.

[949] In this country the subject of comparative mythology and the origin of theistic notions has been exhaustively treated by Herbert Spencer, Andrew Lang, J. G. Frazer, and others. Nevertheless, it cannot be determined whether the fear of ghosts or the innate bent of the human mind to speculate as to casuality is the germ of religious systems. Their development has, no doubt, always been much indebted to the ascendancy to be gained as the reward of successful imposture in such matters.

[950] Avowed atheists were rare among the Greeks, as there was always some personal risk in ventilating opinions which clashed with the popular superstitions. Some, however, incurred the odium of holding such views. Of these the most noteworthy was Diagoras, who is said to have impiously chopped up his image of Hercules to boil his turnips; Athenagoras, Apol., 4. The jaunty impiety of Dionysius, tyrant of Syracuse (*c. 400* B.C.), was celebrated in antiquity. After pillaging the temple of the Locrian Proserpine, he sailed back home and, finding the wind favourable, remarked to his companions, "See what a fine passage the gods are granting to us sacrilegious reprobates." He seized the golden cloak from the shoulders of Jupiter Olympus, observing that it was "too heavy for summer and too cold for winter, whereas a woollen one would suit him well for all seasons." Noticing a gold beard on Æsculapius at Epidaurus, he removed it, saying, that it was "improper for him to wear it, since his father, Apollo, was always represented beardless." Whenever in the temples he met with statues proffering, as it were, jewels and plate with their projecting hands, he took possession of the valuables, asserting that it "would be folly not to accept the good things offered by the gods." The pious were aghast at the example of such a man enjoying a long and prosperous reign and transmitting the throne to his son; Cicero, De Nat. Deor., iii, 34; Lactantius, Div. Instit., ii, 4, etc. With a view to such instances, Plutarch wrote a treatise to prove that "the mills of God grind slow, but very sure." Euhemerus and Palaephatus transformed mythology into history by a rationalizing process, assigning the origin to popular exaggeration of common occurrences.

[951] A system of verbal trickery originated with the Eleatics, of which Zeno (*c. 400* B.C.) was the chief exponent. Their catches were generally ingenious;

that disproving the reality of motion is best known—"If a thing moves, it must do so in the place in which it is, or in a place in which it is not; but it cannot move in the place in which it is, and it certainly does not move in a place in which it is not; therefore there is no motion at all;" Diogenes Laert., Pyrrho, 99, etc. See Plato's Euthydemus for a sample of ridiculous word-chopping.

[952] There were six principal sects which achieved a sort of permanency and retained their vitality for several centuries. They may be characterized briefly: Academics (Plato), sceptical and respectable; Peripathetics (Aristotle), inquisitive and progressive; Stoics (Zeno of Citium, Chrysippus), ethical and intense; Cynics (Antisthenes, Diogenes), squalid, morose, and sententious; Epicureans, tranquil enjoyment and indifference; Cyreneans (Aristippus), pure hedonism with discretion. In general the Epicureans are wrongly associated with the last conception.

[953] Aristotle (c. 350 B.C.) was the first to perceive the importance of collecting facts and disposing them into their proper groups. Thus zoology, botany, anatomy, physiology, mineralogy, astronomy, meteorology, etc., began to take form in his hands, each being relegated to a separate compartment for consideration as a concordant whole and to receive future additions.

[954] Even with his limited outlook Aristotle had sufficient astuteness to divine that nature might become the "slave of man," and expresses himself clearly to that effect; Metaphysics, i, 2. Such a claim may provoke a smile from the modern who reviews the mild conquests of the embryo science of his day.

[955] A few of their utterances may be quoted:

Ἐχθρὸς γάρ μοι κεῖνος ὁμῶς Ἀϊδᾶο πύλῃσιν,

Ὅς χ' ἕτερον μὲν κεύθῃ ἐνὶ φρεσὶν ἄλλο δὲ εἴπῃ.

Iliad, ix, 312.

Ἔργον δ' οὐδὲν ὄνειδος, ἀεργίη δέ τ' ὄνειδος.

Op. et Dies, 311.

Μὴ κακὰ κερδαίνειν, κακὰ κέρδεα ἶσ' ἄτῃσιν.

Ibid., 352.

[956] From the Golden Verses of Pythagoras; Epictetus, iii, 10.

[957] Hence Socrates would not save his life by flight from Athens after his condemnation, although his friends had made everything secure for his escape; see the Crito.

[958] Plato, Gorgias, 55, etc.; Protagoras, 101, etc.

[959] Isocrates, Ad Nicoclem, 61. This maxim, in slightly differing forms, has been attributed to Confucius and many others. Pythagoras enjoined his disciples to love a friend as oneself; see Bigg, Christian Platonists, London, 1886, p. 242. "Love your fellow men from your heart," says Marcus Aurelius, viii, 34.

[960] Cicero, De Officiis, iii, 8. In this treatise the author is for the most part merely voicing the sentiments of the Stoic Panaetius.

[961] Epictetus, ii, 2.

[962] Ibid., i, 18.

[963] Marcus Aurelius, xii, 12.

[964] Seneca, Epist., 47; De Beneficiis, 18, etc. To a master who ill-treats his servants Epictetus addresses himself: "Slave! can you not be patient with your brother, the offspring of God and a son of heaven as much as you are"; i, 13.

[965] Tuscul. Disp., ii, 17.

[966] Epist. 7.

[967] Lucian, Demonax.

[968] It was, however, prohibited early at Thebes; Aelian, Var. Hist., ii, 7.

[969] Pand., XXV, iii, 4; see Noodt's Julius Paulus, etc., 1710. Aristotle upheld the custom without scruple; Politics, viii, 16.

[970] Then Valentinian proscribed it with a penalty, but the legislation was tentative, and the practice was scarcely suppressed until modern times; Cod. Theod., V, vii; Cod., VIII, lii, 2; cf. Lactantius, Div. Inst., vi, 20. It was palliated by the institution of the brephotrophia; see p. 82.

[971] Odyssey, xx, 55.

[972] See Lysias, Orat., Ὑπερ τοῦ ἀδυνάτου, etc., Plutarch, Aristides *ad fin.*

[973] See p. 81.

[974] Trajan appears to have established orphanages and homes for the children of needy parents; see Pliny, Panegyric., 27, etc. The fact is also indicated by coins (ALIMENTA ITALIAE), and a sculptured slab found in the Roman forum; Cohen, ii, p. 18; Middleton, Rome, etc., Lond., 1892, p.

346. Faustina, wife of Antoninus Pius, also busied herself in a similar way, as is evidenced by well-known coins (PUELLULAE FAUSTINIANAE); Cohen, ii, p. 433.

[975] Isis and Serapis, after a stormy career which lasted more than a century, became finally seated in the city under Vespasian; see "Isis" in Smith's Classical Dictionary and similar works. But the greatest run was on Mithras, a sun-god extracted from the Persian mythology, who grew in favour from the time of Pompey until his worship reached even to the north of Britain. Quite a literature exists under his name at present; see Cumont, Mysteries of Mithras, Lond., 1903. For the account of a regular invasion of Syrian deities see Hist. August., Heliogabalus.

[976] Polybius complains of the rising scepticism at Rome in his time; vi, 56. I need not reproduce the oft-quoted lines of Juvenal (ii, 149), but the following are not generally brought forward:

Sunt, in fortunae qui casibus omnia ponunt,

Et nullo credant mundum rectore moveri, etc.

xiii, 86.

Such unbelief, however, did not penetrate beyond the upper social stratum; and even at Athens in the second century those who scouted the ancient myths were considered to be impious and senseless by the multitude; see Lucian, Philopseudes, 2, etc. The voluminous dialogues of Cicero are sufficient to prove how practised the Romans had become in tearing the old mythology to pieces. But the pretence of piety was kept up in the highest places. "The soul of Augustus is not in those stones," exclaimed Agrippina in a moment of vexation when she found Tiberius sacrificing to the statues of his predecessor; Tacitus, Ann., iv, 52.

[977] There were many grades of charlatans from Apollonius of Tyana, who seems to have been a genuine illusionist or mystic, to Alexander Abonoteichos, an impudent impostor, and Marcus, an infamous rascal; Philostratus, Vit. Apol.; Lucian, Pseudomantis; Irenaeus, i, 13.

[978] But he never left Rome and the duties were performed by Pomponius Flaccus; Tacitus, Ann., ii, 32; vi, 27, etc. Jn. Malala mentions one Cassius, p. 241.

[979] That is, sufferers from epilepsy, St. Vitus's dance, mania, etc., diseases which might be cured by hypnotic suggestion, neuroses of various kinds. This popular fallacy was not held universally, but was derided by the more educated, including the medical faculty; see Philostorgius, viii, 10.

[980] Thus a century later, when a true messianic note was struck, half a million of Jews rushed frantically to destruction in the wake of Barcochebas, the leader of their revolt under Hadrian, though not without the satisfaction of dragging 100,000 Gentiles to their doom at the same time. Some exegetes are tempted to see in John, v, 4, an allusion to this war, and hence to find a date for that gospel (the bridge, via Philo Judaeus, between Judaeism and Hellenism), *c.* 140.

[981] Rufus (or Fufius) and Rubellius are probably meant; Lactantius, De Morte Persec., 2. See the differing statements in the Chronicles from Jn. Malala onwards; also articles on biblical chronology in recent encyclopaedias, Chron. of Eusebius, Consular Fasti appended to Chron. Paschal., etc. By the synoptical gospels the ministry of Jesus seems to have lasted one year only, but two, three, and even four years have been assumed from the later composition of John, *e.g.*, in Jerome's chronicle, *sb.* A.D. 33.

[982] It is, however, improbable that any Christian could have given a consecutive account of the life of Jesus prior to 120 or thereabouts. The newly-discovered Apology of Aristides seems to be the earliest evidence for the existence of gospels. It was presented to Hadrian, perhaps, *c.* 125. On the other hand First Clement, moored at 95, but with an incorrigible tendency to rise to 140, is clearly by a writer who possessed no biography, but merely Logia of Jesus.

[983] They were coated with inflammable matter, pitch, etc., and used for torches to illuminate the public gardens at night (Nov., 64); Tacitus, Ann., xv, 44; Suetonius, Nero, 16, etc.

[984] Dion Cass., lxvii, 14; Eusebius, Hist. Eccles., iii, 18, *et seq.*; cf. Lactantius, De Morte Persec., 3; Suetonius, Domitian. Clement, a cousin of this emperor, appears to have been put to death for being a Christian, and has been claimed by some as one of the first popes.

[985] Pliny, Epist., x, 97, 98. This correspondence and, indeed, the whole book which contains it has been stigmatized as a forgery by some investigators; see Gieseler, Eccles. Hist., i, 33, for refs. The same suspicion rests, in fact, on every early allusion to the Christians. It certainly seems strange that they should be such unfamiliar sectaries to Trajan and Pliny if they were well known at Rome under Nero and Domitian. Much less can we believe that in the destruction of Jerusalem Titus was actuated chiefly by a desire to extinguish Christianity, or that he had weighed the differences in theological standpoint between Jews and Christians; Sulp. Severus, Hist. Sacr., ii, 30. Such is history "as she was wrote" at that epoch. The whole evidence that Christians were popularly known and recognized politically during the first century is scanty and unsatisfactory. Trajan achieved a great reputation, which never died out even among the Christians, perhaps on

account of the tolerant attitude attributed to him on this occasion. He was prayed out of hell by one of the popes along with one or two other noted pagans whom the Church was anxious to take under its wing.

Quivi era storiata l'alta gloria

Del roman prince, lo cui gran valore

Mosse Gregorio alia sua gran vittoria:

Io dico di Traiano imperadore; etc.

Dante, Purg., x; Parad., xx.

[986] Hence the anti-Christian philosopher Celsus (*c.* 160) exclaims: "You say that no educated, wise or intellectual person need approach you, but only those that are ignorant, silly, and childish. In fact you are able to persuade the vulgar only, slaves, women, and children"; Origen c. Celsum, iii, 44.

[987] Minucius Felix, Octavius, 12, etc. Their gloomy austerity is strongly brought out by Tertullian in his tract De Spectaculis.

[988] Tertullian, De Idololatria, 17, *et seq.*; De Corona Militis, 11; Origen c. Celsum, viii, 55, 60, *et seq.* Not only did they refuse the quasi-divine honours to the Emperor, but they would not even join in the illumination and floral decoration of their houses required of all loyal citizens during imperial festivals; Tertullian, De Idololatria, 13, *et seq.*; Ad Nationes, i, 17; Theophilus, Autolycus, i, 11, etc. The causes of the unpopularity of the Christians can be studied very completely with the aid of Gieseler (Eccles. Hist., i, 41), who has brought together numerous extracts and references bearing on the subject. As was natural under the circumstances, atrocious libels began to be spread abroad against them, such as that they worshipped an ass's head, that the sacrifice of new-born infants was a part of their ritual, etc.; Tertullian, Apology, 16; Minucius Felix, 9, etc.

[989] Origen c. Celsum, viii, the latter half especially. As early as 500 B.C. Xenophanes had said "God is the One," but this was recondite philosophy which could not penetrate to the masses, and, if preached openly, would have aroused popular fanaticism; Aristotle, Metaphysics, i, 5.

[990] The prohibitive campaign was almost confined to Lyons and Vienne in Gaul; Eusebius, Hist. Eccles., v, 1, *et seq.* The animus against the Christians was so intense that slaves were even allowed to inform on their owners, ordinarily a criminal act; Pand., XLVIII, xviii, 1, 18, etc. The Acts of the Martyrdom of Polycarp (*c.* 155-161), after holding their ground so long, are now at last beginning to be classed as spurious; see Van Manen in Encyclop. Biblica, *sb.* Old Christ. Literat.

[991] See Tertullian's Address to the Martyrs; also Cyprian's restrained efforts to modify the reverence paid to them; Epist., 22, 83, etc.; cf. Eusebius, Martyrs of Palestine; Lactantius, De Morte Persec.; Neander, Church Hist., ii.

[992] Ten persecutions were reckoned by those who wished to make up a mystic number to accord with the ten plagues of Egypt, Revelat., xvii, etc., but the specification of them does not correspond in different writers. After a certain date, which cannot be accurately fixed, there was always local animosity against the sect, the practical issue of which varied relatively to the temper of the populace and the provincial governor; see Gieseler, i, 56.

[993] Lactantius, De Morte Persec., 48; Eusebius, Eccles. Hist., x, 5. Advanced critics, however, are now beginning to doubt the authenticity of this decree as presented by the Fathers of the Church; see Seeck, Gesch. d. Untergangs d. antiken Welt, 1895, ii, pp. 457, 460.

[994] At present it appears that some nourish a hope of the reality of miracles being still believed in by supposing them to have occurred as an "extension of the natural." In this way it may become credible that cartloads of baked bread and cooked fish—vertebrate animals with all their physiological parts—suddenly sprang into existence out of the air. A travesty of the ridiculous, not an extension of the natural, is the more proper description of such assumptions. Natural phenomena, observed, but so far ill understood, lie in quite a different plane from contradictions of natural law in which consists the essence of legendary miracles.

[995] The more timorous critics still cling to one or two of the Epistles grouped together under the name of St. Paul, but the advanced school has decided to reject them in their entirety; see Van Manen, Encycl. Biblica, *sb.* "Paul." I may exemplify the general discrepancy of views still prevailing in this field of research by a single illustration: "It has now been established that the latter (Epistles of Ignatius) are genuine"; Encycl. Britan., *sb.* "Gospels" and "Ignatius": "certainly not by Ignatius"; Encycl. Biblica, *sb.* "Old Christ. Lit." Such opposing statements will continue to be put forward as long as we have Faculties of Divinity at Universities filled by scholars who are constrained to treat historical questions in conformity with the requirements of an established ministry; and so long shall we be edified by the spectacle of men engaged in balancing truth and error in such a manner as to pretend not to be refuting the latter, so that in perusing their treatises we must either suspect their candour or distrust their judgement. Yet in not a few instances the men may be observed exulting amid the ruins of the fortress which they had entered to hold as an invincible garrison.

[996] A. D. Loman decided in 1881 that Jesus had not been a real personage, but he now thinks he went too far; Encycl. Biblica, *sb.* "Resurrection." Edwin

Johnson, author of *Antiqua Mater*, 1887, has marshalled the evidence against his existence very fully and fairly, but in some of his later work he has gone too far, and such exaggerated scepticism, while it may often amuse, can scarcely succeed in convincing. Jn. M. Robertson, author of A Short History of Christianity, 1902, and previous works of some magnitude from similar studies, argues on the same side. Havet says, "Sa trace dans l'histoire est pour ainsi dire imperceptible"; Le Christianisme, iii, 1878, p. 493. Bruno Brauer concludes that "the historic Jesus becomes a phantom which mocks all the laws of history"; Kritik d. evang. Geschichte, 1842, iii, p. 308; see also Frazer's Golden Bough, 1900, iii, p. 186, *et seq*. Disregarding the Gospels, a form of narrative which could not be accepted by us as historical in connection with any other religion, the slight allusions to Jesus in known writers (Josephus, Tacitus, Suetonius), are evidently mere hearsay derived from the Christians themselves. Hegesippus, a lost church historian (*c.* 170), gives some details as to the death of "James, the brother of the Lord," and also states that some poor labourers of Judaea, for whom a descent from the Holy Family was claimed, were brought before Domitian and dismissed as of no account; fragments in Eusebius, Hist. Eccles., iii, 20. Remarkable is the silence, in his voluminous writings, of Philo Judaeus, a philosophico-theological Jew of Alexandria, a prominent citizen, and a man of middle age at the time of the Crucifixion. So close to the scene itself he could scarcely have failed to have heard of any popular agitation centring round a Messiah at Jerusalem. When Augustus was told that Herod had executed two of his sons he observed that "it was better to be Herod's pig than his son." In ignorant repetition at a later date this remark was construed into an allusion to the slaughter of the innocents; Macrobius, ii, 4. Several (non-extant) Jewish historians, Justus Tiberiensis for example, made no mention of Jesus. Still worse is the case for the Apostles; they are not noticed outside the N. T. unless in Acts conceded on all hands to be apocryphal. Most singular is it that no descendants of theirs were ever known. Towards the middle of the second century when the Christians loom into view as a compact body of co-religionists we should assuredly expect to find relations of the Apostles, direct or collateral, moving with extraordinary prestige among the Saints on earth. But, beyond a vague allusion to two daughters of Philip (Eusebius, Hist. Eccles., iii, 39), there is no trace of any such individuals. The descendants of Mahomet alone were numerous a century after his death, but the Twelve proved as barren of progeny as if they had never existed. With respect to the canon of the N. T. it is known that it was formed almost as at present before the third century, a great many similar works being put aside as apocryphal or unsuitable. Those selected were altered to some extent to meet the requirements of doctrine; Origen c. Celsum, ii, 27; Dionysius of Corinth in Eusebius, *op. cit.*, iv, 23, etc. They were, in fact, edited from time to time in the interests of orthodoxy or heresy, interchangeable terms, as is shown by Origen, Epiphanius, and Jerome; see Nestle's Textual Criticism, Lond., 1899. Much of the Apocrypha remains to this day, including circumstantial accounts of the childhood of Jesus; see Clark's Ante-Nicene Library, in which Tatian's Diatessaron (*c.* 170, an Arabic version only remains), shows the absence of texts now found in the Gospels, especially that relating to the Church being founded on a rock (Peter). The striking likeness between the legend of Buddha (*c.* 500 B.C.), and the life of Jesus has been set forth by several Orientalists; see Seydel, Die Buddha-Legende und das Leben Jesu, 1884. The resemblance to early Egyptian folklore may be seen in Griffith's High Priests of Memphis (story of Khammuas), 1900 (from recent demotic papyri). Some interesting questions are raised in Mead's Did Jesus Live 100 B.C.? (on Talmudic legends or libels). It must be borne in mind that scarcely a MS. of a classical author (excepting some scraps recently recovered in Egypt) exists, which has not passed the pen of monkish copyists. Hardouin taxes them with having forged nearly all patristic literature, both Greek and Latin. They had, he says, suitable materials for various ages, parchments, inks, etc., and executants who practised various styles of writing. In recording his conclusions he deprecates the accusation of insanity. Such is the deliberate verdict of a Roman Cardinal whose learning is indisputable, and whose discrimination in other matters has not been impugned; Ad Censur. Vet. Script. Prolegomena, Lond., 1766. At any rate the acknowledged forgeries make up an enormous bulk, Gospels, Acts, Epistles, laws, decretals, etc. It seems scarcely possible that the question as to the existence of Jesus and the Twelve can ever be definitely disposed of; and it must take its place beside such problems as to whether there was ever a Siege of Troy, a King Arthur, etc. In the cases of Pope Joan and William Tell, local and contemporary records were obtainable sufficiently comprehensive to prove a negative; but no evidence is likely to come to hand close enough to exclude the credible details of the Gospel narrative from the possible occurrences at Jerusalem during the period. The English reader now possesses in the Encyclopaedia Biblica, a repertory in which Biblical investigations are treated in a manner as free from bias and obscurantism as is attainable at the present time. Such a work has long been needed in English literature, and marks a national advance. But much more remains to be done, and within a score or two of years we may see such discussions take up a stable position between the advanced critics who still feel obliged to entertain some illogical propositions, and the rather wild free-lances who would dissipate all marvel-tainted evidence by their uncompromising scepticism, in which they sometimes do more harm than good by their disregard of critical sanity. By that time a liberal application of the critic's broom will have swept many documents now held up to public respect into the limbo to which they properly belong.

[997] Previous to the overthrow of Biblical and other ancient cosmogonies by the extension of natural knowledge the historic inquiry as to the truth of supernatural religion was paramount. As recently as the fifties of the last century a sceptic, if asked to give reasons for his disbelief, might have answered that it was due to the absence of witnesses of known position and integrity to attest the occurrences; and that if such evidence were forthcoming he should certainly consider that Christianity rested on foundations which could never be shaken. Let us see whether it is in our power to prove that if a religion based on miracles could pass such an ordeal it would not necessarily even then hold an impregnable position. In 1848 certain phenomena, termed the "Rochester knockings," occurring at a place in New England, impelled a wave of credulity as to spiritual manifestations throughout Christendom, which has not wholly subsided up to the present date. Prof. Robt. Hare, an eminent chemist and electrician, was attracted to investigate the matter with the firm intention of exposing the folly. But he became convinced instead, and by the aid of a lady who could produce "raps," apparently unconnected with her person, he devised a code of signals from which resulted a couple of bulky volumes devoted by the professor to explicit details of the doings in, and the beauties of, the spirit-land, the whole recounted by deceased relations of his own; Spiritualism Scientifically Demonstrated, New York, 1855. But the spirits did not for long restrict themselves to merely audible signs; they responded generously to the attention paid to them and soon began to reveal their hands, faces, and even their whole persons for physical observation, often pelting the audience with flowers, presenting them with bouquets, and showing themselves to be accomplished musicians in the negro mode by performances on unseen instruments. Although their deeds were never dark, yet they always insisted on darkness as indispensable for the perpetration of them. In 1852, after the craze reached England, many men of academical and scientific repute observed and attested incredible phenomena, of which Prof. Challis of Cambridge said that, if the statements had to be rejected, "the possibility of ascertaining facts by human testimony must be given up." Mr. A. R. Wallace, the congener of Darwin, became a convert, and bore witness to the miracles of Mrs. Guppy, her floral materializations, etc.; Modern Miracles and Spiritualism, 1874, etc. (I cannot omit to mention that this author, at one time at least, was an anti-vaccinationist). Sir W. Crookes, the celebrated scientist, had séances in his own house, where he walked and talked with a young lady from the Orient, dead a century before, subjected her to a quasi-medical examination, and possessed himself of a lock of her hair; Researches on the Phenomena of Spiritualism, 1870. The professors of Leipzig University received the celebrated medium, Dr. Slade, in their private study on several occasions, when he satisfied them of his ability to perform the impossible by producing untieable knots, passing matter through matter, and

causing writing to appear on slates from invisible correspondents; Transcendental Physics, by Prof. Zöllner, Lond., 1883. Other observers who upheld the reality of spiritual achievements are Sir R. Burton, Mr. Cromwell Varley, F.R.S., Dr. Lockhart Robinson, Lord Lindsay, etc. The list of veracious witnesses is, in fact, a long one and a weighty. Yet all these eminent men have been deceived by cunning impostors. See the Reports of the Societies for Psychical Research, English and American, which have been issued regularly for nearly twenty years. Hallucinations, ghost-stories, and hypnosis have been exhaustively investigated, but no spirits have ventured to materialize themselves whenever conclusive tests were insisted on. At the most it has been demonstrated that telepathy, a kind of wireless telegraphy between brain and brain, may occur under favourable but rare conditions. Whenever trickery was excluded the pretended mediums were invariably unsuccessful. The redoubtable Dr. Slade, when he found that dupes failed him, retired from the profession, and shortly after, on meeting a friend who challenged him, replied, "you never believed in the old spirits, did you?" The absurdities which were effective among the credulous when their superstitions were appealed to were often a ludicrous feature. A stone picked up by the wayside and ejected adroitly from the medium's pocket during a dance is looked upon as a supernatural occurrence. See Truesdell's ridiculous exposure of Slade and other charlatans of that class; Bottom Facts of Spiritualism, N.Y., 1883. The career of an English impostor has been unveiled throughout by a confederate in Confessions of a Medium, Lond., 1882. The literature on both sides is very large and is still accumulating. Several spiritual journals are published with the support of thousands of believers in Europe and America, etc. This modern illustration teaches us very conclusively: (1) That had the Gospels come down to us as the acknowledged writings of some of the best known and trustworthy men of antiquity, their contents would still have to be discredited as originating in fraud or illusion: (2) That devotion to a branch of science, or even to science generally, is not essentially productive of any critical insight into matters theological or professedly supernatural: (3) That phenomena of cerebration, normal, aberrant, and perhaps supranormal (exalted sensitiveness), may easily be utilized for purposes of imposture; and are a proper subject for methodized psychical study. Since a contemporary religion, supported by a mass of direct and definite evidence thus collapses before a strict scrutiny, we must ask what truth could reside in those generated in the womb of Oriental mysticism, for which no solid foundations can be perceived? When we see that even scientists do not always succeed in persuading themselves that nothing is credible but fact, *quod semper, quod ubique, quod omnibus demonstrabile sit*, how little reliance can be placed on popular reports and unauthentic tracts. Even if we had not spiritualism to hand, a practically similar lesson might be taught from a consideration of Shakerism,

Mormonism, Harris's Brotherhood of the New Life, the Zion Restoration Host, with its reincarnated Elijah, etc. See Oxley's Modern Messiahs, 1889, for many interesting details as to popular illusionists who have assumed the prophet's mantle.

[998] Timaeus, 9, *et seq*. Plato is not here inventing, but for the most part merely co-ordinating previous notions, especially those of the philosopher whose name is affixed to the dialogue. Reference to some other dialogues is necessary to complete the picture of his religion and theology.

[999] Parmenides; Republic, vi, 19; Plotinus, Enneads, vi, 9.

[1000] That is fire, air, water, and earth; not our chemical elements.

[1001] The original (?) Trinity here invented consists of: 1. The ποιητής, πατήρ, or δημιουργός. 2. Νοῦς. 3. Ψυχή. From the spurious Epinomis Νοῦς may be equaled with Λόγος.

[1002] Phaedo, 19, 25, etc.

[1003] Thus the period of eclecticism was entered on, for an account of which see Zeller's Eclectics, Lond., 1883. It began about the age of Cicero, but a definite system did not crystallize out of it till the time I am treating of.

[1004] Born at Lycopolis in 205; died in Campania, 270.

[1005] There was no creed in Neoplatonism, and, therefore, what was believed has to be deduced from a study of the Enneads of Plotinus, so-called as consisting of a series of books, six in all, each containing nine treatises. The logical germ of the conception is that the One emits continually the Nous or intelligence; and the latter the Soul. The Soul animates the world, but becomes lost should it allow itself to coalesce with matter by yielding to sin. The subject has been treated exhaustively by Vacherot, L'école d'Alexandrie, Paris, 1846; and by Zeller, Philosophie der Griechen, iii, Leipzig, 1881. Neither of these works has been translated, but there is an excellent summary by Bigg (Neoplatonism, Lond., 1892), who has dealt with some phases of the movement at length in his Christian Platonists of Alexandria, 1886. According to Bigg's expression, the Christian Father, Clement Alex. (*c.* 190), "separated the thinker from the thought, and thus founded Neoplatonism." Numenius, who was, perhaps, a Jew, made some advances in the definition of the Platonic trinity; and Plotinus was accused of borrowing from him; see Bigg's latter work, pp. 64, 250, etc. Ammonius Saccas, a porter of Alexandria, was the teacher of Plotinus, and is considered to be the immediate begetter of Neoplatonism.

[1006] Philo Judaeus (*c.* 20) is the first known to have taught this doctrine of ecstasy, but it is not certain that the Neoplatonists utilized his works. He also was the first to corrupt the rigid monotheism of the Jews by assuming the

Platonic (?) Logos as a necessary mediator between Jehovah and the world; see Harnack, History of Dogma, Lond., 1892, i, p. 115, etc.; also Bigg as above, and the Histories of Philosophy by Zeller, Ueberweg, etc.

[1007] The details of the life of Plotinus are due to Porphyry, who gives the most succinct account of his doctrine, and describes his excursions into the higher sphere by means of self-hypnosis. The whole field of modern spiritualism seems to have been cultivated by the Neoplatonists, and, indeed, by other mystics long before; allusions by Plotinus himself will be found in Enneads, v, 9; vi, 7; iii, 8, etc. Porphyry relates that during the six years of his intimacy with him, his master attained to ecstatic union on four occasions. It will be seen, therefore, that Plotinus was very abstemious in indulging in such a luxury; he would have much to learn from modern improvements under which Mrs. Piper and other trance-mediums enter the vacuous realm regularly day by day; see the Psychical Society's Reports; cf. Bigg, Christian Platonists, etc., p. 248; also Myers' Classical Essays, 1883, p. 83, *et seq.*

[1008] "Only the cultured," he remarks, "can aspire to the summit and upwards; as for the vulgar crowd, they are bound down to common necessaries"; Enneads, II, ix, 9.

[1009] The Stoics began this allegorizing of the ancient books; see Zeller (Stoics, Epicureans, and Sceptics, Lond., 1892) for an account of their conceits. Philo Judaeus performed a similar service for the Pentateuch, of which the Jews do not seem to have believed much literally in his day; nor, in fact, did the early Christian Fathers; see Origen, Comment. in Genesim, etc. He notices, amongst other things, the difficulty which arises from the production of light before the sun was created; Gen., i, 3, 16. Porphyry's treatise on the Cave of the Nymphs (Odyssey, xiii, 102) remains to show the method of exegesis adopted by the Neoplatonists in order to demonstrate the divine inspiration of the old Greek poets. Kingsley's novel, "Hypatia," gives a good picture of Neoplatonism in some of its popular aspects.

[1010] A treatise emanating from the school of Iamblichus is extant, viz., The Mysteries of the Egyptians, an exposition supposed to be written by Abamon in answer to a sceptical letter from Porphyry to Anebo, assumed characters apparently. It includes a whole system of Neoplatonic magic and theurgy, and describes the various appearances of daemonic phantasms with the accuracy of one accustomed to be familiarly associated with them. Objectively the series descends from the celestial light which defines the personality of a god to a turbid fire indicative of the form of a lower daemon, perhaps of malignant propensities. There is a recent edition of this work in English, probably a venture addressed to spiritualistic circles.

[1011] Irenaeus, i, 23; Hippolytus, vi, 7, etc. His contests with St. Peter were a favourite subject in early Christian literature; see Ordericus Vitalis (ii, 2), who has extracted some amusing incidents as to their rivalry at Rome, etc. In the Clementine Homilies and Recognitions, which form a kind of religious novel, at the time put forward as genuine, he fills the stage as the villain of the piece, but is considered to be merely a pseudonym for St. Paul, a name which typified a policy to which the author of the composition was opposed. See the article on Simon in any comprehensive encyclopaedia of recent date.

[1012] Mansel's Gnostic Heresies (1875) supersedes to a great extent the larger treatises of Matter and others, as it embodies a discussion of details more recently derived from Hippolytus, etc. Their sects increased rapidly in number, from the thirty-seven dealt with by Irenaeus (c. 185), to the eighty refuted by Epiphanius (c. 350). There were two main schools of Gnostics, the Syrian and the Alexandrian. The former was frankly dualistic, but the Egyptian assimilated Buddhistic notions, which saw in matter the essence of evil; only, however, when vitalized by the celestial emanations after they had become impoverished, as the result of their descent to an infinite distance from the throne of light. In general the attitude of Gnostics towards Christianity was rejection of the Jewish creator as an evil demiurge, and the acceptance of Jesus as an emissary from the god of love to rescue the world from sin and darkness. Their Christology was docetic; that is, the Saviour was merely a phantom who appeared suddenly on the banks of the Jordan, in the semblance of a man of mature age. Their greatest leader, though not a pure Gnostic, was Marcion of Pontus. His bible consisted of the Pauline Epistles, and a Gospel said to be Luke mutilated, but more justly recognized as an independent redaction of the primitive tradition. Marcion's Jesus said, "I come not to fulfil the law, but to destroy it"; see Tertullian, Adv. Marcion, iv, 7, 9. The modern Christian might imagine that his faith is dualistic, owing to the power and prominence given to the devil, but such a view would be inexpiable heresy. Satan and his crew are merely rebellious angels, whose relations to Jehovah are similar to that of sinful men in general, so much so that some of the Fathers in the early Church held that Christ would descend into Hell to be crucified there a second time for the salvation of devils; see Origen, De Principiis, I, vi, 2, 3; Labbe, Concil. (1759), ix, 533, can. 7, etc.

[1013] Unless it should be maintained that Christianity germinated in Gnostic soil, the most vigorous growth which overshadowed and in the end annihilated its weaker associates, a not untenable hypothesis.

[1014] The two portly folios devoted to the history of Manichaeism (Amst., 1734), by Beausobre, must now be supplemented by more recent, though less extensive, works, owing to the activity of modern scholars among Oriental sources. St. Augustine was a Manichaean for eight years, and the most reliable details are to be collected from his writings after he became a Christian, and issued diatribes against his former teachers. Socrates gives a short life of Mani, fabulous in great part most likely; i, 22; the latest researches are those of Kessler. The best summary will be found in Harnack, Hist. of Dogma, iii, p. 317, to which is appended a bibliography of the subject.

[1015] An old Persian notion; see Xenophon, Cyropaedia, vi, 1.

[1016] "Not the devilish Messiah of the Jews, but a contemporaneous phantom Jesus, who neither suffered nor died"; Harnack, Encycl. Brit., *sb.* "Manichaeism."

[1017] The text of his edict, with references to the sources, is given by Gieseler, Hist. Eccles., i, 61. The enactment, however, is regarded with suspicion, and is never mentioned unless accompanied by a query as to its genuineness. See also Haenel, Cod. Theod., 44*.

[1018] See the laws against mathematicians, etc., for so were sorcerers and witches designated at the time, from the Antonines onwards; Cod. Theod., IX, xvi; Cod., IX, xviii.

[1019] As Harnack remarks (*loc. cit.*), it commended itself successfully to the partly Semitic inhabitants of North Africa, among whom was Augustine. But it permeated Europe as well, and in a more Christianized form flourished among such comparatively modern sects as the Cathari, Albigenses, Bogomils, etc. Its fate in these quarters is traced out by Gieseler and other church historians. But the Manichaean pedigree of these sects is not now accepted so freely as formerly; see Bury's Gibbon, vi, p. 543. At one time all heretics were stigmatized as Manichaeans in the vituperation of the orthodox, especially when their views approached the docetism held by all Gnostics, as in the case of the Monophysites; Labbe, Concil., v, 147, etc.

[1020] Justin. Apol., i, 11; Eusebius, Hist. Eccles., v, 16; see Gieseler, *op. cit.*, i, 41, 48, etc. The belief in the Millennium was, doubtless, the most potent influence in segregating the first Christians from their fellow subjects. It was conceived by some that as the world was created in six days it would last for six thousand years, and the seventh thousand would be distinguished by the reign of Christ on earth; see the Church Histories and Harnack's article "Millennium," in Encycl. Brit., etc. As the chronology was uncertain the critical transition might be revealed at any moment. Christian writers now began to date from the creation of the world as per Genesis; some made it about 5500 B.C., so that the Millennium should have been entered on during the reign of Anastasius. But according to others it should have begun under Nero or Trajan. Michael Melit. (Langlois); Jn. Malala, p. 428, etc.

[1021] See Apostolical Constit., ii, 25; Hatch, Early Church, pp. 40, 69, etc. The Emperor Julian was rather exasperated at finding that the Christians took the wind out of his sails by their indiscriminate charity, and so cultivated the good will of all the lower classes; Epist. (frag.), p. 391 (H). He seems to be addressing some Pagan priest.

[1022] See The Teaching of the Twelve Apostles, 11, *et seq.*; Gieseler, *op. cit.*, i, 30. It is uncertain whether the first assemblies were convened after the pattern of the Jewish synagogue or the guild meetings of the Empire; probably after one or the other according to local affinity.

[1023] It may be imagined that this transformation was not effected without a conflict when parties with opposed views found themselves at the parting of the ways. This rupture was called Montanism, from Montanus, a Phrygian who, with two "prophetesses," proclaimed a renewal of the original dispensation. The movement spread to the West, where the celebrated Tertullian became one of its most ardent advocates. See Gieseler, *op. cit.*, i, 48, etc., or Harnack in Encycl. Brit., *sb. nom.*

[1024] Origen c. Celsum, iii, 9.

[1025] Some details of the catechetical course are known. The student was first taken through the "science" of the period until, like Socrates, he found that he knew nothing. Then the current of Jewish-Christian legend and mythology was allowed to flow, and everything was lighted up instantly as by an electric illumination; Gregory Thaumaturgus, Panegyr. in Origen, 5, *et seq*. Almost the strongest argument the Fathers found for the acceptance of their creed was the failure of Greek philosophical speculation to explain the universe. Many of them dwell at great length on this subject; see Tatian, Athenagoras, Lactantius, etc. One of the best summaries of ancient metaphysics is given by Hippolytus in his first book against heresies. But Clement and Origen were more concerned to correlate the two, thinking there was something divine in both. Eusebius is on similar ground in his Praep. Evang., etc.

[1026] As late as 160, or so, the Christians were taunted with having no visible places of worship; Origen c. Celsum, viii, 17, 19, etc.; Minucius Felix, 10. About a century later the handsome churches began to be erected; Apostolic Constit., ii, 57; Eusebius, Hist. Eccles., viii, 1; x, 4, etc. An inventory of the actual contents of a church at Cirta, in N. Africa, *c.* 300, is extant; Routh, Reliquiae Sacrae, ii, p. 100.

[1027] See the account of Hierocles, the hostile proconsul, in Lactantius, Div. Inst., v, 2; De Morte Persec., 16. He and the Emperor Galerius appear to have been the prime movers of the Diocletian persecution in 303; cf. Eusebius, *op. cit.*, viii, 2, etc. After several years, however, Galerius found the task of stamping out Christianity beyond him, and issued an edict of toleration. Hence there was really no call for Constantine to legislate anew. This Hierocles was one of those who set up the idealized Apollonius of

Tyana as an avatar of the Deity, and tried to exalt him as an object of adoration above Jesus. But the attempt failed; Apollonius was a real personage with a familiar name; Jesus was a dream; see the controversial tract of Eusebius against Hierocles.

[1028] Cod. Theod., XVI, vii, 1; x, 1, 7, etc., and Godefroy *ad loc.* About this time (380) Gratian discarded the dignity of Pontifex Maximus, which the previous Christian emperors had continued to assume; Zosimus, iv, 36.

[1029] A civil war was opened throughout the East by many bishops, who proceeded to demolish the temples at the head of gangs of monks and other enthusiasts. On both sides infuriated mobs fought zealously for their religion, and much slaughter resulted. The most violent commotion was occasioned by the destruction of the great temple of Serapis at Alexandria (389); see the ecclesiastical historians: Socrates, v, 16; Sozomen, vii, 15; Theodoret, v, 21, etc. Such doings became official under Arcadius; Cod. Theod., XVI, x, 16 (399); cf. Gieseler, i, 79.

[1030] In 367 Damasus and Ursinus fought a battle in one of the Roman churches for the papal seal; 137 corpses were removed next day from the pavement of the sacred edifice. "I am not surprised at the contention," says Ammianus, "when I consider the splendour of the dignity. The successful aspirant is enriched by the offerings of matrons, rolls about in his chariot sumptuously apparelled, and surpasses the profusion of royalty in his banquets"; xxvii, 3. As the Vicar of God, bishops professed to stand above temporal princes; Apostol. Constit., ii, 34. The Bishop of Tripolis declared to the Empress Eusebia (*c.* 350) that he would not visit her unless she descended from the throne to meet him, kissed his hands, and waited his permission to reseat herself after he had sat down, etc.; Suidas, *sb.* Λεόντιος. St. Martin of Tours (*c.* 370) was waited on at table by the Empress; he handed the cup to his chaplain, thus giving him precedence over the Emperor; Sulp. Severus, Vita St. M., 20; Dial., ii, 6. See further Gieseler, *op. cit.*, i, 91.

[1031] See the original church historians. Theodoret's account is the most definite and satisfactory; i, 2, *et seq.* Recently Arianism has been treated by Gwatkin in a separate work. Harnack's exposition of it is, as usual, most lucid and interesting; Hist. Dogma, iv. This is the great controversy in which the celebrated words *Homoousios* and *Homoiousios* were combined to distinguish the contending theories:

D'une syllabe impie un saint mot augmenté

Remplit tous les esprits d'aigreurs si meurtrières,

Et fit de sang chrétien couler tant de rivières, etc.

Boileau, Sat. xii.

Homoean and *Anomoean* denote Arian sub-sects who differed more or less from orthodoxy. In fact, the Arian heresy has never really died out, and is now represented by Unitarianism.

[1032] "Tradendi ratio sicca est, memoriaeque potius, quam intelligentiae accommodata"; Mosheim, Eccles. Hist., IX, ii, 3. The first great theological debates concerned the mutual relations of the persons of the Trinity in their celestial abode; and were decided against those who confounded the persons (Sabellians, Monarchians) or divided the substance (Arians). Such momentous matters being settled as finally registered in the so-called Athanasian Creed, the Fathers descended to earth and busied themselves in analyzing the mystic conjunction of the Godhead with the flesh, viz., the Incarnation of Jesus. These controversies were determined by the ejection from the fold of Orthodoxy of those who maintained the existence of but one nature or one will in the God-man (Monophysites, Monotheletes), and also of a small party who propounded the incorruptibility of the body of Jesus (Aphthartodocetae). The erection of this fabric of dogma was essential to Orthodoxy, the underlying conception of which was that God became man so that man might become God; ii Clement, 9; cf. Bigg, *op. cit.*, p. 71. Hence if the Saviour were made out to be merely a sham human being the whole scheme of redemption must fall through at once. The last step led them to consult about the mundane relatives of Jesus, and ended in the dogma that Mary's was an asexual birth, the Immaculate Conception, and that, as she could never have been sullied by any carnal conversation, the brothers of Jesus, as represented, must merely have been his cousins. But the Church did not approach some of these latter considerations till a later age.

[1033] His laws have already been referred to. For the result as represented by an educated Pagan, see Libanius, De Templis. This Council enacted that the Bishop of CP. should hold the next rank to the Roman Pontiff; Socrates, v, 8 (Concil., can. 3). About this time the title of Patriarch began to be restricted to the higher bishops; *ibid.* Constantine's pagan temples at CP. were now ruined; Jn. Malala, p. 345.

[1034] The chief source for the Council of Chalcedon is Evagrius, ii, 1, *et seq.* By Canon 21 the equality of the Byzantine Patriarch with the Pope was affirmed; Labbe, Concil., vii, 369; cf. Cod. Theod., XVI, ii, 45, etc.

[1035] Evagrius, iii, 13, *et seq*. It was composed by Acacius, the Patriarch of the capital.

[1036] See pp. 104, 180. To the Monophysites, Anastasius is, of course, "the pious and orthodox Emperor": see John of Nikiu (Zotenberg); Zachariah of Mytilene (Hamilton), etc.

[1037] Cod., I, v, 12; Codinus, p. 72; Procopius, De Aedific, i, 4. See Ducange, CP. Christ., *sb. nom.*, for a collection of passages relating to St. Mocius.

[1038] In 423 Theodosius II considered that Paganism was virtually extinct, so little in evidence were those who still adhered to the old religion; Cod. Theod., XVI, x, 22. But subsequent events proved that his confidence was premature. I have anticipated the use of the word "Pagan" (*paganus*, rustic, villager) as a term of reproach to those who had not been illuminated by Christianity. In this sense it is first found in a law of Valentinian I: Cod. Theod., XVI, ii, 18 (365). It arose at a time when the urban population exhibited a sharp contrast to the country people in the matter of religion. Long after the former had been converted *en masse*, polytheism lingered in the rural districts, the scattered inhabitants of which did not come into touch with the Christian propagandists and their new creed for a considerable time. Hence the idea of a country fellow became synonymous with that of a worshipper of the gods long since despised.

[1039] The history of their migration and subsequent activity at the local source of their inspiration will deserve our attention in a future chapter.

[1040] Valentinian I and the succeeding emperors legislated definitely against them; Cod. Theod., XVI, v, 3, 18, 40, 43, 59; cf. Cod., I, v. The whole title against heretics contains sixty-six laws, a monument of Christian bigotry and intolerance. The novelty of the Christian doctrines and the constant dissensions of ecclesiastics as to the proper mode of apprehending them, caused all classes to be infected with a mania for drawing theological distinctions, *ex. gr.*, "If you require some small change, the person you address will begin to argue about 'begotten and unbegotten'; should you ask the price of bread you will hear that the Father is greater and the Son inferior; or in reply to an inquiry whether your bath is prepared, the attendant will define for your benefit that the Son was made out of nothing"; Gregory Nys., Orat. De Deitate, etc., 2 (in Migne, i, 557). Yet sometimes a prelate would assume a jocular tone in the pulpit when speaking on these grave questions. Thus Eudoxius, Bishop of CP., began his discourse one day with the assertion, "The Father is impious, but the Son is pious." The congregation seemed awe-struck, but he at once continued, "Be not alarmed; the Son is pious because he worships the Father, but the Father worships no one"; Socrates, ii, 43. Marrast has devised some scenes to bring out the absurd way in which theological hair-splitting disturbed everyday social relations at this period; *op. cit.*, p. 89.

[1041] Chrysostom mentions the fact with exultation. Objectors fear that the race may die out as the result of the widespread celibacy, but the Saint knows better; the women who remain will be rendered more fecund by the Deity, and thus the numerical complement of mankind will be maintained. He also knows that there is a countless host of heaven, asexual, who are propagated in a passionless manner by divine ordination; In Epist. Rom. Hom. xiii, 7 (in Migne, ix, 517); De Virginitate, 14, *et seq.* (in Migne, i, 544); cf. Ambrose, De Virginitate, 3; Rufinus, Hist. Monach., 7 (in Migne, 413).

[1042] Monks are enjoined by Theodosius I "deserta loca et vastas solitudines sequi atque habitare"; Cod. Theod., XVI, iii.

[1043] The literature of early monkish life, descriptive and laudatory, is very extensive; see Gieseler, Eccles. Hist., i, 95, 96, etc. The most striking picture will be found in Evagrius, i, 21; iv, 33, etc. He is lost in admiration of them; they suppressed their natural appetites so rigidly that they looked like corpses wandering away from their graves. Some lived in dens and caves where they could neither stand nor lie. Some dwelt in the open air almost naked, exposed to excessive heat or cold. Others rejected human food and took to grazing like cattle, shunning human beings as if they were wild beasts. Both sexes embraced such lives of unremitting castigation. Some of the males made a practice of repairing from time to time to the cities in order to demonstrate their sexual frigidity by bathing in the public baths amongst nude women. They applied themselves to prayer, of course, until they brought themselves to the verge of exhaustion; cf. Sozomen, vi, 28, *et seq.* One Apelles had a conflict with the devil similar to that related of the English St. Dunstan.

[1044] The celebrated Simeon Stylites was the inventor of this sublime method of serving the Deity. From 420 he lived on columns near Antioch for thirty-seven years; Evagrius, i, 13; see Gieseler, i, *loc. cit.*, for reference to fuller accounts, separate biographies, etc.

[1045] He was contemporary with Athanasius, who wrote an extant life of him; see Sozomen, i, 13, etc.

[1046] Sozomen, iii, 14.

[1047] Socrates, iv, 23; Sozomen, i, 12, *et seq.* Previous to Christianity there were at least two communities of Jewish ascetics in the near East, the Essenes, who dwelt west of the Dead Sea, and the Therapeutae, who lived by Lake Moeris, near Alexandria. The first have been described briefly by Pliny (Hist. Nat., v, 15) and the second by Philo Judaeus in a separate tract (De Vita Contemplativa) respecting the authorship and date of which, however, opinion continually fluctuates; I do not know whether at present it is on the crest of the wave or in the trough of the sea. These solitaries consisted of males and females, and were recruited regularly by persons who became sick of the world and determined to fly far from the madding crowd. About them generally see Neander, Church Hist., Introd.

[1048] Socrates, iv, 21; Gregory Nazianz., Laud. Basil (in Migne, ii, 577).

[1049] Nicephorus, Cal., xv, 23; see p. 78. Not psalmody, however, says Card. Hardouin, but restless application to work. Manufacture of fictitious documents he insinuates, doubtless.

[1050] Cod., XII, i, 63; Orosius, vii, 33; Jerome, Chron., an. 375; cf. Socrates, iv, 24.

[1051] The histories of monachism are numerous and voluminous, especially those composed some two or three centuries ago. Helyot's Hist. des Ordres Mon., Paris, 1714, etc., in 8 vols., may be read for amusement as well as instruction.

[1052] Epicurus, the unavowed disciple of Leucippus and Democritus, the earliest atomists, conceived the coalescence of the particles to result from their rushing onwards always under the influence of a certain natural deflection which led to their meeting continually so as to become conjoined. As an Academic, and, therefore, a sceptic, Carneades could not accept this or any other theory, but in criticizing its fortuity, he remarked that it might have been perfected, or, at least, made more intelligible if Epicurus had conferred some faculty of will or intention on his atoms; Cicero, De Finibus, i, 6; De Fato, 11. With our increased knowledge of physics, we may now venture to supply the deficiency in accordance with the suggestion of Carneades. Not even in the process of crystallization can the motion of the atoms or molecules be considered as fortuitous, since they seem to be borne towards each other under the influence of some irresistible desire. The recent investigators strongly uphold the vitality of the process.

[1053] The question of abiogenesis or spontaneous generation, remains still indeterminate. Substances in transitional stages between the vital and the non-vital state have not been observed; perhaps because such matter is too inconspicuous to have been discovered so far and recognized, or, it may be, that the swarm of germs by descent is now so great, that the incipiently organic at once becomes their prey, and forms, perhaps, their constant pabulum. If identical atoms underlie all kinds of matter, and the recent *début* of electrons brings the proof appreciably nearer that it is so, we are still at a loss to explain why they should at one time, by their association, exhibit vital phenomena, and at another reveal to us their versatility in aggregating under the species of gold, sulphur, etc. The statement in the text might run that the chemical compounds combine with each other in greater complexity to form the elements of protoplasm.

[1054] That the effective origin of evolution consists in will capable of responding to a stimulus, being an essential attribute of matter, is a conclusion to which we are led necessarily by a consideration of the subject. When an amoeba protrudes a process, incited from within or without by some desire, it is already on the way to evolve itself into a higher form; and when a hygienist essays to preserve or prolong life by his studies in bacteriology, etc., in his immeasurably higher sphere, he literally does no more. The earlier evolutionists, Huxley, for example, were inclined to hold that the potency of cosmic evolution became evanescent progressively with the elaboration of purposive intelligence and social institutions, but such a view is manifestly erroneous, and would not now, I presume, be maintained by any contemporary scientists.

[1055] Our means of astronomical research are not sufficiently definite to enable us to explain conclusively the appearance of previously unobserved stars (*e.g.* Nova Persei, 1901), but there is good reason to suppose that these new lights sometimes signal to us the catastrophe of millions of beings more or less similar to ourselves. We are, however, well acquainted with the convulsions of nature, which often bring swift destruction to thousands of those dwelling on this small globe; for instance, the Mont Pelée eruption of 1903, which claimed some 40,000 victims. It might indeed be imagined from the occurrence of such disasters that animated nature is merely a kind of surface disease of the earth, which undergoes a spontaneous cure from time to time by means of earthquakes, floods, volcanic action, etc. Certainly, if we are the only result of the activities of this solar system, there would seem to be much superfluous expenditure of power and materials. The conception of God, when cleared of all irrelevancy, is merely that of a perpetual source of energy; and that we must find in the medium we exist in or nowhere. It is nugatory to talk of beginnings and endings when dealing with the infinite, unless as regards phases of phenomena; if there had to be an end of the universe, there would never have been a beginning.

[1056] Amongst some follies, the Stoic philosophers, in their pantheistic conception of nature, reached the highest level which has yet been attained in the expression of theocratic dogma. With them, the universe is the very body of the divine essence, and the good and wise man is in no way inferior to the sublimest manifestation of it. He is rightly called a god upon earth, and his intellect is an efflux of the Deity. "Back to the Porch for your ideas of God and nature," the modern philosopher may cry to his age. "You are gods yourselves, and nature is your realm to conquer and hold in subjection." The religion of the future will be more akin to Stoicism than to any other doctrine which has been formulated by thinkers in the past—a high ethical code upheld by a pride of race and a devotion to the evolution of humanity. The Stoic would not now be ready to make his own quietus with a bare bodkin should the currents turn awry. He would stand to his post till the last hour, working for the advancement of science. "Les stoiciens n'étaient occupés qu'a travailler au bonheur des hommes, à exercer les devoirs de la société: il semblait qu'ils regardassant cet esprit sacré qu'ils croyaient être en eux-mêmes, comme une espèce de providence favorable qui veillait sur le genre humain"; Montesquieu, Esprit des Lois, xxiv, 10. See Plutarch, De Stoic. Repug., 13; Adv. Stoicos, 33; Seneca, De Provid., 1; Epist., cvi; cxvii, etc.; Epictetus, ii, 8, 9; Lactantius, Div. Inst., i, 5, 27, etc.

[1057] Accepting the identity of the evolutionary process at all grades of its prepotency, we may suppose that future advancement will be the result of deliberate effort; and that the more determinate such effort, the more rapid must be the progress. While the aptitude of our faculties must be increased by their being constantly exercised in study and research, the knowledge attainable by such work may ultimately win for us some controlling influence over our physiological constitution. The wild dreams of mediaeval alchemists now seem to us less unreal since we have had experience of the properties of radium; and the vision of an *elixir vitae*, which illuded those investigators, appears more realizable in the light of recent research. The arrest of senility may come within the range of the future therapeutist; and a new Demeter may subject the modern Triptolemus to some alchemical fire, to render him proof against mortality. Less remotely, the systematic administration of sexual associations would exert a powerful influence over mental and bodily development; and it would be physiologically correct if famous stallions should stand to cover brood mares in the human as well as in the equine world. The Spartans realized something of this in practice; Plutarch, Lycurgus. The tendency to equalization of the sexes which has been growing of late years, is undoubtedly a forward movement on the path of evolution. The possibility of man in the future being endowed with greatly increased intellectual power must not be lost sight of. Exceptional gifts of genius, in some cases uniquely manifested, and the occurrence of "prodigies," especially in relation to mathematics, music, and art, teach that the mental faculties of the human race may yet be evolved in a much higher degree. The limitations imagined by Greg, which are, perhaps, generally entertained, must now be contemplated with suspended judgement: "Two glorious futures lie before us: the progress of the race here, the progress of the man hereafter. History indicates that the individual man needs to be translated in order to excel the past. He appears to have reached his perfection centuries ago.... What sculptor has surpassed Phidias? What poet has transcended Homer?" etc.; Enigmas of Life, 1891, p. 177. This is an evident misconception of the pace at which evolution moves; such short periods count for nothing. In evolutionary time, Homer and Phidias are our contemporaries. We know nothing of the final state of such beings as ourselves after they have passed through some millions of years, to which most probably the life of this planet must extend. They may well attain to some condition resembling that of the "gods" of Epicurus, who existed with a "quasi corpus, quasi sanguis," etc. The chemist and biologist have a wide field before them in which they will yet make many conquests.

[1058] Compare the account of the soldier Ammianus with those of the church historians; Socrates, iii; Sozomen, v; Philostorgius (an Arian), vii; Theodoret, iii, etc. These are honest writers and, although they often relied on mere hearsay, most of the matter they bring forward is historical. On the other hand the Church History of Eusebius, who was infinitely above them in abilities and learning, contains little but popular report and legend. It is improbable that Julian inflicted any physical persecution on the Christians, but no doubt his subordinates did so on the strength of his attitude towards them and he afterwards got all the credit of it.

[1059] It is generally suggested that the constant immigration of barbarians and their wholesale collocation in the army must have gradually undermined the civilization of the Empire. But a great state is able to digest an enormous quantity of such accretions; and in the pride of their recent elevation such new citizens would have become more Roman than the Romans themselves. The great Transatlantic Republic has been built up during three centuries by the immigration of alien barbarians. For a good summary of the peaceful settlement of barbarians in the Roman territories see Bury, *op. cit.*, i, p. 31.

[1060] See Gieseler (*op. cit.*, i, 99), where the assimilation of heathenism is well summarized and instanced. Augustine (*c.* 400) draws a striking picture of the impostors, who, in the garb of monks, tramped the country selling sham relics, phylacteries, etc.; De Op. Monach., 28, 31, etc.; Epist. ad Jan. (118). Jerome, in his diatribe against Vigilantius, unwittingly makes a display of the gross superstition which that earnest reformer sought to suppress. Bayle's article on Vigilantius (Dictionnaire, etc.) is a full and interesting account of the subject, but there is more still in Gilly's V. and his Times, Lond., 1844.

[1061] The first victims of ecclesiastical rancour were the Priscillianists, who arose in Spain about 380. They were tainted with Manichaeism, and two bishops persuaded the tyrant of Gaul, Maximus, to put several of them to death in 385. Generally the Fathers of the Church were shocked at this execution, but the utility of subjecting heretics to the capital penalty was soon perceived and the practice thenceforward became an intrinsic part of Christian discipline. The result is well known to students of Church history and the religious wars waged against the Paulicians, Albigenses, Huguenots, etc., and the horrors of the Inquisition are familiar subjects in popular literature. During three centuries in Spain (1471-1781), the first and the last scene of the judicial slaughter of heretics, nearly 250,000 persons were dealt with by the Inquisitors, a circumstance which Galton considers to have been equivalent to the suppression of national genius and to account for "the superstitious and unintelligent Spanish race of the present day"; see Hereditary Genius, 1869, p. 359. The same reasoning would, of course, apply to any process, such as is occurring in Russia at the present day, by which the more active and effective members of a community are being constantly weeded out. Paganism was not, of course, absolutely free from intolerance; and the cases of Socrates, Anaxagoras, etc., will occur to every one. Even Cleanthes, the Stoic, denounced Aristarchus of Samos for running counter to the popular religion when he put forth some astronomical anticipations of the Copernican system; Plutarch, De Facie in Orbe Lunae, 6. Even Cicero in his "Laws" (ii, 8) decidedly proscribes nonconformity with the state religion. Polytheism was tolerant because it was comprehensive and could easily assimilate all kindred beliefs. Thus a hospitable reception was ensured to any new arrival who was fairly accredited as a member of the Olympian family.

[1062] Seven Crusades to Palestine were undertaken between 1096 and 1270. During that period more than 7,000,000 persons are said to have started from Western Europe on their way to the East. Perhaps the weeding out of the worst fanatics in this way may have conduced to subsequent progress.

[1063] Dante (1265-1321) may be considered as the first prominent figure of the Renaissance; Wycliffe (1325-84) of the Reformation, but Arnold of Brescia (*c*. 1100-55) has some claim to the credit of being the first Protestant.

[1064] In the daily press of March 15, 1896, we read the utterance of a R. C. prelate when speaking of the Anglican clergy: "Do they claim the power to produce the actual living Jesus Christ by transubstantiation on the altar, according to the claims of the priesthood of the Eastern and Western Churches?" Persons who address a public audience in the Metropolis in this manner are not considered to be insane nor are they classed as charlatans. Concomitantly with such proceedings we find that the greatest of English encyclopaedias is published with introductory articles in which it is allowed that the old religion is now a mere phantasm on the stage of reality. At the present moment every form of religious belief rests secure and stable on the broad back of popular ignorance; and it remains for posterity in ages to come to solve the problem as to how long humanity will have to wait for the evolution of that elevation of mind which will decline to pay the tribute of hypocrisy and reticence for the assurance of a stipend.

[1065] Sooner or later the progress of colonization is always resisted by the aborigines, but the numbers of them who fall in war would soon be regenerated and their gradual extinction is due to the restrictions imposed on them by civilization or to their becoming addicted to its vices. The decrease of the U. S. Indians (303,000, 1880; 266,000, 1900; previous decrease unknown) and of the Maoris (100,000, 1780; 46,000, 1901) is partly due to conflicts with the whites, but that of the Hawaiians (200,000, 1780; 31,000, 1900) results solely from the immigration of higher races. Similarly the Tasmanians have become extinct in the last half of the nineteenth century. The peaceful pioneer of civilization, perhaps a missionary, is more deadly to the native races than periodical invasions by an armed force.

[1066] The ecclesiastical dictatorship of the Byzantine emperors, for which the term "Caesarpapism" has been coined, is specially illustrated by Gfrörer, Byzant. Geschichte, Graz, 1874, ii, 17, *et seq*.

[1067] All the chronographers connect his death with a thunderstorm, and it appears at least probable that he was affected with brontophobia in his later years. He is even said to have built a chamber to retire into, for fear of being struck by lightning; Cedrenus, etc.

[1068] Theodore Lect., ii, 7, etc.

[1069] It appears that he set up a private chair or stand in one of the churches, from which he used to address a crowd to gain converts for his doctrine. He was ejected thence by the same Patriarch, who shortly afterwards had to crown him; Theophanes, an. 5982; Suidas, *sb.* φατρία; see p. 104.

[1070] Evagrius, iii, 34.

[1071] He tried to obtain its acceptance in 496, and again 508; Victor Ton., an. 496; Theophanes, an. 6001, etc. He even tried to convert the Pope, Anastasius II; Theodore Lect., ii, 17.

[1072] He favoured the Reds, a mere appendix of the Greens, and so kept himself free from any absolute partisanship; Jn. Malala, xvi. Rambaud (*op. cit.*, 4, 5) is successful in proving by texts that the Demes did not represent definitely any political or religious party; and the notion of comparing them to a sort of popular house, with "supporters of the government," and an "opposition" cannot be substantiated. They were rivals in the games and threefold rivals for the Emperor's favour, in the Hippodrome, for interpreting his will to the people, and for conveying to him the popular sentiment. Thus they had a place in the administration, but not one that can be paralleled in any modern constitution. They were practically indifferent to creed or policy. The numbers recruited under each colour at CP. might be from 900 to 1,500; Theophylact Sim., viii, 7.

[1073] See p. 155. But the exactions of Marinus the Syrian, P.P. who committed the local supervision of the taxes to so-called *vindices* of his own creation, instead of to the Decurions, ultimately branded A. with the opprobrium of being a grasping character: Jn. Lydus, De Magistr., iii, 36, 46, 49; Evagrius, iii, 42, etc.

[1074] The large sum he left in the Treasury has already been alluded to; see p. 163.

[1075] The closest personal view of him is to be got from Cyril Scythop., Vit. S. Saba, 50, *et seq*. He was surnamed Dicorus (double-pupil), because his eyes differed in colour.

[1076] Procopius, De Bel. Pers., i, 10; De Aedific., iii, 2, etc.; Jn. Lydus, De Magistr., iii, 47, *et passim*.

[1077] Especially Evagrius and Cyril Scythop., both of whom condemned him as a heretic.

[1078] Marcellinus Com., an. 518. Now Uskiub, a flourishing Turkish town, nearly on the same site. The whole district has recently been explored by Evans; Antiquarian Researches in Illyricum, Archaeologia, xlix, 1885.

[1079] The Balkans. See generally Tozer's Travels in the Turkish Highlands, 1869, i, 16, etc.

[1080] Procopius, De Aedific., iv, 1. It seems that they are still represented by villages called Taor and Bader; see Tozer, *op. cit.*, ii. Append.

[1081] See Tozer's narrative of his journey through the Pass from Prisrend to Uskiub; *loc. cit.*

[1082] Novel. vii, 1. The extensive remains of the Latin occupation still to be seen are described by Evans, *op. cit.*

[1083] Procopius, De Bel. Vand., ii, 16.

[1084] *Ibid.*, Anecdot., 6. The names of the other two are given as Zimarchus and Ditybistus, but I see no reason to call them his brothers as is sometimes done. Justin was cowherd, or swineherd, or field labourer according to Zonaras, xiv, 5.

[1085] Procopius, *loc. cit.*

[1086] According to Alemannus (pp. 361, 461), however, Zimarchus as a centenarian (!) was active in important posts; Theophanes, an. 6054-5. cf. Jn. Malala, xviii, p. 490

[1087] Jn. Antioch. (Müller, Frag. Hist. Graec., v, p. 31); Procopius, *loc. cit.*

[1088] Procopius, De Bel. Pers., i, 8.

[1089] Theodore Lect., ii, 37; Const. Porph. De Cerim., i, 93, etc. His title was Count of the Excubitors.

[1090] Jn. of Antioch., *loc. cit.*, p. 35.

[1091] Procopius, Anecdot., 6.

[1092] *Ibid.*, De Aedific., iv, 1.

[1093] *Ibid.*, Anecdot., 12; Theophanes, an. 6024. The name seems to have been common at this epoch; see Socrates, v, 21, etc.

[1094] The girl's name was Vigilantia; Procopius, De Bel. Vand., ii, 24, etc. Probably her mother's name.

[1095] Corp. Insc. Lat., v, 8120.

[1096] Inferred from subsequent history. The point is discussed by Ludewig, *op. cit.*, viii, 5; cf. Alemannus, p. 437, *et seq.*

[1097] Victor Ton., an. 520; Const. Porph., *op. cit.*, i, 93.

[1098] The circumstances and date of the adoption are not recorded, but that it must have taken place appears evident from Cod., II, ii, 9; Novel. xxviii, 4, etc. Ludewig argues against it in the face of facts.

[1099] Almost certainly: the correct form would have been Justinus Sabbatianus, but the Byzantines were ignorant or varied old rules *ad lib.* There seems to have been no classical Justinian, but two of that name flit across the stage under Honorius; Zosimus, v, 30; vi, 2.

[1100] See pp. 103, 104.

[1101] From Chron. Paschal. and Theophanes it might be argued that there was an interregnum, but the contemporary accounts of Peter Magister (Const. Porph., *loc. cit.*) and Cyril Scythop. (*op. cit.*, 60) prove that Anastasius died early in the morning on July 9, and that Justin was elevated on the same day. Some give Justin the credit of having betrayed the cause of the eunuch by his astuteness, but it appears rather that his greatness was thrust upon him; Jn. Malala, xvii; Evagrius, iv, 12; Zonaras, xiv, 51, etc.

[1102] The official record of the election by Peter Magister (*loc. supra cit.*) has been preserved. It was Justin's own duty to announce publicly that the throne was vacant. The Circus was immediately filled and, as there was no known claimant to the succession, a wild scene ensued. First one of Justin's subordinates was set up on a shield by a company of the guards, but the Blues, disapproving, made a rush and dispersed the throng. Then a patrician general was seized on by a body of the Scholars, but the Excubitors attacked them and were dragging the unlucky officer away to lynch him when he was rescued by the Candidate Justinian, who was watching the tumult. Upon this the crowd scurried round Justinian himself, but he declined the dangerous distinction, being doubtless aware that a decisive election was maturing behind the scenes among responsible representatives. Still, however, the attempts to create an emperor went on, until at last the doors of the Cathisma were thrown open and Justin appeared, supported by the Patriarch, the Senate, and the chief military officers. All then perceived that an emperor had been chosen by legitimate methods, and both factions with the rest of the populace applauded the new monarch in the usual way: "Justin Augustus, may you be victorious! Reign as you have lived!" etc. It will be observed that Justin did not ascend the throne as the emperor of the Blues or the Greens, but that both Demes joined in their acquiescence. This apparently was always the case unless some party usurper, such as Phocas, managed to seize the reins of power; see Theophanes, an. 6094.

[1103] Procopius, Anecdot., 6. Nearly all the chronographers note his illiteracy. A certain Marinus painted in one of the public baths a sequence of pictures in which he portrayed the career of Justin from his youth upwards. For this he was taken to task by the Emperor, but he extricated himself by explaining that his intention was an ethical one, in order to teach the people that in the Byzantine Empire a man might raise himself by his talents from the dunghill to the first position in the state; Zachariah Mytil., viii, 1.

[1104] Theodore Lect., ii, 37, etc. The name Lupicina was, of course, the popular sobriquet for a prostitute, being connected with *lupa, lupanar*, etc.

[1105] Victor Ton., an. 523; Cyril Scythop., *op. cit.*, 68.

[1106] Marcellinus Com., an. 527. He also took over his uncle's post of Count of the Excubitors; Hormisdas, Epist., 37.

[1107] Procopius, Anecdot., 6; De Bel. Vand., i, 9; Jn. Lydus, De Magistr., iii, 51, etc.

[1108] Zonaras, xiv, 5.

[1109] Procopius, Anecdot., 6. He was probably the *ex officio* president of the Consistorium. It was generally anticipated that Anastasius would have chosen a successor from one of his three nephews, Hypatius, Pompeius, and Probus, all of whom he had raised to important positions. His failure to do so is accounted for seriously by a singular story. Being undecided as to which of them he should select to inherit the Empire, he arranged that they should dine together at the Palace on a certain day in an apartment by themselves. Here he provided three couches, on which, according to custom, they would take a siesta after the meal. One of these he designated in his own mind as the Imperial bed, and kept watch in order to see which of them would occupy it. As it happened, however, two of the three threw themselves down together on the same couch, and the significant position remained vacant. Judging that a higher power had ruled the event, he then prayed that his successor might be revealed to him as the first person who should enter to him next morning. This proved to be that very likely officer of his household, Justin, a result which appears to have satisfied him; Anon. Vales., 13. Such relations cannot be rejected in this age on the grounds that so-and-so had too much good sense, etc. On the contrary, they serve to indicate the mental calibre of the time. The slaughter of several "Theos" as possible successors by Valens (Ammianus, xxix, 1) may be remembered, and Zeno is said to have executed an unfortunate silentiary anent of a silly prediction; Jn. Malala, xv; Theophanes, an. 5982. But Justin and Justinian, being arrested on two occasions, as it is said, were providentially preserved by visions which enjoined their release; Procopius, Anecdot., 8; Cedrenus, i, p. 635, etc.

[1110] Procopius, Anecdot., 6; Jn. Malala, xvii (the fuller transcript by Mommsen, Hermes, vi, 1885, p. 375); Zachariah Mytil., viii, 1, etc. The cruel fate of Theocritus is specially indicated by Marcellinus Com., an. 519. Before the death of Anastasius, Amantius was indulged with a pre-vision of his destiny, having seen himself in a dream on the point of being devoured by a great pig, symbolizing, of course, Justin the swineherd.

[1111] The massacres of Monophysites in Asia Minor are described at length with the names of numerous sufferers by Michael Melit. (Langlois). Among them, two stylites with their pillars were hurled to the ground.

[1112] Jn. Malala, xvii, etc.

[1113] *Ibid.* It was proposed that he should become one of the two Masters of the Forces *in praesenti*.

[1114] Zachariah Mytil., viii, 2. This was the church in which the great Council of Chalcedon was held. Evagrius gives a picturesque description of it.

[1115] Zachariah Mytil., viii, 2; Procopius, Anecdot., 6. After this Justinian spoke of him as his "most distinguished brother"; Hormisdas, Epist., 55.

[1116] In the government of the Church he showed great activity, traces of which will be found in Concil. and Baronius, etc., during these years.

[1117] Jn. Malala, especially in Hermes, *loc. cit.*

[1118] Procopius, *loc. cit.*; Evagrius, iv, 3; Victor Ton., an. 523. As to the *Delphicum*, or banqueting room, see Procopius, De Bel. Vand., i, 21.

[1119] Marcellinus Com., an. 520. Theophanes says he was killed in an *émeute* by the Byzantines to avenge those who perished through his insurrection under Anastasius, but this is evidently a report circulated later on to cover Justinian's guilt. Zonaras mentions both versions of the murder.

[1120] Const. Porph., De Them., i, 12.

[1121] Memorials of this consulate still exist, and samples of the diptychs are preserved at Paris and Milan; Corp. Insc. Lat., *loc. cit.* Unfortunately they are simple in design and do not attempt a likeness of Justinian. From them we learn that at this time he had assumed the names of Flavius Petrus Sabbatius Justinianus; for reproductions see Molinier, Hist. gen. des Arts, etc., Paris,

1896, and Diehl, *op. cit.* Perhaps the later diptych in Gori represents him; see p. 50. As to the adulatory attempts to fasten the name of Anicius on Justin and his nephew in order to connect them with the most distinguished Roman family of the age, see Ludewig and Isambert (*op. cit.*), who have discussed the question at length. Justinian and St. Benedict, a contemporary, are brought into relationship and presented as scions of the same race as the existing royal house of Hapsburg.

[1122] Marcellinus Com., an. 521. Trajan, after his conquest of the Dacians, exhibited 10,000 gladiators and 11,000 animals in the Colosseum; Dion Cass., lxviii, 15. Under Claudius I a naval battle for sport on Lake Fucinus brought 100 ships, manned by 19,000 combatants, into play; Tacitus, Ann., xii, 56; Dion Cass., lx, 33. Real warfare among the Grecian states was often on a less extensive scale. Justinian's display cost about £150,000, his first considerable draught on the savings of Anastasius.

[1123] Const. Porph., De Them., i, 12.

[1124] Procopius, De Aedific., i, 4; Codinus, p. 87; see p. 37. cf. Chron. Paschal., an. 605

[1125] A history of the reign of Justin is enumerated among the works of Hesychius of Miletus, but nothing remains to us but the jottings, more or less brief, of the chroniclers. Nicephorus Callistus (*c.* 1400) has rolled into one nearly all previous Church historians.

[1126] Jn. Malala, xvii; cf. Marcellinus Com., an. 523, etc. Theodotus, the P.U. of CP. was especially severe in his repressive measures and went too far in executing a man of rank. On the strength of a serious illness of Justinian it seems likely that he even aimed at the purple, but Justinian recovered and immediately brought him to trial for his excesses. By the influence of Proclus he escaped with exile; Procopius, Anecdot., 9; Jn. Malala, xvii; cf. Alemannus, p. 368.

[1127] Paulus Diaconus, Hist. Miscel., xvii.

[1128] *Ibid.*; Marcellinus Com., an. 525; Theophanes, an. 6016, etc.

[1129] Paulus Diac., *loc. cit.*; Anon. Vales., 16. These writers, however, represent Justin as conceding everything demanded, although the statement is at variance with the general tenor of their own account, and there is no trace of a wave of leniency in the literature of the East. That John got the credit of having betrayed his trust in the interests of orthodoxy is shown by a spurious letter in which he is seen urging the Italian bishops from his prison to persecute the Arians; Labbe, Concil., viii, 605.

[1130] Pliny (Hist. Nat., vi, 15) adverts to the common error of calling them Caspian, instead of Caucasian. Properly the Caspian, also Albanian Gates (now Pass of Derbend), were situated at the abutment of the Caucasus on the sea of that name. There were other Caspian Gates south of that sea in Hyrcania.

[1131] On the Russian military road from Vladikavkaz to Tiflis. It rises to 8,000 feet.

[1132] Pliny, Hist. Nat., vi, 12; Procopius, De Bel. Pers., i, 10. An old way of blocking dangerous passes; Xenophon, Anab., i, 4.

[1133] Jn. Lydus, De Magistr., iii, 52, *et seq.*

[1134] *Ibid.*, Procopius, *loc. cit.*

[1135] Jn. Lydus, *loc. cit.*

[1136] Zachariah Mytil., viii, 5. Cavades demanded 500 lb. of gold (£20,000) each year.

[1137] Al Mundhir (Nöldeke).

[1138] Zachariah Mytil., *loc. cit.*; cf. Procopius, De Bel. Pers., i, 17.

[1139] Zachariah Mytil., *loc. cit.* This account seems to emanate from a contemporary native of Syria; cf. Procopius, De Bel. Pers., ii, 28. Al Lât and Al Uzzâ, names of a lascivious duality, held sway at Mecca till overthrown by Mahomet. This Arab, like most of his tribe, appears to have possessed a subtle wit, a circumstance which was utilized for the invention of a skit pointed at the Monophysites. It was related that two bishops of that sect, paying him a visit in the hope of converting him to Christianity, found him apparently in a state of great despair. On being questioned, Alamundar replied that he was shocked at having just heard of the death of the archangel Michael. The missionaries assured him that the death of an angel was an impossibility. "How then," exclaimed the Arab, "can you pretend that Christ, being very God, died on the cross, if he had but one divine nature?" The bishops retired discomfited; Theodore Lect., ii, 35, etc.

[1140] Rufinus, x, 10; Socrates, i, 20, etc. A Christian captive, a female, won over the royal family by miraculous cures, etc.

[1141] In the classical period Iberia was the usual name for Spain among the Greeks.

[1142] Jn. Malala, xvii, etc. The tables (see p. 90) of his cloak, were embroidered with the likeness of Justin.

[1143] Jn. Malala, xvii, etc.

[1144] See p. 176.

[1145] Jn. Malala, *loc. cit.*, etc.

[1146] Khosrau (Nöldeke); also called Nushirvan (Anosharwán), as Zotenberg always names him in his translation of Tabari.

[1147] Procopius, De Bel. Pers., i, 11. He even tried to make out that it was a cunningly devised plot to annex the Empire to Persia. The power of Proclus, who seems to have been an alarmist, is clearly brought out by this incident.

[1148] Procopius, *loc. cit.* Theophanes (followed by Clinton, Fast. Rom.) places this affair in 521, a date which removes it altogether out of its setting; 525 is the most likely year.

[1149] Hypatius and Probus, the nephews of Anastasius.

[1150] Procopius, De Bel. Pers., i, 12.

[1151] Procopius, De Bel. Pers., i, 12. As, however, the Roman guard could only be victualled by the active co-operation of the Lazi, and after a short time they proved too lazy to bring in provisions to the fort, it was evacuated and left to the Persians; *ibid.*

[1152] *Ibid.*

[1153] "Sidus cometes effulsit; de quo vulgi opinio est tanquam mutationem regnis portendat," etc.; Tacitus, Ann., xiv, 22; cf. xv, 47. As Milton expresses it:

Satan stood

Unterrified, and like a comet burn'd,

That fires the length of Ophiuchus huge

In the arctic sky, and from his horrid hair

Shakes pestilence and war.

Paradise Lost, ii.

[1154] The fullest account of these calamities is given by Jn. Malala, xvii.

[1155] Cedrenus and Zonaras place it in this reign. Jn. Malala a little later.

[1156] This was not the first occurrence of the kind, and all the chronographers are anxious to record that a slab now came to light with a punning inscription or prophecy, which may be rendered in English as, "The river Skip will skip some evil skippings for the townspeople"; as anxious as they are to note the peregrinations of a Cilician giantess, over seven feet high, who tramped the Empire, begging a penny at all the workshops for showing herself. After its restoration Edessa was called Justinopolis in legal acts.

[1157] Procopius puts it as high as 300,000; De Bel. Pers., ii, 14.

[1158] Jn. Lydus, De Magistr., iii, 54.

[1159] Zachariah Mytil., viii, 4.

[1160] Nearly all these particulars are due to John Malala, who, from the amount of detail he supplies about his native city, may be called the historian of Antioch. From him we learn that the Olympic games continued to be celebrated at Antioch, but were finally suppressed in 521 by Justin, for reasons similar to those which about half a century ago led to the abolition of Donnybrook Fair.

[1161] Cedrenus, i, p. 641. Perhaps he is only speaking figuratively.

[1162] Jn. Lydus, *loc. cit.*

[1163] Evagrius, iv, 6. Jn. Malala (xviii, p. 443) puts the re-christening in 528. He adds that Justinian remitted three years' taxes to several of the towns then damaged by earthquakes.

[1164] His death is said to have resulted from the recrudescence of an old wound in the foot at the age of seventy-five (Jn. Malala) or seventy-seven (Chron. Paschal.). The higher number is to be preferred, as Procopius says that at his accession he was τυμβογέρων, that is, an old man "with one foot in the grave"; Anecdot., 6; cf. Alemannus, p. 385.

[1165] The age of Justinian is not satisfactorily known, but Cedrenus and Zonaras give him forty-five years at his coronation. I need only allude to the reputed life of Justinian by his so-called tutor, Bogomil or Theophilus, quoted implicitly by Alemannus, a historical puzzle for nearly three centuries, but at last solved a few years ago; see Bryce, English Hist. Rev., 1887. It is little more than a MS. leaflet (in the Barberini library at Rome), and proves to be devoid of any sort of authenticity. The chief non-corroborated statement is that Justinian spent some time at Ravenna, as a hostage, with Theodoric the Goth. Justinian himself was, in fact, a barbarian of some tribe, and the bogus name given him, *Uprauda*, seems to have some affinity with "upright" and "Justinian."

[1166] The characters of Helen, Andromache, and Penelope, as they appear in the Iliad and Odyssey, have taken a place permanently in modern literature.

[1167] See Plutarch's account of the legislation of Lycurgus. A king of Sparta was fined by the Ephors for marrying a wife of poor physique for money, instead of choosing a strapping young lady with a view to having a vigorous family; *ibid.*, Agesilaus; Athenaeus, xiii, 20. The Spartans applauded the adulterous union of Acrotatus and Chelidonis, because they seemed to be physically well matched for the production of offspring; Plutarch, Pyrrhus. In fact Lycurgus thought that wives might properly be lent to suitable mates for breeding purposes. As an example of noble character in the female, the conduct of Chelonis is recorded: also the resolution and bravery of the female relatives of Cleomenes when they all met their death at Alexandria; *ibid.*, Agis; Cleomenes.

[1168] On the Athenian women in general, see Becker-Göll, Charicles, Excurs.

[1169] To a female visitor from another country it seemed that the Lacedaemonian women ruled the men; Plutarch, Lycurgus; cf. Aristotle, Politics, ii, 9. He makes out that things were muddled at Sparta, owing to interference by the women.

[1170] Herodotus, vii, 99; viii, 87, etc. Several of her ruses in war are mentioned by Polyaenus, Stratagems, viii, 53.

[1171] Pliny, Hist. Nat., xxxvi, 5, etc. The fragments of it to a large amount are now in a special room of the British Museum, together with attempted restorations in the solid and on the flat. It was delightfully situated on the Bay of Halicarnassus, a sight in itself, and a point of sight for a splendid prospect of sea, contained in a circuit of rising coast, covered with specimens of Greek architecture. Herodotus himself hailed from this town.

[1172] Polyaenus, Stratagems, viii, 60.

[1173] Athenaeus, xiii, 10.

[1174] Diodorus Sic., xix, 52; 11; 51; Justin, xiv, 5, 6, etc.

[1175] Laodicea in Phrygia (and elsewhere), by Seleucus after his mother Laodice; Thessalonica by Cassander, and Nice (Nicaea) in Bithynia, of ecclesiastical fame, by Lysimachus, from their wives. These were generals and successors of Alexander, *c.* 320 B.C.

[1176] The most illustrious lady of this age was Phila, wife of Demetrius Poliorcetes (her third marriage). She acted the part of political adviser and ambassadress; and was amiable and pacific as well as intellectual; Plutarch, Demetrius; Diodorus Sic., xx, 93. A flatterer of D. raised a temple to her, and called it the Philaeum; Athenaeus, vi, 65.

[1177] Justin, xxxix, 1, 2.

[1178] *Ibid.*, 4. These queens flourished *c.* 100 B.C.

[1179] Justin, xxvi, 3. He was called Demetrius the Handsome, son of the D. above-named, but not by Phila. She stood at the door of the chamber, while the ministers of her vengeance were operating within, calling out to them to spare her mother (*c.* 250 B.C.). Her own fate was to be put to death by her son, Ptolemy IV of Egypt, in 221 B.C.

[1180] That is, her hair cut off and suspended in the temple of Aphrodite to propitiate divine favour for her husband (Ptolemy III), during his Syrian war, *c.* 245 B.C. It became a constellation according to the adulators of the day, as is shown in the poem of Catullus, a translation from the Greek of Callimachus.

[1181] The constitution of the Roman family can be apprehended readily by running through the consecutive expositions in Muirhead's Private Law of Rome, Edin., 1886, pp. 24, 64, 115, 248, 345, 514. In law the mother and children were practically the slaves of the *paterfamilias*: he could divorce his wife at pleasure, and yet 500 years elapsed before a husband made use of this power, so potent was the high ethical code which sustained the Republic.

[1182] The story or legend of Cloelia used to be well known. Being delivered as a hostage, with a number of other maidens, to Porsena, she encouraged them to escape, and headed the band in swimming across the Tiber. But they were all punctiliously returned (*c.* 508 B.C.); Livy, ii, 13; Plutarch, Publicola, etc.

[1183] Portia, daughter of Cato, and wife of Brutus, the assassin of Caesar, aspired to be the confidante of her husband, but, distrusting her feminine nature, she refrained from soliciting him to trust her, until, by stabbing herself in the thigh, she felt satisfied of possessing sufficient masculine strength of mind to become the repository of state secrets (44 B.C.); Plutarch, Brutus, etc. See Shakespeare's delineation of her in *Julius Caesar*, where she recounts her action to Brutus.

[1184] The accomplishments of Cornelia, the fifth wife of Pompey, are given in detail by Plutarch. She was well read in literature, played the lyre, had made progress in geometry, and fortified herself by the study of philosophy. Julia, the mother of Mark Antony, is called "a most learned woman" by Cicero, Catiline, iv, 6. Greek culture was fashionable at this time among the Romans. But an earlier Cornelia (*c.* 330 B.C.) became famous in infamy as the centre of a female society for poisoning men of note; Livy, viii, 18.

[1185] Tacitus, Ann., xiii, 5.

[1186] Hist. Aug. Heliogabalus, 2, *et seq*. She "lived the life of a prostitute," and she also instituted a "petty senate" of females, which prescribed the fashions of the day to women. Manners, dress, jewellery, style of carriages, choice of draught-animals, horses, asses, or oxen, etc., were the subject of their jurisdiction.

[1187] *Ibid.*, 17, *et seq.* Both were murdered, and their bodies dragged through the streets by the Praetorian guard, before their reign had lasted quite four years.

[1188] She was a daughter of the great Theodosius. The turning-point in the fall of the Western Empire was the sacking of Rome by Alaric in 410. From about 425 her authority was paramount at Ravenna, the provisional capital or rather refuge of the mouldering government. Most information about her is contained in Zosimus, vi, 12, and Procopius, De Bel. Vand., i, 3, *et seq.*

[1189] I have several times had occasion to mention this princess. There is no consecutive history of this period, but merely scraps to be collected from brief chronicles, Church historians, and fragments of lost works, etc.

[1190] See pp. 103, 302.

[1191] Const. Porph., i, 93; see p. 303.

[1192] Jn. Malala, xv.; Theophanes, an. 5967, *et seq.*

[1193] Tacitus, Ann., iv, 19; the case of Sosia Galla. Cf. the account of Salonina and her gorgeous appearance, riding in the van of the army with her husband Caecina; *ibid.*, Hist., ii, 20.

[1194] Tacitus, Ann., iii, 33.

[1195] *Ibid.*, i, 69.

[1196] *Ibid.*, ii, 55, 74; iii, 17, etc. As she acted with the secret approval of the Court, she was acquitted at a mock trial (20), but a dozen years later, on the death of her accessories, she anticipated her fate by suicide; *ibid.*, vi, 26.

[1197] *Ibid.*, iii, 33. Plutarch (De Mul. Virt.), has collected twenty-seven instances of the notable doings of women, and Polyaenus (Stratagemata, viii) has repeated most of them, and added almost as many more. The latter record extends up to about 170.

[1198] Herodotus, i, 199. This applies to Babylon and Cyprus, but there were several other places, and the custom was carried by the Semites as far west as Sicca Veneria, in Numidia, N. Africa; Valerius Max., ii, 6 (15). See the commentators on the passage of Herodotus; Strabo, XVI, i, 20, etc. At all times the simplicity of devout females was liable to be abused, several instances of which are recounted. For example, an ancient rite ordained that a Phrygian damsel should on the eve of her marriage bathe in the Scamander, whilst invoking the river-god to accept her virginity. In this custom on one occasion a youth of the neighbourhood found his opportunity. Hearing of the nuptials of a young lady who was socially unapproachable to him, but of whom he had long been enamoured, he bedizened himself with reeds and water-flowers and posted himself in a recess to await her coming. On her entering the water he came forward thus in the guise of the divinity she was supposed to meet, and the guileless maid permitted him to embrace her without resistance, devoutly unconscious of anything being wrong. Subsequently, as she was walking in the bridal procession, her eyes fell upon him among the spectators, whereupon she made him a profound obeisance and pointed him out to those who accompanied her as the genius of the sacred stream; Aeschines, Epist., 10. This was an isolated and comparatively blameless case, but later on some of the semi-Christian charlatans managed such matters wholesale; see the account of Marcus in Irenaeus, i, 13.

[1199] Strabo, VIII, vi, 20

[1200] Athenaeus, xiii, 25. St. Augustine was of the same opinion: "Aufer meretrices de rebus humanis, turbaveris omnia libidinibus"; De Ordine, ii, 4 (in Migne, i, 1000).

[1201] Athenaeus, xiii, 46. Nicarete of Megara is noted as being a disciple of Stilpo of the same town, a philosopher who achieved a great and lasting reputation; *ibid.*, 70; Diogenes Laert. in Vita, "A wife is legally countenanced in sulking and keeping to the house, but a hetaira knows that it is only by her social talents that she can attach friends to herself"; Athenaeus, xiii, 7.

[1202] The names of these biographers are preserved, viz., Aristophanes of Byzantium, Apollodorus, Antiphanes, Ammonius, and Gorgias of Athens, but their works are lost; Athenaeus, xiii, 21, 46. The first-named composed as many as 135 lives, and Apollodorus exceeded even this number. The gist of their writings, however, seems to have been preserved by Athenaeus in his thirteenth book; and among the moderns, Jacobs has attempted to reconstruct all the principal biographies; Attische Museum, 1798-1805. The accounts of them are almost wholly made up of anecdotes as to their witty remarks and rejoinders. But at least one modern author has written biographies of courtesans; see Devaux-Mousk, Fleurs du Persil, Paris, 1887 (with portraits and autographs).

[1203] Plutarch, Pericles, etc. At the same time it was not beneath her to become a procuress, and it is said that all Greece was supplied with girls by her agency. It was even maintained that the immediate cause of the Pelopennesian war was the abduction of one of these girls imported from Megara; Athenaeus, xiii, 25; Plutarch, *loc. cit.* Parallels to Aspasia are not altogether wanting in very recent times. Thus of Cora Pearl (*née* Crouch, of Plymouth) we read: "For some time she excited the greatest interest among all classes of Parisian society, and ladies imitated her dress and manners"; Dict. Nat. Biog., *sb. nom.*

[1204] Memorabilia, iii, 11.

[1205] Diogenes Laert., Epicurus; Cicero, De Nat. Deor., i, 33; see an imaginary letter of hers in Alciphron, ii, 2.

[1206] Athenaeus, xiii, 37, 38, 56. Timotheus, when it was thrown in his teeth that his mother was a prostitute, replied that he was very much obliged to her for making him the son of Conon. The son of Pericles by Aspasia was legitimated and became a general.

[1207] *Ibid.*, 40, 38. Hieronymus, the last king of Syracuse, is said to have married a common prostitute, but their issue did not succeed to any crown; *ibid.* In modern times the assumption of the premiership of Bavaria by the notorious Lola Montez (*née* Gilbert of Limerick) will be remembered. "She now ruled the kingdom of Bavaria, and, singular to say, ruled it with wisdom and ability. Her audacity confounded alike the policy of the Jesuits and of Metternich"; Dict. Nat. Biog., *sb. nom.* Her *régime* did not, however, last more than a year, being unable to stem the tide of revolution in 1848. More fortunate was the *castrato* singer, Farinelli, who retained a position differing little from that of prime minister under Philip V of Spain and his successor for nearly twenty-five years. The reign of courtesans in the seventeenth century, when the aristocratic blood of France and England was enriched by "legitimated princes" and peers under Louis XIV and Charles II is too well known to need comment here; but the acquisition of governmental power at the hands of Louis XV by Jeanne Vaubernier (Countess Du Barry), a low-class strumpet, doubtless helped decidedly to bring that disgraceful epoch to a close; see Voltaire's *Louis XIV* and *Louis XV*, etc.

[1208] Athenaeus, xiii, 38; Alciphron, ii, 1.

[1209] Athenaeus, xiii, 60. Here, again, a parallel is afforded by Cora Pearl. During the war of 1870 she transformed her house into an "ambulance," where she spent her time and money to the amount of £1,000 in nursing wounded soldiers. Afterwards she claimed to be reimbursed, but £60 only was granted to her by the government; see her Mémoires, Paris, 1886. Ultimately she was expelled from Paris.

[1210] *Ibid.*, xiii, 7, 31.

[1211] *Ibid.*, xiii, 70; Polyaenus, viii, 45, etc.

[1212] Athenaeus, xiii, 34.

[1213] *Ibid.*, xiii, 54. A figurative memorial, a lioness tearing a ram; Pausanias, ii, 2.

[1214] *Ibid.*, xiii, 59; Aelian, Var. Hist., ix, 32. Crates, the Cynic, said that it was an advertisement of the profligacy of Greece.

[1215] Athenaeus, xiii, 69; and another at Babylon, the seat of his governorship. Plutarch (Phocion) says it cost about £7,000, and was poor value for the money, but Pausanias extols it; i, 37.

[1216] Athenaeus, xiii, 34.

[1217] *Ibid.*, vi, 62. Plutarch tells us that he fined the Athenians £70,000, which he handed over to Lamia and the rest of his harem to buy *soap*!

[1218] A *licentia stupri* was issued to each woman by the *aediles*; Tacitus, Ann., ii, 85.

[1219] Plutarch, Sulla.

[1220] *Ibid.*, Pompey.

[1221] Plutarch, Lucullus.

[1222] In the year 19 Rome was shocked by Vistilia, a married woman of noble birth, applying for a licence. She was banished, and a law passed to prevent the repetition of such an occurrence; Tacitus, Ann., ii, 85. Half a century later probably no notice would have been taken, but the ethics of the day varied regularly with the character of the reigning emperor.

[1223] Dion Cass., lxvi, 14. As a proof of the meanness of Vespasian, he relates that Titus expostulated with his father on the unseemliness of maintaining a tax on the collection of urine, whereupon the Emperor, drawing a handful of gold from his pocket, tendered it to his son, saying, "Smell, does it stink?" cf. Suetonius, 23.

[1224] Socrates, v, 18. The punishment of an adultress at this epoch took the ridiculous form of impounding her in a narrow cabinet next the street, where she was forced to prostitute herself to all comers. Every time she received a companion a jingling of little bells was kept up to publish the circumstance to passers by. At the same period immense underground bakeries were run by contractors for the supply of the Steps (see p. 81), and they hit on a remarkable expedient for procuring slaves to work in them. Taverns served by prostitutes were set up contiguous to the vaults; and customers, chiefly strangers, were lured into a compartment, from which they were suddenly lowered into the cavity beneath, by a sinking floor. There they ended their days in enforced labour, being never again allowed to see the light. A bold soldier of Theodosius, however, being thus entrapped, drew a dagger and fought his way out. He then laid information, which brought about the destruction of all such infamous dungeons; *ibid.*

[1225] In the Middle Ages the absence of judicious and uniform legislation is one of the most marked features, and in every province the extremes of sociological phenomena are commonly to be observed. Side by side with measures for the total abolition of prostitution we find brothels tolerated as a regular department of royal palaces. In 1546, for example, prostitution was suppressed at Strasbourg, and at Toulouse in 1587. On the other hand, from the eleventh century onwards, a community of courtesans was maintained as part of the establishment of the kings of France. They were placed in the charge of an officer, named *le Roi des Ribauds*. His position, however, was low, and his right to eat at the same board with the other members of the household was disputed; see Rabutaux, La Prostitution (*au moyen âge*), Paris, 1851, ff. 16, 21, 32, 33. Again, it is well authenticated, though almost incredible, that in the sixteenth century nobles and generals of the south of Europe kept in the camp elegantly caparisoned goats for amatory purposes; see Bayle, *sb*. Bathyllus.

[1226] See p. 89.

[1227] Our knowledge of these facts in detail is due to Procopius (Anecdota or Hist. Arcana), but sufficient corroboration from other sources is not wanting. The question as to the authenticity of this work of Procopius has been finally set at rest by the recent researches of Dahn and Haury. It is doubtless as true as all history in detail, *i.e.*, vitiated by prejudice, ignorance, and mistakes. The life and literary activity of P. will be noticed later on.

[1228] Procopius, Anecdot., 10.

[1229] This was a staple piece of "gag" for centuries, and is another instance of the uniformity of Byzantine life during long periods; see Tertullian and Gregory Naz., as quoted by Alemannus, *op. cit.*, p. 380.

[1230] See Mirecourt (Les Contemporains, Paris, 1855, 78) for an amusing account (with portrait) of Lola Montez, and her bold procedure in dispensing with her *maillots*, "to the delight of the gentlemen of the orchestra," when dancing at Paris. Some may still remember the popularity of "the Menken," as Mazeppa at Astley's, the result of her having been counselled to turn "to account her fine physique"; see Dic. Nat. Biog., *sb. nom.*, for her career and distinguished associates. Her apology, protesting against the performance being denounced as an exhibition of nakedness, was published, and is extant. This hetaira approached somewhat to her Greek prototypes, and issued a volume of poems, which, if not equal to Sappho's, had a merit of their own. The same significance cannot, however, be attached to such displays as at the present day. The indiscriminate bathing was only just passing into disrepute, and ingenuous exhibitions of that kind were still possible. See, for instance, Aristaenetus (i, 7), where a "modest" young lady trips down to the beach, coolly divests herself of her clothing, and asks a young gentleman, who happens to be reclining there, to keep an eye on her things while she is in the water. This author, waiting *c.* 500, could scarcely have deemed such an incident preposterous in his time. As to naked women in the theatre, in addition to the notices already given from Chrysostom, see In Matth. Hom. xix, 4 (in Migne, viii, 120).

[1231] Her proceedings are described by Procopius, with the openness and detail which was natural to the age in which he lived. For this, however, he has been censured, to the damage of his historical credit, as if he thereby proved himself to be a dissolute person, unusually experienced in the vices of the times. But the charge is unjust, and might be urged with greater force against almost all of the Christian fathers who continually inveigh against abuses of the sexual instinct, in the intricacies of which they show themselves to be far better versed. Beginning with the Epistle of Barnabas they never tire of decrying circumstantially all sexual relations, especially those who "medios viros lambunt, libidinoso ore inguinibus inhaerescunt"; Minucius Felix, 28; cf. Arnobius, Adv. Gen., ii; Lactantius, Div. Inst., vi, 23, etc. Their rigid text is "genitalem corporis partem nulla alia causa nisi efficiendae sobolis accepimus"; *ibid.* Nor was it regarded as proper that the knowledge and discussion of such matters should be ordinarily thrust out of sight; on the contrary they were included in the category of topics habitually invested with interest to "society." Thus the polished Agathias in an amatory epigram (28), after lamenting the pangs and torments of love, makes his point with:

Πάντ' ἄρα Διογένης ἔφυγεν τάδε, τὸν δ' Ὑμέναιον

ᾔειδεν παλάμῃ, Λαΐδος οὐ χατέων.

This graphic effusion duly found its place in that book of "elegant extracts," compiled for the delectation of the Byzantine drawing-room, the Greek Anthology, where it remains enshrined amid a crowd of companions, at least ten times as remote as itself from modern ideas of decency.

[1232] One example of her unusual turpitude may be reproduced. After enlivening a party of ten or more young men for a whole evening, she "παρὰ τοὺς ἐκείνων οἰκέτας ἰοῦσα τριάκοντα ὄντας ἂν οὕτω τύχοι, ξυνεδυαζετο μὲν τούτων ἑκάστῳ"; Procopius, Anecdot., 9. Unconsciously she was emulating the activities of the Empress Messalina five centuries previously:

Claudius audi

Quae tulerit: dormire virum cum senserat uxor ...

Intravit calidum veteri centone lupanar ...

Excepit blanda intrantes, atque aera poposcit:

Mox lenone suas jam dimittente puellas,

Tristis abit; etc.

Juvenal, Sat. vi, 115, *et seq.*

Pliny discusses her proclivities in the inquiring mood of a physiologist; Hist. Nat., x, 83.

[1233] This is in direct opposition to the established views of Byzantine superstition; see p. 119.

[1234] The age of Theodora is nowhere mentioned, but Ludewig and Isambert favour 497. Nicephorus Cal. (xvi, 39) says that she was born in Cyprus, an assertion which cannot be contradicted, but which is, on the whole unlikely, and some of his collateral statements are erroneous. The following information *pour rire* has found its way into so considerable a work as Hefner-Altneck's Trachten: "Theodora was the daughter of Acacius, Patriarch of CP., and was trained by her mother (!) for the theatre, in which she distinguished herself by her art as a pantomimist"; i, p. 124. The Patriarch Acacius was doubtless a celibate. The whitewashing of Theodora has, of course, been undertaken, but late, not till 1731, by Ludewig. She was, in fact, in bad odour with the Church, and the worst that could be said of her was acceptable. Recently a further attempt has been made by Débidour (L'Impératrice Theodora, Paris, 1885, Latin Thesis, 1877), called forth by Sardou's well-known play of *Theodora*, in which she is undoubtedly misrepresented. A pendant to this *brochure*, containing all the facts of the defence, will be found in Eng. Hist. Rev., 1887 (Mallet). Present flatterers were, of course, ready to swear that she was an Anician! See p. 308.

[1235] Procopius, Anecdot., 10, 17. His horror at the practice of abortion teaches us that a great revulsion of public sentiment must have taken place since the time of Aristotle, who counsels resorting to it when over-population is threatened; Politics, vii, 16.

[1236] Procopius, Anecdot., 17.

[1237] *Ibid.*, 9.

[1238] Codinus, p. 104 (Anon. of Banduri). This information dates from the early part of the eleventh century, but must have been copied from some earlier document. It is in general agreement with Procopius, Anecdot., 9.

[1239] Socrates, iv, 28. The Novation purists made great headway there; *ibid.*, ii, 30, etc.

[1240] Contiguous to the church of St. Panteleemon, which stood on the Propontis to the east of the Theodosian Port; see Notitia, reg. ix and Ducange *sb. Homonoea*. The suburban St. P. is said to be indicated by ruins still existing at the foot of the "Giant's Grave," on the Asiatic side of the

Bosphorus; see Gyllius, De Bosp., iii, 6; Procop., etc., Notitia, reg. ix; Ducange, *sb. Homonoea*; Procopius, De Aedific., i, 9.

[1241] Codinus, *loc. cit.*

[1242] Procopius, Anecdot., 9.

[1243] *Ibid.*, 10. He allows that she was sufficiently well looking, but he also states that her countenance was disfigured by debauchery; *ibid.*, 9. At a later date he praises her beauty as something almost superhuman, but this was intended for the eyes of the Court; De Aedific., i, 11.

[1244] In natural gifts she may have had some resemblance to Cleopatra; see Shakespeare's presentation of the latter:

Age cannot wither her, nor custom stale

Her infinite variety, etc.

Act ii, 2.

[1245] Procopius, Anecdot., 9; cf. John of Ephesus, Com. de Beat. Orient. (Van Douven and Land), p. 68, where the words occur, "ad Theodoram τὴν ἐκ τοῦ πορνείου, quae illo tempore patricia erat." She is often mentioned in this work in a laudatory strain, with which this sentence, as Diehl (*op. cit.*) forcibly observes, is decidedly incongruous. Probably, therefore, it has been introduced by a copyist, but of what date I cannot surmise.

[1246] Probably she now took up her residence in the palace of Hormisdas; see pp. 37, 309.

[1247] As shown by subsequent events; Theophanes, an. 6019; Victor Ton., an. 566; Jn. Malala, xviii, p. 430; *ib.*, an. 6020.

[1248] Her position was now very similar to that of Caenis under Vespasian; see p. 336.

[1249] See p. 108.

[1250] Procopius, Anecdot., 10; the law itself, Cod., V, iv, 23 (De Nuptiis). This relaxation, however, was quite in accordance with the development of Christian sentiment. Thus Chrysostom expresses it: "Inflamed by this fire (Christian repentance) the prostitute becomes holier than virgins"; In Matth. viii, Hom. vi, 5 (in Migne, vii, 69).

[1251] Procopius, Anecdot., 9. The spurious life by Theophilus (see p. 320) tells us also that Justinian's mother, her name Biglenitza (Vigilantia), opposed the marriage, not on account of unchastity, but because Theodora was too clever and addicted to magic, etc. There is no historical mention of this Vigilantia.

[1252] *Ibid.*, 10.

[1253] Jn. Malala, xvii, etc.

[1254] According to Michael the Syrian, Jacobite Patriarch of Antioch, Theodora was the daughter of an "orthodox" (*i.e.*, Monophysite) priest, who would not part with his daughter until Justinian had pledged his word not to coerce her to conform to Chalcedon! See Chabot's trans. from the Syriac, 1901, ix, 20. She built St. P. (p. 344) on the site of her chaste pre-nuptial life.

[1255] Procopius, Anecdot., 1. Aimoin (Hist. Franc., ii, 5), a western author of the eleventh century, but in great part fabulous, relates that Belisarius and Justinian entered a brothel and chose there two prostitutes, Antonina and *Antonia*, sisters, whom they subsequently married. If this is not merely loose hearsay emanating originally from a reader of Procopius, it shows the sort of stories which were popularly current on the subject. Although the anecdote is scarcely far-fetched, it is rendered impossible by the fact that the ages of the two men differed by something like a score of years.

[1256] Later we hear from Procopius (De Bel. Goth., i, 5) that in 535 he had just become old enough to receive a separate command in the army; which probably indicates that he had then attained to the age of eighteen, the period when a young Roman was freed from his guardian (*curator*) and became *sui juris*. About nine years earlier (*c.* 526, De Bel. Pers., i, 12) Belisarius is referred to in very similar terms, so that the relative ages of these two characters can be determined with tolerable accuracy. Belisarius was then "πρῶτος ὑπηνήτης."

[1257] Antonina and her son Photius are personages almost peculiar to Procopius and do not come to light noticeably in the ordinary chronographers.